APPLETON-CENTURY HANDBOOKS OF LITERATURE

Albert C. Baugh, *Editor*

CONTEMPORARY
ENGLISH
LITERATURE

CONTEMPORARY
ENGLISH
LITERATURE

By

Jeha **MARK LONGAKER**
Professor of English

AND

EDWIN C. BOLLES
Assistant Professor of English

UNIVERSITY OF PENNSYLVANIA

APPLETON-CENTURY-CROFTS, Inc.

NEW YORK

PREFACE

THE ORGANIZATION of material in this book conforms with that of the other books in this series. After a brief consideration of the historical background and time-spirit of the different phases of the contemporary period, the method of procedure is topical. Within the topical divisions of poetry, novel, drama, and miscellaneous prose, the arrangement is generally chronological. In the treatment of particular movements and groups, however, it has seemed more practicable at times to proceed from a discussion of major figures to those of lesser importance. In the many instances in which an author's works extend to several literary forms, the works, regardless of type, are considered in the principal entry of the particular author. Thus Hardy's novels and poetry, Galsworthy's novels and dramas are considered under the entries of Hardy and Galsworthy respectively.

The general bibliographies are arranged according to literary type, with subdivisions indicated in so far as they prove helpful. The reference works on poetry, for example, are subdivided into anthologies, biographical and critical studies, and discussions of poetic theory and principle. In the bibliographies of individual authors, the order of arrangement is generally from comprehensive treatment to the treatment of particular facets of the author's life and works. The chronologies of authors' works and the lists of bibliographical items are often selective rather than exhaustive; and in the reference works, reviews and newspaper notices are not included. Only places of publication other than New York and London are listed in the bibliographies.

Publishers have been generous in granting permission for

the use of a few quotations and of photographs, and acknowl-
edgment of indebtedness is made in connection with their
use. Dr. A. C. Baugh, with his vast resources as editor and
literary historian, has been of invaluable assistance in the
preparation of this handbook.

M. L.
E. C. B.

CONTENTS

CONTENTS

ILLUSTRATIONS

POETRY & FICTION
1890–1914

Victoria, 1837-1901
Edward VII, 1901-1910
George V, 1910-1936

ENGLAND AT THE TURN OF THE CENTURY

DURING TWO decades before war swept away the last vestiges of the nineteenth century, the high tide of the greatest empire since Rome flowed through the streets of London. It bore the whole harvest of the effort begun in the days of Elizabeth in war, trade, science and colonization, bringing to the upper classes born to enjoy those fruits what was rightly called "the lordliest life on earth." In the brilliant pageantry of the Diamond Jubilee of 1897 it became a spectacle of armed power, of proud young dominions and subject peoples accepting their overlord, and of English-men quickened with an imperial consciousness that had not been felt at the Golden Jubilee ten years before. In the center was the Queen, now visibly near the end of her days but still a great symbol of sovereignty, within whose reign the vast majority of her subjects had passed their whole lives. Around her the nation was more loyal and prosperous than it had ever been. No wonder the Englishman thought of his life as "ageless, effortless, ordered" and destined to go on indefinitely as it had been. The solemn warning of Kipling's "Recessional" he took to be fine rhetoric.

Of course, the price of all this splendor was high and there

was great inequality in the sharing of the returns. There
were furtive doubts that imperial trade and the gold of the
Rand *were* adequate returns for the energy of the blood
that the empire had drained away. Victorian conservatism
could easily become inertia, and in many ways the life and
mind of England were lagging dangerously behind the times.
Gladstone died in '98, the last of the great statesmen who
for so long had supported the throne. The new men did
not seem to be of their stature and there were no soldiers
who had served in a major war. Yet except among the artistic
and literary "decadents" for whom a *fin de siècle* exhaustion
was often merely an amusing pose there was no evidence of
the cultural decline that often accompanies the end of an
era. If Victorian conservatism had not lost its weight, neither
had Victorian optimism lost its drive. Self-criticism is a sign
of vitality. There were vigorous critics, and among the young
a healthy dissatisfaction with the existing order and a will
to change.

For nearly a generation, chiefly under Gladstone's leadership, and against the grain of the governing class as a whole,
England had been moving toward democracy. An extension
of the franchise to all householders and the adoption of the
ballot had given political responsibility to a large part of
the working class who now had effective representation in
Parliament. In 1891 primary schooling was made free and
compulsory for all. The restrictions that had closed the
armed and civil services and the universities to all but the
elect had been removed and many more careers opened to
merit, but there still were many preserves into which no
outsider could hope to break. Power was passing to the
people but on the surface of life this would not have been
noticeable. The Englishman taught by long tradition to
know his place and give loyal service was not to be found in
the servants' hall alone; he was the laborer to whom a shilling a week might mean a bitter strike, the seaman at two-

pound-ten a month or the genteel married clerk at "thirty bob a week" whose case was as bad as theirs. It is not so much by gains as by what had been set going that the democratic trend of the nineties is to be measured. The effort begun by Ruskin, Toynbee, and Morris to awaken the social conscience of the middle class was bearing fruit. Organized settlement work and social services were replacing the sporadic, lady-bountiful charity of the past. The YMCA had been active in London since 1880 and the Salvation Army for twenty-five years longer. Among the intellectuals the Fabian Society, erected by Sidney Webb, G. B. Shaw, and H. G. Wells on foundations laid by William Morris, was bringing socialism to the middle classes in terms more acceptable than those of the militant Social Democratic Federation whose meetings the police suppressed. There was no relaxation of class boundaries, emphasized by so many fine distinctions of possession, occupation, conduct, taste, and accent, but an increasing awareness throughout the classes of their proper share in a society that embraced them all.

An important social movement was the demand of women for greater freedom. Under an act of 1883 married women now controlled their own property and women's colleges had been established at Oxford and Cambridge in the seventies, but otherwise they were as restricted and dependent as their grandmothers. Suffrage was not yet a major issue, but younger women were resolved to have greater economic and social independence. Tennis gave them a sport in which they could meet men on equal terms, the bicycle a cheap and manage-able means of getting about, and the telephone and type-writer a wide new field of employment and enterprise. By the end of the century there were twenty-eight women's clubs in London. It was these that started the whole world playing bridge. Tennis, cycling, the "pop" concert, and the "hop" with its lively new waltzes and two steps resulted in a pleasanter, less formal social life for young men and women alike.

In the mechanical world high speed and electricity marked the end of the Queen's reign as steam had marked its beginning. In 1895 the Scottish expresses were making an average of 63 miles an hour and five years later an experimental, turbine-driven destroyer, H. M. S. *Viper,* achieved 33⅓ knots. The *Lucania,* fastest of the Cunarders, had run from Queenstown (Cobh) to New York in five days, eight hours, but in 1897 lost the Blue Ribbon to the *Kaiser Wilhelm der Grosse,* of the North German Lloyd.

Electric light, elevators, telephones, and trams were changing city life and 1900 saw the opening of the "Tupenny Tube," the electric subway that soon superseded the smoky steam Underground Railway that had carried a generation of Londoners in hideous discomfort. Motor cars had appeared on the continent in the early nineties but until 1896 had been kept from English roads by a law requiring them to be preceded by a man on foot carrying a red flag. By 1900 both cars and motorcycles were coming into use, though England remained far behind France in their development.

London was changing but was still a stately and wholly English city without the huge stores, office buildings, blocks of flats, and sky signs of later years. Its modern architecture was dull but, except for some deplorable attempts to interpret Ruskin, inoffensive, and where Nash's crescent curved down Regent Street to the new Eros in Piccadilly Circus, wholly satisfying. There was a clatter in the roadways of horses drawing buses, hansoms, smart cabs, and, in the season, carriages of the nobility with hammer cloths and footmen. On the sidewalks men were top-hatted and black-coated, and women, if not chic, elaborate from ostrich plumes to sweeping hems. Flower girls, pavement artists, and pathetic singers gave local color to its everyday streets and on a Bank Holiday the coster in pearlies drove his family out on the donkey barrow. It was a vital but hardly a beautiful city: the Pre-Raphaelites and the Aesthetes had left little mark on it outwardly, though many of its interiors had Morris furniture and wallpapers, the kind of ornament approved by Wilde, and the kind of picture approved by Whistler. Except for literature the arts were at slack water as the century ended. In its bars and shops, its parks and drawing rooms, its theaters and music halls, its millions lived a vigorous, unintellectual life gladly leaving the higher exercises of the mind to those odd, brainy people in Chelsea who enjoyed Ibsen and Wagner, studied at the Slade, or repeated James Whistler's asperities. Around the busy center where the pulse of life was strong sprawled an ignoble flatness of men or wretched neighborhoods that never saw the Lord Mayor's coach or the scarlet pomp of guard mount. Looked at anywhere London might appear monotonous, ugly and vulgar, but in the smoky gold of its autumn days its streets became spacious and its sombre buildings robed themselves in a dignity of light befitting a great capital.

Since Waterloo England had had eighty years of peace. Her armies, small and wholly professional as they had been since the time of the Stuarts, fought their brief campaigns far away. The most imposing of these, the Crimean War (1854-56), was not by our standards a serious affair. The year after the Diamond Jubilee, Kitchener broke forty thousand dervishes at Omdurman with half their numbers and a handful of casualties. So the public gave only casual attention to the trouble that for two years had been growing between the Uitlanders (English) of the Rand and the Boers of the Transvaal Republic. The possibility of serious consequences and the injustice of England's attitude toward the Boers were ignored before the aggressive imperial policy of Joseph Chamberlain and the prospects of wealth offered by the ambitious schemes of Cecil Rhodes. And even when the quarrel issued in a declaration of war in October, 1899, no one was alarmed. As a military force the Boers were not impressive, a rural militia rather like so many Pennsylvania farmers. Surely "Sixty thousand horse and foot going to Table Bay" would easily take care of them. The following months piled up a black record of defeats in which the English forces were outgeneralled and outfought. Modder River, Spion Kop, and Sanna's Post became sinister names as the losses of men and guns mounted and the army learned belated lessons in modern tactics and the use of machine guns. The country fell into a grim mood that was not lifted until the relief of Mafeking (May 18, 1900) loosed an hysteria of celebration such as was not seen again for eighteen years. The work of Lord Roberts who had replaced Buller in the South African command, and the army's dearly bought knowledge of fighting in the veldt had turned the tide toward victory and it now seemed that the war might be quickly ended.

With Mafeking Night returned the spirit of careless jingoism in which England had entered the war. Union Jacks were everywhere, music halls blared windy imperialism and contempt of the enemy, and in the streets children bought rubber pigs called Dying Boers that when blown up collapsed again with an agonizing squeal. It was a silly season in which the lean khaki men, new figures in London, had no part. Neither had an important minority of the nation that had distrusted the imperial spirit from the start. A solid body of Little Englanders denounced the war and all it stood for, the unscrupulous exploitation that had engendered it, the domination of foreign peoples, militarism, and the control of empire by commercial interests. They included most of the men of letters and had the support of one or two newspapers strong enough to risk an unpopular liberalism. Their opinions had ultimate influence but at the time they were politically ineffective.

The Queen throughout the darkest days of the war had

scrupulously fulfilled her public duties and even added to them. She lived to see the hope of victory become a certainty and then, tired out, died in January, 1901. She was succeeded by her son Albert Edward, now a man of sixty, who was crowned in August as Edward VII.

The immediate business in hand was the winding up of the Boer War which had degenerated into stubborn guerrilla fighting of the commandos (light columns of the Boer militia) which required a large and expensive force for its suppression. This was achieved in May, 1902, the Boers surrendering and acknowledging themselves subjects of the King. In 1910 the Boer republics (Transvaal and Orange Free State) were incorporated with the English colonies in the Union of South Africa with dominion status.

During his short reign of nine years King Edward gained the title of Peacemaker because he maintained the surface calm of Europe and averted for some time a danger of which his people were very imperfectly aware. Queen Victoria, of the House of Hanover and married to the beloved Albert of Saxe-Coburg-Gotha, had been deeply attached to the pacific, politically divided Germany of her youth; she had applauded the achievement of the Reich in the stress of the Franco-Prussian war. But her grandson, the Kaiser Wilhelm II, taking over the splendidly organized state that Bismarck had created for him, had quickly become truculent toward all Europe and toward England in particular:

> Dere's Grandma tinks she's nicht small beer
> Mit Boers und such she'll interfere
> She'll learn none owns dis hemisphere
> But Me—und Gott!

Already possessing the finest army in the world, he proceeded to build a navy that involved England in a costly armament competition. German competition cut seriously into England's shipping and trade; German diplomacy was hostile. Edward understood his nephew and since England had not an ally, or a real friend, among the nations, went to work personally to establish the good relations that made possible the Triple Entente with France and Russia that was his diplomatic masterpiece. It was by no means a checkmate to German designs but it delayed the European crisis for some years.

Soon, though it took a long time to penetrate the public mind, the danger of a German war became apparent. As early as 1903 a book called *Modern Warfare* by an anonymous artillery officer ("Ubique") discussed in detail the composition and tactics of a British expeditionary force to meet the Germans in Belgium and in the same year Erskine Childers' novel *The Riddle of the Sands* told of the discovery by two English yachtsmen of a German base on the Frisian coast for the invasion of England. In 1906 a melodrama *An Englishman's Home* startled London audiences with a realistic picture of a German invasion and the shooting of English civilians. Yet so completely did the success of the Triple Entente lull these early alarms that when the war at last came in 1914 it was a genuine shock to a majority of the nation. Fortunately through favoring the appointment of his friend R. B. Haldane to the War Office in Campbell-Bannerman's liberal cabinet of 1906, the King assured the reorganization of the army and the creation of the Territorial reserve which enabled the nation to meet the shock.

Though Edward was much more liberal than his mother, his reign was on the whole one of social conservatism. The traditional life of the aristrocracy and country gentry was unimpaired as Sassoon shows it in *Memoirs of a Fox-Hunting Man* (1927). For the middle classes it was an idyllic time. If incomes were small by modern standards, the means of culture were cheap and abundant. Travel, except in the most backward countries, was comfortable and unhampered by passports and official restrictions. Carnegie libraries and

EDWARDIAN LONDON

excellent cheap reprints were making the best books available to virtually all. The gramophone brought music into the homes of those who could not play. Motor cars made golf and week-ending national institutions.

Cheap newspapers, spectacular sports, and the cinema were the doubtful benefits of the working class. The establishment of the *Daily Mail* in 1896 by Alfred Harmsworth (afterward Lord Northcliffe) marked the beginning in England of modern popular journalism. The Boer War, creating a vast demand for sensational news, made his fortune. His papers became the media for mass advertising and the promotion of popular sports. Now began the national popularity of professional (soccer) football and an increased spectator and gambling interest in sports of all kinds. Sir Thomas Lipton turned the America's Cup races, which had been the diversion of wealthy noblemen like Lord Dunraven, into a gigantic advertisement for tea. And every game, fight, and race had its crowds of devotees in the readers of the halfpenny press. The cinema, cheaper and more varied, began to draw the crowds from the music halls, and working-class pleasure resorts such as Douglas and Blackpool grew astonishingly.

In 1906 was launched H. M. S. *Dreadnaught,* that with her ten twelve-inch guns and twenty-one knots speed effected a revolution in naval construction and tactics. The *Lusitania* and in 1907 her sister, the *Mauretania,* followed. Designed to serve as auxiliary cruisers, these were the most famous ships of the Cunard Line and for years holders of the Atlantic record. The sinking of the *Lusitania* in May, 1915, was influential in arousing American sentiment toward entry into the First World War on the side of England. By 1909 motor buses and taxicabs had appeared in the streets of London and rapidly changed the character of its traffic so that by the end of Edward's reign horse-drawn vehicles had all but disappeared. In the same year Blériot's flight from

Calais to Dover awoke the nation to the new danger of invasion by air and stimulated interest in aviation, in which England had hitherto been far behind France and the United States.

The arts of the new century were also beginning to take shape. In literature, as is shown elsewhere in this book, the Edwardian era, if not especially progressive, was undeniably vigorous; the young men whose early work had appeared in the nineties were now developing into mature writers, some eight or ten of them destined to make great names. Granville Barker was notably raising the standard of the London theater, while the Abbey Theater, Dublin, and later the Manchester Repertory Theater became two strong centers of dramatic progress outside the capital. An old theatrical art, the dance, began to be studied with a new seriousness in the interpretations of Isadora Duncan and Adelaide Genee. Painting, which had grown insipidly pretty, began to recover strength in the hands of Augustus John, William Orpen, Henry Nevinson, Muirhead Bone, and others. Elgar in music and Lutyens in architecture, if not exactly among the great, did substantial work. In 1902 King Edward founded the Order of Merit for those, chiefly artists and writers, to whom titles would be unacceptable or inappropriate. In 1905 it was conferred on Meredith, then in his seventy-eighth year. Bridges, Masefield, Galsworthy, and Hardy are among those who have since received it.

Politically the reign began with the conservative wing of the Unionist party in power under the premiership of Lord Salisbury. They had been put there by the "khaki vote" in the election of 1900 to end the Boer War as quickly as possible, but that done, they remained in office until 1905 when the Liberals carried Campbell-Bannerman's government into office. It was now that the men who were to direct the politics of the First World War began to rise to leadership— Arthur Balfour, Herbert Asquith, David Lloyd George, and

Sir Edward Grey. Women's suffrage and the attack upon the power of the House of Lords became important issues.

In April of 1910 the King returned from abroad in poor health. He wished to go on as usual but his condition grew rapidly worse, then critical, and on May 6 he died. The Prince of Wales was proclaimed as George V.

King Edward had great personal dignity and love of State ceremonial; otherwise he was wholly unlike his mother. Frivolous in youth, he had become a cynical man of the world, fond of good living and far from exclusive in the formation of his private circle. He travelled widely, amusing himself in all the brighter resorts of the continent. His example brought about a marked increase of smartness and extravagance in fashionable life and a breaking down of the Victorian ideal of respectability. But he used his personal influence at home and abroad on the whole wisely and for the good of his country, and his reign was the last happy period in the history of modern England.

George V was crowned in June, 1911. It was in one of England's rare hot summers in which the brooding atmosphere seemed an emanation of an unrest that was everywhere palpable. There were widespread strikes among dockers, seamen, and railway workers that required the presence of troops in London and other cities where there was some ugly fighting. At the same time the appearance of a German warship off Agadir, Morocco, nearly precipitated a European crisis. In Westminster, Parliament was less troubled by the Parliament Bill which took the last of its real power from the House of Lords than by the Suffragettes, who from agitation had begun a campaign of violence that was to continue to the outbreak of the war. Altogether it was an ominous coronation year, though from morning to night hurdy-gurdies filled the streets with the strains of "My Hero" from the season's hit *The Chocolate Soldier*. In the fall the King and Queen sailed to India for the great

Durbar at Delhi, the first ceremony of its kind held by a British sovereign.

The next three years passed in alarms and unrest. Labor troubles got steadily worse. Ulster, alarmed at the prospect of Irish home rule, was armed and drilling in all but open rebellion. In April, 1912 the great new White Star liner *Titanic* (46,800 tons) sank in collision with ice on her maiden voyage westward with a loss of 1635 lives. The investigation of the disaster showed a scandalous negligence in the building and operation of large passenger vessels. The next year brought a scandal of another sort. It became public that the Chancellor of the Exchequer, the Attorney General, and other cabinet ministers had been dealing unethically in American Marconi shares. The affair was whitewashed in a Select Committee of Parliament, but it remained an unpleasant symptom of the extravagance that was driving the fashionable world, often recklessly, into the stock market. It was a jar to the credit of the Liberal party that since 1906 had survived two elections.

Throughout England as the nation approached the August Bank Holiday of 1914 the old order appeared, if not disintegrating, at least to be cracking badly. The reserve that had surrounded aristocratic life was being discarded: fashionable youth was dancing foxtrots and tangos in restaurants and hotels; its presence at Henley or Cowes, at races, hunt meets, and garden parties was photographed for the press. Its traditional superiority was becoming mere snob prestige. The conservatives were shocked by green wigs at London parties, the brutality of Masefield's poems, and cubism, which then seemed the final insanity in art. The new king did not have the great influence of his father. A younger son, he had been bred to the navy without expectation of succeeding to the throne. A quiet, self-effacing man, he was utterly conscientious in his duty but without much effect on the lives of his subjects. The ordeal of the war had not yet created the affectionate respect that attached them to him strongly in later years.

All Europe had been aware for years of *"der Tag"* for which Germany waited to declare her power and fulfil her destiny. When it came, of course, it looked like something else. On June 28, 1914, an Austrian Archduke, Francis Ferdinand, was assassinated at Sarajevo by a Serbian nationalist. Austria sent a crushing ultimatum to Serbia, which, over Russia's protest, led to war. Russia mobilized, then her ally France, then Germany. Most Englishmen realized that their country would become involved, but they expected it to be only in the naval sphere which was traditionally hers. Sir Edward Grey, Foreign Secretary, made desperate efforts to limit the war he could not stop, feeling, like all the cabinet, that England was too distraught with politics and labor trouble to embark securely on a major war. But the invasion of Belgium on August 4, forced England to meet her obligations under the Triple Entente. War was declared and the first British Expeditionary Force crossed the Channel. Grey said: "All over Europe the lamps are going out."

PREMIERS

Lord Salisbury (Unionist), *1895-1902*
A. J. Balfour (Unionist), *1902-1905*
Sir H. Campbell-Bannerman (Liberal), *1905-1908*
Herbert Asquith (Liberal), *1908-1914*

POETRY

POETRY, by its very nature, has always reflected and at times augmented the spirit of its age. In the period from 1890 to 1914, poetry was especially responsive to the rapidly shifting environment which is part of the time-spirit. Although 1890 marks no upheaval in life and letters, nor even so much as the publication date of a significant literary work, it was in the closing decade of the nineteenth century that a perceptible disquiet began to manifest itself in the arts, including poetry. The disquiet of the *fin de siècle* was the result of many factors, not the least of which was the restlessness of an age grown tired of its own conventions. The Victorian Age had been long and fruitful. A great romantic tradition had been established at the start which flourished under the momentum of the works of Wordsworth, Coleridge, Byron, Shelley, and Keats. As the mid-century passed, however, with the industrial revolution well under way, and with the discoveries of the scientists and preachments of the philosophers casting doubt into what had for long been an unrippled pool of thought, there was an increasing tendency to use literature as a means to moral and didactic ends, and to bring it to the level of those who, it was believed, might profit most by its lessons. The major poets Tennyson and Browning, working in the great tradition, had by reason of strong individual genius brought it to new heights; but there were many prolific writers who gave to the period little of its greatness but much of its prevailing tone. As the century advanced, a monotony, or at least a lack of variety was evident in the art forms, with moral baggage burdening the vehicles which were designed especially to reach the vast middle classes. Verse patterns, diction, and imagery were standardized into conventions which suffered from overuse. Victorian literature has been immoderately praised and disparaged, but the fact remains that the age was weary of itself before it came to an end.

Even before the century was drawing to a close, in limited circles there was a recognition of a need for change. The Pre-Raphaelites, for example, had set out deliberately to try to respiritualize art by going to the past for themes in order to escape from moral and didactic purpose; and in the works of Rossetti and Swinburne, both poets of extreme talent, the romantic movement flamed anew. Other manifestations of unwillingness to follow the prevailing pattern appeared, although the instances were isolated and without a carefully deliberated effort to escape the conventions of the times. George Meredith in *Modern Love* (1862) and *A Reading of Earth* (1888) was clearly out of tune with an age which kept marital love on a pedestal from which it was to be hymned with epithalamia or regarded with reverence, and which viewed nature from an ornate gazebo to see it only in its rose-bowers and unmixed benevolence.

By 1890 the disquiet had become so pronounced that organized movements began to flourish in which there was a calculated effort to break away from the themes and manner of the time-weary age. The so-called Yellow Nineties, a name derived from the once-notorious periodical which flourished in the early part of the decade, *The Yellow Book,* witnessed the rapid growth of what has been variantly termed the Art for Art's Sake School, the Aesthetic Movement, and the Decadence. Adopting the earlier Pre-Raphaelite conviction that art should be respiritualized, some of Walter Pater's precepts, and devices of manner from the French symbolists, the poets of the Aesthetic Movement created a revolt against the Victorian conventions which possesses both historical and literary significance. Manifestations of the revolt appeared in many forms, including the drawings of Aubrey Beardsley and Charles Conder, and the prose tales of Hubert Crackanthorpe and George Egerton; and in much of the verse of Ernest Dowson, Arthur Symons, and Oscar Wilde the most distinctive features of the decadence appeared.

Almost concurrently a group of Irish authors, becoming increasingly aware of the rich storehouse of themes which lay virtually untouched in the old Gaelic legends, and, like the poets of the aesthetic school, unsympathetic to the conventional refinements of recent British verse, set deliberately to work to revive the Gaelic tales, not only to bring the heroic age of Ireland into high relief, but also to find avenues of escape from Victorian confines. The movement which has been called the Celtic Renaissance was probably more the result of a new nationalistic spirit than a reaction against Victorianism, but in the development of the movement there was a conscious effort on the part of its leaders to remain independent of English and Victorian influence. The idea of a Celtic literary revival was so appealing, and the need for change was evidently so great, that during the early phases of the movement more than a few talented London writers who had little on which to base their claim to Irish ancestry were readily led to attach themselves to the "Celtic fringe" and seek inspiration in Gaelic themes. It was William Butler Yeats who was the pole-star of the revival, both as publicist and poet. *The Wanderings of Oisin and Other Poems* (1889) and the verses in *Poems* (1895) illustrated the uses to which Gaelic lore could be put, and gave momentum to a movement which flourished until after the First World War and continues to exist.

As Richard Le Gallienne has pointed out, "The last ten years of the nineteenth century properly belong to the twentieth century, and, far from being 'decadent,' except in certain limited manifestations, they were years of an immense and multifarious renaissance. All our present conditions, socially and artistically, our vaunted new 'freedoms' of every kind—including 'free verse'—not only began then, but found a more vital and authoritative expression than they have found since, because of the larger, more significant personalities engaged in bringing them about." * Without an organized movement to give them objectives and support, but with positive literary personalities which made them leaders rather than followers, poets appeared during

---

* *The Romantic 90's* (1925), p. 136.

the nineties to produce verse which contrasted sharply with what had gone before and was still in vogue. William Ernest Henley in his verses *In Hospital* (1888), *London Voluntaries* (1893), and *A Song of Speed* (1903) treated themes which many of his immediate forebears would have considered unfit for poetry. The graphic portrayal of his experiences in Lister's Infirmary in Edinburgh, "half workhouse and half jail," was scarcely palatable to a generation of readers who turned away from a realistic contemplation of suffering and death. Not only did many of Henley's themes come as a shock, but the muscularity of his manner led many a conservative, accustomed to the refined diction and easily scanned measures of Tennyson, to view with concern the level to which poetry had descended. When *A Song of Speed* appeared, with its irregular lines thrust in apparently confused procession across the page, there were those who insisted that in neither content nor certainly in manner could such a piece be called poetry. It was Henley who as editor of the *National Observer* first published the *Barrack Room Ballads* of Rudyard Kipling. Those verses were greeted with delight by the younger and more buoyant spirits of the time, who liked their virility of subject and presentation, but the conservatives and the followers of the aesthetic school were as one in their judgment of what was termed coarseness in Kipling's manner.

It was during the nineties that Thomas Hardy made his first bid for recognition as a poet, as did A. E. Housman. The gnarled and blunt manner of Hardy's *Wessex Poems* (1898), with the recurrent theme of the preponderance of ill, came as something unsalutary to many readers who preferred to close their eyes to realities while reciting Pippa's Song in Browning's *Pippa Passes*. The structural beauties in A. E. Housman's *A Shropshire Lad* (1896) made his work more acceptable than Hardy's, although it was not only among the die-hards that the conviction was expressed that such verse should not be placed into the hands of the young. "The black, vicious melancholy" attributed to the poetry of Hardy and Housman was a deterrent to the reception of their works which was not overcome until the twentieth century was well advanced. It is interesting to note that Housman's *A Shropshire Lad,* published in 1896, reached only its fifth small printing in 1905, whereas Sir Henry Newbolt's *Admirals All* (1897) went through twenty-one printings in a few years. Hardy's *Wessex Poems* fared even worse than Housman's volume in the ten years after its publication.

Of those who were particularly opposed to the questionings and misgivings of Hardy and Housman concerning the unmixed benevolence of nature and the divine plan, the devout Roman Catholics stood ready to reaffirm their faith. The Victorian conflict not only strengthened the faith of many Catholics, but during the closing decades of the nineteenth century, it led many perplexed men and women, in their eagerness to find something to which to cling, to embrace zealously the Church of Rome. Many of the decadents, especially Ernest Dowson and Lionel Johnson, found in their conversion a source of inspiration; but it is in the verse of Francis Thompson and Alice Meynell that the devotional urge found its choicest expression. The force of their work, especially that of Thompson, and the increased output of peculiarly Catholic poetry in the new century have led a few historians to consider these manifestations a sign of a Catholic literary renaissance.

Throughout the revolts and counter-revolts which occurred in the reaction against Victorianism, many conservatives, either out of the firm conviction that traditional forms have ample variety, or out of apprehension of change, continued to follow the old main current. Of the many traditionalists, Austin Dobson, Sir William Watson, Robert Bridges, Laurence Binyon, and Alfred Noyes have illustrated with varying degrees of persuasiveness and effect that good poetry does not depend on the magic of novelty.

The turn of the century saw the aesthetic movement well spent; in fact, before the first decade of the new century had passed, a reaction set in which has been called the First Georgian Revolt. This revolt had few of the aspects of an organized movement, and the poets who made up the very loosely knit group often had aims other than that of avoiding the extremes to which the decadents had gone. Although there was a strict avoidance of an exploration of the nuances of sensation, especially that which suggested the sinister and the carnal, there was also an effort to keep away from the overused rhythms and lofty diction of the Victorians, and to reject themes which were didactic and hortatory. The works of this scattered group, who were essentially traditionalists, illustrate not a return to Victorian morality, but a return to wholesomeness. Some of the early works of W. W. Gibson, Lascelles Abercrombie, and J. Elroy Flecker belong to this reaction. These poets and others who have been somewhat arbitrarily identified with the First Georgian Revolt by reason of their appearance in Edward Marsh's *Georgian Poetry* did their most distinctive work independent of any reaction or movement.

It was during the first decade of the new century that the realism and muscularity which were a part of Henley's manner were carried to new provinces and heights by John Masefield. *The Salt Water Ballads* (1902), *Ballads* (1903), and especially *The Everlasting Mercy* (1911) employed themes and diction which were more pronounced in their naturalism than anything which the earlier reactionaries had shown. When in "A Consecration," he declared, "Mine be the dirt and the dross, the dust and scum of the earth!" he warned his readers that here would be poetry different from the sweetness and light of most of his predecessors. Masefield's realism shocked many of his readers, who were resentful not only because the dirt and dross appeared, but that the poet had placed such stress on them. The advancing century was becoming more accustomed to colloquial and even gross diction in verse, for specialists in calling a spade a spade were beginning to appear on all sides; but in 1911 when *The Everlasting Mercy* appeared, Masefield's apparent satisfaction in using realism as an end in itself was not generally approved.

It was against the extremes of realism and the frequent slip-shod technique of its practitioners that a counter-reaction set in which is at times called the Second Georgian Revolt. These so-called Georgian Revolts were little more than the efforts of individual poets, all of whom were essentially traditionalists, to demonstrate the strength and beauty which can be achieved without forsaking the time-tested conventions. Ralph Hodgson and Walter de la Mare were identified with this movement, although their greatest works are the result of highly individualized genius rather than of a clearly defined reactionary spirit. It is with the lesser figures in the motley assortment which were brought together by Edward Marsh in his anthologies *Georgian Poetry* that the most reactionary tendencies appear. The "dust and scum" of Masefield become the moonlight and roses of John Drinkwater, John Freeman, and W. J. Turner. There is little vitality and strength in most of these Georgian poems—at least when they are compared with Masefield's—but in them there is a serene sort of beauty which is in part dependent on a rigorous stylistic discipline. Without becoming conspicuously fastidious in their attention to form, the better poets whom Marsh brought into his collections were perfectionists to whom the file was more essential than the sledge. It was not until the outbreak of the war that the realists and the Georgians were brought for a time under one banner, at least insofar as they both found inspiration in a common theme.

THE AESTHETIC MOVEMENT

Although the nineties were marked by a restlessness which manifested itself in literature at large, the aesthetic movement was the most calculated effort to break away from the main current of Victorianism. By 1890 there was sufficient sentiment against the utilitarian spirit which permeated much of the immediately preceding and current literature to constitute a revolt which, as the decade advanced, became a wide and productive movement. In such gathering places as the Crown—a latter-day Mermaid Tavern—groups of young artists and poets talked far into the night about art for art's sake, Walter Pater's dicta, and the necessity *pour épater le bourgeois*. It was a period of art cults and clubs of which the short-lived but famous Rhymers' Club, which had as its members such young poets as Ernest Dowson, Lionel Johnson, Arthur Symons, and William Butler Yeats, was outstanding. Fastidiously designed and illustrated periodicals such as *The Yellow Book* and later *The Savoy* were issued presumably to rescue art from what the editors and contributors felt was its increasing concern with practical ends. In spite of the fact that the nineties cannot be labeled prevailingly decadent, for there were countercurrents constantly at work, it was during this interval that the aesthetic movement reached its zenith and fell into sharp decline.

The poetry which emerged has often been called decadent, largely by reason of the fact that in its most characteristic expression it showed much of the strain for the unusual which is part of an age grown weary of its conventions. Decadence appears in any art which is the result of a complex and highly developed civilization, but the decadence of the nineties was the outgrowth of a definite aesthetic philosophy. As an essential declaration in its creed, the aesthetic school rejected all objectives which were didactic and hortatory. In addition to a rejection of all utilitarian purpose, the creed insisted upon a stress on form—not a care-fully molded conventionalized form save in the fundamental principle of stress—but a form which must be first, last, and always richly musical, and the more unusual—one might even say exotic—the better. For this part of their belief the practitioners of the aesthetic group went to the French sym-bolists, and especially to Paul Verlaine who in his "Art Poétique" had stated:

> Music above everything
> And odd music at that—
> Vaguer and more soluble than air,
> Without anything in it that burdens or is set.

With beauty as its chief objective, the decadents explored the responses to the senses, which in themselves were ex-alted as the most fertile source for response to beauty. The senses, however, dulled by the commonplace, had to be stimulated, even agitated, by a deliberate search for subtle, unusual effects: the result should produce nuances of sensu-ous response. It was here that decadence began to take on an unhealthy visage. Tiring of the fragrance of new-mown hay and even attar of roses, the poet in quest of nuances of sensation turned to patchouli and the fever plants of the south. Arthur Symons pointed out in his once-provocative essay "In Defense of Patchouli" that stimulation often lay in the less obvious sensory responses, and Oscar Wilde, in both precept and example, indicated that nature was an unproductive field in which to find poetic content. The char-acteristics which appeared in the poetry thus motivated have been summed up by Holbrook Jackson in *The Eighteen Nineties* (1914): "Perversity, Artificiality, Egoism, and Curi-osity ... characteristics not at all inconsistent with a sincere desire 'to find the last final shade ...' "

Obviously poetry motivated by a beauty drawn almost en-tirely from the senses cannot be robust; its roots cannot be strong, if it has roots at all. Preserving its creed, it cannot reconcile God's ways to man, nor can it provide man with a philosophy, substantial and abiding, which will reconcile him to life's ironies and nature's laws. But it can be beautiful, exquisite, and haunting; and the poetry of Ernest Dowson was all of these.

Ernest (Christopher) Dowson (1867-1900) was born in Lee, Kent, of parents of literary interests and connections, but neither of whom was physically strong nor temperamentally stable. Complete maladjustment, traceable to his lack of formal schooling and discipline, the atmosphere of despair in his home, and tuberculosis, was the essential tragedy in Dowson's life. When both of his parents committed suicide, the life-weariness which was part of his birthright became more pronounced; and in spite of his half-hearted efforts to find something to which to tie the frayed ends of his life in writing and his association with the Bohemian circles in London and Paris, he was never successful in making the right adjustments with circumstances which beset him relentlessly. Habits of irregularity were thrust upon him, and he, with little strength of body or will to combat ill fortune, was tired of the struggle long before his death.

He wrote two novels with Arthur Moore, *A Comedy of Masks* (1893) and *Adrian Rome* (1899), did much translating from the French for Leonard Smithers, the publisher, and produced a dozen tales in prose, most of which appeared in *The Yellow Book* and *The Savoy*. All of his prose, especially that in "The Princess of Dreams" and "The Visit," has distinction and beauty. Although Dowson, himself, gave support to the conclusion that his poetry was composed of "verses making for mere sound, and music, with just a suggestion of sense, or hardly that..." much of the spirit of the decadence and of his own personality can be read into the lines. The love poems, among which are the justly famous "Cynara," and the devotional poems, such as "Extreme Unction" and "Nuns of the Perpetual Adoration," show Dowson's wavering "between heaping garlands upon the altars of Aphrodite and lighting candles to the Blessed Virgin." Although the devotional poems have more than their tonal beauty to commend them, for the essential voice of the poet one must go to the verses in which a life-weariness is expressed. Although such a sentiment was part of the decadent spirit, in the light of what is known about the circumstances surrounding Dowson's life, poems such as "A Last Word" and "They are not long, the weeping and the laughter" must be regarded as the expression of sincere feeling. It is true that his volume and range are slight, and his voice is never strong. As a true decadent, he was unconcerned with conveying a message. In his darkly beautiful lyrics, however, there are imagery and phrasings which are consummate, and melodies which are haunting.

VERSE: *Verses* (1896), *The Pierrot of the Minute, A Dramatic Phantasie in One Act* (1897), *Decorations: In Verse and Prose* (1899), *Poems*, ed. Arthur Symons (1905), *Poems*, ed. Desmond Flower (1934). PROSE: Novels with Arthur Moore: *A Comedy of Masks* (1893), *Adrian Rome* (1899), *Dilemmas: Stories and Studies in Sentiment* (1895), *The Stories of Ernest Dowson,* ed. Mark Longaker (1947).

Mark Longaker, *Ernest Dowson* (Phila., 1944); Victor Plarr, *Ernest Dowson, 1888-1897: Reminiscences, Unpublished Letters, and Marginalia* (1914); John Gawsworth, "The Dowson Legend," *Transactions of the Royal Society of Literature of the United Kingdom* (March, 1939); Arthur Symons, A Memoir, in *Poems* (1905).

Arthur Symons (1865-1945) was a directing force to the aesthetic movement as editor, critic, and poet. Born in Wales of Cornish parents, he was trained in provincial schools under excellent masters before taking up residence in Paris where he became familiar with the current art movements and many of the leading poets. On his return to England, he wrote reviews of the performances at the better music

halls, of concerts and operas, and contemporary continental
literature. An habitué of the Crown, a member of the
Rhymers' Club, well informed about all the arts, Symons
was well equipped at the time of the demise of *The Yellow
Book* to take on the editorship of the new art magazine *The
Savoy* which Leonard Smithers and Aubrey Beardsley were
ready to put out. He wrote a vast number of critical essays
during the nineties and later, some of the best of which appear in *The Symbolist Movement in Literature* (1899) and
Dramatis Personae (1923); and he added much to the volume
and direction of decadent verse. Such pieces as "A Revenge"
and "The Café Singer" in *Days and Nights* (1889) are both
decadent and melodramatic, and virtually all the poems in
Silhouettes (1892) have a heady scent about them which
leaves the senses cloyed. "To One in Alienation" in *London
Nights* (1896) treats the theme which Dowson used in the
"Cynara" poem, but Dowson's genuine delicacy and rich
melody are absent. In some of Symons' later verse, however,
notably in "Modern Beauty" and "Night" there is no longer
a preoccupation with the nuances of sensation. His last
poems show a restraint unusual for one who had written
Silhouettes, but in spite of the fact that they are interesting
pictorially and good technically, they lack the surge which
carries poetry to the heights. As a critic, Symons will continue to have some value, and his influence in giving shape
to the aesthetic movement can scarcely be overestimated.

VERSE: *Days and Nights* (1889), *Silhouettes* (1892), *London Nights*
(1895), *Amoris Victima* (1897), *Images of Good and Evil* (1899),
Lyrics (1903), *The Fool of the World and Other Poems* (1906),
Wanderer's Song (1909), *Knave of Hearts* (1913), *Lesbia and Other
Poems* (1920), *Love's Cruelty* (1923), *Jezebel Mort and Other Poems*
(1931), *Collected Poems,* 3 v. (1924). PLAYS: *Tragedies: The Har-
vesters, The Death of Agrippina, Cleopatra in Judea* (1916),
Tristan and Iseult (1917), *The Toy Cart* (1919). CRITICAL STUDIES:
An Introduction to the Study of Browning (1886), *Studies in Two
Literatures* (1897), *The Symbolist Movement in Literature* (1899),

Studies in Prose and Verse (1904), *Studies in the Seven Arts* (1906), *William Blake* (1907), *The Romantic Movement in English Poetry* (1910), *Dante Gabriel Rossetti* (1910), *Studies in Elizabethan Drama* (1919), *Charles Baudelaire: A Study* (1920), *Dramatis Personae* (1923), *Studies on Modern Painters* (1925), *A Study of Thomas Hardy* (1927), *Studies in Strange Souls* (1929), *A Study of Oscar Wilde* (1930), *A Study of Walter Pater* (1932). ESSAYS AND SKETCHES: *The Loom of Dreams* (1901), *Cities of Italy* (1907), *London, a Book of Aspects* (1908), *Parisian Nights* (1926), *Confessions, a Study in Pathology* (1930), largely autobiographical; *Wanderings* (1931).

W. G. Blaikie-Murdoch, *The Work of Arthur Symons: An Appreciation* (1907); T. E. Welby, *Arthur Symons* (1925); Max Wildi, *Arthur Symons als Kritiker der Literatur* (Leipzig, 1929).

An active member of the Rhymers' Club, a regular patron at the Crown, and a frequent contributor to *The Yellow Book*, **Lionel Johnson (1867-1902)** was one of the most talented figures of the aesthetic movement. Born in Kent, he showed even in extreme youth a desire to be well informed in all branches of culture-history. At New College, Oxford, he was so slight of stature that "he had more than once been taken for a schoolboy up for a scholarship examination," but he already had the reputation of being a wit and poet. Down in London, instead of following the profession of law which had been suggested to one of his alert mind and persuasive tongue, he became a free-lance critic and an habitué at the pubs where art was discussed. Interested in all sorts of movements, he readily attached himself to the group who were the forerunners of the Irish Literary Revival, and for a time insisted on his Celtic origin and cultivated a brogue. In 1891 his conversion to the Catholic Faith gave him a new source of inspiration for his verse. Johnson died at the age of thirty-four as the result of a fall.

The collected edition *Poems* brought out in 1915 contains some verse which did not appear in *Poems* (1895), but the total volume is not large. In their richness of decoration and melody, they have much of the essential quality of the decadence, although they never approach the ornate. A dignity and restraint, traceable to his admiration of classical literature, appear even in the treatment of themes in which a lesser poet would have weighted his lines wtih baroque imagery. Although the senses play a part in his verse, especially that of sound, Johnson's discipleship to the aesthetic ideal was more intellectual than sensory, save in such poems as "To Morfydd" in which he loses himself in the rich music of the refrains. In the short poem "The Precept of Silence" he has caught the spirit of man's fundamental loneliness in lines that are both melodic and subdued. The earnestness of the devotional poems is accentuated by a manner which can often be called abrupt. Although melodic, "Mystic and Cavalier" with its interrogative and exclamatory lines is more intent on making the theme articulate than on decorating the manner. In spite of the fact that Johnson's poetry reflects his statement: "In my library, I have all the knowledge I need of the world," and that his volume and range are slight, there is more real genius evident than in the works of most minor poets.

VERSE: *Poems* (1895), *Ireland* (1897), *Collected Poems* (1915). PROSE: *The Art of Thomas Hardy* (1894), *Post Liminium* (1911), *Reviews and Critical Papers* (1921).

At present there is no sustained biographical and critical study of Lionel Johnson. See Clement Shorter, *Lionel Johnson: A Memoir*, no. 34, Vigo Cabinet Series (Elkin Mathews, n.d.); Dixon Scott, "Lionel Johnson's Prose" in *Men of Letters* (1923); Cornelius Weygandt, "Lionel Johnson: English Irishman" in *Tuesdays at Ten* (Philadelphia, 1928); Ezra Pound, Introduction to *The Poetical Works of Lionel Johnson* (1915); H. V. Marrot, Introduction to *A New Selection of the Poetry of Lionel Johnson* (1927).

Although much of his decadent poetry appeared before the nineties, **Oscar Wilde (1856-1900)** was definitely of the aesthetic school. It was his literary philosophy as well as

Pater's which gave momentum to the decadents, and it was his early poetry which illustrated and exalted the art-for-art's-sake principle. A brilliant essayist, a clever playwright and writer of tales, and a versatile and talented poet, Wilde stands out as one of the most vivid figures of the nineties. Born in Dublin, the son of a distinguished surgeon and a talented mother, Oscar Fingal O'Elahertie Wills Wilde, after a pampered childhood was sent to the Portora Royal School, Enniskillen, and Trinity College, Dublin, before matriculating at Magdalen, Oxford. His early successes with writing supported his inclination to be regarded as an esthete; and his talent, which included a cynical, epigrammatic wit, helped him to apply his statement: "The first duty in life is to be as artificial as possible." *Poems* (1881) and the plays which he wrote in the nineties were widely acclaimed among those of fastidious and progressive tastes as the work of rare genius. It was at the height of his popularity in the theatre that Wilde's unfortunate sexual maladjustment brought him into difficulty through the ill-advised suit which he brought against the father of Lord Alfred Douglas. After two years imprisonment, he left England to live on the continent, chiefly in Bernaval, Paris, and Naples. An outcast from England, but not without friends who recognized his talents and charm, Wilde died in Paris in 1900.

Although not so widely known as the plays and some of the verse, Wilde's prose is a strong illumination of the author and his precepts. His aesthetic creed, and, in fact, his general philosophy are to be found in *Intentions* (1891) and *De Profundis* (1905). Of the prose narratives, *The Picture of Dorian Gray* (1891) illustrates Wilde's skill at using the framework of a story for expressing his views on art and life. The plays, with the exception of the sensuous poetic drama *Salome* (1893), are cleverly designed examples of the Comedy of Manners. The problems presented in *Lady Windermere's Fan* (1892), *A Woman of No Importance*

(1893), and the trimly turned trifle *The Importance of Being Earnest* (1895) are never seriously considered or answered, nor are the characters completely realized. The lines given to them, however, are sprightly and often scintillating. In his poetry, Wilde shows considerable range and varying degrees of emotional depth. The themes vary from political precept to devotional sentiment, and from the revelation of a mood to the sociological implications in "The Ballad of Reading Gaol." His manner, often derivative, ranges from the adjective-laden lines in "The Sphinx" to the delicately restrained style of "Requiescat." His last poem "The Ballad of Reading Gaol" stands apart from much of the earlier poetry in the real substance of its theme and the sincerity of its expression. There is small doubt that Wilde had genius, but after the passing of a half-century, it is even more strongly affirmed that some of it was misdirected.

VERSE: *Poems* (1881), *The Sphinx* (1894), *The Ballad of Reading Gaol* (1898). PLAYS: *Vera, or the Nihilists* (1882), *The Duchess of Padua* (1884), *A Florentine Tragedy* (1885), *Lady Windermere's Fan* (1892), *Salome* (1893), *A Woman of No Importance* (1893), *An Ideal Husband* (1895), *The Importance of Being Earnest* (1895). PROSE STORIES AND ESSAYS: *The Happy Prince and Other Tales* (1888), *Lord Arthur Saville's Crime and Other Stories* (1891), *The Picture of Dorian Gray* (1891), *A House of Pomegranates* (1891), *Intentions* (1891), *The Soul of Man Under Socialism* (1891), *De Profundis* (1905).

Stuart Mason, *A Bibliography of Oscar Wilde* (1914); Hesketh Pearson, *Oscar Wilde: His Life and Wit* (1946); Frances Winwar, *Oscar Wilde and the Yellow Nineties* (1940), with bibliography; Robert H. Sherard, *Life of Oscar Wilde* (1906, rev. ed., 1928); O. T. Hopkins, *Oscar Wilde: A Study of the Man and His Work* (1916); Frank Harris, *Oscar Wilde: His Life and Confessions* (2 v., 1918); Arthur Symons, *A Study of Oscar Wilde* (1930); G. J. Renier, *Oscar Wilde* (1933); Boris Brasol, *Oscar Wilde, the Man, Artist, and Martyr* (1938); Lord Alfred Douglas, *My Friendship With Oscar Wilde* (1932), *Without Apology* (1938), and *Oscar Wilde:*

A Summing-Up (1940); Vincent O'Sullivan, *Aspects of Wilde* (1936), Edouard Roditi, *Oscar Wilde* (1947), in which Wilde's stature as a critic is considered; George Woodcock, *The Paradox of Oscar Wilde* (1949). See also Roditi's article, "Oscar Wilde's Poetry as Art History" in *Poetry,* LXVII (1945), 322-337; A. H. Nethercot, "Oscar Wilde and the Devil's Advocate," *PMLA,* LIX (1944), 833-850.

John Davidson (1857-1909) was associated with the decadents, but his most mature work shows a complete severance from the spirit of the aesthetic school. He contributed poems to *The Yellow Book* and was a member of the Rhymers' Club, the later meetings of which he attended irregularly. His attachment to the art movements of the nineties was probably more the result of his desire for sympathetic understanding and companionship than of any conviction of the soundness of the objectives of the art-for-art's-sake movement. Even before he came to London, his mind was too speculative and rapacious to allow him to lose himself in responses to the senses, and as the decade advanced and turned into the new century, his philosophical inquiries engaged him to such an extent that they became his preoccupation.

Born at Barrhead, Renfrewshire, Davidson after a troubled childhood left school at the age of thirteen to work in a chemical laboratory where he probably got his first inkling of a purely chemical cosmos; and at fifteen he was a pupil-teacher at Barrhead. For eleven years he was a teacher in the Scottish provinces, during which interval he read widely in the classics and Elizabethan literature, and it was at this time that his first acquaintance with Nietzsche and other philosophical writers began. In 1889 he came to London to try to establish himself as a professional man of letters. Of his early years in London little is known save that he wrote much and published little, and that he was often sick and poor. In spite of his association with the writers of the aesthetic school, he found so little encouragement from publishers that he was forced into journalism. Poverty, a constantly ailing body, and an unsatisfying philosophy became insurmountable obstacles in his later years. One day in March, 1909, he did not return to his home in Penzance where he had lived in lowly circumstances. Some time after his disappearance, his body was washed up by the sea.

Davidson wrote three novels, six plays, many essays, some of which served as prefaces to his volumes of verse, a considerable amount of journalistic hackwork, and twelve books of poems. The prose is often dated in both content and style. In his preferred medium verse, there are two main tendencies revealed: an occupation with romantic themes in which a four-line ballad stanza is often employed and in which the manner has some of the decoration of the decadents; and a philosophical speculation cast usually into blank verse in which there is little attempt at adornment. The well-known "Ballad of a Nun" and "Ballad of Hell" illustrate his best and most distinctive work in the first group, and the "Testaments" show his trend of thought and manner in the second.

As a prophet and seer, Davidson never appealed to wide audiences and it is improbable that future generations will go to the "Testaments" to bring light out of their darkness. Even his zeal, which extended at times to fanaticism and high-pitched rhetoric, must be put aside in the final estimate of his works in which his cosmogonic passion made of him more the vehement prophet than the poet. Some of his early poems, especially the ballads, and many of the pieces in *Fleet Street Eclogues* (1893), will continue to be read; and such reflections of a courageous mind and spirit as those in "The Unknown" should be read by those who are too readily inclined to dismiss the poet's philosophical works as zeal without intellect.

VERSE: *In a Music Hall* (1891), *Fleet Street Eclogues* (1893, rev. ed., 1909), *Ballads and Songs* (1895), *The Last Ballad* (1899), *The Testament of a Vivisector* (1901), *The Testament of a Man God Forbid* (1901), *The Testament of an Empire Builder* (1902), *The Testament of a Prime Minister* (1904), *The Testament of John Davidson* (1908). NOVELS: *Laura Ruthven's Widowhood,* with C. J. Wills (1892), *The Wonderful Mission of Earl Lavender* (1896), *Miss Armstrong's Circumstances* (1896). SKETCHES: *A Random Itinerary* (1894).

Davidson stated that he wished no biography written. His wish thus far has been carried out. C. A. and H. W. Stonehill, *Bibliographies of Modern Authors,* second series (1925); H. Fineman, *John Davidson: A Study of the Relation of his Ideas to his Poetry* (Phila., 1916); Gertrud von Petzold, *John Davidson und sein geistiges Werden unter dem Einfluss Nietzsches* (Leipzig, 1928); Petronius Applejoy, "A View of John Davidson Against a Nineties Background," *Catholic World,* CLIV (1932), 552-561.

Richard Le Gallienne (1866-1948), although spending much of his time in the United States since 1918, did his most distinctive creative work while still in England. Born in Liverpool in 1866 and educated at Liverpool College, he was down in London during the nineties, already well established in literary circles. A reader for John Lane and Elkin Mathews, one of the founders of the Rhymers' Club, a prolific reviewer, Le Gallienne contributed to the stream of decadent verse which the age produced. His account of the period in *The Romantic Nineties* (1926) is an illumination not only of the spirit of the times but of the author at this stage as well. His *Poems* (1892) are definitely of the *fin de siècle* tone, although he is never so lyrical as Dowson or so deliberate with sensory effects as Symons and Wilde. His later work in verse including *The Lonely Dancer* (1913) and *The Junkman and Other Poems* (1921) is different from the poems written during the nineties in both theme and manner, but his voice is never strong. Poetry, when it came to him, came as a sort of digression. His chief talent was critical. In America, he is perhaps best known for his numerous re-

views in which all literary forms are his province, and for
such delicately told stories as *The Quest of the Golden
Girl* (1896).

VERSE: *My Lady's Sonnets* (1887), *Poems* (1892), *An Elegy, and
Other Poems, Mainly Personal* (1895), *New Poems* (1910), *The
Lonely Dancer and Other Poems* (1913), *The Junkman and Other
Poems* (1921), *The Magic Seas* (1930). PROSE: *George Meredith:
Some Characteristics* (1890), *Prose Fancies* (1894), *The Quest of the
Golden Girl* (1896), *The Sleeping Beauty and Other Prose Fan-
tasies* (1900), *Attitudes and Avowals* (1910), *Vanishing Roads and
Other Essays* (1915), *The Romantic Nineties* (1926), *There was a
Ship* (1930).

THE CELTIC RENAISSANCE

The nineties, characterized by revolts and literary movements, saw the rapid growth of the Irish literary revival.
Although the ultimate sources of the movement probably
can be traced back into the middle of the century, it was
with Standish O'Grady's works, especially *The History of
Ireland: The Heroic Period* (1878) that interest in the literary past of Ireland was given new momentum. At the start,
the movement had as its main objective the retelling of
Celtic legends and stories. A new literary consciousness developed out of this purpose which was to find expression in
a large number of prose and verse narratives in which the
old Gaelic heroes were reanimated and given a new significance and in which the magic of the Irish imagination
played a distinctive part. In its more advanced stages, the
movement did not confine itself only to a recognition and
use of Ireland's literary past, but it expanded into an exploration of the significance of the political scene, and became increasingly concerned with the sociological problems
of peasant and laborer. Such concerns, according to some of
the figures in the movement, were beyond the boundaries
of the purpose of the revival, but they were a natural outgrowth of a recognition of a new national consciousness.

The natural magic of the Celt appeared in the expression of this consciousness, regardless of theme; but it was in the poetry and dramas which were unhampered by utilitarian baggage that a strangely lighted world, somewhere between myth and reality, began to emerge. The tenuous themes and moods, often expressed in symbols drawn from the imagination rather than from reality, and the atmosphere of other-worldliness, led Yeats and some of his associates to speak of the early phases of the movement as "the Celtic Twilight." A mysticism which was often without the mark of the Church appeared in the retelling of the old legends and in the literature which was concerned with mood. The general tone of the style was archaic, or at least quaint, in that Gaelic elements frequently were introduced in order to add to the atmosphere of a remote past and the mood of unreality. At the beginning and up until the First World War, the revival was given direction by authors of exceptional talent, with the result that the poetry and drama of the Celtic Renaissance have undoubtedly enriched contemporary literature and literature at large.

The outstanding figure in the Celtic Renaissance was **William Butler Yeats (1865-1939)**. To identify Yeats with a movement, or even with a national literature, however, is inadequate and misleading, for his work, in spite of the distinctively Celtic quality of much of it, is so varied in theme and manner that it cannot be labeled by a sufficiently inclusive phrase. There are many sides of Yeats, some of them apparently anomalous, but all of them essentially poetic. He advanced steadily in intellectual scope and depth, but the lyric note he never lost. Although some of his later works seem heavy with thought and difficult of comprehension, his artistry can never be questioned. A masterful technician and a severe self-critic, he produced little which does not have on it the stamp of his finest talent. Fundamentally a romantic, he nevertheless applied the discipline of the classicist to his work, especially in his mature poems. There is apparent traffic with the modernists in some of the later pieces, but this is more of a reflection of his many-sided poetic person-ality than an expression of loss of faith in the objectives and manner of the tradition-alists.

WILLIAM BUTLER YEATS

William Butler Yeats was born at Sandymount, a sub-urb of Dublin, in 1865, the son of John Butler Yeats, an artist of considerable talent. A younger brother, Jack Yeats, became well known as a painter, and one of the sis-ters was distinguished as a bibliophile and the founder of the Cuala Press in Dublin. From his own report the poet was unhappy as a boy. "I re-member little of my child-hood but its pain," he wrote. "I have grown happier with every year of life as though gradually conquering something in myself...." Sensitive and probably a little stubborn, he found his early schooling under the tutelage of an elderly woman distasteful, and it was not until his father took him in hand that he learned to read. "I was always near the bottom of my class," he reported, "and always making ex-cuses that but added to my timidity." Intermittently, how-ever, he was an avid listener to the tales and legends which were told to him in the heavy brogue of northern Ireland where he was often sent for long sojourns with relatives while his parents moved back and forth between Dublin and London. When he was eight, he was taken by his par-ents to London where he attended the Godolphin School in

Hammersmith. After seven years in London schools where he overcame much of his early timidity, he was taken to Dublin where his father then made his residence, and until he was eighteen he followed a classical training at the Erasmus Smith School. In spite of the fact that he showed much interest in literature, especially in the English poets, even to the extent of writing a considerable amount of verse in the manner of Spenser, it was decided that he enter the Metropolitan School of Art. Although he showed talent in art, he had developed a compelling interest in writing; and frequently, according to his own report, he neglected his sketching and reading in art history in order to write and destroy page after page of verse. Recognizing the seriousness of his interest in writing, and encouraged by the publication of some of his verse in the *Dublin University Review* and later in the *Irish Monthly,* he decided even against strong parental objection to abandon art as a profession and devote his energy and talent to writing.

During his twenties he spent most of his time in London which he believed was better suited than Dublin as an environment for a man of letters. London during the eighties and nineties was the scene of much literary activity; and Yeats, no longer the timorous schoolboy, became a zealous participant in the art groups which sat at the Crown and the Cheshire Cheese. He was active in the affairs of the Socialist League, he attended seances and joined clubs which were concerned with Theosophy and the arcana of the East, he rarely missed a gathering at the Fitzroy Settlement; and all the while he was contributing stories, articles, and poems to the London and Dublin journals. With his inborn and cultivated interest in Irish folklore, he was a major figure in founding the Irish Literary Society and in circulating the information that there was an Irish literary rebirth. Nor did his interest in Irish literature end with publicizing its significance. Already in 1889 *The Wanderings of Oisin* appeared, in which Celtic figures from the dim past move about "the Firbolgs' burial mounds." Although indebted to Standish O'Grady for some of the material in this poem, Yeats embroidered the tale with a richness of phrase and melody which led many readers to see at once the poetic resources of Irish legend. With *The Countess Kathleen and Various Legends and Lyrics* (1892) he gave additional momentum to the movement which was under way and to his own reputation as a poet. It was soon after the publication of *The Countess Kathleen* that the Rhymers' Club set aside "Celtic Nights," and Lionel Johnson began to affect a brogue. The time was ripe for a great poet to express the beauty of Irish legend and mood, and Yeats, with his energy and genius, was at hand.

Back and forth between London and Dublin, he helped to organize the Irish National Literary Society, and by 1900 he brought to fulfillment an idea which for long had been an increasingly vivid dream: the founding of an Irish National theatre. Assisted by Lady Gregory and Douglas Hyde, Yeats made possible the Abbey Theatre in Dublin from which there came some of the best plays and players of the present century. Yeats was not content to be only an organizer and for a time the manager: the creative impulse in him was too strong for him to be only a propagandist and critic. The Abbey Theatre had its ups and downs during its early years, but all along Yeats brought to it his enthusiasm, his skill at organization, and his splendid talent as a dramatist.

Although his love for Maud Gonne, the famous Irish beauty and zealous nationalist, was unrequited and left him disconsolate for long, after the First World War, Yeats's life was a progression of literary successes. Many distinctions were to come to him in recognition of his services to Ireland and his literary genius. The University of Dublin conferred degrees on him, and on his seventieth birthday, he was honored by a great banquet as Ireland's most celebrated figure.

From 1922 to 1928 he was a senator in the Irish Free State, in which role he maintained a discerning conservatism which served as a check and balance to some of the policies of his more outspoken colleagues. He married Miss Georgia Lees in 1917 out of which union a son and daughter were born. In 1923 he was awarded the Nobel prize for literature, Oxford presented him with the degree of Doctor of Literature, and on his visits to America he was given distinctions and honors. Already in the twenties he often referred to himself as an old man, for many of his contemporaries were gone; but there was little diminution in his intellectual curiosity and energy. He retained his enthusiasm for literature and life until his death in 1939.

In Yeats's personality there were combined the zeal of youth and the discipline of maturity. Always a poet, he existed in the land of faery, but he was endowed with an unusual amount of practical wisdom which gave balance to his life and works. Those who knew him intimately recall a man of great intensity, sensitive and bold in turn, with a pronounced eagerness of countenance and mind. One could not be in his presence without feeling something of his greatness.

Although his talent was essentially poetic, Yeats frequently employed the medium of the drama. He was one of the very few playwrights in recent times who could make poetry effective from behind the footlights. One of his earliest plays, *The Land of Heart's Desire* (1894), with its theme drawn from Celtic folklore of a girl whose soul is lured to "the land of heart's desire" by a fairy child, reaches a high poetic plane in both conception and in many of the lines. *Kathleen ni Houlihan* (1902), written in prose, has interest and power even when its symbolic significance is removed; and in the character of Michael Gillane, Yeats has drawn a memorable portrait. In *A Pot of Broth* (1902), written with Lady Gregory, he attempted farce which is obviously not his chief stock in trade. His later plays show an advance in design, occasionally at a loss to the lyric quality; but *The Shadowy Waters* (1904), one of his particular favorites, and *Deirdre* (1906) show his finest work as a dramatic poet. Both of them possess much lyric beauty, but it is in *Deirdre* in which he combines great dramatic effectiveness with the loftiest poetry.

It was in the province of nondramatic poetry, however, that he did his most distinctive work. His creative period, extending over almost half a century, falls into more or less readily distinguishable intervals. The division indicated by Herbert Palmer in *Post-Victorian Poetry* (1938) is illuminating:

1. The period in which he was occupied with mythology and richly embroidered verse, when, though variable in technique, he concentrated mainly on wavering rhythms. It was the period of the Celtic Twilight.

2. A middle period, which commenced shortly before the War, when he wrote more intellectually and with greater austerity. His rhythms harden, and are more in line with the Elizabethan texture of verse.

3. A later period which commenced some years after the War, when affected by the cult of the Modernists he becomes increasingly cerebral and obscure. He is still Yeats, but inclined to be academic and sometimes a little sour. The English poet who seems to have most affected him is John Donne.*

The period in which he did his finest work is a question whose answer depends largely on one's preferences in poetry. There are critics of the traditionalist school who insist that Yeats's greatest contribution to literature was made before 1914, whereas those of modernist leanings are prone to disparage the earlier works as the product of an only relatively fruitful apprenticeship, and to point to *Later Poems* (1924) and "The Tower" (1928) as the full flower of his genius.

* Reprinted with the permission of J. M. Dent and Sons.

Fortunately the differences in his poetry are not so sharply pronounced as to make a middle ground in the judgment of his works untenable.

Certainly the early narratives in which Celtic legend is the theme are told with a beauty and grace which few readers can overlook or mistake for rhetoric. Nor can the richly descriptive passages in such an early poem as "The Wanderings of Oisin" be dismissed as eloquence. There are lines which are profusely embroidered and even purple, but their beauty is rarely obscured by the weight of decoration. "The Rose of the World," "Into the Twilight," "The Song of the Faeries" in *The Land of Heart's Desire,* and the much anthologized "Lake Isle of Innisfree" are representative of his early manner.

In the later works, the symbolism is often derived more from the mind than from the imagination and the emotions; and much of the decoration of the earlier poems gives way to compression of phrase. The rhythms of "Down by the Salley Gardens" and "The Song of Wandering Aengus" appear less frequently, and in their place more austere cadences are employed. His images, no longer highly colored, continue to retain an intensity which was a faithful part of his poetic temperament. "The Tower" (1928) affords a good example of the later Yeats. "The early rainbows" are gone, and if there was a romantic rhetoric in his poetry, it certainly is gone. If his imagination and mind led him at times into symbolism which is remote and obscure, the result cannot be traced to a conscious effort on his part to be ingenious, much less difficult. As an influence on his age, and as an author of range and depth, the stature of Yeats is undoubtedly that of a major poet.

VERSE: *Mosada: A Dramatic Poem* (1886), *The Wanderings of Oisin and Other Poems* (1889), *Poems* (1895), *The Wind Among the Reeds* (1899), *In the Seven Woods* (1903), *Poems, 1899-1905* (1906), *The Golden Helmet and Other Poems* (1912), *Responsi-*

bilities and Other Poems (1916), *The Wild Swans at Coole, Other Verses, and a Play in Verse* (1917), *Michael Robartes and the Dancer* (1920), *Later Poems* (1922), *The Cat and the Moon and Certain Poems* (1924), *The Tower* (1928), *The Winding Stair and Other Poems* (1933), *Collected Poems* (1933), *The King of the Great Clock Tower* (1934), *New Poems* (1938), *Last Poems and Plays* (1940). PLAYS (in verse and prose): *The Countess Kathleen* (1892), *The Land of Heart's Desire* (1894), *The Shadowy Waters* (1900), *Cathleen ni Houlihan* (1902), *Where There is Nothing* (1902), *The Hour Glass* (1903), *A Pot of Broth* (1904), *The King's Threshold* (1904), *Deirdre* (1907), *The Unicorn From the Stars and Other Plays,* with Lady Gregory (1908), *Four Plays for Dancers* (1921), *Wheels and Butterflies* (1934), *Collected Plays* (1934). ESSAYS: *Ideas of Good and Evil* (1903), *Discoveries, a Volume of Essays* (1907), *Poetry and Ireland,* with Lionel Johnson (1908), *Synge and the Ireland of his Time* (1911), *The Cutting of an Agate* (1912), *Essays* (1924), *Letters on Poetry to Dorothy Wellesley* (1940). MEMOIRS: *Reveries over Childhood and Youth* (1915), *Four Years* (1921), *The Trembling of the Veil* (1922), *Autobiographies,* includes *Reveries over Childhood and Youth* and *The Trembling of the Veil* (1926), *Estrangement* (1926), *Reflections from a Diary Kept in 1909, The Death of Synge and Other Passages from an Old Diary* (1928).

A. J. A. Symons, *A Bibliography of William Butler Yeats* (1924); Joseph Hone, *The Life of William Butler Yeats* (1942); Richard Ellman, *Yeats, The Man and the Masks* (1948); Norman Jeffares, *W. B. Yeats: Man and Poet* (1949); Donald A. Stauffer, *Golden Nightingale* (1949); T. R. Henn, *Lonely Tower* (1950); Forrest Reid, *W. B. Yeats: A Critical Study* (1915); C. L. Wrenn, *William Butler Yeats: A Literary Study* (1920); Louis MacNeice, *The Poetry of W. B. Yeats* (1941); J. H. Pollock, *William Butler Yeats* (Dublin, 1935); V. K. N. Menon, *The Development of W. B. Yeats* (1942); Cornelius Weygandt, "W. B. Yeats" in *The Time of Yeats* (1937); J. P. O'Donnell, *Sailing to Byzantium: A Study of the Later Style and Symbolism of W. B. Yeats* (Cambridge, Mass., 1939); James Hall and Martin Steinmann, eds., *The Permanence of Yeats* (1950); R. P. Blackmur, "The Later Poetry of W. B. Yeats," *Southern Rev.,* II (1936), 339-362; Morton Zabel, "Yeats at Thirty and Seventy," *Poetry,* U.S., XLVII (1936), 268-277; W. K. Tindall, "The Symbolism of W. B. Yeats," *Accent,* V (1945), 203-212; Kenneth Burke, "On Motivation in Yeats," *Southern Rev.,* VII (1942),

547-561; Cleanth Brooks, "The Vision of W. B. Yeats," *Southern Rev.*, IV (1938), 116-142; D. S. Savage, "The Æstheticism of W. B. Yeats," *Kenyon Rev.*, VII (1945), 118-134.

George Russell (1867-1935), better known as A.E., although not so widely read as Yeats, played an important part in the Irish Literary Revival as both publicist and poet. Stephen Gwynn, in writing about the contributions which Yeats and A.E. made to the movement, observed:

These two men were to dominate the entire literary revival, and affect the whole intellectual life of Ireland in their time . . . Both were mystics. But whereas in George Russell mysticism appeared inseparable from his being, with Yeats it had the aspect of an exotic cult. Russell was of service to Ireland through the philosophy which radiated through his nature. It was in part a love of beauty, but more truly a love of humanity, of the divine in human nature.

Both poets drew much of their inspiration from the magic of Ireland's past, but whereas Yeats in his reanimation of tales from the Heroic Age was narrative and descriptive in manner, especially in the earlier poems, A.E. was always reflective. His effort in drama for the Irish Playhouse, a version of the Deirdre theme, although satisfactory, indicated that playwriting was not his most fruitful province. He lacked Yeats's ability to weave beautiful designs on a sustained narrative theme, and in spite of the fact that he was an admirable decorator in words, few of his poems were motivated to produce only vivid sensuous response. He shared with Yeats a fondness of symbolism, but the symbolic in A.E. is almost always remote and possessed of less warmth than that of his contemporary, for his symbolism is that of the soul striving to maintain communication with the eternal and divine. "I know I am a spirit," he wrote in the preface to *Homeward,* "and that I went forth from the self-ancestral to labours yet unaccomplished; but filled ever and again with homesickness I made these songs by the way."

Born in 1867 in Lurgan, County Armagh, George William Russell attended school in Dublin, and on account of his talent in drawing, he was sent to the Metropolitan School of Art at the age of sixteen. Although recognition came to him chiefly as a writer, he never forsook pictorial art, for there are more than six hundred paintings, chiefly in oil, which he gave away or sold for a pittance. When Yeats first met him at the art school, Russell was already interested in the cults of the East, Theosophy, and the Bhagavad-Gita. Recognizing in himself a dual personality, Russell allowed his real name to represent the practical side of his nature, and A.E. the mystic and poetic. The two distinct sides of his nature are plain, for the same man who wrote "Oversoul" and "Reconciliation" was the chief organizer of the Irish Agricultural Society, a competent authority on soil conditioning, and editor of *The Irish Homestead* from 1904 to 1923. Into both spheres he brought zeal, intellect, and talent. Many distinctions came to him in his late years, including honorary degrees from Dublin University and Yale; and he was offered a senatorship in the Irish Free State. This he refused, for he did not like the turn of political events in the twenties. It was his opposition to what was going on in Irish politics which led him to spend his last years in England where he died in 1935.

In addition to his play *Deirdre* (1902), written at the request of the Irish National Dramatic Company for their spring festival, Russell wrote a considerable amount of prose, some of which remains uncollected. *Some Irish Essays* (1906), *Imaginations and Reveries* (1915), and *Song and Its Fountains* (1932) which heightens an appreciation of his poetry, represent the most characteristic pieces of his literary prose. Although a prolific poet with nearly a dozen volumes of verse between *Homeward: Songs by the Way* (1894) and *The House of Titans and Other Poems* (1934), A.E. has never been widely read outside of Ireland. His mysticism, although deistic, contains Oriental and Celtic elements, and goes farther back than orthodox Christianity. The themes, often symbolic and abstract, are conveyed through measures which are melodic and strongly accented. Although his poetry is charged with meaning, some of it has an abiding appeal largely on account of its tonal quality. Such poems as "Carrowmore" and "The Twilight of Earth" afford ample proof that A.E.'s contribution to literature extends beyond the active part he played in supporting the Irish revival.

VERSE: *Homeward: Songs by the Way* (1894), *The Earth Breath and Other Poems* (1897), *The Divine Vision and Other Poems* (1904), *By Still Waters* (1906), *Gods of War and Other Poems* (1915), *Voices of the Stones* (1925), *Collected Poems* (1926), *Midsummer Eve* (1928), *The Dark Weeping* (1929), *Enchantment and Other Poems* (1930), *Vale and Other Poems* (1931), *The House of Titans and Other Poems* (1934), *Selected Poems* (1936). DRAMA: *Deirdre: A Drama in Three Acts* (1907). PROSE: *Some Irish Essays* (1906), *The Hero in Man* (1909), *The Renewal of Youth* (1911), *Imaginations and Reveries* (1915), *The Candle of Vision* (1918), *The Interpreters* (1922), *Song and Its Fountains* (1932).

Bibliographies of Irish Authors, "Æ (George William Russell)," *Dublin Magazine,* new series, V (1930), 44-54; Darrell Figgis, *Æ: A Study of a Man and a Nation* (1916); W. K. Magee (pseudonym John Eglinton), *A Memoir of Æ, George William Russell* (1937); Cornelius Weygandt, "George William Russell" in *Irish Plays and Playwrights* (1913); Diarmuid Russell, "Æ (George William Russell)," *Atlantic Monthly,* CLXXI (1943), 51-57.

Some of the younger Irish poets looked upon A.E. rather than Yeats as their leader, and it was through his encouragement and help that a goodly number of talented young men and women were brought into the revival. Of these, none was more deserving of encouragement than **James Stephens (1882-1950)**. It is a familiar story of how Stephens, leading a life of penury and drudgery as a clerk in a solicitor's office, but writing stories and verse all the while, sent A.E. some of his poems with a wistful inquiry concerning their possible worth, and of how the older poet after reading the poems

invited the young man to his home to read his verse before a
roomful of authors already known to fame in Dublin. All
Stephens needed was a start, for he had much to contribute
to the later development of the revival and to literature at
large. Irish to the core and a natural supporter of the purposes which underlay the revival, he was at the same time
capable of showing the entire English-speaking world the
charm of the Celt. Readers who have put the peculiarly
Irish works of Yeats and A.E. aside as too local, and, as a result, too obscure for the uninitiate, have found Stephens'
The Crock of Gold (1912) delightful. It is here, and occasionally elsewhere in Stephens' works, that the American and the
New Zealander with no Irish background can readily see the
quaint, the mystical, the comic, and the poetic which in
various combinations give to Irish literature much of its
appeal.

James Stephens was born in Dublin in 1882. His birthright and early environment were scarcely congenial to a
literary career. It was not until he was in his late teens and
already at work at a variety of unpromising jobs that he
became an avid reader and attended the Abbey Theatre to
witness the dramatized versions of tales from the Heroic Age.
His early marriage and attendant obligations of rearing a
family kept him from venturing far afield in search of inspiring employment, but in his spare time he wrote articles
and verses. Through the help of A.E., Stephens found employment at the National Gallery of Ireland and receptacles
for his writing. After his success with *The Crock of Gold* he
made his residence in London and Paris, with occasional
long sojourns in his native Dublin. Several times during the
twenties and thirties he visited the United States to lecture
and read his verse. In the years preceding his death in 1950,
he continued to write, but his efforts showed little of the
vigor and charm of his early work.

Although a versatile author, Stephens is known most

widely for *The Crock of Gold,* an identification by no means unfortunate, for the story has an easily recognized worth. The manner is beguiling, ranging from the comic to the wistful, and from bold to light, faery touches.

His verse reveals a poet of many voices and varied moods. In *The Renaissance of Irish Poetry* (1929) David Morton says aptly: "He is in succession a poet of nature with quaint and smiling imaginings, a Paddy of coarse humor, and finally a romantic dreamer haunted with a passionate memory of his country's beautiful and legendary past." There is exuberance in much of his early poetry in which there is a reflection of his love for life and humanity. Although interested in Ireland's past as indicated in the free adaptations from the Gaelic in *Reincarnations* (1918), he is apparently as much concerned with what the lowly Thomas said in a pub as with trying to project himself into the spirit of Celtic heroes. The fine poem "The Shell" is a sort of transition between his interest in the real and human and his concern with the abstract and mystical, and the twenty-three cantos of *Theme and Variations* (1930), although not without melody, have little of the buoyancy of the verse in *The Rocky Road to Dublin* (1915). *Strict Joy* (1931), his most mature work technically, contains poems which indicate that Stephens was not only the observer of humanity and a reviver of old tales, but a poet of considerable insight as well.

VERSE: *Insurrections* (1909), *The Lonely God and Other Poems* (1909), *The Hill of Vision* (1912), *The Rocky Road to Dublin* (1915), *Songs From the Clay* (1915), *Green Branches* (1916), *Reincarnations* (1918), *Collected Poems* (1926), *The Outcast* (1929), *Theme and Variations* (1930), *Strict Joy* (1931), *Kings and the Moon* (1938). PROSE: *The Crock of Gold* (1912), *The Demi-gods* (1914), *Deirdre* (1923), *In the Land of Youth* (1924), *Etched in Moonlight* (1928).

"Bibliographies of Modern Authors: James Stephens," *London Mercury,* IV (1921), 193; Edward Davison, "James Stephens" in *Some Modern Poets* (1928); Cornelius Weygandt, "The Riddling

of James Stephens" in *Tuesdays at Ten* (Phila., 1928); George
W. Russell, "James Stephens" in *Imaginations and Reveries*
(1916); Ernest Boyd, "James Stephens" in *Portraits: Real
and Imaginary* (1924); Groff Conklin, "James Stephens, Metrist,"
Engl. Jour., XXV (1936), 268-277.

"Seumas O'Sullivan" (Seumas Sullivan Starkie, 1878-   ),
was born in Dublin with a rich heritage of Celtic lore as part
of his birthright. From youth he was bent on preparing
himself for a literary career, and even in his middle teens
he was seriously concerned with writing verse. Like
Stephens, he came under the influence and encouragement
of A.E., who printed some of his early poems in a collection he made from the verse of the younger writers. Zealously interested in the Celtic revival and one of its major
supporters in the later phases of the movement, O'Sullivan
has brought a fine intellectual vigor to the editorship of *The
Dublin Magazine,* and critical and creative talent to a wide
variety of work. He is well known in Ireland as an erudite
bookman and a discerning critic, but his reputation has
become more than local through some of his fine verse. Small
collections of poems have appeared since *The Twilight
People* in 1905, among which *The Earth Lover* (1909), *Mud
and Purple* (1918) and the volume *Dublin Poems* (1946), in
which many of the earlier poems reappear, are representative. Thus far he has had no traffic with Eastern mysticism
in the manner of Yeats, A.E., and in a lesser way, James
Stephens; and in the poem "Credo" he rejects the mysticism
of the church in the first stanza. Devotional and pagan elements, the latter drawn from Celtic mythology, appear side
by side in his volumes; but he is neither a devotional poet
nor the singer of pagan rites. Much of his verse is the result
of mood in which there is no occupation with the role of
prophet and seer. In his poetry of Dublin, there is much
which suggests the city of yesteryear, especially of the eighteenth century. In such poems as "Nelson Street" and "Mer-

rion Square" he is scarcely the poet of whom A.E. said: "He is the literary successor of those old Gaelic poets who were fastidious in their verse, who loved little in this world but some chance light in it which reminded them of fairyland." O'Sullivan's works as a whole indicate that he had many loves other than the land of faery. When he does linger in scenes of twilight, however, there is something of Walter de la Mare's magic. In manner, he is of the traditionalists, employing for the most part diction and verse measures whose beauty and rhythms have stood the test of time.

Padraic Colum (1881-   ), widely known in America as well as in Ireland, has shown a variety of talents, some of which he has brought to themes quite remote from the Irish scene. His birthright and early training, however, fitted him well for active participation in the Celtic revival. Born away from Dublin in Longford in 1881, he had as part of his heritage something of Irish peasant background and certainly a love of the soil. After what was evidently an adequate education at local schools, he came to Dublin in his late teens to be attracted by the early phases of the Irish National Theatre. His first efforts were with short plays in which he tried to deal with Celtic legend, but the results were satisfying to neither the leaders of the movement nor to him, and, as a result, he turned his talent to themes of contemporary significance. *The Saxon Shillin'*, directed against the enlistment of Irish youth in the British army, was produced in 1903 to the satisfaction of audiences who had become increasingly nationalistic. It was not until he had written *Broken Soil* (1904) and *The Land* (1905), however, that he found his most fruitful province in playwriting. These plays, as the titles indicate, deal with the call of the land which is especially insistent to the rural Irishman. What many consider his finest play, *Thomas Muskerry* (1910), reveals life in a small community in a dramatically effectual way. In all of his plays, Colum is successful with his characterization,

especially in *Thomas Muskerry,* and there are frequent fine
lines which suggest the poetic passages in Synge. Beautiful
as some of the passages are, the dialogue is generally not
possessed of the naturalness which produces the illusion
of reality. Colum's talents, although dramatic, are better
adapted to story-telling and descriptive poetry than to the
stage. In his prose versions of the classical stories of Jason and
the Golden Fleece and the journey of Ulysses, he has written
with a grace and beauty entirely in keeping with the greatness of such themes. Although the tone may be more Celtic
than Greek, the effect, especially in the story of the Argo-
nauts, is highly poetic. It is in his small volume of poems
Wild Earth (1909) that Colum has done his finest work. The
Irish soil is the foundation of these poems, but they are more
than technicolored pictures of peasant life. A rich imaginative force is always at work, and the melodies have a simple
sweetness which is consistently appealing.

Colum's later work in *Dramatic Poems* (1922) and *Creatures* (1927) is distinguished for its imaginative quality, but
in *Creatures* there is a perceptible tightening of line and
lessening of melody. Since the First World War, he has spent
much of his time away from Ireland, living for long intervals
in the United States and the Hawaiian Islands. His *Tales
and Legends of Hawaii* (1924) and *The Bright Islands* (1925)
make good reading and indicate that no matter what the
scene, Colum views it with the sensibilities of a poet.

Winifred M. Letts (Mrs. W. H. Verschoyle, 1882-   )
was born in Leinster and her early life and training were
detached in large measure from the literary atmosphere of
Dublin. It is possible that the tone and direction of her writing would have been what they are without her recognition
of an Irish literary revival. Much of her work is peculiarly
Irish, but she has never felt the urge to use the legends of the
Heroic Age, nor has she made an effort to confine her themes
to any locale and her manner to any particular pattern. She

has called herself "a backdoor sort of bard," for in her early and most characteristic work, *Songs From Leinster* (1913) she dealt with lowly folk whom she had observed at close range and with rich sympathy. A novel, *Rough Way*, which appeared the same year her first volume of verse was issued, is English rather than Irish in both scene and manner. The protagonist, a restless, indecisive young man who in time casts his lot "with the caravan whose goal is the stars" has a certain universality of interest, but the development of the character is by no means strong. *The Spires of Oxford and Other Poems* (1917) was motivated largely by the emotions of the author during the First World War. As the title indicates, it is the departure of the Oxford men rather than the Leinster and Dublin men which gave direction to her theme. In 1926 she returned to her earlier province in *More Songs From Leinster*, and although one feels that she is now back where she belongs, there has been a change within her that has dulled the freshness and simplicity of her earlier songs. Such poems as "Blessing," "The Harbour," and "Hallowe'en" in the 1913 collection with their unaffected treatment of the simple folk of Leinster are representative of her finest talent. These poems and others suffer somewhat from sentimentalism, but one is led to believe that this quality is largely an illumination of a side of the Irish temperament. Thus far her work has shown no real range or great depth, but in her limited province of sympathetic observation of Irish life she has produced a score of poems which have an appealing sincerity, simplicity, and melody.

Katharine Tynan (Mrs. Henry Hinkson, 1861-1931), like her younger countrywoman Winifred Letts, was definitely Irish in some of her work, but she dealt with themes which were often quite remote from the major current of the revival. In her autobiographies, *Twenty-five Years: Reminiscences* (1913) and *The Years of Shadow* (1919), she has traced many of the episodes of the Celtic Renaissance and recorded

the part she played in the movement. By reason of the fact
that she was an ardent Catholic, she kept aloof from that
part of the movement which sought to reanimate pagan figures; and with the Eastern cults which interested Yeats, A.E.,
and Stephens she had no concern. She was born in 1861 in
Dublin of parents who were devout in the faith and far
above the average in cultural interests. Her education at the
Convent of St. Catherine at Drogheda gave support to early
literary inclinations and the deep devotionalism of her training at home. Her earliest efforts were in prose in which she
developed a novel-like form to record her observations of the
Irish life with which she was familiar. *The Way of a Maid*
(1895) and other stories with an Irish background make
agreeable reading, but the characterization and plots are
conventional, with no attempt to reveal national characteristics. Her collection of verse *Irish Poems* (1913) has in it
Celtic elements, but such poems as "The Old Magic" and
"The Exile," although they deal feelingly with her love for
Ireland, are an expression of homesickness which comes to
most people, be they Irish or Chinese. Katharine Tynan was
essentially a devotional poet, comparable in some respects to
Alice Meynell, but not always given to Mrs. Meynell's re-
straint. The sentimental musings on the Lamb of God in
"Sheep and Lambs" are of a different school from Mrs.
Meynell's "The Shepherdess"; and lines such as:

> Like the pitter-patter of little feet
> That come no more . . .

from the poem "All Souls" unfortunately remain in the
memory at the expense of much finer lines of which she was
capable. Her most representative work can be found in *New
Poems* (1911), *The Flower of Youth* (1914), *Late Songs* (1917)
and *Evensong* (1922). The outstanding characteristics in
these poems are a gift for melody of the more conventional
sort, a serious meditativeness which at times approached the
mystical, and a refined grace of expression. At the time of her

death in 1931 she was regarded as one of the finest of the
women poets. Her stature as a poet has decreased considerably in recent years, but she continues to hold a place with
the minor devotional writers of the century. Her books of
memoirs, *Twenty-five Years: Reminiscences* (1913) and *The
Years of Shadow* (1919) illuminate much of her contemporaries and herself, and make agreeable reading.

Sister Frances Inés, *Katharine Tynan Hinkson* (Philadelphia,
1952).

The revival manifested itself in many ways and took on
many forms, but it was in the field of the drama that it
reached its highest level. Until the influence of the revival
made itself felt, Irish drama was virtually nonexistent. Literary Irishmen who were interested in the theatre went to
London, where they devoted their talents to playwriting
which had little or nothing to do with Irish themes. But
with the performances of the Daughters of Erin and the Irish
Literary Theatre at the close of the century, a new spirit
began to assert itself; and by 1904, when the Abbey Theatre
was under way, the greatest talents in Ireland were brought
to dramatic literature. Before the first decade of the new
century was spent, a long procession of playwrights had appeared to produce the most significant dramatic literature
of recent times.

Of the dramatists who gave significance to the Celtic
Renaissance, **John Millington Synge (1871-1909)** was the
greatest. He was born at Rathfarnham, near Dublin, in 1871
of parents of good estate and culture. His maternal grandfather had translated Josephus, and his father was familiar
with the classics and nineteenth-century continental literature. At an early age the boy's bent was toward music; and
after he had finished at the schools in Wicklow, he was sent
to Germany with the thought that he might be trained to
become a professional musician. While in Germany he read
widely in continental literature, and it is reported that he

showed much interest in the peasant-dramas of Anzengruber
along with a fondness for the works of Heine. By his mid-
twenties he had given up the notion of becoming a professional musician, for he had
shown an aptitude for writing, and the increasing consciousness of his talent and a
rapidly developing art creed
led him to decide to become
an author. His consciousness
of talent and theories of art,
however, did not provide him
with a fertile province in
which to work; his interests
were varied, and no compelling source of inspiration beck-
oned. It is a familiar story of
how he went to Paris, there to

JOHN MILLINGTON SYNGE   meet William Butler Yeats in
1898, a time at which Yeats
was zealously interested in the Irish revival. Sensing that
the younger man had great talent which was seeking to
attach and express itself, Yeats told Synge to go back to
Ireland, even to the Aran Islands, to find and express a
life "that has never found expression." Synge followed the
suggestion of his countryman, and for the next few years he
lived the life of the Aran Islanders, totally detached from the
art cults of Paris, London, and Dublin. Informed and inspired by his sojourn on the Islands, he returned to Dublin
where during his absence the drama had developed into a
major part of the revival. Although he no doubt would have
found an outlet for his talent elsewhere, it was the flourishing of the theatre with its accent on Irish life that shaped
Synge's literary destiny. The receptacle of the theatre was
open and inviting, he had observations and stories from the

Islands which were ideally suited to the interests and needs of the stage, and with little encouragement from the leaders of the dramatic movement he set out to write plays. From *Riders to the Sea* (1903) to *Deirdre of the Sorrows* (1909) he demonstrated through both one-act and full-length plays his exceptional dramatic and poetic power. In addition to his work as a playwright, he wrote a few poems, twenty-two of which were collected into a volume, *Poems and Translations* (1910), the year following his death.

Although he was essentially a poet in almost everything he wrote, he devoted little of his time to verse. The twenty-two poems which were collected for *Poems and Translations* reveal much of the spirit of the man; and such pieces as "In May," "A Question," and "In Kerry," with their bold, grim lines which often suggest Hardy, are exemplifications of his views of what poetry should be. "It is the timber of poetry that wears most surely," he wrote, "and there is no timber that has not strong roots among the clay and worms. . . . Even if we grant that exalted poetry can be kept successful by itself, the strong things of life are needed in poetry also, to show that what is exalted or tender is not made by feeble blood. It may almost be said that before verse can be human again it must learn to be brutal." Certainly the last lines of "In May" and "A Question" are expressions of this creed.

In the plays there is much which is primitive and even brutal. Characters and situations such as Synge portrayed in his dramas are remotely related to the life that most theatre-goers have observed or experienced. With the exception of *Deirdre of the Sorrows,* the plays deal with sides of contemporary, or at least fairly recent Irish life; but the sides of life which are illuminated are those of isolated, wind-swept regions inhabited by blind tinkers, rogues, and tramps. The characters and the situations are devoid of any suggestion of conventional beauty. In fact, at first glance they seem grotesque and ugly, with nothing to which one can go in one's experience for comparison. In spite of the strangeness and grotesqueness of the characters, and for all of their primitive and brutal ways, through Synge's artistry they become not only convincing but moving. The characters in *Deirdre of the Sorrows,* drawn from the old legend, are of a different mold: they are of the Heroic Age and bear the stamp of greatness. When Naisi bids farewell to Deirdre: "We'll go, surely, in place of keeping a watch on a love had no match and it wasting away," one feels that one has observed for a time figures of noble lineage and spirit.

In dramatic design the plays show inadequacies, for they do not always move directly from a clearly defined unstable situation to an inevitable climax, with suspense heightened along the way. Nor do they confine themselves to a single mood. Any lack of tightness in the design and harmony of tone, however, is more than balanced by the frequent beauty of the lines. Without losing the illusion of reality, Synge gives to his characters lines which are richly poetic. This is especially true in the *Deirdre* play, but the rich inflections appear in the lines of lesser people than Deirdre and Naisi. In Christy's wooing of Pegeen in *The Playboy of the Western World* there are speeches which increase in beauty with each rereading. Synge did much to bring the drama away from the drawing room and court, and his significance in giving direction to folk-drama has been great; but there is much intrinsic worth in his plays which will continue to be recognized long after his part in shaping a dramatic movement has been forgotten.

PLAYS: *Riders to the Sea* (1903), *The Shadow of the Glen* (1903), *The Tinker's Wedding* (1904), *The Well of the Saints* (1905), *The Playboy of the Western World* (1907), *Deirdre of the Sorrows* (1909), *Complete Works* (1935). VERSE: *Poems and Translations* (1910). PROSE: *The Aran Islands* (1907).

P. P. Howe, *John Millington Synge: A Critical Study* (1912); Maurice Bourgeois, *John Millington Synge and the Irish Theatre*

(1913); John Masefield, *John M. Synge: A Few Personal Recollections* (1915); Cornelius Weygandt, "Synge" in *Irish Plays and Playwrights* (1913); Daniel Corkery, *Synge and Anglo-Irish Literature* (1931); A. D. Estill, *The Sources of Synge* (Phila., 1939); L. A. G. Strong, "John Millington Synge," *Living Age,* CCCXIV (1922), 936-960.

Like Synge, **Lady Gregory (1859-1932)** was interested in folk-themes and in the people who give to Ireland much of its characteristic tone, but whereas Synge viewed life with the eye of a poet, she was more the observer and recorder of the life she knew. Her chief talent was expressed as a writer of folk-plays, usually comedies, in which the less somber sides of Irish life were revealed; and as a figure in the Irish literary movement which concerned the theatre, she not only contributed many plays, but she also encouraged young writers to turn their talents to the stage.

Lady Gregory (Isabella Augusta Persse) was born in County Galway in 1859 of parents who were interested in giving their daughter more than the educational advantages of the parochial school. It has been reported that she had an unusual background in classical literature, although some of this probably came to her through her union with Sir William Gregory who was a lover of the classics and a well-known Orientalist. As an Irish M.P., Sir William was concerned with the political scene in Ireland, and especially in the state of affairs in the counties remote from Dublin; and his wife came to share many of his interests in matters political and sociological. No doubt encouraged by her husband, she recognized the need for an organized nationalist movement if conditions in Ireland were to improve. After his death in 1892, she pursued more fully her interests in the folk-history and literature of her countrymen. By the time that the Irish literary movement was under way, she was well equipped in both background and spirit to contribute to its development. Her most significant contribution to the move-

ment was through her plays and the support she gave to the
Abbey Theatre. Her beautiful home at Coole, with its fine
garden and the wild swans on the lake, was a gathering place
for many of the playwrights and players of the Abbey
Theatre group. She continued writing plays and paraphrases
from Irish stories until a few years before her death in 1932.

Lady Gregory was equally successful with both the one-act
and the full-length play. Familiar with the idiom of the
theatre and of the people whom she portrayed, and less given
to fantasy and mysticism than some of her associates in the
movement, she wrote a long list of plays which provide clear
and faithful cross-sections of Irish life. Although she was
appreciative of the witchery and beauty in the old Irish
stories of the Heroic Age, her themes were generally more
down-to-earth than those of Yeats and A.E. Her work has
been identified largely with folk-comedy, but underlying the
situations in her plays there is an illumination of, if not a
solution to, the Irishman's problems. The later pieces in
Three Wonder Plays (1922), and *Three Last Plays* (1928),
are capably handled and make pleasant reading, but they do
not add greatly to the playwright's stature. The widespread
interest once shown in many literary circles for things Irish
has waned perceptibly, and with it, enthusiasm for Lady
Gregory's plays has diminished. Posterity, at least outside of
Ireland, will probably find her plays too localized to encourage their frequent revival.

PLAYS: *Spreading the News* (1904), *Kincora* (1905), *The White
Cockade* (1905), *Hyacinth Halvey* (1906), *The Image* (1910), *The
Full Moon* (1911), *Irish Folk-history Plays* (first and second series,
(1912), *New Comedies* (1913), *Three Wonder Plays: The Dragon,
Aristotle's Bellows, The Jester* (1922), *On the Racecourse* (1926),
*Three Last Plays: Sancho's Master, Dave, The Would-be Gentle-
man* (1928). FOLKLORE: *A Book of Saints and Wonders* (1906), *The
Kiltartan History Book* (1909), *The Kiltartan Wonder Book* (1910).
ESSAYS: *Coole* (1931).

Lady Gregory's Journals, ed. Lennox Robinson (1947); Dawson

Byrne, "Lady Gregory" in *The Story of Ireland's Great Theatre* (1939); Cornelius Weygandt, "Lady Gregory's Plays," in *Irish Plays and Playwrights* (1913).

Although neither a publicist nor an active participant of the Irish literary revival, **Lord Dunsany (1878-   )** has contributed much to the stream of contemporary literature. He stands apart from Yeats, Synge, Lady Gregory, and others who were definitely a part of the movement, and yet in much of his work there is the unmistakable stamp of the Celt. His reputation is almost equally divided as playwright, story-writer, and poet. In all roles he is delightful, for his brightly colored imagination and his evident joy in the expression of his talent give his works an easily recognized charm. He shares with most Celts a fondness for symbolism, but there are instances in which the allegory rather than its underlying meaning is the chief source of the reader's enjoyment. In spite of the fact that there are perceptible Celtic elements in his work, there has been no effort on his part to revive the Heroic Age, or to deal with situations and characters that are peculiarly Irish.

Edward John Moreton Drax Plunkett was born in 1878 of a long line of Irish peers with estates in both Ireland and England. Lord Dunsany is the eighteenth baron of the long line. He was educated at Eton, and with a military career beckoning, he went to the Royal Military College at Sandhurst. His profession led him into the remote corners of the world: he saw action in the South African Campaign, and as Captain in the Royal Inniskilling Fusiliers he served in the First World War. As early as 1905 in *The Gods of Pegana* he showed a genuine talent at writing, and with the passing of time he has shown a considerable versatility of literary interests. He has lectured in America and sojourned in this country for long intervals between the wars.

His earliest work in the field of the drama was with the one-act play, a form with which he has been singularly successful. *The Gods of the Mountain* (1911) is a finely spun poetic drama which he never quite equalled in most of the later short plays. *The Lost Silk Hat* (1914) is a pleasant piece which has been included in many one-act play anthologies, but it lacks the poetic side of Dunsany's fancy. *A Night at an Inn* (1916) shows the playwright's skilful handling of the uncanny without losing plausibility. Until 1921 it was generally agreed among the critics that Dunsany's talent was limited largely to the one-act play, for *The Laughter of the Gods* (1917), one of his first attempts at full-length drama, had in it elements which were not readily manageable; but with *If* (1921) even the most severe reviewers commended the design and technique. The theme of the play—if a man could change his lot by merely wishing, the results would probably be unfortunate—is not without worth, but the charm of the play is dependent largely on the fertile fancy of the author in building up his allegory. The audience is caught in the spell to emerge at the final curtain with the feeling that the dream was the reality.

As a writer of tales, Dunsany shows much of the magic of the Celt. *The Book of Wonder* (1912), and especially *The King of Elfland's Daughter* (1924) contain tales which for all their bright-hued fancy are replete with simplicity and grace. "The Coming of the Troll" is an entrancing piece in which the style combines freshness, dexterity, and delicacy with excellent result. Even when he is dealing with scenes and characters which border on the grotesque, there is nothing sinister or ugly.

As a poet Dunsany has done distinguished if not great work. A representative sampling of his verse is to be found in *Fifty Poems* (1929). The poems in this volume range in theme from descriptions of scenes in Africa, such as "Evening in Africa," to reflections on episodes in the First World War, such as "To the Fallen Irish Soldiers," to illuminations of mood as in "Snow on the East Wind." It is in such a poem as "The Watchers," with its note suggesting Walter de la Mare's "The Listeners" that Dunsany has done his finest work in verse.

PLAYS: *Five Plays: The Gods of the Mountain, The Golden Doom, King Argimines and the Unknown Warrior, The Glittering Gate, The Lost Silk Hat* (1914), *Plays of Gods and Men: The Tents of the Arabs, The Laughter of the Gods, The Queen's Enemies, A Night at an Inn* (1917), *If* (1921), *Alexander and Three Small Plays: Alexander, The Old King's Tale, The Evil Kettle, The Amusements of Khan Kharuda* (1925), *The Old Folk of the Centuries* (1930), *Lord Adrian* (1933). STORIES: *The Gods of Pegana* (1905), *Time and the Gods* (1906), *The Sword of Welleran and Other Stories* (1908), *A Dreamer's Tales* (1910), *The Book of Wonder* (1912), *Fifty One Tales* (1915), *Tales of Wonder* (1916), *Tales of War* (1918), *Tales of Three Hemispheres* (1919), *The King of Elfland's Daughter* (1924), *The Charwoman of Shadow* (1926), *The Blessings of Pan* (1927), *The Curse of the Wise Woman* (1933), *The Man Who Ate the Phoenix* (1949). SKETCHES AND STUDIES: *Nowadays* (1918), *Unhappy Far-Off Things* (1919), *The Travel Tales of Mr. Joseph Jorkens* (1931), *Mr. Jorkens Remembers Africa* (1934), *If I Were Dictator* (1934). VERSE: *Fifty Poems* (1929), *Ulysses, Bound to the Mast* (1949).

Edward H. Bierstadt, *Dunsany the Dramatist* (1917); Cornelius Weygandt, "The Dramas of Dunsany" in *Tuesdays at Ten* (Phila., 1928); Barrett H. Clark, "Lord Dunsany" in *A Study of the Modern Drama* (1925).

Lennox Robinson (1886-   ) became an active figure in the Celtic Renaissance as a very young man, and he has been a sustaining force to interest in the revival for almost half a century. He has compiled anthologies of Irish verse, he edited Lady Gregory's *Journals,* he was the stage manager of the Abbey Theater from 1910 to 1914, and he was an outstanding contributor to the Irish drama in the middle and later period of the revival. The son of a clergyman, Robinson from youth had decided that writing was to be his career; but it was not until he saw the Abbey Players that he considered the medium of the drama. He had barely turned

twenty-two when his play *The Clancy Name* (1908) was produced at the Abbey Theatre. This was followed by *The
Crossroads* (1909), *Harvest* (1910), and *Patriots* (1912). The
themes in these plays are distinctively Irish, and to a certain
extent they were aimed at correcting conditions in Ireland.
The element of propaganda is there, especially in *Pátriots,*
but it does not become obtrusive, nor does it impair the
value of the plays as human documents. Of the later plays,
The Whiteheaded Boy (1920) and *The Far-Off Hills* (1931)
are illustrative of the high plane to which Robinson can rise
with realistic comedy.

   Conal O'Riordan (1874-   ), whose early works appeared
under the name Norreys Connell, succeeded Synge as the
director of the Abbey Theatre in 1909. An injury which left
him a cripple made it necessary for him to give up his intention of making the army his career; but his zealous interest
in literature, for which he had shown considerable talent as
early as his middle teens, was a ready substitute, and for over
fifty years he has been writing in a wide variety of literary
forms. During the nineties, he was associated with the decadents, especially Dowson and Johnson, but he never gave
himself over to their creed or their way of living. In one of
his early novels *A Fool and His Heart* (1896) he indicated
the pitfalls and tragedies which awaited the artist who made
his permanent residence in Bohemia. With the heyday of
the Celtic revival, O'Riordan was easily led to devote his
talent to the theatre, and from 1908 to 1914, he was one of
the outstanding figures of the middle generation of playwrights. *The Piper* (1908), although designed as an allegory,
was a forthright disclosure of the less commendable traits in
the Irish character, especially its inconsistency in practical
things. Aimed as a corrective, it could scarcely have attained
its end, for it lacks the sharpness of characterization and the
excellent lines of Synge's *Playboy of the Western World*
with which it is often compared. *Time* (1909), and *Shake-*

speare's End, and Other Irish Plays (1912) are further illustrations of O'Riordan's insight into Irish character and history. In "An Imaginary Conversation," one of the "Other
Irish Plays" in the collection of 1912, there is an engaging
restoration of a scene from the past in which Robert Emmet
and Tom Moore come to life with lines that are skilfully
handled. In fact, O'Riordan's chief talent is in the restoration of historical scene rather than in providing correctives
to conditions in Ireland. His *Soldier Born* (1927), published
in America as *Yet Do Not Grieve* (1928), and *Soldier of
Waterloo* (1928) are fine fusions of history and fiction with a
style which at times suggests George Meredith.

St. John Ervine (1883-   ), like O'Riordan, had been in
England during his formative years before he became director of the Abbey Theatre in 1915. Like his predecessor, he,
too, has written novels of which *Mrs. Martin's Man* (1914),
Changing Winds (1917), and *The Wayward Man* (1927) indicate his most characteristic themes. His plays, of which there
are many, are not limited in background to Irish scenes and
characters, although his earlier works for the theatre such as
Mixed Marriage (1911), *The Magnanimous Lover* (1912), and
The Orangeman (1914) are concerned directly with Irish
problems, both religious and political. The later plays by
which he is well known, *Jane Clegg* (1914), *John Ferguson*
(1915), and *The First Mrs. Fraser* (1929) are not so local in
appeal; in fact, the last-named play has nothing distinctively
Celtic in it. Of the middle generation of Irish playwrights,
Ervine is pre-eminent as a dramatic craftsman and as a vivid
portrayer of character. The figures whom he creates in both
plays and novels are convincingly motivated throughout,
whether they are Irish or of other nationality; and by reason
of the fact that they are usually not given to such elemental
passions as the characters in many of the Irish plays, they are
more readily recognizable by the majority of theatre-goers
and readers.

Many of the plays which appeared in the middle and later stages of the revival dealt with the problems which beset contemporary Ireland, and in the plays of **Sean O'Casey**

(1884-   ) some of these problems become a powerful motivating force. Probably by reason of his birth and rearing among scenes of poverty and unrest in Dublin, O'Casey was singularly equipped to portray graphically the disquiet and distress of large groups of his countrymen. To him, the old Gaelic legends meant little, and for the mysticism of some of his predecessors in Irish literature, especially A.E. he has expressed a marked distaste. Instead of lingering in the land of faery, he grapples with issues of the

SEAN O'CASEY

present with a realism that is often stark. His autobiographical works, *I Knock at the Door* (1939), *Pictures in the Hallway* (1942), *Drums Under the Window* (1946), and *Inishfallen Fare Thee Well* (1948), are not only a vivid illumination of the man and his times, but also a declaration of his artistic creed. The plays *Juno and the Paycock* and *The Shadow of a Gunman,* published together in 1925, *The Plough and the Stars* (1926), *The Silver Tassie* (1928), and *Within the Gates* (1933) are representative of his most characteristic themes and treatment. In spite of their localized settings and their vigorous concern with recently current issues in Ireland, O'Casey's plays show a concern with humanity which gives them a universal interest.

* * * * * * * *

In August, 1914, after years of bitter struggle, Home Rule for Ireland was enacted, its operation being suspended until after the war. Two years later at Easter, 1916, a serious rebellion broke out in Dublin which disclosed a new militant party, Sinn Fein, determined upon independence. The outbreak was suppressed after six days but the country remained uneasy and in 1919 there was renewed violence which even the infamous Black and Tans, recruited from the toughest of the discharged veterans, could not control. After eighteen months of terror, the Irish Free State was created by treaty. The new state was self-governing under the Crown and included all of the island south of Protestant Ulster, now known as Northern Ireland. In 1927 the republican faction won control of the government and abolished the oath to the English Crown. Ten years later, under a new constitution, full independence was achieved by the republic of Eire.

From the days of Swift to those of Shaw, Irish letters were really Anglo-Irish, not a remote branch but in the main stream of English literature. In Yeats, Synge, and those who worked with them for the revival and the Abbey Theater the beginnings of a cleavage appear. Their treatment of Irish themes from an Irish instead of the conventional English point of view and their development of the resources of Irish idiom, very different from comic dialect, to give a natural expression to Irish sentiments mark their work off from anything that went before it. Joyce chose to be a cosmopolitan, and his countrymen disowned him for it. None of them expressed so much of Ireland as he, but he did it only by transcending national limitations. At some time toward 1930 —any date chosen must be conventional—the work of Oliver St. John Gogarty, Peader O'Donnell, Sean O'Faolain and Liam O'Flaherty shows a quality that marks it as distinctly not English. Irish literature has become a distinct entity. It is not a matter of politics, or of subject matter and idiom merely, but as with the coming of age of American writing, the achievement of an independent national character and feeling that no longer conforms to a now foreign tradition. Its later literary history must be treated separately from that of England.

William Ernest Henley (1849-1903)

Although the major part of Henley's work was done before the turn of the century, there are many qualities in his verse which are definitely un-Victorian and which anticipate the characteristics which are loosely labeled modern. With the issues which gave Tennyson and Browning much of their inspiration and theme, he was unconcerned; and against the deliberate aestheticism of the Pre-Raphaelites and the decadents of the nineties, he took a positive stand. For the man Henley, one must have considerable admiration, for this "booming, bursting, bumptious" personality, as Edith Sitwell called him, although a cripple from youth, was not an invalid in spirit.

In the sequence "In Hospital," with the themes drawn from his bedfast days at Lister's Infirmary in Edinburgh, Henley's stark realism was an innovation unpalatable to many Victorian readers. The poems in *London Voluntaries*, and "A Song of Speed" are more interesting for their venturesome metrics and diction than for their impressionistic effects. Henley's range was slight, and in spite of the fact that he is more than a one-poem author—the celebrated "Invictus"—G. B. Shaw was sound in his conclusion that "when Henley had such an experience as the Hospital to go on, he wrote well; otherwise, his case was one of manner without matter." His manner, however, illustrates a fine sense of pictorial values, virile words, interesting versification, and an unmistakable gusto.

A Book of Verses, including "In Hospital" (1888), *London Voluntaries and Other Verses* (1893), *Poems* (1898), *Hawthorn and*

Lavendar (1901), *A Song of Speed* (1903), *Collected Works,* including essays and prefaces, 6. v., (1908).

John Connell, *William Ernest Henley* (1949); Jerome H. Buckley, *William Ernest Henley* (Princeton, 1945); Kennedy Williamson, *W. E. Henley: A Memoir* (1930); L. Cope Cornford, *W. E. Henley* (1913); H. B. M. Watson, "William Ernest Henley," *Athenaeum,* VI (1903), 11-14; J. C. Bailey, "The Poetry of William Ernest Henley," *Monthly Rev.,* XXIV (1903), 261-265; W. W. Grey and L. Cope Cornford, *Notes to "Lyrica Heroica"* (1912).

Thomas Hardy (1840-1928)

Although Hardy's work in the novel was completed by 1897, most of his verse appeared after the turn of the century. His fiction is probably more widely known than his poetry, but had he been given to George Meredith's cleverness of phrase, he, too, might have said: "Fiction is my kitchen wench; poetry my muse." Hardy's verse is a more compact and illuminating revelation of the essential man than his prose. His wife and biographer, Mrs. Florence Hardy, observed: "Speaking generally, there is more autobiography in a hundred lines of his poetry than in all of the novels." As both novelist and poet, he has a secure place among the greatest authors of our times.

He was born June 2, 1840, on the border of Bockhampton Heath, about three miles from Dorchester, Dorset, the son of a mason and builder. There is little in his heredity to account for his genius and bent of mind. The environment in which he was born and reared, however, had a pronounced bearing on his novels and poems. His biographers have pointed out that it is almost impossible to think of Hardy without associating him with that part of southern England, Dorsetshire, which he called Wessex. Dorset has been retenanted with Clyms and Eustacias, Judes and Bathshebas; Puddleton Heath, near Bockhampton, has been identified with Egdon Heath; and Dorchester has Casterbridge as its second name. That Hardy, like his character Eustacia

Vye, "imbibed much of what was dark in its tone" may account in some measure for what has been called his peculiarly twilight view of life.

For a time his parents thought that he might be trained for the clergy, and there was talk of his going to Cambridge. But he was not eager for university life, and even in his late teens he had no inclination toward dogmatic religion. At sixteen, he went to work with John Hicks, an architect of Dorchester, who taught him little, but who helped him to determine to follow the profession of architecture. At twenty-two he was in London, doing miscellaneous work in drafting rooms and taking evening courses at King's College under Sir Gilbert Scott, a Gothic expert. Although he himself said: "I was a child till I was sixteen; a youth till I was twenty-five; a young man till I was forty or fifty," during his twenties he had already pondered long and earnestly over the inner significance of life. His questionings and reflections he cast into verse; and the thought that they might have worth caused him to neglect his profession of architecture, and by 1869 to launch out into literature. He found his poems generally unsalable, but noting the success of Meredith with fiction when the latter had had little response from his verse, Hardy set to work on a novel. Meredith, recognizing his earnestness and talent, helped him considerably both with criticism and encouragement. From 1871 until 1897 he rose to one of the highest places in English fiction, starting with *Desperate Remedies* (1871) and ending with *Jude the Obscure* (1896). *The Well-Beloved* appeared in 1897, but Hardy's determination to forsake the novel dated from his distress over the bitter reviews which appeared on the publication of *Jude*. Volumes of verse began to appear before the close of the century, and by 1925 nine fairly large books had been issued. The *Collected Poems* (1931) contains virtually everything included in the earlier volumes, with the exception of the massive poetic drama *The Dynasts* which had

HARDY'S BIRTHPLACE

appeared in three parts in 1903-6-8. Too much significance
should not be attached to the dates of publication, for many
of the poems were written much earlier. His last works were
produced at Max Gate, Dorset, where he led a secluded life
until his death in 1928.

Hardy's prose is of considerable volume: eleven novels and
three collections of short stories. The novels vary in interest
and merit, but even in the early works such as *Desperate
Remedies* (1871) and *Under the Greenwood Tree* (1872),
there is an unmistakable sense of design. With the culminating situation always in view, Hardy fitted his characters,
settings, and plots into a well-centralized development in
which all of the parts are skilfully integrated. His portrait
gallery of characters is exceptionally wide, and in the principal figures there is always a three-dimensional quality
which indicates a penetrating observation of the cause and
effect of human action. His characters are shaped both by
their inner natures and the external circumstances which
surround them. They are not masters of their fate; in fact,
circumstance plays a large part in the direction of their lives;
but they often contribute to the outcome of events by forces
which lie within their own natures. Eustacia Vye, Damon
Wildeve, and Clym Yeobright in *The Return of the Native;*
Bathsheba Everdene, Gabriel Oak, and Farmer Boldwood in
Far From the Madding Crowd; Tess and Angel Clare in *Tess
of the D'Urbervilles;* and Jude and Sue in *Jude the Obscure*
are all memorable characters, not only for what they did but
for what they were. They may antagonize the reader—in fact,
they often do—and few of them can be called endearing; but
they compel the reader's interest and sympathy by reason of
their poignant reality. They represent universal types in
their strength and weakness, but they are strongly marked
individuals in their efforts to surmount the obstacles which
their temperaments and circumstance put in their way.

Even finer than his characterization is his handling of

setting. Although his backgrounds lack variety, for he deals almost exclusively with Wessex, there is ample latitude for a man of Hardy's penetrating observation to relieve any monotony. As a local colorist, he has few equals. Not only can he create atmospheres which in themselves become a powerful force in the motivation of the characters, but he can take specific events and places which are part of the background, and with a fine sense of graphic detail, create scenes which cause the reader to become an eye-witness to rural and community life in Wessex. The fine description of Egdon Heath in *The Return of the Native,* the insight into rural life in *The Woodlanders* and *Far From the Madding Crowd,* and the revelation of the inner spirit of the community in *The Mayor of Casterbridge* are only a few illustrations of Hardy's ability to create vivid settings.

It is Hardy's handling of plot which has aroused most discussion and antagonized many readers. The precept in one of his earlier poems "In Tenebris": "If a way to the Better there be, it exacts a full look at the Worst. . . ." finds expression in almost all of his novels. His characters are thrust into circumstances over which they can exercise small control, and from which they rarely escape. Jude, with his yearning for education, is beset by obstacles which Hardy makes insurmountable; Tess, with a chance for happiness, places a letter which might have given her peace from her past under the door of Angel Clare's room, to learn when it is too late that the letter was concealed under the carpet; and Eustacia, in her attempt to escape from the heath which has been her Hades, falls into the weir and is drowned. It is true that these characters are in themselves tragic figures who contribute much to the fate which finally overtakes them; but with the author's manipulation of circumstances, all controlled by the forces of ill, they have small chance to overcome the obstacles which confront them. The plots of the novels suffer by reason of the relentless application of his belief in the preponderance of ill in the world, but their poignancy as records of man's struggles remains unmitigated.

Not only are the novels masterpieces of design, but the style often rises to a high plane of poetic prose. It is true that the manner is at times heavy and cumbersome, as if the author is straining at the bonds of his medium; and there is nothing which can be called sprightly. With cleverness, there is no traffic, and there are passages which lack conciseness and finish. Some of the episodes are overwritten to such an extent that the effect approaches melodrama, and his belief in the forces of evil in the world gave support to a noticeable inclination to stress the bitter episodes in the lives of his characters. The suicide of Father Time in *Jude,* the aftermath of the burial of Fanny in *Far From the Madding Crowd,* and the killing of Alec D'Urberville in *Tess* are memorable on account of the explicit morbid detail with which they are described. Over and against such inadequacies are his sustained cadences in the chapter "Queen of the Night" in *The Return of the Native,* the fine restraint in the closing passages of *The Woodlanders,* and the artistic sincerity which marks all of his work.

Hardy's poetry is in large measure a continuation, an illumination and a distillate of the novels. In fact, many of his poems have been called condensed novels, for in their compact development there are themes and characters which might readily be put into the longer prose medium. Such poems as "The Newcomer's Wife," "The Dance at the Phoenix," and "The Turnip Hoer" are made of the same stuff as the novels; and the outcome of the characters' struggles against the caprices of circumstance is the same. They are skilful in their compression of unstable situation; and by reason of their lean development, the climaxes and tragedies come with a suddenness that is often shocking. The last line of "The Newcomer's Wife" has a directness and force which cause the reader to wish for a few stanzas in preparation for it. The verse schemes in these pieces are simple; and the diction is unembellished by any rhetorical devices of imagery which might relieve their starkness. They are not great poetry, for their themes are limited to what the reader hopes are isolated experiences in the life of man; but in their plain, sturdy lines there are poignancy and power.

Hardy's greatest poetry is not that in which he traces in compressed form life's ironies, or in which he is the iconoclast in dogmatic religion, or even when he is crying out against the futility of war, as in his poem "The Pity of It"; he undoubtedly attains his greatest heights when he is seeking the reasons for life's wounds and anguish. Here he is no longer recording life's ironies through specific episodes, but attempting to penetrate the cause and to find "a way to the Better." Here he becomes not a prophet and seer, but a cosmic poet, dealing with the universal and ageless problems which beset men's minds and souls. To Nature's questioning, in the poem under that title, "We wonder, ever wonder, why we find us here!" he replies, "No answerer I"; but the struggle through which he has gone before making the admission is implicit in the poem; and in that struggle there are nobility and greatness. Such poems as "Hap," "A Young Man's Epigram on Existence," and the long poetic drama "The Dynasts" are of cosmic theme, and "The Dynasts" is of cosmic scope. It is on a plane with "Paradise Lost" and "Prometheus Unbound" in its loftiness of theme, and certainly in its depth and sincerity of purpose. Its length, and its complexity of conception and design, keep it from being widely read; but it is one of the most magnificently conceived poems of our times. That it lacks the lyric beauty of Shelley's "Prometheus Unbound" is against its consummate greatness; and despite the elevated tone and unmistakable power in its entirety, there are passages which are heavy with the effort to convey his theme.

Hardy has not been "the idle singer of an empty day,"
nor has he created a dream world in which one is surrounded
by the beauties of sight and sense and in which one is contentedly lost. He is not an opiate to the mind and soul, nor
does he stimulate a desire to reform the institutions to which
man is accustomed. He is, amongst the recent poets, one of
the least musical. But as Siegfried Sassoon has said: "Men
are alive only when they struggle. When they grow aware of
the futility of their effort, and yet strive to fashion something
from it, they become noble and tragic; such was Hardy."

VERSE: *Wessex Poems and Other Verses* (1898), *Poems of Past and
Present* (1902), *Time's Laughingstocks and Other Verses* (1909),
Satires of Circumstance (1914), *Moments of Vision and Miscel-
laneous Verses* (1917), *Late Lyrics and Earlier* (1922), *Human
Shows, Far Phantasies, Songs and Trifles* (1925), *Yuletide in a
Younger World* (1927), *Winter Words in Various Moods and
Metres* (1928), *Collected Poems* (1931). POETIC DRAMA: *The
Dynasts: A Drama in Three Parts* (1903-6-8). NOVELS: *Desperate
Remedies* (1871), *Under the Greenwood Tree* (1872), *A Pair of
Blue Eyes* (1873), *Far From the Madding Crowd* (1874), *The Hand
of Ethelberta* (1876), *The Return of the Native* (1878), *The Trum-
pet-Major* (1880), *A Laodicean* (1881), *Two on a Tower* (1882),
The Mayor of Casterbridge (1886), *The Woodlanders* (1887), *Tess
of the D'Urbervilles* (1891), *Jude the Obscure* (1896), *The Well
Beloved* (1897).

A. P. Webb, *A Bibliography of the Works of Thomas Hardy, 1865-
1915* (1916); C. J. Weber, *The First Hundred Years of Thomas
Hardy, 1840-1940: A Centenary Bibliography of Hardiana* (Water-
ville, Me., 1942); Florence Hardy, *The Early Life of Thomas
Hardy, 1840-1891* (1928), *The Later Years of Thomas Hardy, 1892-
1928* (1930); C. J. Weber, *Hardy of Wessex: His Life and Literary
Career* (1940); Ernest Brennecke, *The Life of Thomas Hardy*
(1925); R. T. Hopkins, *Thomas Hardy's Dorset* (1922); W. T.
Rutland, *Thomas Hardy: A Study of His Writings and Their
Background* (1938); Ruth Firor, *Folkways in Thomas Hardy*
(Phila., 1931); Patrick Braybrooke, *Thomas Hardy and His Philos-
ophy* (1924); A. P. Elliott, *Fatalism in the Works of Thomas Hardy*
(Phila., 1935); H. Garwood, *Thomas Hardy: An Illustration of the
Philosophy of Schopenhauer* (Phila., 1912); H. C. Webster, *On a*

Darkling Plain: The Art and Thought of Thomas Hardy (Chicago, 1947); Samuel Chew, *Thomas Hardy, Poet and Novelist* (rev. ed., 1928); Lascelles Abercrombie, *Thomas Hardy: A Critical Study* (1919); Lionel Johnson, *The Art of Thomas Hardy* (1894, expanded with a bibliography by John Lane, 1923); Edmund Blunden, *Thomas Hardy* (1942); Lord David Cecil, *Hardy the Novelist* (1943); Mary Ellen Chase, *Thomas Hardy: From Serial to Novel* (Minneapolis, 1927); Roland Williams, *The Wessex Novels* (1925); A. J. Guerard, *Thomas Hardy: The Novels and Stories* (Cambridge, Mass., 1949); J. G. Southworth, *The Poetry of Thomas Hardy* (1947); E. C. Hickson, *The Versification of Thomas Hardy* (Phila., 1931); Jacques Barzun, "Truth and Poetry in Thomas Hardy," *Southern Rev.*, VI (1940), 179-192; Hugh Molson, "The Philosophies of Hardy and Housman," *Quarterly Rev.*, CCLXVIII (1937), 205-213; A. B. Hopkins, "The Dynasts and the Course of History," *South Atlantic Quarterly*, XLIV (1931), 432-444; J. G. Fletcher, "The Spirit of Thomas Hardy," *Yale Rev.*, XIII (1924), 322-333.

A. E. Housman (1859-1936)

The age which reflected on Thomas Hardy's "In Tene-bris" with its forthright line: "If a way to the Better there be, it exacts a full look at the Worst," was given additional incentive to question life's unmixed benevolence in the slender volumes of A. E. Housman. But whereas Hardy sought to find the ultimate sources of the world's ills, Housman was largely concerned with a recognition of them and a way to ease their pain; and whereas Hardy was often gnarled and rugged in expression, with little in his verse that can be termed melodic, in Housman there is a constant song quality. Although in much of their verse there is a common theme, there is nothing to indicate that either influenced the other.

Alfred Edward Housman was born March 22, 1859, at Bournheath, Worcester, the son of Edward Housman, a solicitor, and one of seven children among whom were Laurence Housman, the poet and playwright, and a sister Clemence whose talents were recognized by editors and publishers of the nineties. Shropshire, the county with which he has become associated by reason of the settings and place names in many of his poems, and the title of one of his

volumes, was never his home. It was an adjacent county, the land beyond the horizon. After learning the rudiments of Latin and Greek at the Bromsgrove School, he went up to St. John's College, Oxford, on a scholarship where he remained from 1877 to 1882. Although qualified for a degree, he did not receive it until 1892, at which time he forsook his work as a Higher Division Clerk in the British Patent Office to become Professor of Latin at University College, London. In 1911 he became Kennedy Professor of Latin at Trinity College, Cambridge, where he remained until his death in 1936.

A. E. HOUSMAN

Authorities in classical literature agree that Housman was a scholar of considerable note, not only for his contributions to the *Classical Quarterly* and *Classical Review*, but also for his excellent editions of Juvenal, Lucan, and the five books of the *Astronomica* of Manilius. Although the point need not be labored, there seems to be ample evidence that Housman went to school under the Latin poets, for in his works there are the qualities of conciseness, lucidity, and restraint, qualities usually associated with the classical manner.

In 1896, four years after he had become Professor of Latin at University College, London, when he was thirty-seven, a small volume of sixty-three poems appeared under the title *A Shropshire Lad*. Twenty-six years later, in 1922, forty-one poems appeared under the significant title *Last Poems*. A few months after his death in 1936, forty-eight poems were issued by his brother Laurence entitled *More Poems*. The appearance of this volume came as a surprise to his readers, for in the preface to the volume *Last Poems,* he had said: "I publish these poems, few that they are, because it is not likely that I shall ever be impelled to write much more. I cannot be expected to be revisited by the continuous excitement under which in the early months of 1895 I wrote the greater part of my other book, nor could I well sustain it if came." Although there is nothing strikingly different in either theme or manner from the poems of the earlier collections, the pieces which Laurence Housman collected for *More Poems* are not inferior to the average of the already published poems; in fact, they add to Housman's stature as a poet and to the reader's enjoyment. Many of them belong essentially to the same time as that at which the poems in *A Shropshire Lad* were written; and although the name Terence does not appear, they often express a young man's concern with the preponderance of ill in the world.

In spite of the fact that Housman's province is limited, there are many classifications of his poems to invite the reader; but the most illuminating division, and one that often goes unrecognized, is that there are poems not only of darkness but poems of light. Mr. Charles Williams in *Poetry at Present* (Oxford, 1930) writes to the point when he says: "Not every poem is explicitly concerned with the 'much less good than ill.' A reader who opened *A Shropshire Lad* at the beginning could read the first sixteen poems without finding in it more than an occasional stanza of darkness, and without necessarily holding it to be more than dramatic or semidramatic. For those sixteen contain love songs, a ballad lyric, and one or two of as exquisite nature poems as any in English, especially the famous 'Loveliest of trees, the cherry now'...." A fairly long list of poems could be compiled from the three volumes in which life's ironies have little part. "Reveille" is a sinewy call for action and courage; "Oh, When I Was in Love with You" tells of the ennobling power of love; "Epithalamium" points out the blessings of friendship; and "The Chestnut Casts its Flambeaux, and the Flowers," with all of its lamenting of man's sad lot, is poignantly insistent that trouble can be borne. The poet offers no solution for escape, but in many of the poems there is the comforting assurance that in the face of the misery in the world there are beauties in nature, in friendship, and in love which give man courage to bear his unfailing burdens.

Although "the hemlock fascination of the poet's self-centered, self-pitying, and abject pessimism" has been over-stressed by a generation of readers who needed support for their own misgivings about the world's goodness, there is no doubt that the poems of darkness outweigh in both quantity and intensity the poems of light. The allegory in the closing lines of "Terence, This is Stupid Stuff" leaves one fully aware of the poet's recognition of life's ills; and such poems as "When Smoke Stood Up From Ludlow," "Bredon Hill," and "The Culprit," among many others, have a sombreness which cannot be escaped. Frustration, futility, hopelessness all play a part in the quietly bitter resignation out of which these poems take shape. Despair and tragedy, often made more bitter by abrupt anticlimax, are the end of many a rose-lipt maiden and light-foot lad. The impermanence of youth and beauty becomes the sentiment for laments in which there is little to suggest Herrick's advice of "Gather ye rosebuds while ye may." No doubt, as his brother Laurence observed: "He would have liked the laws of God and man to be kinder than they are; and a great deal of the anger and bitterness of his verse is due to the fact that they are so much the other way."

It is probable that the sentiments of the poems would have attained only a mild response had they been presented with less grace and melody. To the mature poetry reader who has been made completely aware of life's ills through experience, Housman's themes exercise little fascination, but the manner is so compelling that in many instances the thought becomes secondary in arousing and sustaining interest. Even the most bitter themes are made palatable as the poet in an apparently effortless way expresses his mood. The manner is consistently appealing by reason of its seeming simplicity and artlessness. The diction and stanzaic patterns are always in keeping with the changing moods of youth beset by the contemplation of life's scheme. Although the manner is always simple and direct, there is ample evidence to indicate that it was cunningly deliberated and painstakingly revised. Only a perfectionist in style could achieve such effects with the simplest words and verse measures. The note is seldom strong and resonant; rather it suggests a shepherd's pipe heard at a distance in autumn.

In spite of the fact that many of the poems were designed to reflect the moods of troubled youth, in them there are an unfailing dignity and restraint. Bitter as they sometimes are, they are never vituperative; and one never feels that the poet is consciously straining to give emphasis to his sentiment. The dignity and restraint of the diction are often put to severe tests in the many instances in which everyday language and colloquialism are introduced as a realistic part of the presentation, but in no instance do the colloquial and the poetic get in each other's way. The two stanzas which begin, "The fairies break their dances" in *Last Poems* are an example of the poet's remarkable skill at blending two apparently hostile levels of diction. To a lesser artist, the effect could readily descend to parody and jingle, but with Housman the results are always poetic.

In the Leslie Stephen Lecture, delivered by Housman at Cambridge in 1933 under the title "The Name and Nature of Poetry," the poet compared his art to a secretion:

"... whether a natural secretion, like turpentine in the fir, or a morbid secretion, like the pearl in the oyster." The creative process in Housman, it would seem, was the result of his sympathetic understanding of the troubles which beset all "ill-treated fellows" to which mankind at large belongs. Pessimistic, but not misanthropic, he set out as a sort of self-deliverance to reflect the moods of an imaginary character who had, as he observed, "something of my temper and view of life." To this reflection he brought a severely disciplined economy of phrase, simplicity of diction and verse, and a haunting music.

VERSE: *A Shropshire Lad* (1896), *Last Poems* (1922), *More Poems* (1936), *Collected Poems* (1939). PROSE: *The Name and Nature of Poetry* (1933).

Theodore G. Ehrsam, *A Bibliography of A. E. Housman* (Boston, 1941), supplemented by Robert W. Stallman, "An Annotated Bibliography of A. E. Housman: A Critical Study," *PMLA,* LX (1945), 463-502; Grant Richards, *A. E. Housman, 1897-1936* (1942); A. S. F. Gow, *A. E. Housman: A Sketch* (1936); Laurence Housman, *A. E. Housman: Some Poems, Some Letters, and a Personal Memoir* (1937); see also Laurence Housman's Introduction to *More Poems* (1936); Katherine Symons, and others, *Alfred Edward Housman: Recollections* (Bromsgrove, 1936); Percy Withers, *A Buried Life: Personal Recollections of A. E. Housman* (1940); O. Robinson, *Angry Dust: The Poetry of A. E. Housman* (1950); H. W. Garrod, "Housman: 1939," *Essays and Studies,* XXV (1939), 7-21; John Sparrow, "Echoes in the Poetry of A. E. Housman," *Nineteenth Century,* CXV (1934), 243-256; Hugh Molson, "The Philosophies of Hardy and Housman," *Quarterly Rev.,* CCLXVIII (1937), 205-213; Stephen Spender, "The Essential Housman," *Horizon,* I (1940), 295-301; A. F. Allison, "The Poetry of A. E. Housman," *Rev. Eng. Studies,* XIX (1943), 276-284.

SOME DEVOTIONAL POETS

A considerable amount of devotional poetry has been written in England since 1890. Oscar Wilde, Ernest Dowson, and Lionel Johnson found some of their inspiration in the

Church, as did Katharine Tynan Hinkson, Dora Sigerson Shorter, and Alice Meynell; and more recently Alfred Noyes, Roy Campbell, and T. S. Eliot have found compelling themes in religion. Although the major part of his work was done before 1900, **Francis Thompson (1859-1907)** became widely known as a devotional poet after the turn of the century. Born at Preston in Lancashire, the son of a physician who had become a zealous convert and a woman who had had the intention of becoming a nun, the boy was reared in an atmosphere congenial to his parents' wish that he become a priest. After seven years of preparation at St. Cuthbert's at Ushaw, he was told by his advisers that he should withdraw and undertake a different career. His failure to qualify for the priesthood was a source of acute and lasting grief to him and his parents. Since his father was a physician, it was decided that he go to Owens College, Manchester, to prepare himself to become a doctor. Physically and temperamentally ill-suited to such a profession, and with his ideal of becoming a priest shattered, Thompson became addicted to drugs, left medical school after successive failures, and went to London to sink in time to the level of a tramp. When he was still presentably clad, he sought warmth in the public library where he read poetry and occasionally wrote on paper he had salvaged from the streets.

It is a familiar story of how Wilfrid Meynell and his wife Alice, coeditors of *Merry England,* received early in February, 1887, some tattered manuscripts on blue wrapping paper. The unpromising appearance of the manuscripts caused Meynell to put them aside, and it was not until nearly a year had passed that he glanced at them, to be at once impressed by the contents, especially the stanzas entitled "The Passion of Mary." After much difficulty, he arranged for a meeting with the writer which was the beginning of Thompson's rescue and his real beginning as a poet. The Meynells gave him courage and hope, inspiration, and a receptacle for his verse. They sent him to a hospital to be treated for his affliction, and from there to the priory at Storrington. Later, after staying with the Meynells in London, Thompson went to the Capuchin Monastery at Pantasaph, Wales, where he mingled with the monks, and where he often saw Coventry Patmore who offered him guidance and encouragement. By 1896 he returned to London to work occasionally at journalism until his death in 1907.

His most widely known poem "The Hound of Heaven," first printed in *Merry England* in July, 1890, is autobiographical in that it records the poet's experiences in the years following his rejection for the priesthood. While trying to find peace through all the well-known channels—in science, in nature, and in an apostleship to beauty—his soul was being pursued by the Hound of Heaven, a daring symbol for God's search for the souls of men. As a devotional document the poem may have only a limited usefulness to some readers; but for power of theme, intensity of purpose, artistry of conception, and rapture of ultimate realization, "The Hound of Heaven" has a high place in English poetry.

The shorter poems such as "Lilium Regis" in which the lily of the king is God's Holy Church; the sonnet "Ad Amicam," the first in a sequence of fifteen, in which the poet expresses the peace which comes to those whose souls have been found; and "In No Strange Land" in which his mystic relationship with the divine becomes very real, are characteristic of Thompson's finest work in the devotional lyric. For an illumination of the poet's belief in the sanctifying grace which attends the innocence of children, "Daisy" has deservedly found its way into most of the anthologies.

Thompson is neither a poet of thought, nor a poet of melody and beauty for their own sake, although melody and beauty of imagery are pronounced characteristics. He is essentially an inspired devotional poet in whose works can be found an authentic mysticism, an intensity of purpose and feeling, and lyric rapture. At times this lyric rapture found expression in a beautiful simplicity: in such poems as "Daisy," "Little Jesus," and "In No Strange Land" there are directness and ready comprehensibility in diction and imagery. In the "Sister Songs" and some of the sonnets, however, his expression often lacks discipline, with the result that extravagances of imagery appear which border on the turgid. Despite his easily recognized lack of restraint, amongst devotional poets and poets at large, Thompson has a secure place.

VERSE: *Poems* (1893), *Songs Wing to Wing* (1895), *Sister Songs: an Offering to Two Sisters* (1895), *New Poems* (1897), *The Hound of Heaven* (first separate ed., 1908), *Selected Poems* (ed. Wilfrid Meynell, 1908), *Youthful Verses* (privately printed, Preston, England, 1928), Terence Connolly, ed., *Collected Poems* (1932). PROSE: *Health and Holiness* (1905), *Shelley* (1909), *St. Ignatius Loyola* (1909), *Selected Essays* (1927), Connolly, ed., *Literary Criticism by Francis Thompson: Newly Discovered and Collected* (1948).

C. A. and H. W. Stonehill, *Bibliographies of Modern Authors*, second series (1928); Everard Meynell, *The Life of Francis Thompson* (rev. ed., 1925); R. L. Megroz, *Francis Thompson: The Poet of Earth in Heaven* (1927); T. H. Wright, *Francis Thompson and his Poetry* (1927); Cornelius Weygandt, "Francis Thompson" in *Tuesdays at Ten* (Phila., 1928); K. T. Hinkson, "Francis Thompson," *Fortnightly Rev.*, LXXXVII (1910), 349-360; W. S. Blunt, "Francis Thompson," *Academy*, XI (1907), 88-96; C. H. S. Wilson, "Francis Thompson, Poet of Childhood," *Dalhousie Rev.*, XIV (1935), 474-478.

The importance of **Alice Meynell (1847-1922)** is two-fold: she presided over a generation of writers and she wrote verse and prose in which there is considerable distinction. To George Meredith she presented "the image of one accustomed to walk in holy places." Of Thompson's mysticism, however, there is little, and the variety of themes indicates that she was not exclusively a devotional poet.

Born Alice Thompson in 1847 into a serene home of parents interested in the arts, she possessed literary inclinations

as a part of her birthright. Sojourns with her parents in Italy,
tutors of more than average capabilities and culture, an
atmosphere of refinement in her home, and her conversion
to Catholicism at the age of twenty, were the background out
of which her personality and talent developed. Even in her
teens she wrote poetry, but it was not until 1875 that a small
collection *Preludes* appeared in which she was perceptibly
influenced by Mrs. Browning and Christina Rossetti. In 1877
she married Wilfrid Meynell, a young man occupied with
editing conservative periodicals, a man of undoubted taste
and literary perception whose talent was more largely critical
than creative. With him she became the coeditor of *Merry
England,* and for years she shared his work, helping with
reviews and submitting essays and poems. Her writing was
not confined to the periodicals which she and her husband
edited, for Henley printed some of her work in the *National
Observer,* and some of it appeared in the *Spectator* and the
Saturday Review. In addition to all the activity as editor and
contributor, she became the mother of eight children, most
of whom were to show considerable talent; and she was a
source of inspiration and encouragement to those who sat in
her drawing room at Palace Court in London and her hos-
pitable home in Sussex. Richard Le Gallienne said of her:
"The touch of genuine asceticism about her seemed but to
accent the sensitive sympathy of her manner, the manner of
one quite simply and humanly of the world, with all its
varied interests, yet not of it. There was the charm of a
beautiful abbess about her, with the added *esprit* of intellectual sophistication. However quietly she sat in her drawing room of an evening with her family and friends about
her, her presence radiated a peculiarly lovely serenity, like
a twilight gay with stars." Although in her late years her
speech became slow and without its earlier keenness of
phrase, she was never pedantic. She died at her home in
Sussex in 1922.

A glance at a list of her published works indicates that she was more fluent in prose than verse. Her critical standards, illustrated in many reviews, reveal her insistence on discipline and moderation. Nimbleness of phrase for its own sake she deplored, and she was quick to detect any sort of artificiality, of manner. Sentimentality and overwrought effects were high on her *index prohibitorum*, along with any inclination away from the precise and discriminating. Her essays in which the purpose was other than critical show a careful application of the discipline she advocated in her reviews. They are subjective without becoming really personal, and in spite of their easy, informal air, they are always dignified. In them there is nothing of Lamb's delight in the confession of human frailty, and nothing which approaches the boisterousness of Stephen Leacock. There are light passages, to be sure, in which a fresh and, at times, unexpected humor comes to the reader; but there is no deliberate attempt to be whimsical, much less coy. Without becoming austere, Mrs. Meynell's essays reflect her serene personality and her intellectual and stylistic discipline.

Although the greater volume of her work was in prose, at intervals—some of them long—little volumes of verse, much of which had appeared in magazines, were issued. In the collected edition of 1923, which contains little more than a hundred pages, there is more variety in theme and manner than is implied in Edith Sitwell's description of her poems as "limp exhortations to virtue." The assurance and dignity of the manner can scarcely be called limp; and although Mrs. Meynell no doubt wanted the world to be a better place than it often is, she was not a reformer. Were it not for the delicate richness of feeling in many of her poems, she might have become a victim of her own restraint and self-imposed discipline. There are no great emotional surges, and there is no lavish imagery as one encounters in Thompson. In such a poem as "Renouncement" she escapes from the charge of lack of warmth, but generally the reader has the impression of emotion well leashed. The intensity of her religious emotion appears in such well-known poems as "The Shepherdess" and "Christ in the Universe," but it is a serene, intellectualized emotion rather than rapture. A perfectionist in form, Alice Meynell illustrated in her poetry the quiet richness of her spiritual life in a fashion which appeals to readers of the most exacting tastes.

VERSE: *Preludes* (1875), *Poems* (1893), *Other Poems* (1896), *Later Poems* (1901), *The Shepherdess and Other Verses* (1914), *Poems of the War* (1915), *A Father of Women* (1917), *Last Poems* (1923), *Collected Poems* (1923), *Complete Poems* (1940), *The Poems of Alice Meynell* (Centenary ed., 1947). PROSE: *Colour of Life and Other Essays* (1897), *Second Person Singular and Other Essays* (nd), *Spirit of Place and Other Essays* (1899), *Childhood* (1913), *Essays* (1914), *Selected Essays* (1926).

C. A. and H. W. Stonehill, *Bibliographies of Modern Authors*, second series (1925); Viola Meynell, *Alice Meynell* (1929); Annie K. Tuell, *Mrs. Meynell and Her Literary Generation* (1925); Alfred Noyes, "Alice Meynell" in *Some Aspects of Modern Poetry* (1924); Roy Eldridge, "The Poetry of Alice Meynell," *Catholic Rev.*, CXVI (1922), 150-160; G. K. Chesterton, "Alice Meynell," *Dublin Rev.*, CLXXII (1923), 1-12.

Although **Gerard Manley Hopkins (1844-1889)** wrote in the age of Tennyson, his poetry did not come to the attention of the public until 1918 when Robert Bridges, then poet-laureate, issued the *Poems of Gerard Manley Hopkins* with copious notes. At the time little attention was paid to the volume, and it seemed as if Hopkins' posthumous bid for recognition would be ignored. By the mid-twenties, however, with zealous modernists engaged in finding precursors for their tendencies in verse, Hopkins became widely known among the technicians in versification and among readers of devotional poetry. In fact, a cult developed which has been inclined to magnify the significance of his work.

He was born in Ireland in 1844, and after a somewhat

undisciplined youth, he became attached to the Jesuits to pursue the tradition of the order as a scholar and teacher. As an instructor in Greek language and literature at University College, Dublin, he lived in a rarified atmosphere of the classics and his own highly introspective and egocentric nature. Of an ingenious, inquisitive turn of mind, and possessed of talent in both writing and drawing, he devoted much of his time in his middle and late years to an attempt to make his reflections articulate and to experiments with verse measures. Possibly feeling that he had not mastered his theories sufficiently to present his poems to the public, he allowed them to accumulate, along with a large mass of explanatory material in which he stated his theories and objectives. Hopkins died in 1889 when, according to Robert Bridges, "he was beginning to concentrate the force of all of his luxuriant experiments in rhythm and diction, and castigate his art into a more reserved style."

Hopkins is a difficult poet to comprehend. The difficulty can be traced not only to his oblique thought, but also to the fact that his medium is too confined for his feeling. One of his editors observed that his is "a passionate emotion which seems to try to utter all its words in one." Furthermore, he is given to a manner highly elliptical and to imagery which is without ready association. His "sprung rhythms," in which stress rather than quantity in the verse line is a fundamental principle, provide another difficulty to the reader who is accustomed to only the conventional verse patterns. Behind all of his experimentation, however, there was method; and even in his more irregular pieces, the informed reader can see justification. "No doubt my poetry errs on the side of oddness," he wrote. "I hope in time to have a more balanced and Miltonic style. But as air, melody, is what strikes me most of all in music, and design in painting, so design, pattern, or what I am in the habit of calling *inscape* is what above all I aim at in poetry. Now it is the virtue of design, pattern, or inscape to be distinctive, and it is the vice of distinctiveness to become queer. This vice I cannot have escaped." Although interesting to the technician, and possibly significant in theme to those who can comprehend his spirituality, Hopkins' intrinsic worth should not be magnified.

VERSE: *Poems,* ed. Robert Bridges (1919), revised and enlarged ed. Charles Williams (1931), *Complete Poems,* ed. W. H. Gardner (1947). PERSONAL PAPERS: *Letters,* ed. C. C. Abbott (2 v., 1934), *Further Letters,* ed. C. C. Abbott (1937), *Notebooks,* ed. H. House (1936).

W. H. Gardner, *Gerard Manley Hopkins* (2 v., 1944, 1949); E. E. Phare, *The Poetry of Gerard Manley Hopkins: A Survey and Commentary* (1933); John Pick, *Gerard Manley Hopkins: Priest and Poet* (1942); Eleanor Ruggles, *Gerard Manley Hopkins: A Life* (1944); Harold Whitehall, "Sprung Rhythm," *Kenyon Rev.,* VI (1944), 333-354.

Wilfrid Scawen Blunt (1840-1922) belonged to the Meynell circle, and in spite of his interest in Mohammedanism in the years following his diplomatic assignments in the Near East, he was essentially more of the West than the East. According to Wilfrid Meynell, he returned to the Catholic faith in his last years, a faith from which he had never more than superficially departed. His attachment to the Moslem religion, it would appear, was more academic than spiritual, and only a temporary stage in a widely varied life. "I have lived my life in full," he wrote. "No life is perfect that has not been lived youth in feeling, manhood in battle, old age in meditation." And T. E. Welby, reflecting on Blunt's full life, observed: "To have married Byron's granddaughter, bred Arab horses, and been admired by Henley and George Wyndham is to have made a great deal of life." A considerable amount of self-illumination is contained in *My Diaries* (1919), in which there is much which has to do with Blunt's attitude toward British foreign policy, especially in the Near

East, and some reflections on religion and literature. Blunt's chief distinction was as a poet. Although not widely read today, his verse is of considerable volume and variety. His best poems are reflective rather than narrative and dramatic in which manner, however, most of his talent sought expression. Among the reflective poems, especially those in *Poems* (1923) there are moods and sentiments which might be called devotional, although Blunt's inspiration was drawn from sources different from those of Thompson and Mrs. Meynell. Of mystic exaltation there is nothing. It is rather an intense satisfaction and reverence in meditating on the handiwork of the Creator. In spite of the fact that the odes of Pagan Arabia illustrate a considerable side of the poet, it is in such sonnets as "On the Shortness of Time" that he has done his finest work.

VERSE: *The Love Sonnets of Proteus* (1882), *The Wind and the Whirlwind* (1888), *Esther* (1892), *Stealing of the Mare* (1892), *Griselda* (1893), *Seven Golden Odes of Pagan Arabia* (1908), *Poems* (1923). PROSE: *The Future of Islam* (1882), *Gordon of Khartoum* (1911), *My Diaries: Being a Personal Narrative of Events, 1888-1914* (1919).

Edith Finch, *Wilfrid Scawen Blunt* (1938); Sister Mary Joan Reinehr, *The Writings of Wilfrid Scawen Blunt* (1940).

Rudyard Kipling (1865-1936)

A conclusive judgment of Rudyard Kipling's worth is still to be made. Some indication of his popularity is afforded by the estimate that more than 3,500,000 copies of his books were sold by his American publishers between 1895 and 1935. The critical disparagement which is at times implied in such notices of an author's popularity is not always applicable to Kipling, for in spite of the fact that his works have appealed to many classes of readers, he cannot be dismissed as only a prolific and clever writer who gave the public what it wanted.

Joseph Rudyard Kipling was born December 30, 1865, in Bombay, India, the son of John Lockwood Kipling, a sculptor and authority on the Hindu plastic arts, and Alice Kipling, the daughter of a distinguished Wesleyan clergyman. Kipling's birthright augured well for the future; and when at an early age he showed a fondness for all manner of stories and displayed a lively imagination, his parents agreed that he was marked for a career with his pen. When he was six, he and a younger sister were sent to England to school, to live at Southsea with an elderly relative whose manner was austere and whose home Kipling was to call "the House of Desolation." It was relief for him to be sent to the United Services College at Westward Ho where he remained for four years. His stories in *Stalky and Co.* (1899) afford a pleasant picture of the school and its life at the time, and one can detect in the character Beetle lineaments of the author. Although the training he received at Westward Ho was no great contributing factor in his development, he edited six numbers of the school paper and contributed stories to it. As early as 1881, he had published *School Boy Lyrics*.

RUDYARD KIPLING

At seventeen, he returned to India where through his father he obtained congenial work on the staff of the Lahore *Civil and Military Gazette* to which he brought enthusiasm and energy, combined with a talent for writing lively articles and stories. The *Gazette* in turn provided him with a receptacle into which to place his writing and a rigorous apprenticeship in giving readers what they want. By the time he was twenty-two he was adequately trained to fill the post of assistant editor of the *Pioneer* at Allahabad, at the time the greatest of the Anglo-Indian papers. Because he was not always submissive to editorial policy, he was in time given "more assignments at a distance than in the immediate vicinity of the office"; and after several years of moving about India procuring good copy, he was sent by the *Pioneer* as correspondent-at-large to England, and later to Australia, New Zealand, and South Africa. Soon after his arrival in England he sent some of the verses which he later collected for *Barrack-Room Ballads* to W. E. Henley who was enthusiastic about their merit and issued them promptly in the *National Observer*. On his return to London in 1892 after extensive travel for the *Pioneer,* Kipling was ready to give up professional journalism, and collect some of his stories and verse for publication in book form.

While looking after the issue of his books, Kipling met Wolcot Balestier, a young American critic, whose sister Caroline he married in 1892. He came with his wife to live at her home in Brattleboro, Vermont, until 1896. According to report, "He adopted Vermont, but Vermont never adopted him," and, not without bitterness, he and his wife left America to search for a good place for a permanent home. After an interval of travel, they settled at Rottingdean, Sussex, which Kipling grew to like to such an extent that in his later years he rarely went far from the boundaries of his garden. In 1907 he won the Nobel Prize for literature, not for any particular or recent work, but on account of his achievements over a period of years. There was a perceptible falling off of volume after 1910, but his vigor of manner persisted and he was by no means written out. To the end he produced valuable additions to both his verse and prose, especially during the First World War; and his autobiography, *Something of Myself,* written late in life, is full of his characteristic strength. He died at his home in Sussex in 1936.

As a personality Kipling was dynamic and uncompromising. He never adopted half-way measures. It is not difficult to tell where Kipling stood; and since his political conclusions were more the result of personal feeling and instinct than of the conservative and at times equivocal deliberations of the Foreign Office, he laid himself open to criticism. It is as a poet of imperialism that Kipling drew the chief attacks, including Max Beerbohm's caricature of a little bespectacled man in a helmet, blowing a tin trumpet and waving a British flag. It is no doubt true that in his later years Kipling was somewhat of an opinionated recluse, attacking the established order but mistrusting political change, and often with his mind closed to the worth of his literary contemporaries, but his sincerity and forthrightness cannot be questioned.

Although Kipling is more widely known through his verse than his prose, in the tales and novels there is much which is characteristic of his talent and which continues to appeal to a wide class of reader. The pieces in *Soldiers Three* (1888), though an engaging anticipation of what he was later to do for the soldier in his verse, are not so finely written as the stories in *Plain Tales From the Hills* (1888). These tales reveal much of the author's understanding of Anglo-Indian life and his sense of vivid pictorial detail as well as his talent for compelling narrative. Of the stories which have an Indian background, "Without Benefit of Clergy" and "The Man Who Would be King" are among the best. *The Jungle Book* (1894) and *The Second Jungle Book* (1895) are classics in a sense, for these stories, designed largely for children but appealing to all ages, are excitingly and delightfully told. *Wee Willie Winkie* (1888), though agreeable, is not so compelling to the imagination as are many of the stories in the *Jungle Books,* nor does it have the fine narrative artistry of *Puck of Pook's Hill* (1906).

The novels *The Light That Failed* (1890), *Captains Courageous* (1897), and *Kim* (1901) are entirely plausible in character and plot, but *The Light That Failed* lacks the force of great tragedy. *Captains Courageous,* though appealing as a story and illuminating in its description of the background of the fishing fleets of the North Atlantic, is undistinguished by any really memorable passage of prose. *Kim,* with its setting in India, has striking passages of description; and although the plot is loosely woven, Kim and the old lama are a picturesque, endearing pair as they move through the bazaars and along the Grand Trunk Road.

Kipling's verse reveals a writer of many themes, moods, and manners. There are poems, for example, in which he is the romanticist of modernity and the machine age. In "M'Andrew's Hymn" he shows very persuasively that the drama and glamor of the sea did not disappear with the advent of the steamship. "The Bell Buoy," with its onomatopoetic refrain, dramatizes vividly the struggles between the forces of the sea and a product of man's mechanical ingenuity. In "The King" he gives the most eloquent expression to his belief of the presence of romance in the here-and-now of reality. In much of his verse, especially in "The Rival," "La Nuit Blanche," "The Explorer," and "Mary, Pity Women," he demonstrates a remarkable talent for projecting himself into different types of character, thinking their thoughts and using their idiom. In "Mary, Pity Women" the manner in which the poet expresses the anguish of the poor, disillusioned girl whose lover is leaving her an expectant mother goes beyond clever mimicry. In such well-known pieces as "The Ladies," "Pink Dominoes," and "Tommy" he seeks not only a skilfull imitation of a point of view and the idiom of his characters, but an expression of his own shrewd wisdom. In many of these pieces the wisdom is of a practical worldly sort, with its application limited to particular circumstances, and with cleverness rather than profoundness in the manner and tone. "The Recessional," "If," and "L'Envoi" are still recited, at times probably more for their rhetoric which is not too well concealed than for their lofty sentiment. Unfortunately some of Kipling's finest lyrics are ignored for those in which there is something the reader mistakes for greatness, but what is in reality only a tuneful jingle conveying a clever theme. The poems "A Nativity" and "My Boy Jack" have a dignity and beauty which puts them into a different class from the overworked measures in "Boots" and the cleverness in "Pink Dominoes." Many of Kipling's themes have already been put aside as dated, but his versification, generally vigorous and martial, exercised at times at the expense of consummate tonal effects, continues to give pleasure; and his diction and imagery, comprehensible and usually down to earth, delight readers who prefer the explicit to the subtle and cerebral.

VERSE: *Departmental Ditties* (1886), *Barrack Room Ballads and Other Verses* (1892), *The Seven Seas* (1896), *Recessional and Other Poems* (1899), *The Five Nations* (1903), *Rewards and Fairies* (1910), prose and verse; *Songs From Books* (1912), *The Years Between* (1919), *Sixty Poems* (1939), *Rudyard Kipling's Verse* (definitive ed., 1940), *The Novels, Tales, and Poems of Rudyard Kipling* (35 v., 1939). PROSE: *Plain Tales From the Hills* (1888), *Soldiers Three* (1888), *The Light That Failed* (1890), *Many Inventions* (1893), *The Jungle Book* (1894), *The Second Jungle Book* (1895), *Captains Courageous* (1897), *The Day's Work* (1898), *Stalky and Co.* (1899), *Kim* (1901), *Just-so Stories* (1902), *Puck of Pook's Hill* (1906). AUTOBIOGRAPHY: *Something of Myself* (1937).

L. H. Chandler, *A List of Magazines, Newspapers, Periodicals ... Containing Items of the Work of Rudyard Kipling, ... Attributed to Him, and Items by Others About Him or About his Work* (1933); Frederick Ehrsam, *Bibliographies* (Boston, 1941), pp. 121-160; Mrs. Flora V. Livingston, *Bibliography of the Works of Rudyard Kipling* (Cambridge, Mass., 1927; supplement, 1938); Hilton Brown, *Rudyard Kipling* (1945); R. T. Hopkins, *Rudyard Kipling: A Character Study* (1921); G. C. Beresford, *School Days With Kipling* (1936); F. F. Van de Water, *Rudyard Kipling's Vermont Feud* (1937); Edward Shanks, *Rudyard Kipling: A Study in Literature and Political Ideas* (1938); R. A. Durand, *A Handbook to the Poetry of Rudyard Kipling* (1914); Anne Weygandt, *Kipling's*

Reading and Its Influence on His Poetry (Phila., 1939); Sir George McMunn, *Rudyard Kipling, Craftsman* (1938); W. M. Hart, *Kipling, the Story-Writer* (Berkeley, Cal., 1918); Lionel Stevenson, "The Ideas in Kipling's Poetry," *Univ. Toronto Quar.*, I (1932), 467-489; Basil Williams, "Rudyard Kipling," *Nineteenth Century*, CXIX (1937), 291-302; Edith Merrielies, "Time and Mr. Kipling," *Virginia Quar. Rev.*, XI (1935), 37-46; T. S. Eliot, Introduction to *A Choice of Kipling's Verse* (1941).

John Masefield (1878-)

John Masefield, the present Laureate, cannot be placed in any tradition or school. He himself observed that his earliest verses "reflected clearly my enthusiasm for certain English poets, for Chaucer first, then Keats, then Milton, then Shelley." Later he fell under the magic of Swinburne's melodies and the beauty of the earlier work of William Butler Yeats, and there is no doubt that Synge's dicta and plays provided a pronounced though temporary influence. There is no consistent reflection of any of these, however; and although there is an eclectic element in the total body of his work, there is a clear indication of his poetic individuality.

JOHN MASEFIELD

The wide variety in Masefield's work can be traced in some measure to his rich and varied experience. He was born in Ledbury, Herefordshire, the son of a solicitor and a woman of gentle ways, both of whom died when the boy was still young. Of the circumstances of his youth little is known, although it is reported that he was restless if not unhappy. In his middle teens he went to sea, and before he was nineteen he had touched the principal ports of the Western Ocean. His experiences on ships and with seamen played an important part in his development, for in the poem "Biography," he wrote:

> Yet when I am dust my penman may not know
> Those water-trampling ships which made me glow ...
> And yet they made me.*

For long intervals he remained ashore, working for a time in a rug factory, then on a farm, and under an assumed name in Luke O'Connor's saloon in New York. That he spent his spare moments aboard ship and in O'Connor's bar reading the English poets, and that even in his teens he felt a keen awareness of his literary mission, are surmises, however, that are in need of modification. It is no doubt true that he viewed many of his experiences with a kind of poetic detachment, and that even in his early twenties he had tried to write what he called "pictures in verse." Some of his early efforts he had printed in *The Speaker* and *The Outlook;* and through the encouragement of J. L. Hammond, editor of *The Speaker,* Masefield became a regular contributor of reviews, stories, and verse to Hammond's journal. In 1904 he filled for some months a post on the *Manchester Guardian,* but even before this association, he had issued *Salt Water Ballads* (1902), and the following year a sort of companion piece *Ballads.* At the time these collections were only moderately successful; it was not until 1911 that he attracted wide attention and even notoriety with his first sustained narrative poem *The Everlasting Mercy.* With the Victorian conventions of refinement still strong, some of the passages in the poem shocked many readers who insisted that the piece was deliberately crude, and not poetry at all. But Masefield, firmly believing in the dictum of Synge that "the strong

* From *Poems.* Copyright, 1935, by The Macmillan Co. and used with their permission.

things of life are needed in poetry ... before verse can be human again it must be brutal," was not discouraged by the comments of the traditionalists and prudes. By the time *The Widow in the Bye Street* (1912), *Dauber* (1913), and *The Daffodil Fields* (1913) appeared, he had convinced most of his readers that he had more to offer than a shock. Over the protests of Stephen Phillips that the standards of literature were being endangered, Masefield was awarded the Edmond de Polignac prize for poetry by the Royal Society of Literature. With this encouragement, Masefield continued to write much: scarcely a year passed without another volume of verse or prose, and sometimes both. At the death of Bridges in 1930, Masefield was appointed Laureate. The significance of the appoinment was noted at the time; a Labor government chose for laureate a poet definitely of the people. Since his appointment, he has continued to write much, although his most ineffectual work is in the field of occasional verse. At his home at Boar's Hill near Oxford, surrounded by a fine library and pictures of ships for which he has more than a ship fancier's attachment, Masefield in his late years no doubt looks back on a life rich in experience, and with the satisfaction of knowing that he has used his energy and talent well.

As a personality, he is more winning than dynamic and impressive. To his role of poet, he attaches a lofty importance, but he has discarded all the posturings and mannerisms of dress and elocution which for long have done poetry a disservice. He is no believer in poetry for the few; he has never presumed to suggest to his readers that their background is limited and their taste questionable, or that he is the one to lead them from darkness to light. Although he has political convictions, he has not used them to try to point out new Utopias. "Reformers do best," he has said, "when they keep their efforts to themselves, their families, and their parishes." As Laureate he has been appreciative of his responsibility, but during the war years his sense of obligation produced no propaganda or flag-waving.

Although his major work is in verse, he has written a considerable amount of prose, none of which is particularly outstanding. The stories in *A' Mainsail Haul* (1905), and in the later sustained narratives *Sard Harker* (1924) and *Odtaa* (1926) are full of authentic detail in recording background, but in characterization and plot there is no great power. Compared to his early verse, both the themes and style of the prose narratives are conventional. His plays have more distinction than his stories, although he has contributed little which is truly great to the English drama. *The Tragedy of Nan* (1909), strongly influenced by Synge, is perhaps his finest effort for the theatre. *The Tragedy of Pompey the Great* (1910) suggests an Elizabethan drama in some of its external aspects, but the full power of the tragedy is unrealized in spite of a few admirably handled scenes. Masefield is nearer to his real *métier* in the short poetic dramas *Philip the King* and *Good Friday,* for apparently his talent as a poet is less restricted when he has only one act to manipulate than when he has undertaken a larger and more complex dramatic form.

It is in his poetry that Masefield has found his most complete and finest expression. In his earliest poems, *Salt Water Ballads* (1902) and *Ballads* (1903), he did some of his most distinctive work. What Kipling had done for the ordinary British soldier, Masefield was qualified to do for the seaman. He was the first English poet who had been a true deep-water sailor. In his prefatory lines to *Salt Water Ballads,* he declared:

> Others may sing of the wine and the wealth and the mirth
> The portly presence of potentates goodly in girth;—
> Mine be the dirt and the dross, the dust and scum of the earth! *

* From *Salt Water Poems & Ballads.* Copyright, 1916, by The Macmillan Co. and used with their permission.

In the light of such a declaration of intent, one might feel that a vehement socialist was about to condemn the unfairness of the class system, but Masefield is not the reformer: he is the describer and interpreter of the sea and its men, and although the "dirt and the dross" enter in some of the pieces, "the music, the colour, the glory, the gold" play a part in the poet's illumination of his subject. Such poems as "A Valediction," "A Wanderer's Song," and the well-known "Sea-Fever," without losing anything of faithfulness of observation and authenticity of phrase, are on a higher plane than that of the pieces in which the author is concerned chiefly with the scum and in which he at times "mistakes brashness for strength." In *Ballads* there is a continuation of the spirit of the earlier series, with a perceptible lessening of stress on the dross in both sentiment and diction. "Spanish Waters" and "Cargoes" are as richly poetic as anything Masefield has done.

In 1911 *The Everlasting Mercy* appeared, the first of a long series of sustained narrative poems. Although the conversion of Saul Kane may not be psychologically convincing to some readers, and the character may have too much of Masefield's own sentiment in him to be entirely consistent, the story has undoubted power. It may be taken, as has been suggested, "as one more footnote to the varieties of religious experience." Compact throughout in unfolding the action, the style ranges from a gross realism to a lofty lyric tone in which simplicity and directness are not forsaken. In *The Widow in the Bye Street,* the unadorned manner fits the theme admirably, and although the way is strewn with the pitfalls of sentimentality and melodrama, the poet with few exceptions escapes them on account of his intentness on the theme. *Dauber* (1913) is a moving story of the sea, rich in vivid descriptive detail, with a somewhat ill-timed tragedy at the end. *Reynard the Fox* (1919), with its fine illumination of the English countryside, has been aptly judged as "a damned good run, but a bank holiday field." In the other long verse narratives, *The Daffodil Fields* (1913), *Right Royal* (1920), and *King Cole* (1921) Masefield offers additional evidence of his versatility in background and invention of theme, but the style of these poems, like that of the earlier narratives, is uneven. The later poems which deal with Arthurian characters do not run to the same length as *The Daffodil Fields,* and they are not so intent on the narrative element. Much of the vigor of the earlier poems is missing, and all of the brashness. They are essentially of the nineteenth-century tradition, with something of Tennyson's mildness, and with diction and imagery quite remote from that in *The Everlasting Mercy.*

Although Masefield's principal talent lies in narrative verse, he has written a considerable number of reflective poems. "A Creed" and "Beauty," written comparatively early, reach a high level, although the latter poem is somewhat disfigured by a weak ending. Of the many sonnets, there is none which stands out as particularly fine: they are capable rather than consummate. His occasional poetry, written chiefly after he became Laureate, has little of the facility and vigor which characterize the major part of his work. The very special kind of talent which is required for good occasional poetry he does not possess. His poem written at the time of the death of George V is as helpless as Masefield can be with his pen; and his lines "On the Ninetieth Birthday of Bernard Shaw," although no doubt sincere, dwindle off into a commonplace unworthy of either Shaw or Masefield. Despite the merit of much of his later work, Masefield is identified with the *Salt Water Ballads* and the narrative poems written before 1925, and it is here that his most important contribution to English poetry lies.

VERSE: *Salt Water Ballads* (1902), *Ballads* (1903), *Ballads and Poems* (1910), *The Everlasting Mercy* (1911), *The Story of a Roundhouse and Other Poems* (1912), *The Widow in the Bye*

Street (1912), *The Daffodil Fields* (1913), *Dauber* (1913), *Philip the King and Other Poems* (1914), *Good Friday and Other Poems* (1916), *Lollingdon Downs and Other Poems* (1917), *Rosas* (1918), *Reynard the Fox* (1919), *Enslaved and Other Poems* (1920), *Right Royal* (1920), *King Cole* (1921), *The Dream* (1922), *Midsummer Night and Other Tales in Verse* (1928), *South and East* (1929), *The Wanderer of Liverpool* (1930), both prose and verse; *Minnie Maylow's Story and Other Tales and Scenes* (1931), *A Tale of Troy* (1932), *Collected Poems* (1935), *A Letter From Pontus and Other Verse* (1936), *Tribute to Ballet* (1937), *The Country Scene* (1939), *Gautama the Enlightened and Other Verse* (1941), *Thanks Before Going* (1946), *On the Hill* (1949). PLAYS: *The Tragedy of Nan and Other Plays* (1909), *The Tragedy of Pompey the Great* (1910), *The Faithful* (1915), *Melloney Holtspur* (1922), *A King's Daughter* (1923), *The Trial of Jesus* (1925), *Tristan and Isolt* (1927), *The Coming of Christ* (1928), *End and Beginning* (1933), *A Play of St. George* (1948). NOVELS AND TALES: *A Mainsail Haul* (1905, enlarged, 1913), *A Tarpaulin Muster* (1907), *Captain Margaret* (1908), *Multitude and Solitude* (1909), *The Street of Today* (1911), *Sard Harker* (1924), *Odtaa* (1926), *The Hawbucks* (1929), *The Bird of Dawning* (1933), *The Taking of the Gry* (1934). HISTORICAL NARRATIVE: *Gallipoli* (1916), *The Battle of the Somme* (1919), *The Nine Days' Wonder* (1941), on the evacuation of Dunkirk. STUDIES: *William Shakespeare* (1911), *John M. Synge, a Few Personal Recollections With Biographical Notes* (1915), *John Ruskin* (1920), *Chaucer* (1931), *Poetry* (1931). AUTOBIOGRAPHICAL: *In the Mill* (1941), *So Long to Learn* (1952).

Charles N. Simmons, *A Bibliography of John Masefield* (1930); Gilbert Thomas, *John Masefield* (1933); Cecil Biggane, *John Masefield, a Study* (Cambridge, Eng., 1924), J. E. Brown, *John Masefield* (Exeter, Eng., 1939); W. H. Hamilton, *John Masefield: A Critical Study* (1922); N. I. White, "John Masefield: an Estimate," *South Atlantic Quar.*, XXVI (1932), 189-200; G. H. Clark, "Various Mr. Masefield," *Saturday Rev.*, XXXI (1923), 1-12, and "John Masefield, Poet Laureate," *Dalhousie Rev.*, XII (1932), 25-46; Anton A. Raven, "A Study in Masefield's Vocabulary," *Modern Language Notes*, XXXVII (1922), 148-153.

THE TRADITIONALISTS

Existing in a different sphere from Kipling and Masefield, and finding their themes and styles largely in the province which had proved fertile to the Victorians and the Romanticists before them, a long procession of poets has appeared in the past fifty years who might with reasonable accuracy be called traditionalists. Their sources of inspiration, their manner of apprehending their themes, and the rich and wide variety of stanzaic patterns and verse schemes all indicate that a following of the main line of English poetry need not necessarily result in derivative content, threadbare verse-measures, and cliché-ridden imagery. Derivative notes appear, to be sure, in both theme and manner; and on occasion, one might wish for a manner of expression a little more daring and less given to regularity of design; but even in the more conservative of the traditionalists, there are instances in which a striking freedom of apprehension and manner appears. Among those who have followed the main line with relative consistency, Austin Dobson, William Watson, Stephen Phillips, Laurence Binyon, Robert Bridges, T. Sturge Moore, Alfred Noyes, and Sir Henry Newbolt are to be named. Many others, including the Georgians, were essentially traditionalists, although in most of these instances there are distinctive qualities which set the poets somewhat apart from those who followed the main line.

Austin Dobson (1840-1921), like many of the writers of the late nineteenth century, was interested in poetry for its own sake. Instead of attempting to cultivate the nuances of sensation as did the poets of the aesthetic school, however, he found adequate sources of inspiration in the refinements of living and in the brighter aspects of the past, especially in the England and France of the eighteenth century. Although serious at times, his talent was not directed toward a questioning of primary cause and a solution for the world's ills. His most characteristic work shows a lightness and delicacy in both theme and manner.

Henry Austin Dobson was born in Plymouth in 1840 of parents who were sufficiently well-to-do to indulge their tastes in travel, reading, and the arts. There was a French strain in the family which no doubt accounts for his familiarity with French literature and a manner of expression which can be called peculiarly French. Furthermore, some of his schooling was completed in France where he augmented his natural inclination to enjoy the wit and deftness of phrase which are part of the French manner. From his late teens until he was sixty-one he held progressive posts with the London Board of Trade, work which evidently allowed him ample time to indulge his tastes in reading. When Theodor de Banville issued his *Petit Traité de la Poésie Française* in 1872, in which the author pleaded for the revival of some of the earlier forms such as the triolet, villanelle, rondel, and rondeau, Dobson had already experimented with many types of verse-measure; and in 1878 he produced an essay "Some Foreign Forms of Verse" in which he illustrated the beauties of the artificial forms and indicated how they could be employed agreeably in English poetry. With a remarkable facility for meter and rime, Dobson began to turn out volumes of verse which were read with delight by a widening group. Although his most characteristic work was done before the turn of the century, he remains widely read by those who enjoy *vers de société*. During his later years, he did not forsake verse entirely, but he devoted much of his interest to prose essays in which he was especially successful in catching at least the external spirit of the eighteenth century and in maintaining the lightness of phrase which is such a distinctive quality in his verse. Dobson died in 1921.

In the collected edition of his verse, which is well over 500 pages, the themes are varied: narrative, descriptive, reflective, but never hortatory; and still his range is slight. His sentiment, when it touches the reader at all, touches him only momentarily. One is inclined to feel thát in Dobson's case the theme is often subordinated to the verse; and the verse by reason of its lightness and delicacy was never meant to be the vehicle for profound thought and feeling. The French forms such as the triolet and rondel scarcely adapt themselves to content other than the light and pleasant; and even when Dobson forsakes the French forms, as he often does, the verse maintains a lightness of key. Although it is true that Dobson was "only a most accomplished writer of verse," with little to offer the reader who is seeking light on the verities of life, there is much pleasure to be derived from listening to his graceful melodies and watching his delicate figures move under the crystal lustres of an eighteenth-century drawing room. It is an atmosphere of dainty porcelain figurines, brocaded drapery and wig powder, brought to the reader through apparently effortless verse. "A Gentlewoman of the Old School," and "The Ballad of Beau Brocade" are well nigh consummate in their quaint charm. They possess what has been called an "archaic gentility" which requires an artistry not easily attained. For facility and grace of manner, Austin Dobson's verse holds a high place in English literature.

Vignettes in Rhyme and Vers de Société (1873), *Proverbs in Porcelain and Other Verses* (1877), *Old World Idylls* (1883), *At the Sign of the Lyre* (1895), *Poems on Several Occasions* (1895), *Collected Poems* (1923).

Alban Dobson, *Austin Dobson* (1925); "Austin Dobson: Some Letters From His Friends," *Cornhill Mag.*, LXIV (1927), 569-585; Edmund Gosse, "Austin Dobson," *Quarterly Rev.*, CCXXXVII (1920), 33-67; Cornelius Weygandt, "Austin Dobson, Augustan," in *Tuesdays at Ten* (Phila., 1928).

The charm of Austin Dobson's verse was recognized by many of his poet-contemporaries, of whom **William Watson (1858-1935)**, later Sir William Watson, was one who paid tribute to his friend in stanzas which began:

> Yes! urban is your Muse, and owns
> An empire based on London stones.

It was Watson's chief purpose in poetry to recognize the beauties in other poets, especially those of the great romantic tradition. Little interested in novelty of theme and manner, and in the experiments of his contemporaries with new media in versification, he entered feelingly into the spirit of Burns, Wordsworth, and Keats. His talent may be called critical as well as poetic, for he brought to his own verse a severe self-discipline and a rich appreciation for the great poets of England's past.

William Watson was born at Burley-in-Wharfdale, Yorkshire, in 1858, of landed gentry who provided him with the traditional training of sports, the classics, Eton, and later the University. Probably the same instinct for reform which appeared often in the Romanticists Burns and Shelley inspired him to appraise and at times attack British policies and institutions. As early as *Ver Tenebrosum* (1885), in which he attacked the foreign policy in Egypt, he gained recognition in political circles which he maintained through many parliamentary crises. He was not linked with any faction, nor did he attempt to curry favor, for generally he was of the opposition. When Alfred Austin, the Poet Laureate, died in 1913, Watson, who had been for long considered a likely candidate for the post, was passed over in favor of Robert Bridges. His failure to attain the laureateship did little to make him less critical of British policies. Stubbornness and obstinacy became part of his life and work. Before the First World War, he made a lecture tour in America in which his traditionalist creed was plainly and repeatedly declared. His lecture "The Poet's Place in the Scheme of Life," printed in 1913, is an amplification in prose of the theme in his poem "Apologia." In much of his later critical work in both verse and prose, he antagonized the modernists by what seemed to them to be unreasonable attacks on their efforts. His spirited defense of British character and policies during the First World War led to his being knighted in 1917. Watson died in 1935.

His poems all show dignity, artistic sincerity, and well-disciplined measures which are at times genuinely melodic. His admirable critical faculty kept his style on a consistently high level; but it was also responsible in part for his inadequacies in creative theme. His work is often more rhetorical than inspired, more conventional than impassioned, more critical than imaginative. "The Tomb of Burns," "Shelley's Centenary," and "Wordsworth's Grave" are fine examples of the poet's ability to merge himself with the spirit of the poets of the past. It is in such pieces that his appreciative sense extends to a rapture which is in itself poetic. Although the poems in which he pays lyric tribute to his great forebears are representative of Watson's most characteristic theme, there are varied subjects and manners in his work. Of these, such a graceful, airy manner as that in the song which begins "April, April, laugh thy girlish laughter," and the fine compression in the four-line epigrams are noteworthy. In spite of the fact that the greater part of his work has chiefly its manner to commend it, and that he wrote far too much that is lacking in genuine inspiration, the poems in which he attains lyric expression in dealing with the great tradition and the epigrams have an easily recognized worth.

VERSE: *The Prince's Quest and Other Poems* (1880), *Epigrams of Art, Life and Nature* (1884), *Wordsworth's Grave and Other Poems* (1890), *Lachrymae Musarum and Other Poems* (1892), *Shelley's Centenary* (1892), *Poems* (1892), *The Eloping Angels: A Caprice* (1893), *Odes and Other Poems* (1894), *The Father of the Forest and Other Poems* (1895), *Hymn to the Sea* (1895), *The Hope of the World* (1897), *New Poems* (1902), *The Poems of William Watson* (2 v., 1904), *Sable and Purple With Other Poems* (1910), *The Muse in Exile* (1913), *Retrogression and Other Poems* (1916), *Poems Brief and New* (1925), *Selected Poems: With Notes by the Author* (1928). PROSE: *Excursions in Criticism: Being Some Prose Recreations of a Rhymer* (1893), *Pencraft: A Plea for the Older Ways* (1916).

J. A. Spender, Introduction, *The Poems of William Watson* (2 v., 1904); H. B. Forman, "William Watson," *English Illustrated Magazine*, XXVIX (1903), 541; J. Hoops, "William Watson," *Englische Studien*, LXXI (1936), 155-162.

Among the poets who at the turn of the century were antagonistic to the increasing preoccupation with realism and new verse forms was **Stephen Phillips (1868-1915)**, who in the early years of the 1900's was extravagantly acclaimed one of the greatest poets of the age. William Watson, fond of traditional content and form, found Phillip's poetry much to his liking; and many others who viewed the vigorous and realistic pieces of Kipling and Masefield with distaste proclaimed Phillips a latter-day Shakespeare. His star has almost entirely waned, but it is not difficult to determine the reasons which contributed to his vogue. He brought to readers and theatre-goers a brightly hued world of the past in which Ulysses, Herod, Mariamne, and Paolo and Francesca moved about uttering phrases which were heavy with imagery and occasional beauty. As J. C. Squire observed: "Phillips tended to make all his characters minor poets."

Stephen Phillips was born at Oxford in 1868 of parents who were accustomed to the finer things of life, including classical literature. Soon after he had finished at the University, Phillips went on the stage where he remained for six years, being an indifferent actor, but learning the fundamentals of the theatre which he was later to put to practical use. After forsaking his career as an actor, he became an army tutor, a rôle of which he soon tired. Even as a student at Oxford, he had indulged his talent for writing verse; and by 1890, he and his cousin Laurence Binyon issued a joint volume of their verses entitled *Primavera*. With *Christ in Hades*, published along with *To Milton Blind* in 1896, Phillips began to attract notice; and with the poetic drama *Paolo and Francesca* (1899) he rose to fame. Through 1902, which witnessed the completion of *Ulysses, The Sin of David,* and *Nero,* Phillips was widely acclaimed. He told Hesketh Pearson that he had written *"Paolo and Francesca* for love, *Herod* for popularity, *Ulysses* for money, and *Nero* for all three." He realized his objectives, for his poetic dramas brought him popularity and money; but unfortunately their manner shows inadequacies which keep them from permanent worth. He continued to write verse and short plays until his death in 1915, although he never attained the success he had found with *Paolo and Francesca* and *Herod.*

Phillips's most characteristic and best work is found in his poetic dramas, and of these *Paolo and Francesca* is undoubtedly his greatest work. The elevation of the theme and the author's sensitivity to its beauty made for a lyrical drama of a high order. It is in the later poetic dramas and the short lyrics that Phillips's diction and imagery show a perceptible labor. His efforts to attain the enraptured at times become heavy; purple passages show through the columns in the Greek and Roman scenes, and what was meant to be lofty approaches the turgid. In his later work, he evidently was well aware of his inability to capture the sublimity of occasional passages in his poetic dramas, for in his poem "A Poet's Prayer" in *New Poems* (1907) there is a plaintive lament for "those absences of fire" which had flamed in *Paolo and Francesca.*

Christ in Hades (1896), *Paolo and Francesca* (1899), *Herod* (1900), *Marpessa and Other Poems* (1900), *Ulysses* (1902), *The Sin of David* (1902), *New Poems* (1907), *Pietro di Siena* (1910), *Lyrics and Dramas* (1913), *Armageddon* (1915), *Harold* (posthumous, 1927).

Hesketh Pearson, "Stephen Phillips" in *Modern Men and Mummers* (1921); Cornelius Weygandt, "The Rise and Fall of Stephen Phillips" in *Tuesdays at Ten* (Phila., 1928), F. W. Chandler, "The Verse Dramas of Stephen Phillips" in *Aspects of Modern Drama* (1914).

Although Stephen Phillips's cousin **Laurence Binyon (1869-1943)** never rose to the height of popularity to which Phillips rose with *Paolo and Francesca,* he was a poet of considerable talent who possessed one qualification for high attainment which his cousin often lacked—restraint. Like Phillips, he believed that poetic themes and vehicles which sought novelty and escape from the established order were out of keeping with his talent; in fact, Harold Monro observed that his work showed "the persistent loyalty to all main traditions."

LAURENCE BINYON

Born at Lancaster in 1869, Binyon early demonstrated an interest in literature and the arts, especially painting. While at Trinity College, Oxford, he won the Newdigate Prize for poetry in 1890. The same year he and Phillips brought out the joint volume *Primavera* which is unmarked by distinction in either instance. The poems were conventional in both theme and manner, with little to distinguish them from merely competent verse. Until the First World War, and to a certain extent later, Binyon's interests and talents were to a large extent academic. He was extraordinarily well informed in matters that concerned the fine arts, an interest which led him in 1919 to write an illuminating essay entitled *Eng-*

lish Poetry in Its Relation to Painting and the Other Arts.
Although his critical canons were eclectic and there is
no effort to define a theory or a distinctive creed, his judgments are always discerning and thought-provoking. Already
in 1893 he held the distinguished post of Head of the Department of Printed Books and Deputy Keeper of Prints and
Drawings in the British Museum. As a sideline he did a
considerable amount of editing, including his fine edition of
Boswell's *Life of Johnson.* He came to the United States
after the First World War for a sustained visit, during which
time he was guest professor of poetry at Harvard College.
Unlike Phillips, Binyon's range and talent continued to develop with the years. Although never a prolific poet, Binyon's literary interests and talent remained consistent until
his death in 1943.

The greater part of his poetry appears in the two volumes
The Collected Poems of Laurence Binyon issued in 1931.
This collection brings his work up to 1928, with the exception of some eight or nine plays in verse, and a few minor
omissions. One volume contains the narrative poems; the
other, the lyrical. The earlier poems, both narrative and
lyrical, are marked by a conventional and academic tone.
They have dignity and restraint to commend them, but the
creative surge is almost entirely absent. Such pieces as "The
Autumn Crocus," "Nightfall," and "Montenegro," although
well-mannered and pleasing, seem to be little more than
literary exercises. As early as his *London Visions* in 1908,
however, there is an increasing sharpness of discernment
and feeling. Without forsaking his belief in the worth and
beauty of traditional themes, and without losing his sense
of restraint and stylistic dignity, he widened his range to
include themes which were concerned with the realities of
life. During the First World War, he became aware of
themes which bore no relationship to his carefully turned

verses on Tristan's death and the lagoons of Venice. In spite of the fact that he saw no real action, the War brought him out of the past for a time to produce such interestingly conceived poems as "Strange Fruit" and "The Zeppelin." The two long odes, "The Sirens" and "The Idols," written between 1920 and 1929, illustrate his most mature achievement. "The Sirens" is a lyrical exposition of the forces of enchantment and hope which keep man forever on the quest, the inner voices which make life not only tolerable, but noble and beautiful. Although academic and conventional for the most part, Binyon's poetry at large, and especially in the later pieces, shows artistic sincerity, and an unfailing, richly modulated tone. His prose studies of the pictorial arts remain substantial guides and engaging essays.

VERSE: *Lyrical Poems* (1894), *Odes* (1901), *London Visions* (1908), *The Secret* (1920), *The Sirens* (1927), *Collected Poems* (2 v., 1931). PROSE: *Painting in the Far East* (1908), *Japanese Art* (1909), *The Drawings and Engravings of William Blake* (1922), *English Water Colors* (1933).
Bibliographies of Modern Authors, "Laurence Binyon," *London Mercury,* II (1920), 114; J. G. Southworth, "Laurence Binyon," *Saturday Rev.,* XLIII (1935), 341-355.

Robert Bridges (1844-1930), Poet Laureate from 1913 to 1930, followed the main traditions in English poetry in the larger part of his work. By reason of the small output of verse during the first fifteen years of his laureateship, he was at times referred to as the poet whom the Muse forgot. Surrounded as he was in his later years by such dynamic and prolific writers as Kipling, Masefield, Noyes, and Yeats, he was the forgotten man. At Chiswell House at Boar's Hill near Oxford, detached apparently from the world of observation and experience and from the political issues of his day, Bridges seemed to be without compelling poetic urge. All the while, however, he was crystallizing the sentiments and re-

flections of a long life into the conclusions of his longest
and most mature poem *The Testament of Beauty* (1929).
Although Bridges' *métier* was established even before he

ROBERT BRIDGES

became laureate, *The Testament of Beauty* added im-
measurably to his stature as a
poet and refuted the notion
that the Muse had passed him
by.

Robert Seymour Bridges
was born in 1844 at Walmer
on the Kentish coast among
scenes of serenity and general
well-being. When he was ten,
he was sent to Eton where he
remained from 1854 to 1863.
He was a good student, distinguishing himself especially in
classical studies; but he was also an active participant in the
sports and pastimes of the great English public school. Immediately after leaving Eton, he went up to Corpus Christi,
Oxford, where his already lively interest in the classics was
given additional breadth and depth. Even as a young man,
he was attracted to classical dignity and restraint; and it is
largely for this reason that he did not incline toward the
creed and expression of the Pre-Raphaelites who at the time
were attempting to respiritualize art. His interest in the
classical was a natural development for one of his preferences and tastes. By the time he left Oxford he had written
much verse, most of which was derivative, but in which he
himself recognized a proficiency of expression which led
him to adopt poetry as at least a spiritual profession. After
Oxford, he travelled extensively, with apparently no purpose other than to widen his horizon. Eight months he spent
in Germany, later to travel in Egypt and Syria; and before

he returned to England, he had left few of the principal cities on the Continent untouched. There is no poetic record of his responses to what he experienced on his travels, but in his later poetry one is often startled at the breadth of his information.

His first volume, *Poems* (1873), was little more than a pamphlet in which the lyrics were written in a conventional descriptive manner, but they showed the discipline of careful craftsmanship. It was during the seventies that he experimented with some of the infrequently used classical measures and with the intricate French forms. He apparently had little to say and no great emotional surge to try to capture, but he had delight in seeking artistic perfection. It was perhaps his realization of inadequacy of theme which led him to widen his range of experience and to take up the study of science and later medicine. He became a student at St. Bartholomew's, and later a physician at the Children's Hospital, Great Ormond Street. In spite of his success in the medical profession, by 1882 he gave it up permanently. From 1882 until 1905 he lived at Yattendon, years devoted to his now compelling urge to write. From 1905 to 1906 he was in Switzerland, returning to England to build Chiswell House near Oxford, where he lived the remaining years of his life.

When Alfred Austin died in 1913, after a long and comparatively fruitless laureateship, Bridges was given the honor largely on account of his conservatism. He accepted the laureateship largely on his own terms, and evidently he held to his terms, for there was almost a total abstaining from the composition of ceremonial odes and occasional poetry. He fell into a period of inactivity upon his appointment, devoting much of his time to the Society for Pure English, to prose essays, and to editing an anthology, *The Spirit of Man* (1916), which reveals his tastes clearly, as does his later anthology, *The Chiswell Book of Poetry* (1924). His monumental work *The Testament of Beauty,* which did not appear until 1929, occupied much of his time in his later years. He died in 1930.

It has been observed that "with Robert Bridges there died a distinct poetic type. He was the mild-mannered gentleman of quiet reflection, with definitely Victorian standards of morality and life, with classical interests and discipline in his art, aware of the strides of science but showing a mild distaste for modernity, shocked at the advance of Socialism, and believing in the ultimate good of Nature's scheme." In his last poem he fused some of the modern spirit and manner into his "loose alexandrines," but there is more of the nineteenth century in Bridges, the man and the poet, than of the present.

Despite the period of inactivity in the years following his appointment as laureate and contrary to general impression, Bridges was a comparatively voluminous poet. His work may be divided into the narrative poems in which he dealt generally with classical themes, the miscellaneous lyrics, and his long philosophical poem *The Testament of Beauty*. In the first group, *Prometheus the Firegiver: A Mask in the Greek Manner* (1883), *Eros and Psyche* (1885), and *Achilles in Scyros* (1892) are representative. The themes are developed in such delicate descriptive detail, the action is so quietly though lucidly recorded, the imaginative force is so carefully restrained, that without the implication of a philosophy of beauty, the poems deserve a very high place among the procession of works which have utilized classical legend.

Among the miscellaneous lyrics, of which there are many, Bridges' contribution to the sonnet sequences in English poetry, *The Growth of Love*, has much merit in its demonstration of the poet's technical skill. Of the brief lyrics such poems as "Elegy" and "Nightingales" in *Shorter Poems* (1890) are characteristic of the best of the poet's attainments. "Elegy" is melodic to the point of suggesting Swinburne, with a Shelley-like grace and beauty; and the theme is of sufficient depth to free the poem from any identification with mere rhetoric. "Nightingales" is exceptionally fine in its adaptation of verse to theme, and in its expression of wonder at the sources of beauty which have made possible the bird's song. In handling the French forms such as the triolet and rondeau, Bridges illustrates his deft craftsmanship and his ability to apply the lightest of touches to sentiments which require more grace than depth in their expression. These pieces, however, despite their skilfull handling, are not of the same level as "A Dead Child," in which his fine restraint, both emotional and stylistic, is demonstrated, and the familiar "Nimium Fortunatus," which compresses much depth of thought and feeling into seven brief stanzas.

His final work, the long *Testament of Beauty* has a loftiness of theme and an elaborateness of design which invite comparison with the great philosophical poems in the language. In execution, however, the poem falls short of greatness. The conclusion that "the wise will live by faith . . . faith in the Order of Nature and that her Order is good" is arrived at only after many intricate circumlocutions. Some of the passages seem plainly digressional, and the elaborateness of design is at times an obstacle to ready comprehensibility. Bridges recognized that his content was not consistently poetical, but his unfailing dignity of expression keeps the manner always above the commonplace. The poem is cast into a form of rimeless verse—loose Alexandrines, Bridges called his lines—a form well adapted to the content, but scarcely melodic.

Robert Bridges will probably not be remembered for *The Testament of Beauty,* for it is not easy reading; and as Louis Untermeyer remarked when it appeared, "It is likely to be more discussed than examined." It is rather when Bridges is dealing with beauty in the concrete, when he catches the rapture of the love of Eros and Psyche in delicate melodies and contemplates the starry woods from which the Dorian nightingale has come that he has contributed most to the reader's enjoyment and to the finest in English poetry.

Poems (1873), *The Growth of Love* (1876, enlarged ed., 1889), *Prometheus the Firegiver* (1883), *Eros and Psyche* (1885, rev. ed., 1894), *Shorter Poems of Robert Bridges* (1890, enlarged ed., 1931), *Demeter, a Mask* (1905), *Poetical Works of Robert Bridges* (1912, enlarged ed., 1930), *Ibant Obscuri: an Experiment in the Classical Hexameter* (1916), *October and Other Poems* (1920), *New Verse* (1925), *The Testament of Beauty* (1929), *Selected Poems* (1941). There are eight PLAYS, published separately as follows: *Nero I* (1885), *Palicio* (1890), *Return of Ulysses* (1890), *Christian Captives* (1890), *Achilles in Scyros* (1890), *Humours of the Court* (1893), *Feast of Bacchus* (1894), *Nero II* (1894). Bridges wrote a considerable amount of prose on widely varied subjects, most of which is to be found in *The Collected Essays, Papers . . . of Robert Bridges* (10 v., 1927-36).

George L. McKay, *A Bibliography of Robert Bridges* (1933); Nowell Smith, "A Check-list of the Works of Robert Bridges," *Book Collectors' Quarterly*, XVI (1934), 30-40; Albert J. Guerard, *Robert Bridges: A Study in Traditionalism in Poetry* (Cambridge, Mass., 1942); Francis Brett Young, *Robert Bridges: A Critical Study* (1914); G. S. Gordon, *Robert Bridges* (1932); Edward Thompson, *Robert Bridges* (1944); J. M. Kelshall, *Robert Bridges: Poet Laureate* (1924); Oliver Elton, "Robert Bridges and *The Testament of Beauty*," *English Assn. Pamphlets*, LXXXIII (1932), 15 pp.; Nowell Smith, *Notes on "The Testament of Beauty"* (1931); Cecily Boas, "The Metre of 'The Testament of Beauty,' " *London Mercury*, XXII (1930), 147-153; Herbert C. Lipscomb, "Lucretius and 'The Testament of Beauty,' " *Class Jour.*, XXXI (1935), 77-88; Harold A. Larabee, "Robert Bridges and George Santayana," *American Scholar*, I (1932), 167-182; Edward Davison, "Robert Bridges: Poet Laureate of England," *English Jour.*, XIV (1925), 749-760.

Poets other than Bridges have found a rich source of inspiration in classical themes, and of them **T. Sturge Moore (1870-1944)** ranks high on account of his fine insight into the classical spirit and his delicately balanced verse. Although he has employed themes from many epochs of the past, including stories from the Old and New Testaments and sentiments from the Elizabethans, his finest province is that of Greek and Roman mythology. It is in the poetic rendering of classical legend that his talent finds its choicest expression and his unfailing restraint in diction and imagery its most appropriate application. *Pan's Prophecy, Aphrodite Against Artemis,* and *Danaë,* his most characteristic and finest works, are an exquisite contribution to poetry at large.

Thomas Sturge Moore was born at Hastings in 1870 of parents who fostered the boy's early inclination toward the pictorial arts. Versatility of expression was evident even in his teens; and in later years he showed marked talent as both poet and artist. He was a designer of book plates and covers, including some of the covers for books by William Butler Yeats; and he was a wood engraver of considerable reputation. His capabilities were critical as well as creative, for he wrote excellent appreciations on Correggio, Dürer, and Blake, besides a number of appraisals of the works of more recent artists. His poems, most of which were originally published in fastidiously designed pamphlets, show infinite pains not only with the composition but also with the visual appeal which they create. In spite of his fastidious taste and severe critical standards, Moore produced much in the field of the graphic arts and wrote enough poetry on varied themes to fill two sizable volumes.

A glance at the titles of his major poems indicates at once where the poet's chief interest lies, for most of them suggest themes which belong to remote times. *The Rout of the Amazons, To Leda and Other Odes, Theseus, Medea, and Lyrics, Absolom, Mariamne,* and *Judas* all indicate his occupation with classical and Biblical stories. In a smaller way he has been successful with his adaptations from the Elizabethans, especially in his imitations of Thomas Campion and Ben Jonson. The piece which begins, "Come, my Celia, let us prove" has an authentic ring. Although his miscellaneous lyrics which forsake the classical spirit are often musical, Moore's best efforts are attained with content in which there is a narrative and descriptive framework on which he can weave his designs. Such brief lyrics as "Silence Sings," "The Dying Swan," and "Aforetime" make agreeable reading on account of their unfailing felicity of phrase and assurance of expression, but they do not reveal Moore's most distinctive talent. It is not that he requires a theme on which to develop a consecutive narrative, for he himself wrote to the point in his introductory note to *Danaë:* "This is the story 'such as youthful poets dream on summer eves by haunted streams,' and the poem like such dreams has no fixed order or progress, but begins and begins again, and is broken off rather than ended." To the classical legends he brings a lyric treatment which seeks the implicit beauty in the tale rather than a versified retelling. With a high regard for his source of inspiration, he makes no effort to modernize the lofty tone of the originals, nor to introduce interpretations which might strike a false note. Although the renderings are often severely classical in tone, they escape from the academic and fastidious by reason of their rich imagery and cadence. He writes with a dignity quite in keeping with his artistic regard for poetry of the great tradition, but in such passages as Phaedra's lament at unrequited love, and the chorus songs of Clymene, Doto, and Malis in *Aphrodite against Artemis* there is a fine lyric quality. In the poetic treatment of classical theme Moore has a high place in English literature.

VERSE: *The Vine Dresser and Other Poems* (1899), *Aphrodite Against Artemis* (1901), *The Centaur's Booty* (1903), *Danaë* (1903), *The Rout of the Amazons* (1903), *The Gazelles and Other Poems* (1904), *Pan's Prophecy* (1904), *Theseus, Medea, and Lyrics* (1904), *To Leda and Other Odes* (1904), *Collected Poems* (1904), *A Sicilian Idyll* (1911), *Mariamne* (1911), *The Sea is Kind* (1914), *Judas* (1923), *Poems* (4 v., 1931-1933), *Selected Poems* (1934). PROSE: *Albert Dürer* (1905), *Correggio* (1906), *Art and Life* (1915), *Some Soldier Poets* (1919).

Bibliographies of Modern Authors: "Thomas Sturge Moore," *London Mercury,* III (1920), 100-101; F. L. Gwynn, *Sturge Moore and His Poetry* (Cambridge, Mass., 1942); Jacques Vallette, "Regards sur la poesie de T. Sturge Moore," *Études Anglaises,* VI (1937), 19-27; Arthur McDowell, "The Poetry of Sturge Moore," *London Mercury,* XV (1922), 607-616.

That **Alfred Noyes (1880-   )** is a traditionalist is indicated plainly in his disparagement of the verse of the experimentalists and in his own verse which has kept consistently to the old established channels. He has been one of the most prolific if not one of the most inspired of the twentieth-century poets, and although he has not completely fulfilled the promise which was evident in his early verse, he has contributed much to the enjoyment of readers of all ages who like buoyant rhythms.

Alfred Noyes was born in 1880 in Staffordshire in an environment which was in keeping with a literary career. There were artists in his father's family, and a vice-chancellor of Oxford on his mother's side. His boyhood was pleasant and sheltered, spent largely out of doors, with little concern about the caprices of circumstance and the future. At eighteen he entered Exeter College, Oxford, where in addition to his ability as a varsity oarsman he showed talent in contributing to *The Jester,* a writer-student volume. Although the duties for his tutor were performed adequately, he was by no means a brilliant student. Apparently he did not attach much significance to the degree, for he left Oxford without finishing his examinations. Report has it that he was in London looking after the publication of a volume of verses, *The Loom of Years and Other Poems* (1902) when he should have been writing his examinations. The volume was handsomely printed and bound by Grant Richards with the assurance that its contents would appeal to a wide class of reader. The optimism of author and publisher was well founded, for even Swinburne, whose critical ear had not been dulled by advancing years, enjoyed the poems to such an extent that he invited Noyes to come to his home to read them to him. By 1910, before he was thirty, Noyes had written so copiously that he was ready with a collected edition. As early as 1913 he delivered the Lowell Lectures in Boston, and for a year he was a guest professor of English literature at Princeton University. He has lectured and read his verse in most of the principal cities in both east and west. His winning personality, his fine elocution in reading his own poems, and his sincere forthrightness have made him a platform favorite. He became a convert to the Catholic faith, a step which was implied in poems earlier than *The Torch Bearers* (1930); and he has issued an anthology entitled *The Golden Book of Catholic Verse* (1946) in which there is a well-considered introductory note. His two novels, and his critical essays collected under the title *Some Aspects of Modern Poetry* (1924) are agreeably written, but aside from their stylistic distinction they have little of permanent worth.

Noyes's poems may be divided into those which deal with Elizabethan themes, of which *Drake* (1908) and *Tales of the Mermaid Tavern* (1913) are representative; the fairy tales such as *The Flower of Old Japan* (1903) and *The Forest of Wild Thyme: A Tale for Children Under Ninety* (1905); the miscellaneous lyrics and ballads such as "The Barrel Organ," "Forty Singing Seamen," "The Highwayman," and "A Victory Dance" which appeared in the *Collected Poems* (1927); and *The Torch Bearers,* a trilogy (1922-25-30).

In his treatment of Elizabethan themes, Noyes has done some of his finest work. With the exception of the trilogy *The Torch Bearers, Drake* is his most ambitious poem. Although he considered the theme "worthy of the great Homeric roll of song," *Drake* falls somewhat short as great epic literature on account of its diffuseness and its frequent ineptness of phrase. In the *Tales of the Mermaid Tavern,* Noyes offered additional evidence of partiality for the spacious days of Elizabeth. In the nine tales which go to make up the complete poem, there is a wide variety in content and manner. The tales range from the roistering, Malmsey-bright yarns such as "Black Bill's Honeymoon" to the grisly story of Bess Throckmorton, Raleigh's widow, keeping the severed head of her husband. In adapting verse measure to theme Noyes demonstrates a virtuosity which has rarely been equalled. The diction and imagery are often more facile than exacting, and the lines are often heavy with adjectives.

In the fairy tales, *The Flower of Old Japan* and *The Forest of Wild Thyme,* Noyes gave his readers his first declaration of the precept that discernment often comes from innocence and simplicity, a theme which has been frequently explored, but of which Noyes apparently never tires. The scenes in these poems are pretty and brightly colored, but there is no passage which can be called exquisite or consummate. In fact, some of the passages suggest the cheap modern Japanese importations rather than delicate old miniatures; and many of the author's efforts at simplicity and quaintness are strained.

The miscellaneous lyrics and ballads compose a large and generally agreeable part of Noyes's work. He tells the tragic story of the Highwayman's love for the innkeeper's daughter with a rich cadence that has delighted many a schoolboy; and the imagery, although highly colored, is appropriate to the romantic nature of the tale. In its use of onomatopoeia and crescendo it is well adapted to elocutionary recitation, from which, however, some of its effect has suffered. The rollicking lilt of "Forty Singing Seamen," the buoyant lines in "The Fisher Girl" and the easy rhythm and rime in "Sherwood" give these poems an appeal which, though temporary, is agreeable to readers who are fond of the simpler sound effects in verse. "The Barrel-Organ," with its theme of the effect of an organ-grinder's music on different types and classes of people, is an additional indication of the poet's

talent with rhythm. Although the didactic and satirical are
not Noyes's chief stock in trade, in his attacks on the modernists in "Fashions" and "The Man Who Discovered the Use
of a Chair" he is not ineffectual in his cleverness; and in
"The Victory Dance," with its insistent short lines, he presented a bitter, uncompromising attack on the people who
all too soon forget the havoc of war.

The Torch Bearers, in the form of a trilogy with something of the plan of an epic, has as its theme the reconciliation of science and religion, with great figures in science and
philosophy collectively the hero. It is essentially a devotional
poem, for when in the last book the poet shows the great
scientific discoverers kneeling before the altar, one sees
Noyes moving steadily through the metaphysical experience
which was to bring him into the Catholic Church. The style
of the poem, although lacking in the strident rhythmic
effects of his earlier work, and in places diffuse, is in keeping
with the seriousness of the poet's purpose.

In spite of the fact that the later work of Noyes has been
somewhat disappointing to the critics who before 1910 pre-
dicted true greatness for him, his poetry as a whole has much
to commend it. It is true that he is repetitious in his expression of a gospel of simple faith, that he lacks compression,
that his diction is often more facile than exacting, and that
his rhythms are more lilting than delicate and exquisite; but
Noyes is always wholesome, readily comprehensible, and
gifted with an eloquence of expression in both words and
meter which is appealing to readers who prefer joyful min-
strelsy to the dissonances that are part of a confused and
ailing world.

The Loom of Years and Other Poems (1902), *The Flower of Old
Japan* (1903), *The Forest of Wild Thyme* (1905), *Drake* (1908),
Tales of the Mermaid Tavern (1913), *Collected Poems* (4 v., 1923),
The Torch Bearers (1930), *Collected Poems* (1947).

James E. Tobin, "A Corrected Bibliography of Alfred Noyes,"

Catholic Library World, XV (1945), 181-184; Walter Jerrold, *Alfred Noyes* (1930); David Larg, *Alfred Noyes* (Toronto, 1946); Mabel Vincent, "Alfred Noyes in Retrospect," *Poet Lore,* XLI (1931), 293-304; Barbara Carter, "Alfred Noyes," *Catholic World,* CXXXVI (1932), 51-58.

Sir Henry Newbolt (1862-1938) wrote his finest verse and prose about the sea. He differs from Masefield in that his themes deal with the gold-braided men on the bridge rather than with the seamen in the fo'c's'le; and his sea, although at times stormy, is always beautiful. He was born in 1862, the son of a clergyman, but his paternal grandfather had been a naval captain. From Clifton College, he went to Corpus Christi, Oxford; and for ten years after leaving the University he practiced law. But literature had become to him at least a spiritual profession, for as early as 1898, he had published two volumes of verse, *Admirals All and Other Verses* (1897) and *The Island Race* (1898), and had written many reviews for the literary journals. From 1900 to 1904 he was editor of the *Monthly Review;* and later he produced sound criticism in *A New Study of English Poetry* (1917) and *Poetry and Time* (1919). In 1923 he became official naval historian, largely on the strength of his enthusiasm for the British Navy, and his authoritative accounts of naval warfare of which *A Naval History of the War, 1914-1918* (1920) is representative. His memoirs, *My World as in My Time* (1932), reveal engagingly the personality of the author and his sphere. To the generation which has had its surfeit of wars and which shares Siegfried Sassoon's feeling about war's horrors and futility, the patriotic verse of Newbolt may seem to express an entirely romantic conception of the soldiers' and sailors' lot. There is in Newbolt's verse, however, little that can be called jingoism; in such collections as *Songs of the Fleet* (1910) and *Drake's Drum and Other Songs of the Sea* (1914) there is a love for the sea and its men expressed, but the poems are an outburst of the poet's feelings rather than an attempt to get readers into the mood for enlistment. Most of Newbolt's verse has in it a resonant tone and a red-blooded rhythm which is in some measure comparable to Kipling's. His later verse in *The Linnet's Nest* (1927) and *A Child is Born* (1931) is more subdued in tone, more deli-cate in design and phrase, and according to some of his critics, more essentially poetic than the patriotic verses; but in spite of the merit of the later work, in it one does not find the real voice of Newbolt. For that, one must go to such poems as "Drake's Drum" and the strident measures in *Songs of the Fleet*.

VERSE: *Admirals All and Other Verses* (1897), *The Island Race* (1898), *The Sailing of the Long-Ships and Other Poems* (1902), *Clifton Chapel and Other School Poems* (1908), *Songs of Memory and Hope* (1909), *Collected Poems, 1897-1907* (1910), *Songs of the Fleet* (1910), *Poems New and Old* (1912), *Drake's Drum and Other Songs of the Sea* (1914), *St. George's Day and Other Poems* (1918), *The Linnet's Nest* (1927), *A Child Is Born* (1931). PROSE: *A New Study of English Poetry* (1917), *Poetry and Time* (1919), *New Paths to Helicon* (1927), *My World as in My Time: Memoirs of Sir Henry Newbolt* (1932).

Bibliographies of Modern Authors: "Sir Henry John Newbolt," *London Mercury*, II (1920), 115-116; Coulson Kernahan, "Sir Henry Newbolt," in *Six Famous Living Poets* (1922).

Definitely a traditionalist, but tolerant of any sincere at-tempt to attain beauty and truth in poetry, **Ralph Hodgson (1872-   )** has gained recognition not by frequent and volu-minous publication, but by the excellence of the little he has written. He admits that he cannot understand much that the modernists have produced, but, unlike Watson and Noyes, he is unwilling to declare that the old established order is the only medium for poetry. Although he follows standard verse patterns and employs conventional poetic diction, there is nothing imitative in his verse. In fact, his poetry affords a fine illustration of the originality and freshness which can be brought to the old and tried patterns. His inspiration has run thin in his later years, for since 1917 when he issued a small volume of his collected verse entitled *Poems,* he has written little of real consequence.

Ralph Hodgson (he pronounces his name as if it were Rafe Hodson) was born in Yorkshire in 1872. Early in life he showed a talent for drawing which he was later to put to use in the pictorial department of several London journals. He was art editor of *Fry's Magazine* for a few years; and during the time of his association with Lovat Fraser and Holbrook Jackson at "The Sign of the Flying Fame"—the trade name for a publishing enterprise which issued chapbooks and elegantly printed pamphlets—he assisted with both the literary contents and the pictorial design. It was not until 1907 that his first little volume appeared entitled *The Last Blackbird and Other Lines;* and it was six years later that *Eve, The Bull, The Mystery, and Other Poems* were issued at "The Sign of the Flying Fame." In 1917, the 64-page volume entitled *Poems* appeared, in which virtually everything that Hodgson has written is included. He continued to work on various journals until 1924 at which time he was invited to Sendai University in Japan, to lecture on literature. For over fifteen years he remained in Japan before returning to England by way of the United States. America evidently appealed strongly to him, for he has been living on a farm near Minerva, Ohio, since 1939, occasionally going to eastern cities to lecture and read his poetry. In 1941 he designed and had printed a twenty-page chapbook entitled *The Silver Wedding and Other Poems* with a statement on the back cover "Further chapbooks of verse and prose in immediate preparation." Although the poems in this collection and those which were later printed on single sheets and in the *Saturday Review of Literature* are better than mediocre, they are not on the same high plane as those written before 1917. Hodgson has been married twice, his

second wife an American. In his seventies, he retains his
interest in bull terriers, of which breed he is an expert judge,
and he still likes the out-of-doors and all forms of wild life.
In spite of the fact that he is often regarded as one reticent
to talk about himself and his poetry, he is a delightful con-
versationalist and ready to answer almost any inquiry behind
which there is a sincere interest.

Hodgson's poetry generally reflects the buoyancy and
charm of freshness of the man. From the four lines entitled
"Reason" to the glorious crescendo in "The Song of
Honour," there is an expression of spiritual adjustment as
frank as it is rare. In "Time, You Old Gypsy Man" there is
in addition to a compelling melody an excellent handling
of personification; and "The Gypsy Girl" is a finely spun,
brightly colored little piece in which there is excellent compression without losing richness, and an exceptionally fine
last line. "Eve" and "The Bull," which have found their
way into most of the anthologies of contemporary poetry,
are indicative of Hodgson's freshness of manner, but they
lack the substance of "The Song of Honour" and the fine
compression of most of the poems. It has been pointed out
that Hodgson's Eve "is neither the conscious sinner nor the
symbolic Mother of Men; she is, in Hodgson's candid lines,
any young English girl—filling her basket, regarding the
world and the serpent itself with a frank and child-like
wonder." The temptation and fall are narrated simply, with
no moralizing overtones and only an implied lament that
innocence should fall. "The Bull," along with "Stupidity
Street" and "The Bells of Heaven," show the poet's fondness
for animals. The latter poems are as didactic as Hodgson can
become, whereas the longer poem "The Bull" draws a
graphic, moving picture of the falling of the mighty.

If the pamphlet entitled *The Silver Wedding and Other
Poems* which was issued in 1941 is indicative of what Hodgson has produced since 1917 and may produce in the future,

there is little promise that he will add to his present stature. What he has done, however slight, is on a very high plane; and there is more variety in theme and manner in the 64-page collection *Poems* than can be found in many volumes of greater bulk. Hodgson's variety does not lie in the number of themes and manners he employs, but rather in the varying degrees of intensity he brings to his sources of inspiration. He is never trifling in either the choice of theme or measure; in fact, he has been consistently faithful to what he considers the noble trade of writing poetry.

The Last Blackbird and Other Lines (1907), *The Bull* (1913), *Eve and Other Poems* (1913), *The Mystery and Other Poems* (1913), *The Song of Honour* (1913), *Poems*, a collected ed. (1917), *Hymn to Moloch* (1921), *The Silver Wedding and Other Poems* (Minerva, Ohio, 1941). There have been a few broadsides since 1941, including the four sheets of *A Flying Scroll* (1944, 1945).

Ammon G. Kershner, *Ralph Hodgson* (Phila., 1952).

Some men see shadows rather than sunlight, life's ironies rather than life's joys; and it is refreshing to come upon a poet like **William Henry Davies (1870-1940),** whose early life was spent among shadows, but who always saw the sunshine and the joys. An artificial leg and a life spent in the most squalid retreats did not dampen his boyish love of life. Belonging to no tradition or school, although at times identified with the Georgians, and unaware of the struggle for novelty which was going on among many of the poets of his generation, Davies brought to poetry an unaffected simplicity and child-like innocence of sentiment and thought which were in themselves novel and fresh. His works have been likened to those of Herrick and Blake, but these parallels, although apparent, cannot be sustained for long. His simplicity one can account for, for he was a simple, ingenuous man; but his innocence one wonders at in the light of what he has revealed concerning his life in his autobiographical works. Were it not for the frank, detailed disclosures in *The Autobiography of a Super-tramp* (1908) and *The True Traveller* (1912), one might gather from the major body of his verse that his had always been a sheltered existence, free from care, surrounded if not by plenty, by enough—one to whom Providence had granted the boon of being easily satisfied, and who saw in life only its brightness, its song-birds, its innocent children, its ultimate benevolence.

Born in a public house called Church House in Newport, Monmouthshire, in 1870, of Welsh parents of little attainment and no fast principles concerning the rearing of children, Davies began life after very little schooling as a picture-frame maker, a trade which he gave up for the less confining profession of being a tramp. He sang hymns on Shaftesbury Avenue, London, with hand outstretched; he was a house-to-house beggar in America; he lost a foot when he was jostled from his berth on the couplings of a train on his way to the lush pickings in Alaska; and he rustled up trade for the less mercenary street-walkers of St. Louis and the East End of London. But he had read enough to know that some men when they feel that they have something worthwhile to say, write it down and circulate it for the enjoyment and edification of others. Possessed of a native gift for verse measures and a fine ear for rhythm, and feeling a growing consciousness of a buoyant message of sweetness and light, he began to commit his ideas to the simple stanzaic forms which he knew; and proceeded to circulate them by hawking his little book, done by a job printer, about the streets. His methods of securing customers were as frank and aggressive as his devices for getting meals as he worked the countryside. He learned the names of those who were presumably interested in poetry who might like to have his little volume for a half-crown. George Bernard Shaw, who insisted he "discovered" Davies, found the poet's invitation to become a patron irresistible; and after reading the poems in the collection, he proceeded to find him out. Through Shaw's commendation and encouragement and through his own confidence that he had something to tell the world in verse, Davies began his career as a professional poet. Eight little volumes appeared by 1916, at which time Davies issued his first "Collected Poems." By 1940, he had added considerably to this 1916 volume. The *Collected Poems* of 1940 contain virtually everything he wrote in verse. After his wanderings in many lands, he settled down in the years after 1916 with a Civil List Pension, in time to marry and live in Nailsworth, Gloucester. He died in 1940.

As a philosopher, Davies is not profound; he is only appealing. His zest and buoyancy carried him beyond and below searching universal truths. His cheery gospel of idling and staring is not always salutary, but as Edith Sitwell has said: "He stares with more comprehension than most poets. And he gives us the world as it is, but often it has been bathed in the radiance and dew of a strange innocence."

His verse schemes are almost always iambic, his rime patterns are generally simple, running to the easy abcb stanza, and his diction and imagery are those of a child; but his verse never descends to doggerel or to the prosaic. In fact, for all of its apparent lack of virtuosity, his verse shows a remarkable variety in tonal quality and melody. Good illustrations of his trend of thought and manner can be found in such poems as "Ambition," "Leisure," "Money," "To a Lady Friend," "Death's Game," and "Christ the Man." These poems reveal the poet's thought and sentiment concerning ambition, worldly possessions, love, and religion—four of the dominants in man's life; and they show the originality which may lie in simplicity.

VERSE: *The Soul's Destroyer and Other Poems* (1905), *Nature Poems and Others* (1908), *Farewell to Poesy and Other Pieces* (1910), *Songs of Joy and Others* (1911), *The Bird of Paradise and Other Poems* (1914), *The Song of Life and Other Poems* (1920),

A Poet's Calendar (1927), *Love Poems* (1935), *Collected Poems* (1940). PROSE: *The Autobiography of a Super-tramp* (1908), *The True Traveler* (1912), *Later Days* (1925).

Gwendolen Murphy, "Bibliographies of Modern Authors, W. H. Davies," *London Mercury*, XVII (1928), 301-304; S. J. Looker, "W. H. Davies: His Later Bibliography, 1922-1928," *Bookman's Journal*, XVII (1929), 122-127; and "Man and Super-tramp: W. H. Davies, His Life and Work," *ibid.*, XVI (1928), 363-370; L. Bonnerot, "William H. Davies: Poéte-Vagabond," *Revue Anglo-Americaine*, X (1931), 208-220; Louis B. Duff, "From a Doss House to Parnassus," *Colophon*, XIX (1934), 1-12.

SOME WOMEN POETS

Of the women who have written verse in this century, none is more genuinely poetic than **Charlotte Mew (1869-1928)**. Although her volume is slight, doubtless because of her severe self-criticism, her two small books of verse, *The Farmer's Bride* (1916) and *The Rambling Sailor* (1929), show more range in both theme and manner than is commonly supposed. Occasionally she has handled conventional themes in a conventional manner, as for example in "In the Fields," and the prettily turned "Song" which begins "Love, love today, my dear," but she is never trifling. At times there is a rustic theme and manner, as in "Old Shepherd's Prayer," but she is no imitator of the prettiness of the pastoral mode. Although she is best known for her compressed narratives such as "The Farmer's Bride," it is invariably the lyric manner of recording her theme rather than the story element which is outstanding.

Charlotte Mary Mew was born in 1869, the daughter of an architect who bequeathed to his family little more than an artistic strain. Evidently illness and want were part of Charlotte Mew's lot, and both rumor and internal evidence in her verse hint at an unhappy love affair. Although it is likely that she wrote verse even in her girlhood, Miss Mew's first published work was in prose narrative, the story "Passed" which appeared in the July issue of *The Yellow Book* in 1894. It was not until 1916 that Alida Klemantaski, who became the wife of Harold Monro of the Poetry Bookshop, persuaded Miss Mew to submit some of her poetry for publication. Although recognition was given to her work in both England and America (where in 1921 the poems in *The Farmer's Bride* were published under the title *Saturday Market*), her acute critical sense kept her from releasing any verse which would merely add volume to her work. Thomas Hardy was sufficiently impressed by some of the poems in *The Farmer's Bride* that he named Miss Mew the best woman poet of her time. And it was Hardy, along with De la Mare and Masefield, who was instrumental in securing for her a Civil List Pension. But recognition from such men as Hardy and a widening audience, and the meagre pension, were not enough for her troubled spirit. With the death of her mother and her sister, an increasing life-weariness beset her which left her with little on which to build a plan for her declining years. On March 24, 1928 she committed suicide in a nursing home in London. The year following her death, a small volume of poems which she had been revising for the press was brought out by her friends at Monro's Bookshop under the title *The Rambling Sailor*.

There is no doubt that something of Miss Mew's own troubled life found its way into her poetry. Without being somber, the themes are often touched with premonitions of death and a yearning for the peace which comes with death. Even "The Farmer's Bride" has the sere tone of autumn in it; and the farmer's lament in the closing lines is a poignant cry, full of the heartache of mankind. In her longer narratives such as "The Changeling," in which the theme like that in "The Farmer's Bride" is carried through in monologue, there is the haunting plaintiveness of the child who understands too well her lot.

In all of the narratives there is a fine compression which

permits the inclusion of only the barest essentials of the situation and its development. And still the manner is always warm and intense. Although some of the verse lines exceed twenty syllables, one is constantly aware of the melody. The tones are generally muted, as if they came from a distance, without losing distinctness. The sixty-odd poems which Charlotte Mew saw fit to prepare for the press, although varying in quality, are a small but precious addition to contemporary poetry.

The Farmer's Bride (1916), reprinted in the United States as *Saturday Market* (1921), *The Rambling Sailor* (1929), *Collected Poems* (1949).

Alida Klemantaski (Mrs. Harold Monro), A Memoir in *The Rambling Sailor* (1929); Virginia Moore, "Charlotte Mew," *Yale Rev.*, XXII (1933), 429-432.

Well known in both England and the United States, **Sylvia Townsend Warner (1893-   )** continues to write prose and verse of real distinction. She is probably more widely known for her novels and short stories than for her poems, for her novel *Lolly Willows: or the Loving Huntsman* (1926) was the first selection of the Book-of-the-Month Club; and some of the stories in *The Museum of Cheats* (1947) first appeared in the *New Yorker*. In her prose narratives she is a realist when such an approach suits her ends, as is plain in "View Halloo" and "Rosie Founders" in *The Museum of Cheats;* her realism is often pointed with irony, as in the "Story of a Patron"; and again she can deal effectually with the fanciful as in *Lolly Willows*. The novelist T. S. Powys said to the point: "The secret of Sylvia Warner's success in literature is that she understands exactly how much flavouring to put into a dish—and she never lets the cake burn." It is true that she uses her flavouring—especially irony—with a master hand, and there is no instance in her use of satire in which she loses restraint.

Sylvia Townsend Warner was born in Middlesex in 1893, the daughter of a schoolmaster. There was evidently a background of music in the home, for she has composed music; and from 1916 to 1926, she was one of the editors of the monumental ten-volume work *Tudor Church Music*. Even before her part of this work was completed, she had printed a volume of poems, *The Espalier,* in 1925. This was followed by the novel *Lolly Willows* in 1926, which brought wide recognition to her on both sides of the Atlantic. Almost every year between 1926 and 1935 she was ready with another volume of either prose narratives or poems. Her most recent work might seem to indicate that she is no longer concerned with the world of fancy, but rather with themes and issues which belong to the present. Although the stories in *The Museum of Cheats* (1947) have power and a fine mastery of style, they may not survive so well as some of the poems in *Time Importuned* (1928), *Opus 7* (1931), and *Whether a Dove or a Seagull* (1933), written with Valentine Ackland.

Such poems as "Nelly Trim" and "The Rival" remain more vividly in the memory than anything Miss Warner has done in her short prose narratives. The former, in a haunting ballad measure, is a fine illustration of Miss Warner's talent for blending the unreal with the real, and for handling a blunt theme in a delicate and lyric way. "The Rival" takes on the form of a monologue in an interesting five-line stanzaic pattern in which the farmer's wife laments her lot of being wed to a man who is more attached to the soil than to her. In these poems there is a faint suggestion of the Wessex poems of Hardy; and in the "Four Epitaphs" the suggestion becomes more pronounced. In spite of the fact that Miss Warner is capable of profound thought, in her work there is little of Hardy's concern with the cosmic plan. Her manner varies from the simple and rugged in both diction and verse to the most subtle refinements of basic stanzaic patterns. She is at her best, however, in the compressed narrative poems in which her apparently simple themes convey meanings which are far-reaching, and in which her manner, although bold and direct, is consistently poetic.

VERSE: *The Espalier* (1925), *Time Importuned* (1928), *Opus 7* (1931), *Rainbow* (1932), *Whether a Dove or a Seagull: Poems,* with Valentine Ackland (1933). PROSE: *Lolly Willows; or the Loving Huntsman* (1926), *Mr. Fortune's Maggot* (1927), *The True Heart* (1929), *Elinor Barley* (1930), *A Moral Ending and Other Stories* (1931), *The Salutation* (1932), *After the Death of Don Juan* (1935), *The Museum of Cheats* (1947), *The Corner That Held Them* (1948).

Anna Wickham (1884-　　　) is a striking antithesis to the Victorian "poetesses." Emancipated, resourceful, outspoken, she has little in common with the mild-mannered ladies who wrote conventional verse in the last century. In some measure she resembles the American Dorothy Parker, although she has nothing of the latter's smart sophistication. What she lacks in urbanity and clever phrase, however, she compensates for in forthrightness and strength. She is fearless in the expression of her thoughts, and she has thought much. Poetry is evidently the only fairly satisfying outlet for her, for in "Self-Analysis" she has written that the tumult of her mind gives her a sort of expression which is faulty and harsh, and in which there is some of "the incompetence of pain."

Anna Wickham was born in Wimbledon, Surrey, in 1884 of Australian parentage. At the age of six she went to Australia where during her formative years she led a life less restricted than that of girls in the English provinces. She was educated at the Sydney High School, and along with her classical studies she took lessons in music. At twenty-one she returned to England determined to prepare herself for a career in opera. After studying opera in Paris for a time under De Reszke, she gave up her intention to become a prima donna on account of the endless and exacting discipline such a profession involved and in order to marry

Patrick Hepburn. It was soon after her union with Hepburn that her creative energy found a medium in verse. It has been reported that she wrote nine hundred poems in four years, some of which were later collected for *The Contemplative Quarry* (1915) and *The Man with a Hammer* (1916). During the years immediately following the First World War she continued to write much for a widening audience, but during the thirties there was a perceptible falling off of creative energy, accompanied by a blunt and prosaic manner. In 1939 she was living in Great James Street, London, somewhat embittered by her inability to make proper adjustments with her life and her muse, but forthright and courageous in stating her tastes.

Although there is little in her work which shows consummate workmanship, for she was never a meticulous craftsman, there is a robustness of manner which is almost universally appealing. She herself has said in "The Singer" that were her mind and spirit less troubled, she could doubtless make a lovely poem:

> But I am stung with goads and whips
> So I build songs like iron ships.

The nearest she comes to true lyric beauty is in "Divorce" in which her yearning for freedom from her "little-love's warm loneliness" rises to a fine crescendo in the refrains. With no concern for prettiness of manner, her approach to the thoughts which beset her is arresting in its freshness and forthrightness. The sentiment in "To a Crucifix" is interesting in its attitude toward religious symbols and is representative of the poet's unwillingness to take the old conventions for granted. Although there is considerable variety in her several volumes, Anna Wickham's principal theme is the struggle of a sensitive, idealistic woman brought face to face with the realities of woman's lot. Her protests are uttered incisively and sincerely; and although her phrases are at times striking in their compactness, she never seeks mere cleverness. Even in the verses in a lighter vein such as "Dedication of the Cook," there are no rhetorical embellishments. In spite of the fact that her robust manner is responsible for much of Anna Wickham's appeal, it is the poetic way in which she apprehends her themes that is most important in judging her verse.

The Contemplative Quarry (1915), *The Man With a Hammer* (1916), *The Little Old House* (1918).

Louis Untermeyer, Introduction to *The Contemplative Quarry* (Am. ed., 1921).

Although **Ruth Pitter (1897-   )** reported that she started to write verse in 1902 at the age of five, and had volumes of verse published in 1920, 1927, and 1930, it was not until Alida Monro's anthology *Recent Poetry: 1923-1933* appeared in 1933 that she became known outside a very limited circle. And the curious piece "Digdog" through which she attracted attention is in small way representative of the nature and quality of her verse. Whereas the anthology-piece is almost impossible to understand, the larger part of Miss Pitter's work is lucid and unusually well disciplined; and instead of being an experimentalist in verse measures, as some readers were easily led to believe, in her volumes since 1930 she is essentially a traditionalist who, as Herbert Palmer observed, "walks around in borrowed clothes."

Ruth Pitter was born at Ilford, Essex, the daughter of a school teacher. Her education at the Coburn School, London, according to her own report, was somewhat sketchy, but it was evidently adequate to encourage her to wide reading and to continue her education at college. At the outbreak of the First World War, she interrupted her studies in the middle of the Intermediate year to work for almost two years in the War Office. Later she started a small shop where she made and sold hand-painted trays. Poetry, however, was more than an avocation, and by 1920 she had issued a small volume of verse. It was not until the publication of *A Mad Lady's Garland* (1935), however, that her talent became known in other than limited circles. Many distinctions were to come to her in the thirties: she won the Hawthornden Prize for Poetry; she had Hilaire Belloc, A.E., and Walter de la Mare commend her work highly in the reviews; and James Stephens, in writing the introductory note to her volume *A Trophy of Arms* (1936), stated perhaps extravagantly that as a companion poet to William Butler Yeats at his best, Ruth Pitter should be named. Such a statement need not be taken too literally, but in the light of what she has done in *The Spirit Watches* (1940), and will probably do in the future, she may be considered one of the most important and promising of the contemporary women poets.

There are many moods and themes in her verse, among which the poems which deal with the grotesque, those which reveal her fine observation of nature, and those of mystical insight are most distinctive. In the poems in *A Mad Lady's Garland* there is much which indicates a curious occupation with the incongruous and even repulsive. Of this aspect of her work, A.E. wrote: "I would shrink from the grotesque poetry in *A Mad Lady's Garland* with all the shuddering with which we remove ourselves from the vicinity of cockroaches and earwigs, only Miss Pitter makes the creatures of her fantasy—spiders, fleas, cockroaches, worms, mice, or whatever else—speak so classically, and with so exquisite an artifice, that I am stayed to listen to them, and admit into my house of soul thoughts I would have closed the door upon if they had not come dressed in so courtly a fashion." In "The Coffin-Worm," for example, the poet develops a monologue by a grave-worm to his worm-love in which, for all of the specific morbid detail as the worms settle down to their grisly business, there is an unusual effect of dignity. Miss Pitter's occupation with coffin-worms and their kind is a striking part of her work, but she can deal with the more beautiful manifestations of nature in a fresh and richly imaginative way. In "The Swan Bathing" and "Time's Fool" she brings authentic observation into the descriptive lines which form the background for the development of meditative themes. With nature as such she is not particularly concerned, but she makes certain to keep her images drawn from nature vivid and accurate. Although one feels that Miss Pitter's feet are on the ground and that she sees clearly and honestly what lies about her, there is also the impression that her world is essentially a spiritual world. "The Eternal Image" is a poem of pure vision, with mystical insight, in which there are resemblances to A.E. and the seventeenth-century Vaughn, and in which there is a fine use of *terza-rima*. At 55, Ruth Pitter has shown range and depth along with excellent craftsmanship.

A Mad Lady's Garland (1935), *A Trophy of Arms* (1936), *The Spirit Watches* (1940), *The Bridge* (1945).

Sully-André Peyre, "Ruth Pitter," *Marsyas* (April, 1935), 804-813.

After reading about the spiders and coffin-worms in Ruth Pitter's *A Mad Lady's Garland,* one finds the pastorals of **Victoria Sackville-West (1892-   )** refreshing in their forthright, healthy treatment of English country life. Although Miss Sackville-West does not confine her content to only the agreeable aspects of nature, for she sees the tiger's claw as well as the full-blown rose, she much prefers to see nature's beauty instead of its cruelty. That she is not nature's eulogist is clearly stated in an early passage of *The Land* (1926), and still one feels that she understands and glories in "the sweat, the weariness, the care," and that she is not speaking idly when she says, "The country habit has me by the heart." It is a mistake, however, to identify Miss Sackville-West with only the pastoral mode, for she has written about Persia, Sans Souci, and South Carolina; and even in *The Land* she is as much concerned with human nature as with orchards and bees. Her *Collected Poems* (1933) and her more recent work in both prose and verse indicate a considerable latitude and variety of interests and themes.

Victoria Sackville-West was born at Knole Park, Kent, in 1892, the daughter of Baron Sackville whose name and estate go far back into English history. Although essentially of the same generation and tradition as Edith Sitwell, she was entirely satisfied with the old established order in spite of the fact that in the years following the First World War she realized that the English aristocracy and the old estates could not expect to remain unchanged. In *Pepita* (1937) she engagingly illuminates her attitude toward her ancestors and her birthright, and while indicating the practical inadequacies of the system of bountifully-landed aristocracy in the twentieth century, she is always aware of the nobility and charm which belonged to those who established and sustained the old order. She has travelled widely and has seen England from the outside, with the perspective that comes from a long-range view, but with little diminution of her fondness for the English countryside. As the wife of Harold Nicholson, biographer and diplomat, she has no doubt been concerned with England's policies at home and abroad, but her interests are not essentially political. In 1927, she won the Hawthornden Prize with her poem *The Land,* and since that time she has written much verse on varied themes and a considerable amount of prose, including her venture in murder-mystery, *The Devil at Westease* (1947).

Although she wrote poetry as early as *Poems of West and East* (1917), it was not until *The Land* was issued in 1926 that her work attracted real attention. No doubt the then-current Georgian interest in the English pastoral scene was an incentive to the wide reception of the poem, but the fact remains that long after the Georgian revival of nature as a theme was spent, *The Land* continued to give pleasure to

many readers. In spite of its length, the poem is unpretentious in purpose and manner. In design it suggests James
Thomson's *The Seasons:* the poem is divided into four parts,
each part devoted to a season of the year. The themes within
the seasons range from how to spray against minor pests in
"Spring" to how to make cider in "Autumn." At times the
piece becomes a sort of versified "Practical Hints on Garden-
ing," but the manner rarely descends to a prosaic level. Of
the many other themes she treats, those with a reflective,
philosophical tone and those which have only a piece of
filigree for substance are outstanding. "Insurrection" is not
only self-illuminating, but it shows an understanding and
sympathy for the verities of life, and a genuine intensity of
feeling. "Full Moon" is a dainty little poem, with something
of De la Mare's witchery, and a very fine last line. The verse
is almost invariably deftly spun, and in such a poem as
"Fear" she demonstrates talent as a versifier of fine virtuosity. The novels, including the once popular *The Heir*
(1922) and the recent *The Devil at Westease* (1947), show an
author of well-disciplined technique, animated and reflective
in turn, and satirical without being cynical. She can turn
phrases trimly without any suggestion of smartness. The
themes and characters show variety and depth of observation, but in them there is little compelling emotional attachment for the reader. It is as a poet of varied moods and
themes, with a style that has warmth beneath its serene re-
flectiveness, that Victoria Sackville-West has done her finest
work.

Verse: *Poems of West and East* (1917), *The Land* (1926), *Collected
Poems* (1933). Prose: *The Heir* (1922), *The Edwardians* (1930),
All Passion Spent (1931), *Pepita* (1937), *The Devil at Westease*
(1947).

Florence Boochever, "A V. Sackville-West Bibliography: A Selected
List of Writings by and about V. Sackville-West," *Bulletin of
Bibliography and Dramatic Index,* XVI (Jan.-April, 1938), 93-94,

and (May-Aug., 1938), 113-115; Grant Overton, "The Lady of a Tradition, Miss Sackville-West" in *Arabian Nights Entertainment* (1923); Hugh Walpole, "V. Sackville-West," *Bookman* (London), LXXII (1930), 21-26.

Lady Dorothy (Ashton) Wellesley (1891-   ) is not only difficult to place in any of the recognized categories, but also difficult to judge. Her chief experiences and associations have been literary. Were it not for the enthusiastic praise which William Butler Yeats bestowed on her verse, one might conclude after reading any one of her volumes that she has something of the poet in her, but that it never became quite articulate. The panegyrical Introduction by Yeats to *Selections from the Poems of Lady Dorothy Wellesley* (1936)—with a frontispiece drawing of Lady Dorothy by Sir William Rothenstein—gives the one who is inclined to dismiss her work as that of a minor experimentalist at least momentary pause. Yeats's admiration was further demonstrated in the disproportionate amount of space he allotted to her work in *The Oxford Book of Modern Verse*. She is at her best—or at least her most comprehensible—in her verse which deals with nature, in which there is a suggestion of V. Sackville-West. In the poems in which she is apparently exploring what has been called her "Dream World," however, there is little on which the reader can get a grip, for the reality of unreality with which Coleridge and De la Mare caught the illogical and bizarre images of dreams is missing. Her early work represented in *Genesis, An Impression* (1926), and *Poems of Ten Years, 1924-1934* (1934), so highly praised by Yeats, seems without direction, and the manner shifts capriciously from the conventional to the experimental, with richly decorated phrases standing out from a vocabulary which is generally down to earth. In her later volumes, *Lost Planet, and Other Poems* (1942), and *The Poets, and Other Poems* (1943), there is a clearer indication of purpose, especially in the title-poem of the earlier book; and a more unified and deeper tone is evident. It is possible that the worth which Yeats recognized in her verse will become more evident as she continues to write.

Genesis: An Impression (1926), *Poems of Ten Years, 1924-1934* (1934), *Lost Planet, and Other Poems* (1942), *The Poets, and Other Poems* (1943).

William Butler Yeats, Introduction, *Selections From the Poems of Lady Dorothy Wellesley* (1936), *Letters on Poetry From William Butler Yeats to Lady Dorothy Wellesley* (1940); Herbert Palmer, "Lady Dorothy Wellesley: 'Poems of Ten Years,' " *New Statesman,* VII (1934), 692.

Frances Cornford (1886-   ) has written five small volumes of verse, all of which show distinction. She was born in 1886, the daughter of Sir Francis Darwin and granddaughter of Charles Darwin. It was not until after her marriage to Francis Cornford, Lecturer of Trinity College, Cambridge, that her first volume *Poems* (1910) appeared, although poetry had occupied much of her time in her early twenties. *Spring Morning* (1915) was followed by *Autumn Midnight* (1923) and *Different Days* (1928); and in 1935 *Mountains and Molehills* appeared. In these volumes there is little which can aptly be called either a mountain or a molehill in poetic worth. The themes are varied, to be sure, ranging from the lightly ironic and well-turned triolet "To a Fat Lady Seen From the Train" to the more sombre and searching sestet which begins "My brain is like the ravaged shores . . .", but she is never trifling. Mrs Cornford is a flawless craftsman whose expression of feeling never gets beyond the limits of restraint, and her sense of melody and tone never fails. "Mutely comforting" nature is one of her favorite themes, which she treats in a manner that is both delicate and warm.

Lillian Bowes Lyon (1885-1949) produced small volumes of verse since 1934 when *The White Hare* appeared. *Bright*

Feather Fading (1936), *Morning is a Revealing* (1941), *Evening in Stepney* (1943), *A Rough Walk Home* (1946), and *Collected Poems* (1948) with an introductory note by C. Day Lewis represent her bid for recognition, which up to the present has not been wide. Although she employed irregular measures and free association of images through emotional rather than logical sequence, especially in her later verse, she can scarcely be called an experimentalist since her aims and methods are those with which the reader of contemporary poetry has been long familiar. In her early verse, particularly in the poem which provides the title for the volume *The White Hare,* in both imagery and the use of the short line she suggests Ralph Hodgson. Her most satisfactory work is concerned with what she sees in nature in her region, Northumbria. Here her images are clear and never falter. "The White Hare," although somewhat heavy with adjective, is memorable for the vividness and poignancy with which the theme is developed. In the later pieces such as "Evening in Stepney" and "A Rough Walk Home," in which nature and its metaphors are only incidental to the illumination of emotion in the abstract, Miss Bowes Lyon is not altogether articulate. That some of her latest work, according to C. Day Lewis, "was written under circumstances which would have silenced most poets" may provide a clue to the emotional urge which sought expression in these poems, and a perspective for critical judgment as well.

THE GEORGIANS

During the first two decades of the new century the tendencies which were at odds with Victorianism continued to flourish, but with increasing discipline and restraint. The excesses of the aesthetic school and the more graphic realism of the early Masefield began to show signs of moderation. Extremes in literary reactions are generally most prevalent at the start, and as the first decade of the century passed into the second, English poetry began to strike a balance which led a few of the critics to believe that a golden age in poetry was in the making. In 1912, Edward Marsh brought out his first anthology of *Georgian Poetry* in the Introduction of which he stated: "This volume is issued in the belief that English poetry is now once again putting on new strength and beauty . . . we are at the beginning of another 'Georgian period' which may take rank with the several great poetic ages of the past . . ." The appearance of Marsh's anthology, almost concurrent with the accession of George V, led the reviewers to label those who had contributed to its contents Georgian poets. Additional volumes of *Georgian Poetry* were compiled by Marsh and issued from Harold Monro's Poetry Bookshop in 1915 and 1917; and in 1919 and 1922 two more volumes appeared but without Monro's support and favor. The miscellany *Neo-Georgian Poetry: 1936-1937* (1937) edited by John Gawsworth was only in small part a revival or continuation of the series compiled by Marsh.

To try to list the tendencies which appeared in this series of anthologies is like trying to catalogue the characteristics of a whole generation of poets. The Georgian poets had no pole-star or directing hand: poems by such widely different and highly individual authors as James Elroy Flecker, Walter de la Mare, Lascelles Abercrombie, Gordon Bottomley, John Drinkwater and John Collings Squire were included; and even John Masefield was represented despite the fact that bold realism was high on the *index prohibitorum* of the editor. Although the Georgian poets were all at least presumably devoted to common aims, the results were so heterogeneous when the poets' works at large are considered that one wonders at the editor's ability to select poems from the varied group which would best fit into his definition of Georgian verse. In his efforts, he was not entirely successful, for certainly much which was included only bears out more strongly the fact that poets do not travel in groups, singing their songs according to group standards.

There were, however, several objectives which the Georgian poets had in common and which at least at the start were recognizable. First, there was an unmistakable concern with form. The unevenness of the experimentalists, and the apparent formlessness of the early modernists were deplored as being alien to the poet's craft. Discipline and restraint in diction and imagery were primary requisites, even to the extent of the avoidance of symbolism. Although the lines were to be faithful to observation, especially of nature, realism was suspect, particularly as it applied to the sordid or ugly. In the postwar collections there was a deliberate effort to avoid the issues of the here-and-now, to forget the war and its aftermath, and to return to nature. Were it not for the well-calculated avoidance of the didactic, the poetry in the Georgian anthologies would seem to indicate an attempt to revive the Wordsworthian tradition. In the light of the passage of time and what the individual poets who were identified with the Georgian anthologies did in their more mature work, the term Georgian as it applies to a well-unified group or movement is woven of very thin fabric; but the fact remains that during the early decades of the century there were forces at work in poetry to curb the excesses of the reactionaries and to explore more fully the province of the great tradition.

Identified with the Georgians chiefly on account of the appearance of some of his verse in Marsh's anthologies, but independent of any group or movement, and borrowing little from his predecessors or contemporaries, **Walter de la Mare (1873-   )** has written some of the finest poetry in recent literature. "If there were such a thing as 'pure poetry,'" said Charles Williams, "Mr. de la Mare would seem to be our greatest poet." He has written some thirty-odd volumes, many of which are in prose, including fiction and criticism; and although his work in prose has much merit, it is in poetry that he has done his greatest and most distinctive work.

WALTER DE LA MARE

Walter John de la Mare was born at Charlton in Kent in 1873 of Huguenot, Scotch, and English ancestry. He was educated at St. Paul's Cathedral Choir School in London, after which he was employed in the English branch of the Standard Oil Company for eighteen years. Such employment evidently hampered his essential interests very little, for as early as 1901 he was writing poetry and miscellaneous prose, and since 1908 he has had literature as his profession. In *Songs of Childhood* (1902), his first volume, he used the *nom-de-plume* "Walter Ramal," an anagram of part of his name; but in 1904 with the appearance of his novel *Henry Brocken,* he began to use his own name. In 1910 he won the Edmond de Polignac prize with his poem "The Return," and his reputation as a poet was assured with the publication of "The Listeners" (1912). A sizable two-volume edition of his collected verse was issued in 1928, to which a third volume was added in 1934. His later work has been more largely in prose, which falls into two main categories: the fiction, of which *The Memoirs of a Midget* (1921) attained a very wide circulation; and the criticism, of which his *Lewis Carroll* (1932) and his expanded essay *Poetry in Prose* (1935) are representative.

In his poetry there are three somewhat varied tendencies which may be labelled the verse about and for children, the versified characterizations from Shakespeare, and the shadow poetry. When one considers the poems about and for children, one must recognize that these pieces, for all their apparent jingle and trifling, are always poetic. It has been said that "De la Mare is the singer of a young and romantic world, understanding and perceiving as a child." Such poems as "The Mocking Fairy" and "The Song of Finis" in *Peacock Pie* (1913) have a beauty which removes them completely from nonsense jingles. It is true that some of Lewis Carroll's influence is apparent in such lines as "The Fairy nimbling mambling in the garden," but most of de la Mare's coinings have captured in their combinations of vowels and consonants sounds which have a lyric rather than a ludicrous tone. In the small and difficult province of child vision and expression, the poet in a seemingly artless way has captured scenes of delicacy and beauty, and a song quality which often suggests the far-away voices of children.

In the "Characters From Shakespeare" group, there are interest and merit, especially to the reader who is familiar with Shakespeare's gallery. There are lines such as those at the end of the "Hamlet" which seize upon the very essence of the character and give it a new vitality. The "Mercutio" is exceptionally well turned; in fact, none of them is without discernment and grace of portrayal. As a group, however, they are not representative of de la Mare's most distinctive talent, and in spite of their appeal to those who enjoy association with the characters from Shakespeare's plays, they cannot take a place as poetry with many of his more purely subjective and lyrical pieces.

It is in the poems which deal with the world of shadows and half-lights that de la Mare has risen to supreme heights. There is magic which suggests at times the chilly pale blue light of Coleridge's "Christabel," but the parallel cannot be

sustained for long. It is not a world of brightness and cheer
into which one is cast, nor is it a land of bleakness and
despair. Of excitement and passion there is nothing; the
emotions and senses are lulled rather than stimulated, for
the roses are always fading and the musk has long been
blown. But there are roses, and there are birds and children,
although their voices are sleepy and far away. The poet is
not lamenting the impermanence of beauty; rather he is feeling the passage of twilight into night, and the mood is one of
soul drowsiness. In that strange stage between sleep and consciousness, there is a meeting place where past and present,
unreality and reality join for a time. It is only natural while
lingering in such a sphere that the poet should create something of the ominous and sinister, and although these qualities appear, they are never terrifying. Under his witchery
the sinister in the fading light takes on a rare beauty;
and in spite of the chill of approaching night, in de la
Mare's shadows there is nothing oppressive. Poems such as
"Shadow," "The Dark Chateau," "The Dwelling Place,"
"The Empty House," and "The Listeners" are fine examples
of an expression of a world of shadow. "The Listeners" is
sheer magic which leaves the reader subdued long after the
poem has been put aside.

Walter de la Mare's poetry is that of mood, and as a result
his range cannot include a wide variety of themes in which
stylistic virtuosity is a primary concern. As with every great
poet, however, it is the style as well as the theme which gives
his work permanence; and de la Mare's manner has in it the
qualities which are ideally suited to his moods. To make
articulate a mood such as that in "The Listeners" is the
result of nothing short of genius. He does not hesitate to
employ extra syllables for some of his lines, and he uses rime
only when it suits his purpose. Never diffuse, his word usage,
even when he employs the unusual and archaic, is rich with

suggestion. Although his poetry as a whole varies in texture, it is of a consistently high level; and in the poems which deal with shadows around old houses he has captured moods in a fashion which is truly great.

VERSE: *Songs of Childhood* (1902), *Poems* (1906), *The Listeners and Other Poems* (1912), *A Child's Day: A Book of Rhymes* (1912), *Peacock Pie: A Book of Rhymes* (1913), *The Sunken Garden and Other Poems* (1918), *Motley and Other Poems* (1918), *Poems: 1901 to 1918* (1920), *Story and Rhyme* (1921), *The Veil and Other Poems* (1922), *Down-adown-Derry: A Book of Fairy Poems* (1922), *Ding Dong Bell* (1924), prose and verse, *Selected Poems* (1927), *Stuff and Nonsense* (1927), *The Captive and Other Poems* (1928), *Poems for Children* (1930), *Old Rhymes and New* (2 v., 1932), *The Fleeting and Other Poems* (1933), *Poems: 1919 to 1934* (1936), *Memory and Other Poems* (1938), *Bells and Grass* (1941), poems for children, *Collected Poems* (1941), *Inward Companion: Poems* (1951). PROSE: De la Mare has written much prose, among which the novels *Henry Brocken, His Travels and Adventures in the Rich, Strange, Scarce-imaginable Regions of Romance* (1904), *The Return* (1910), *Memoirs of a Midget* (1921), *At First Sight: a Novel* (1928); the critical studies *Some Thoughts on Reading* (1923), *Desert Islands and Robinson Crusoe* (1930), and *Lewis Carroll* (1932); and the tales in *The Scarecrow and Other Stories* (1945) are representative.

Gwendolen Murphy, "Bibliographies of Modern Authors, Walter de la Mare," *London Mercury,* XV (1927), 526-531; H. C. Duffin, *Walter de la Mare: A Study of His Poetry* (1949); Forrest Reid, *Walter de la Mare: A Critical Study* (1929); R. L. Megroz, *Walter de la Mare: A Biographical and Critical Study* (1924); John Freeman, "The Work of Walter de la Mare," *Quarterly Rev.,* CCXXXVII (1922), 32-47; Storm Jameson, "Mr. de la Mare and the Grotesque," *English Rev.,* XXXIV (1922), 424-430; E. K. Brown, "The Epilogue to Mr. de la Mare's Poetry," *Poetry,* LXVIII (1946), 90-96; B. Ifor Evans, "De la Mare—75," *John O'London's Weekly,* LXVI (May 14, 1948), 230; *Tributes to Walter de la Mare on his Seventy-fifth Birthday* (1948), a collection of essays by Edmund Blunden, Lord David Cecil, J. B. Priestley, and others.

Acquainted with most of the writers included in *Georgian Poetry* and himself an occasional contributor, **Lascelles Abercrombie (1881-1939)** cannot be strictly identified with any group, movement, or tradition; and although he has been called a latter-day Robert Browning, the resemblances are superficial. At times he is as formless as the most ingenious of the modernists, but his themes and the objectives controlling them are largely those of the traditionalist. His most frequently employed medium is a form of verse-drama which by reason of its compression of manner and complexity of thought is better adapted to rereading in the library than to stage presentation.

Born at Ashton-upon-Mersey in 1881 in an atmosphere congenial to theological and literary interests, Abercrombie was educated at Malcolm College and Manchester University. In his twenties, while reviewing for the *Liverpool Courier,* he issued his first volume of poems, *Interludes and Poems* (1908) which was commended by Alice Meynell and Thomas Hardy. By 1910 he made his home at "The Gallows," Ryton, Gloucestershire, where he busied himself by supplying reviews to four of the leading periodicals and by writing verse. Rejected for service in the First World War on account of deficient sight, he became an inspector in a shell factory in Liverpool where he worked twelve hours a day. After the War he was given a Lectureship in Poetry at Liverpool University in which he acquitted himself with such distinction that he was soon sought by other institutions. From Liverpool he went to the University of Leeds, then to London University, and finally to Oxford; and he also lectured at Queen's University, Belfast, the Sorbonne, and Harvard. In spite of the obstacles to creative work after his round of lectureships started, he continued to write poetry until shortly before his death in 1939.

Abercrombie's most characteristic province is narrative verse in which dramatic dialogue and often monologue play a large part. The themes are strikingly varied and unusual. It is true as Herbert Palmer observed that "he takes pleasure in out-of-the-way subjects—especially the weird, the mystical, the horrific, the macabre ... Witchcraft, the end of the world, a legend concerning St. Thomas, the death vision of a friar, Judith's murder of Holofernes ... are among the strange themes which he treats at length and from an individual angle." Although the narrative thread is always there, Abercrombie's chief interest is not in the story he has to tell but rather in the speculations which the situation provokes and the emotional intensity of the theme. In these poems lines are given to the characters which are often out of keeping with their background and attainments, but this lack of realistic treatment is outweighed by the rich poetry in many of the passages.

Emblems of Love (1912), his most ambitious and complex nondramatic poem requires intent application if the meaning of the whole or many of the parts is to be grasped, nor can its theme be reduced to a brief statement without losing the real essence of the poem. Occasionally, as for example in the passage called "Woman's Beauty" from the Vashti section, the reader is led to believe that something of Coventry Patmore's *The Unknown Eros* is about to emerge; but the woman's beauty of which Abercrombie writes is not only the meeting place between God and man, but "the flame within the lantern" by which man recognizes the manifold facets of beauty. The emblems include virtually all forms and stages of love, and their manifestations are approached through history, mythology, and the real and the symbolical. Although the poem represents Abercrombie's loftiest objective, he will probably be read more for his dramatic narratives of which "The Death of a Friar," "The Sale of St. Thomas," and "The New God" reveal a poet of exceptional talent.

VERSE: *Interludes and Poems* (1908), *The Sale of St. Thomas* (1911, expanded 1930), *Emblems of Love* (1912), *Deborah* (1912), *Four*

Short Plays (1922), *Phoenix* (1923), *Twelve Idyls* (1928), *Complete Poems* (1930). PROSE: *Thomas Hardy, a Critical Study* (1912), *The Theory of Poetry* (1924), *The Idea of Great Poetry* (1925).

John Gawsworth, "Lascelles Abercrombie," in *Ten Contemporaries, Notes Toward Their Definitive Bibliographies,* second series (1933); Percy Withers, "Lascelles Abercrombie As I Knew Him," *English,* IV (1943), 174-182; Llewellyn Jones, "Lascelles Abercrombie: Poet and Critic," *No. Amer. Rev.,* CCXX (1924), 319-329.

The longest piece in the second volume of *Georgian Poetry* (1915) was the poetic play *King Lear's Wife* by **Gordon Bottomley (1874-1948).** This play and *Gruach* and *Britain's Daughter* (1921) led Lascelles Abercrombie to say: "It was remarkable enough that Mr. Bottomley should have proved himself capable of worthily inventing a prelude to 'Lear'; it is astonishing that the success should be repeated in a prelude to 'Macbeth.' But it has become clear now that at no time in the history of English poetry since the seventeenth century has the requisite combination of dramatic and poetic talents existed until now in the person of Mr. Bottomley." Resemblances to Shakespeare have been noted in his handling of character, and in vigor he has been compared to John Webster. Other similarities have been drawn between him and more recent poets, including T. Sturge Moore and Lascelles Abercrombie, but Bottomley's mind and talent in spite of these parallels were of a highly individualized order.

Gordon Bottomley was born at Keighley, Yorkshire, in 1874. Of feeble health in his youth and early manhood, his pursuits were largely sedentary. Before the turn of the century he wrote verse, some of which was collected into *The Mickle Drede and Other Verses* (1896) and *Poems at White Nights* (1899). Although the two volumes of *Chambers of Imagery* (1907 and 1912) attracted attention, it was not until his short play *King Lear's Wife* appeared in *Georgian Poetry* in 1915 that Bottomley was regarded as one of the more talented of the poets whom Marsh had brought together in his volume. With the two plays *Gruach* and *Britain's Daughter* (1921) he rose to fame. He received the Benson Medal of the Royal Society of Literature for poetry in 1925, and received an honorary degree of Doctor of Laws from the University of Aberdeen in 1930. His last years he spent virtually in seclusion in one of the sparsely populated regions of Lancashire.

The short plays by which Bottomley is best known, *King Lear's Wife and Other Plays* (1920), *Gruach* and *Britain's Daughter* (1921), and *Lyric Plays* (1932) are dramatically told tales in verse rather than plays for stage production. It would seem that he was more concerned with their poetic content than with their practical adaptability to the theatre. The lines given to the characters are in large measure lyric poems with variations in mood and texture from the bold and even primitive to the delicate and richly burnished. The effect of gorgeousness which R. L. Megroz attributes to these plays is recognizable in many of the passages, although the general impression suggests little heaviness in decoration. In fact, the finest parts of Bottomley's work are commendably restrained, with the vigor implied rather than expressed. Many of the lines bear out his expressed belief that "poetry is fundamentally a matter for the ear," but it need not be inferred from such a statement that he is a poet of pure melody. The thought is there, although at times somewhat elliptically expressed. His poetry which is without narrative theme and design such as that included in *Poems of Thirty Years* (1925) is richly imaginative and agreeably melodic. He can draw vivid images, as for example in "The End of the World," in lines that are both flowing and direct. In spite of the fact that Bottomley's work has generally appeared in fastidiously printed limited editions, he continues to have a deservedly wide circle of readers.

VERSE: *The Mickle Drede and Other Verses* (1896), *Poems at White Nights* (1899), *The Gate of Smaragdus* (1904), *Chambers of Imagery* (two series, 1907, 1912), *A Vision of Georgione, Three Variations on Venetian Themes* (1910), *Littleholme* (1922), *Poems of Thirty Years* (1925), *A Parting and The Return* (1928), *Festival Preludes* (1930). PLAYS: *The Crier by Night* (1902), *Midsummer Eve* (1905), *Laodice and Danae* (1909), *A Riding to Lithend* (1909), *King Lear's Wife* (1915), *Gruach* and *Britain's Daughter, Two Plays* (1921), *Scenes and Plays* (1929), *Lyric Plays* (1932), *The Acts of St. Peter: A Cathedral Festival Play* (1933).

R. L. Megroz, "Gordon Bottomley," *Bookman* (London), LXIV (1923), 177-179; Carl Carmer, "Gordon Bottomley and Poetic Drama," *Theatre Arts Monthly*, VI (Feb., 1930), 151-163; D. A. Robertson, "Gordon Bottomley," *English Jour.*, XV (1926), 177-181.

It was **James Elroy Flecker (1884-1915),** often named as one of the central figures in the Georgian group, who gave expression to one of the more striking dicta of the authors represented in Marsh's *Georgian Anthology:* "The poet's business," he said, "is not to save the soul of man, but to make it worth saving." Realism, especially that which was used to illuminate the ugly aspects of modern life, he deplored; his poetry almost all deals with themes remote from the here-and-now, and it generally suggests a primary concern with form. But the complete Flecker eludes neat labeling, in spite of the fact that in his preface to *The Golden Journey to Samarkand* (1913) he called himself a Parnassian. It is true that he shared the Parnassian interest in technique, but there are many sides to Flecker's work—some of them great.

James Elroy Flecker was born at Lewisham in 1884, the son of the Headmaster of Dean Close School. As a youth he was an avid reader and showed talent in writing; and at Trinity College, Oxford, from which he took his degree in

1906, he wrote a considerable amount of verse. For a year after his graduation from Oxford he taught school at Hampstead, but his eagerness for life and variety led him to enter the diplomatic service. He studied Arabic at Cambridge University, and by 1910 he was sent to Constantinople as vice-consul, later to be transferred to Beirut, where he remained until 1913. He married a Greek woman whom he called Hellé and who was an engaging companion and a source of help and inspiration to him. Advanced tuberculosis caused him to leave his post in Syria for Davos, Switzerland, where after two years he died at the age of thirty-one. His friends found him a man unusually gifted, a good scholar competent in the classical languages and Levantine tongues and lore, and a brilliant talker. During the decade following his death, his work was widely read and commended, and in spite of a perceptible falling off of interest in recent years, his poetry has in it characteristics of permanence.

In his brief though full life, Flecker wrote a remarkably large amount of prose including the well-received novel *The King of Alsander* (1914), a brightly colored romantic drama, *Hassan: The Story of Hassan of Bagdad* published after his death in 1922, and the less colored *Don Juan* (1925); and seven volumes of verse of which *The Golden Journey to Samarkand* (1913) and *The Old Ships* (1915) are representative. J. C. Squire's edition of Flecker's *Collected Poems* (1916), although not inclusive, is an excellent collection of the finest and most distinctive verse. In these poems there is generally an admirable fusion of romantic theme and classical discipline. "The Old Ships" is well-nigh consummate in attaining its rich effect with simple diction and verse scheme. There is something of the sensuousness of Keats in this poem, as in others such as "Gates of Damascus." A more tranquil but equally poetic side of Flecker is to be found in "To a Poet a Thousand Years Hence." Here the simplicity and precision that the poet so much admired but not always attained are in evidence. Although some of the judgments of his poetry which appeared in the years immediately following his death were overenthusiastic, there is small doubt that with Flecker's death there was removed from English poetry one of its greater spirits.

VERSE: *The Bridge of Fire* (1907), *Forty-two Poems* (1911), *The Golden Journey to Samarkand* (1913), *The Burial in England* (1915), *The Old Ships* (1915), *Collected Poems* (1916), *Complete Poems* (1923). PLAYS: *Hassan: The Story of Hassan of Bagdad* (1922), *Don Juan* (1925). PROSE: *The Last Generation: A Story of the Future* (1908), *The King of Alsander* (1914), *Collected Prose* (1920), *Letters of J. E. Flecker to Frank Savory* (1926).

Geraldine E. Hodgson, *The Life of James Elroy Flecker* (1925); Douglas Goldring, *James Elroy Flecker: An Appreciation* (1922); J. C. Squire, Introduction to *Collected Poems of J. E. Flecker* (1916); Herbert Palmer, "James Elroy Flecker: The Poet of the Sun," *Bookman* (London), LXXXII (1932), 282-284; Edward Shanks, "James Elroy Flecker," *London Mercury*, IX (1923), 66-67.

Although **John Drinkwater (1882-1937)** is probably better known in America for his plays *Abraham Lincoln* (1919) and *Robert E. Lee* (1923), he was one of the mainstays in Edward Marsh's *Georgian Poetry*. In fact, he has often been referred to as the typical Georgian pastoral poet, with all the connotations, good and bad, that the label conveys. To identify him with a few biographical plays and a series of pastoral poems, however, is by no means an indication of the volume and variety of his work. Drinkwater was one of the most prolific and versatile of the recent men of letters: playwright, biographer, anthologist, critic, journalist, and verse-writer were some of his roles. In only a few instances did his work attain true distinction, but on the other hand, there is little in his vast output which can be called really bad.

John Drinkwater was born at Leytonstone, Essex, in 1882. After completing the prescribed studies at the Oxford High School, he tried many jobs before settling down with an insurance firm with which he remained for twelve years. Facility in writing and encouragement from his friends, however, led him to give up his work in insurance in order to write reviews and miscellaneous articles for a Birmingham paper. In 1907 he helped to organize the Pilgrim Players, which later became the Birmingham Repertory Theatre of which he became manager in 1913. A half-dozen plays of fair quality grew out of this association, among which the one-act *Cophetua* (1911) and the three-act *Rebellion* (1914) are representative. As early as 1903 he had written verse, some of which was collected and published under the title *Poems;* and by the time Marsh was selecting verse for his *Georgian Poetry,* a great many of Drinkwater's poems were available in periodicals. With a thorough apprenticeship in the theatre behind him, he wrote a long series of biographical dramas including *Mary Stuart* (1921), *Oliver Cromwell* (1921), *Robert E. Lee* (1923), and *Robert Burns* (1925). During the late twenties and early thirties he wrote a number of biographies, and continued to write verse. His two volumes of autobiography, *Inheritance* (1931) and *Discovery* (1932) are agreeable reading in their illumination of the man and his times. Drinkwater died in 1937.

As a playwright, he did his most distinctive work in the field of the biographical drama. His plays appeared at a time when biography was flourishing under an unprecedented vogue. They all make for a pleasant and fairly instructive evening, either in the theatre or the library; and in spite of the author's obvious heightening of episode for effect, the spirit if not the letter of the plays is adequately faithful to history. But even in the best of them, *Abraham Lincoln* and *Oliver Cromwell,* the playwright is more of a popularizer than a discerning interpreter of his subjects; and the lines given to the characters too often take on an inflated quality which makes the effect more theatrical than real. The biographies, including studies of *Byron* (1925), *Charles II* (1926),

Cromwell (1927), *Pepys* (1930), and *Shakespeare* (1933), although not suffering from the overwrought lines of the
plays, are without any particularly searching illumination
of character, but they are well unified and informational in
a general way. The poems are of wide variety of mood and
manner in spite of the fact that they never forsake the conventional. The *Collected Poems* (1922) contains most of
Drinkwater's verse which is worth preserving. As a pastoral
poet, he represents the detachment from the issues of the
present which was a part of the Georgian creed, and his verse
has a conventional sort of beauty in which occasionally there
is an apparent strain for rapture. He lacks the fine observation of Edmund Blunden; in fact, the inaccuracies in "Pike
Pond" led some of the British critics to call him a weekend
naturalist. Perhaps his finest verse is that in the series entitled *Preludes,* narrative love poems in which there are
choiceness of phrase and an easy, supple rhythm. In general,
however, Drinkwater's verse suffers perceptibly by its thinness of theme and its failure to rise sufficiently often to true
lyric intensity.

Verse: *Poems* (1903), *The Death of Leander and Other Poems*
(1906), *Poems of Men and Hours* (1911), *Poems of Love and Earth*
(1912), *Preludes, 1921-1922* (1922), *Collected Poems* (1923), *Summer
Harvest: Poems, 1924-1933* (1933). Plays: *Cophetua: A Play in
One Act* (1911), *Rebellion* (1914), *Abraham Lincoln* (1919), *Mary
Stuart* (1921), *Oliver Cromwell* (1921), *Robert E. Lee* (1923),
Robert Burns (1925), *Laying the Devil* (1933), *A Man's House*
(1934). Biographies: *The Pilgrim of Eternity, Byron* (1925), *Mr.
Charles, King of England* (1926), *Charles James Fox* (1928), *Pepys:
His Life and Character* (1930), *Shakespeare* (1933). Autobiog-
raphy: *Inheritance, Being the First Book of an Autobiography*
(1931), *Discovery, Being the Second Book of an Autobiography*
(1932).

Godfrey W. Mathews, *The Poetry of John Drinkwater* (1925);
Alois W. Roeder, *John Drinkwater als Dramatiker* (Munich,
1927).

Edward Marsh was the collector and guiding spirit of the anthologies of *Georgian Poetry* (1915, 1917, 1919, and 1922), but for more than a decade, **J. C. Squire (1884-   )**—now Sir John—was the chief advocate and support of the Georgian poets and their creeds. As literary editor of the *New Statesman* and as the founder and editor of the *London Mercury*, over which he presided from 1919 to 1934, Squire was in large measure the literary dictator of the twenties. He was so zealous in supporting his favorite Georgians, and in attacking the modernists and other poets whose works he disliked—as for example, his amusing and effective parody on the modernists in *Tricks of the Trade* (1917)—that "the Squirearchy" became a London institution. "Jack Squire's Country Boys" and Squire himself became on occasion the target for the opposition: Osbert Sitwell's *Jolly Old Squire, or Way Down in Georgia* (1922) was only a fairly effective counterattack; and Roy Campbell's *Georgiad* (1931), striking vigorously at the conventional and effete naturalism of Squire's favorites, was somewhat belated, for by 1930 the Georgians had gone their varied ways. Squire and "the Squirearchy," however, had a long and fruitful inning. Standing for a sort of classical discipline in style and a detachment from the political and social issues of the times, Squire was not only an influence on his age, but at his best a very fine poet as well.

John Collings Squire was born at Plymouth in 1884. After completing his formal education at Blundell's School and St. John's College, Cambridge, he became a journalist; and at twenty-nine he had risen to the literary editorship of the *New Statesman*. The articles written under the pseudonym Solomon Eagle were widely circulated and in many places commended for their lucidity and discernment. As early as 1909 he issued a collection of poems, *Poems and Baudelaire Flowers*. In addition to his editorial duties, he wrote enough verse for a dozen small volumes, including some very fine

parodies; collaborated on three plays, including the popular
Berkeley Square (1928); and turned out a vast amount of
literary criticism, much of which was collected into volumes.
He has held many responsible positions as a result of his
energy and ability, and in 1933 he was knighted.

As a critic, Squire was unequivocal, lucid, often discerning
and at times capricious—or at least overenthusiastic in praise
or blame. As a poet, Squire was extremely versatile. The
verse in *Poems and Baudelaire Flowers* (1909) and *The Lily
of Malud* (1917) shows a perceptible Baudelaire influence
and there is more than a little of the tone of the Decadents
of the nineties. In sharp contrast to this verse is his talent as
a parodist. *Steps to Parnassus and Other Parodies and Diversions* (1913) and *Tricks of the Trade* (1917) reveal Squire as
an excellent satirist, with a lively wit that is conditioned
generally by good critical judgment. It is in *The Birds and
Other Poems* (1919), *The Moon* (1920), and *Poems, second
series* (1920) that he did his most distinctive work in the
Georgian vein. It is easy to recognize in these poems the
author's deliberate attempt to fit his talent into the Georgian
pattern. The pastoral mode, so pronounced in the pattern,
is here; but like that in the verse of several of "Jack Squire's
Country Boys," it is the nature of the weekender rather than
that of one to whom nature is all-encompassing. In spite of
the fact that Squire put his own poetry on half-pay, he
handles conventional rhythms gracefully, and his diction
and imagery, although at times artificial, are well disciplined
and often beautiful.

VERSE: *Poems and Baudelaire Flowers* (1909), *The Three Hills and
Other Poems* (1913), *The Lily of Malud and Other Poems* (1913),
Poems, First Series (1918), Second Series (1920), *The Birds and
Other Poems* (1919), *The Moon* (1920), *Poems in One Volume*
(1926). PARODIES: *Imaginary Speeches and Other Parodies in Prose
and Verse* (1912), *Steps to Parnassus & Other Parodies and Diversions* (1913), *Tricks of the Trade* (1917), *Collected Parodies* (1921).

ANTHOLOGY: *Selections From the Modern Poets* (3 v., 1948). PROSE: *Books in General* (3 v., 1918-20-21), *Essays at Large* (1922), *Essays on Poetry* (1923), *Sunday Mornings* (1930).

"Bibliographies of Modern Authors, John Collings Squire," *London Mercury*, II (1920), 347; "Squire of the Squirearchy," leading article, unsigned, *John O'London's Weekly*, LVII (Aug. 20, 1948), 397.

John Freeman (1880-1929) is often associated with that part of the so-called Georgian Revolt which sought to avoid the issues of the present in order to find both sanctuary and salvation in nature. Although his treatment of nature, like that of the other Georgians, lacks penetrating observation and anything which suggests a philosophical approach to the relationship of man and nature, there is much beauty in his pastel shades and delicate measures. His duties as secretary of an insurance company evidently were not too time-consuming, for in addition to twelve books of verse, most of which appears in *Collected Poems* (1928), he wrote a considerable amount of literary criticism including *English Portraits and Essays* (1924) and the excellent *Herman Melville* (1926). It is as a poet that Freeman's chief claim to distinction lies. Some of his critics have placed him very high as a love poet as well as a pastoralist. *Poems New and Old,* in which the love theme appears frequently, won the Hawthornden Prize in 1920. J. C. Squire, who did much to bring Freeman before the public and who edited *Last Poems* (1930) the year following Freeman's death, observed that "every experience was to him, it may be, very intense, because of the imminent shadow of death which overhung him, lending a deeper gloom to discontent and a sharper edge to joy." The lyric "The Moon Bathers," although more distinctly lined than most of his verse pictures, is illustrative of Freeman at his best.

VERSE: *Twenty Poems* (1909), *Fifty Poems* (1911), *Presage of Victory and Other Poems of the Time* (1916), *Memories of Childhood and Other Poems* (1919), *Poems New and Old* (1920), *The Grove and Other Poems* (1924), *Solomon and Balkis* (1926), *Collected Poems* (1928), *Last Poems* (1930). PROSE: *English Portraits and Essays* (1924), *Herman Melville* (1926).

"Bibliographies of Modern Authors, John Freeman," *London Mercury*, I (1920), 497; Edward Shanks, "John Freeman," *London Mercury*, II (1920), 190-194; William Bliss, "The Poetry of John Freeman," *London Mercury*, XXI (1930), 325-337; J. C. Squire, Introduction to *Last Poems* (1930).

Walter James (Redfern) Turner (1889-   ) belonged for a time to the "moonlight" school of J. C. Squire's Georgians, but his more recent work suggests the application of Ver-

WALTER JAMES TURNER

laine's precept in the "Art Poétique," "music above everything." He was born in Melbourne, Australia, in 1889, the son of a church organist. His fondness for melodic tonal effects, shown in much of his verse, was part of his birthright. He was educated at the Scottish College in Melbourne, and at the age of seventeen went to Europe, where, after studying in Germany for a time, he travelled extensively. Before the outbreak of the First World War, he had written music criticism for the *New Statesman*, and a considerable amount of verse, some of which was collected in the volume *The Hunter and Other Poems* (1916). After his military service was over—an experience which produced no verse which can be directly attributed to the War—he became dramatic critic for the *London Mercury* where he was associated with J. C.

Squire and the Georgian poets from 1919 to 1923. At almost yearly intervals small volumes of poems appeared until the mid-thirties; and along with his verse-writing, he found time to write many essays on music and composers, and a few dramas. He visited America in 1929, out of which visit grew *A Trip to New York and A Poem* (1929) and *Miss America, Altiora in the Sierra Nevada* (1930). Although the *Pursuit of Psyche* (1931) and *Jack and Jill* (1934) have added somewhat to Turner's stature, it was in the poems written in the early twenties that he did his finest work. The well known "Romance," with the restlessness which attaches to exotic place names, rarely fails to charm; and such poems as "Search for the Nightingale" and "Ecstasy" are illustrative of his handling of imagery and mellifluous tonal effects.

VERSE: *The Hunter and Other Poems* (1916), *The Dark Fire* (1918), *The Dark Wind* (1920), *In Time Like Glass* (1921), *Landscape of Cytherea* (1923), *The Seven Days of the Sun* (1925), *The Aesthetes* (1927), *New Poems* (1928), *A Trip to New York and a Poem* (1929), *Pursuit of Psyche* (1934), *Jack and Jill* (1934). PROSE: *Music and Life* (1921), *Beethoven* (1927), *Wagner* (1933), *Berlioz* (1934).

Edward Shanks (1892-   ) is often identified with the Georgians and for a time he was included among "Jack Squire's Country Boys." That some of his verse appeared in *Georgian Poetry* and that he was assistant editor of the *London Mercury* while Squire was editor are the principal reasons for this association, which indicates only in part the nature of Shanks' achievements. Born in London in 1892, educated at the Merchant Tailors' School and Trinity College, Cambridge, in the Army and War Office during the First War, he has given his time almost exclusively to literature. In America he is perhaps best known as a critic, especially for his studies of *Hilaire Belloc* (1916), *Bernard Shaw* (1924), and his *Rudyard Kipling: A Study in Literature and Political Ideas* (1938), which is a searching and unpartisan analysis of a large side of Kipling's work. In England he is regarded not only as a sound critic, but also as a poet who has written a considerable amount of verse of distinction, most of which is to be found in *Poems, 1912-1932* (1933). *The Queen of China* (1919) won the Hawthornden Prize and drew the commendation of all the London critics. Shanks' nature poetry is often beautiful, although it is with the more conventional kind of beauty that he deals, and his manner is essentially traditionalist. "A Night Piece" and "The King's Dancer" are exquisitely wrought.

VERSE: *Songs* (1915), *Poems* (1916), *The Queen of China and Other Poems* (1919), *The Shadowgraph and Other Poems* (1925), *Collected Poems, 1909-1925* (1926), *Poems, 1912-1932* (1933). NOVELS: *The People of the Ruins* (1920), *The Richest Man* (1923), *Queer Street* (1932), *The Enchanted Village* (1933), *Tom Tiddler's Ground* (1934). CRITICAL STUDIES: *Hilaire Belloc* (1916), *First Essays on Literature* (1923), *Bernard Shaw* (1924), *Second Essays on Literature* (1927), *Kipling: A Study in Literature and Political Ideas* (1938).

It is difficult to try to explain why **Edward Thomas (1878-1917)** did not qualify for inclusion in Edward Marsh's *Georgian Anthologies,* especially that of 1917 which was devoted largely to the pastoral mode, for Thomas was essentially a nature poet, and a good one. Thomas was of the country, not because he sought deliberately for poetic themes in nature—as was the case with some of the Georgians—but because the rural districts were his natural sphere. He was familiar with the out-of-the-way places in Hampshire and Wiltshire, regions of "eleven houseless miles," and with the simple life in the byways of the countryside.

Edward Thomas was born in 1878 of parents who were of the more prosperous small landowners in Wiltshire. Soon after he completed his work at Lincoln College, Oxford, he turned to literature as a reviewer and writer of biographies, travel books, and nature essays. As a critic for almost twenty years, he was distinguished for his discernment of literary worth and an uncompromising manner. It has been reported that he was unsatisfied with the vehicles into which he had been turning his energy until the American poet Robert Frost, while visiting England in 1912-1914, prevailed upon Thomas to turn his talent to poetry. Some of his early verse, written under the pseudonym "Edward Eastaway" was accepted by the American magazine *Poetry* in February, 1917. His first volume *Poems* (1917) was dedicated to Robert Frost, whom he resembles in both theme and manner, especially in this volume. Soon after the outbreak of the War, Thomas enlisted in the army, to be killed on outpost duty at Arras in April, 1917. A collection of verse, *Last Poems*, appeared posthumously in 1919.

Thomas's most distinctive work is to be found in the poems in which he observes and reflects upon the simple things of the byways of the countryside. Poems such as "Haymaking," "Tall Nettles," and "Thaw" are possessed not only of authentic observation, but also an emotional warmth that derives from the simple and apparently spontaneous expression. The fragrance of a shower on dusty nettles, the sedge-warblers clinging to willow twigs, the speculating rooks looking from the top of an elm "over the land freckled with snow, half-thawed"—these are the essence of Thomas's verse. His stanzaic patterns and meters are often irregular, and it is possible for this reason that Edward Marsh in looking over prospective entries for his Georgian anthologies, rejected the poems of Thomas. The rhythms are generally without strongly marked cadence, so much so, in fact, that there is little to distinguish his lines from prose; but in the approach to the themes, Thomas is always essentially poetic.

Poems (1917), *Last Poems* (1919), *Collected Poems* (1920).

Robert P. Eckert, *Edward Thomas: A Biography and Bibliography* (1937); Walter de la Mare, Introduction, *The Collected Poems of Edward Thomas* (1920).

When **Roy Campbell** (1902-   ) wrote *The Georgiad* (1931), he was not performing merely a literary exercise. To one who compared himself to a volcano: "I too have burned

ROY CAMPBELL

the wind with fiery flags," the well deliberated restraint of the Georgians was a deterrent to true emotional intensity. He recognized the necessity for discipline, but he also felt that poetry which showed only artful structure was without purpose and worth. Furthermore, Campbell's early training and observations in the spacious regions of South Africa led him to smile, not always tolerantly, at the limited range of natural history which the Georgians possessed. He whose pages were strewn with zebras, buffaloes, and eagles found the zoological gardens of the Georgians both small and tame; and the manner of his English contemporaries who dealt with nature he found artificial and effete. Challenging many of the conventions of civilization, but recognizing the breath and variety of traditional verse forms, Roy Campbell has produced a considerable amount of virile poetry in which the "bloody horse" at times gallops without curb.

Ignatius Roy Dunnachie Campbell was born in Durban, Natal, South Africa, in 1902. Although he was later to satirize the conditions and people of South Africa in his long poem *The Wayzgoose* (1928), there is no doubt that much of his unconfined thought and expression can be traced to the spaciousness of the environment in which he was reared. Apparently South Africa in the early decades of the century was a man's country in which there was little opportunity for pampering Parnassian tastes. The boy had the formal school-ing afforded in Natal, and at an early age was attracted by the satirical poets, especially Dryden and Pope. Before he was twenty, he had finished a long poem, *The Flaming Terrapin* (1922) in bold iambic verse which was acclaimed in England as the work of a poet of rare vigor. The Irish poet A.E. was led to observe: "I do not know of any poet who had such a savage splendour of epithet or who can marry the wild word so fittingly to the wild thought." In-volved in dissentions chiefly political in Africa, Campbell went to England in 1926. For a time he found London much to his liking and congenial to his talent, which was encour-aged on many sides, but his native restlessness and unwill-ingness to be confined to sedentary roles led him to southern France, Morocco, and later to Spain, where he distinguished himself as a bull-fighter. Although he has moved about a great deal in recent years and followed many interests, his chief avocation is poetry. Of late he has appeared frequently to read verse over the BBC.

Campbell's poetry can be divided into three types, not always distinct: the satirical verse of which *The Wayzgoose* (1928) and *The Georgiad* (1931) are representative; the de-scriptive poems, chiefly in *Adamastor* (1930), in which South African scenes form an important part; and the symbolical poems of which *The Flaming Terrapin* (1922) is best known. As a satirist Campbell has obviously gone to school under Dryden and Pope, not only in that he frequently employs the heroic couplet, but also in his unequivocal manner of attacking his victims. The opening passages of *The Wayz-goose,* in which he strikes boldly at the South African colo-nists, are a twentieth-century revival of Dryden's manner, even to the device of using a fable. *The Georgiad,* in which he attacks Squire and his Georgians, is amusing in its bold cleverness, especially if one is in agreement with the poet's precepts; but too frequently he fails to check his momentum

with the result that in his headlong rush he goes too far. The
descriptive poems usually have in them reflective elements,
and satire is not always excluded. "Tristan de Cunha" is
not only rich, even overflowing with vigorous epithet, but
it is one of Campbell's finest achievements. The vastness of
the scene is little short of Miltonic, and the awe instilled in
the reader is not easily dismissed. The giant saurian which
tows the ark in *The Flaming Terrapin* is a symbol of the
force which weathers the flood; but here, as well as in most
of the poems, the ultimate meaning is less memorable than
the torrential vigor of the language. There is a wild profu-
sion of adjectives, most of which suggest vast spaces, but the
poet is capable of lines of such delicacy as "White angels
rinsed the moonlight from their hair." His later works show
less riotous imagery, but little diminution of vigor of expression.

VERSE: *The Flaming Terrapin* (1922), *The Wayzgoose* (1928),
Adamastor (1930), *The Gum Trees* (1930), *Choosing a Mast* (1931),
The Georgiad (1931), *Mithraic Emblems* (1932), *Pomegranates*
(1932), *Flowering Reeds* (1933), *Flowering Rifle* (1938), *Talking
Broncho* (1946), *Collected Poems* (1949). PROSE: *Taurine Provence:
the Philosophy, Technique and Religion of the Bull-Fighter* (1932),
Burns (1932), *Broken Record: An Autobiography* (1934), *Light
on a Dark Horse*, Autobiography (1951).

Geoffrey Stone, "Roy Campbell: Romantic, Paradox," *Amer. Rev.*,
VIII (1936), 164-176; L. Bonnerot, "Roy Campbell: un Poéte
Pecheur d'Images," *Revue Anglo-Americaine*, IV (1933), 43-48.

FICTION

VICTORIAN

THE THREE greatest novelists of the waning nineteenth century had all ceased to write by the middle of its last decade.
In 1894, Stevenson died at Vailima at the age of forty-four,
leaving unfinished *Weir of Hermiston*, which even as a frag-

ment shows that he was just entering the maturity of his power. In 1895, Meredith, having won a late and somewhat grudging recognition from the public he despised, published his last novel *The Amazing Marriage*. In 1896, Hardy, disgusted with the abuse that had greeted *Jude the Obscure*, likewise retired from fiction. Meredith and Hardy thereafter devoted themselves to the poetry that from the first had been their love. At the same time the young men who were to be the vanguard of the new century, were publishing their first books. *Almayer's Folly* by Joseph Conrad and *The Time Machine* by H. G. Wells appeared in 1895, *From the Four Winds* by "John Sinjohn"—John Galsworthy—in 1897, and *A Man From the North* by Arnold Bennett in 1898. These four were to dominate fiction through the Edwardian era to to the close of the First World War.

The link between these two generations was formed by a number of writers who began to be noticed in the eighties and with years of creation ahead of them had the misfortune to belong neither to the old century nor the new. Often considered dangerously advanced in their early work, they were, with one or two exceptions, outrun by literary taste so that in their maturity they seemed hopelessly old-fashioned.

The scrupulous naturalism that had been established in France by Flaubert and Zola was represented by several writers of whom George Gissing and George Moore were the best. Gissing after six years of bitter struggle won recognition with *Demos* in 1886, and became the leading portrayer of the world of shabbiness and poverty. Moore, a young Irishman fresh from Paris, appeared first as the author of *A Modern Lover* in 1883 and achieved a success of both estimation and scandal when, in 1894, *Esther Waters* shared the moral censure of Hardy's later novels. The bitter poverty and criminality of London's East End was strikingly presented by Arthur Morrison in *Tales of Mean Streets* (1894) and *A Child of the Jago* (1896), and in Somerset Maugham's first novel, *Liza of Lambeth* (1897). Equally realistic studies of the Jewish quarter by Israel Zangwill began to appear in 1893 with *Children of the Ghetto*.

The life of the Scottish poor, sentimentalized yet not wholly unrealistic in treatment, was the subject of the Kail-yard School of which J. M. Barrie was the leader, with *Auld Licht Idylls* (1888) and the various "Thrums" stories that followed them. Ian Maclaren (Rev. John Watson) wrote half a dozen novels of this school of which *Beside the Bonnie Briar Bush* (1894) is the best known, and S. R. Crockett *The Stickit Minister* (1893). They capitalized the interest in Scotland revived by Stevenson and in the humors of rustic character created by Hardy, making much of local color and quaint dialect. Together with the East End writers they did a great deal for the vogue of the regional novel.

Among cultivated readers Mrs. Humphrey Ward, and for a couple of years, Gerald Du Maurier, led the popular novelists; among the uncultivated Hall Caine and Marie Corelli. Mrs. Ward had startled her contemporaries in 1888 with *Robert Elsmere,* a story of religious doubt and struggle and the most controversial novel of its day. Like her uncle, Matthew Arnold, believing that "conduct is three fourths of life" she dealt with problems of conduct in upper class, and often political, society, occasionally as in *Marcella* (1894) and *Bessie Costrel* (1895) entering the world of the poor. Although considered passé by some critics in the late nineties she continued to hold readers well into the nineteen-hundreds. Du Maurier, an artist who did not discover his literary talent until the end of his life, had a brief hour of glory with the appearance of *Trilby* in 1894. Its vivid picture of art-student life in Paris captured the popular imagination as very few novels do, and formed, with the opera *La Bohème,* which appeared two years later, the basis for a romantic illusion of the Latin Quarter firmly believed in by a whole generation of English and Americans. Richard Le

Gallienne had an equally brief popularity as a novelist with *The Quest of the Golden Girl* (1896). Hall Caine appealed through his eloquent Christian socialism and a strain of Celtic mysticism that covered, for the uncritical, his grave defects as a writer. He reached the height of his popularity with *The Manxman* (1894) and *The Christian* (1897). The quality of Marie Corelli's flashy "spiritual" romances may be indicated by the titles *The Soul of Lilith* (1892) and *The Sorrows of Satan* (1895). Mrs. Ward, Hall Caine, and Miss Corelli—different as they were in quality—were all prolific "best sellers," continuing to write until the nineteen-twenties, though with a faded glory and without the spectacular sales of their brief prime.

Stevenson's legacy of romance was shared by a number of minor writers who though never approaching his stature, produced a large body of adventure stories of real merit and vitality. They were fortunate readers whose youth stood beside Allan Quartermain to meet the shock of the Zulu charge, or crossed swords with Black Michael, or felt the cold horror of the Copper Beeches. There was no sophistication in these adventures, but neither was there a more than allowable quantity of fustian—far less than in their modern counterparts—and the authors knew their subjects and how to tell a story. Henry Rider Haggard had begun in the eighties to exploit the romance of Africa, where he had spent some years, and as his work coincided with the increasing interest in South Africa that reached its peak during the Boer War, enjoyed tremendous popularity. *King Solomon's Mines* (1885), his best and one of the best of its kind, has become a juvenile classic; *She* (1887), which was even more popular, has not lasted so well. The energy of Haggard's work was exhausted by the early nineteen-hundreds but new books of his continued to be published for some years after his death in 1900. Anthony Hope (Hawkins) who aspired to be a serious novelist, is remembered only for that pleasant mélange of *Henry Esmond* and *The Three Musketeers, The Prisoner of Zenda* (1894) and its sequel *Rupert of Hentzau* (1898). These tales of state intrigue and royal romance in the kingdom of Ruritania are saved from absurdity by the author's good breeding and real knowledge of European society. They have outlasted any number of cheap imitations. More thoroughly in the tradition of Dumas were the cloak-and-sword novels of Stanley Weyman. Set chiefly in France of the sixteenth and seventeenth centuries, they were well plotted but weak in characterization. The best was *Under the Red Robe* (1894). Much better than these were the historical romances of A. Conan Doyle, *Micah Clarke* (1888), *The White Company* (1890), and *Rodney Stone* (1896). In 1897 appeared the most successful of all modern "gothic" novels, *Dracula,* by Bram Stoker, a horror classic that in fifty years has lost none of its power to excite and chill.

In the short story Kipling was pre-eminent. Since the amazing year 1888 when he had published in Allahabad and London no fewer than seven volumes (*Plain Tales from the Hills, Soldiers Three, The Story of the Gadsbys, In Black and White, Under the Deodars, The Phantom Rickshaw, and Other Tales, Wee Willie Winkie and Other Child Stories*) he had produced, besides other matter, *Life's Handicap* (1891), *Many Inventions* (1893), and *The Day's Work* (1898). His versatility seemed inexhaustible; his vivid local color and crisp journalistic realism were new and accordant with the high spirits of the years of imperial pageantry. There was much more to him than these superficial qualities, of course, but it was they that gave him his unrivalled popularity. His only successful novel *The Light that Failed* appeared in 1890. Next in popularity to Kipling stood Conan Doyle whose creation of Sherlock Holmes began an era in modern popular fiction. With the appearance in *The Strand Magazine* of the stories that were to become *The Adventures* of *Sherlock Holmes* (1892) and *The Memoirs of Sherlock Holmes* (1894) the first, and greatest, detective of modern English fiction emerged as a character far more subtle, intelligent, and interesting than such simply conceived policemen as Inspector Bucket and Sergeant Cuff. Though the detective story did not attain its full popularity for some years, its first great success was in the cases admirably recorded by Dr. Watson. Another innovation was the early "scientific" stories of H. G. Wells—*The Stolen Bacillus and Other Stories* (1895), *The Plattner Story and Other Stories* (1897), and *Tales of Space and Time* (1899)—appealing especially to those "New Century" minds that looked forward eagerly to an era of realized marvels.

EDWARDIAN

From 1900 until the close of the First World War English fiction was dominated by Conrad, Wells, Galsworthy, and Bennett. Except Conrad they were promptly recognized and the appearance by 1910 of *Nostromo, Tono Bungay, The Man of Property,* and *Clayhanger* seemed to justify the belief that England now had her strongest group of novelists for half a century. The ironic detachment of Conrad's revelations of human weakness, the trenchant criticism and satire of Wells, the skill of Galsworthy in characterization, and Bennett's brilliant regionalism showed abundant variety of power. A new strictness of technique was evident in their work; they were familiar with Russian as with French fiction and had discarded the provincialism and easy going amateurishness that were the blemishes of so many Victorian writers. They were comparatively young men with their best work, presumably, yet to be done.

In view of this great promise, the sudden withdrawal of esteem in the twenties that caused all but Conrad to outlive their reputations and the neglect into which they have since fallen are at first hard to understand. In part it is traceable to a particular defect in each of them. Conrad wrote from within a professional ideal that passed with the sailing ship. Wells and Galsworthy were propagandists who repeatedly sacrificed their art to their causes, and Galsworthy had the added vice of sentimentalism, unforgivable to the following generation. Bennett's irrespressible commercialism would not allow him to write for long at his best, so that at the last his real achievement was clogged with much that was cheap and trashy. More than all this, however, they had all worked in a literary tradition that was passing. As soon as a sufficient body of postwar fiction had appeared for its character to become defined, it was apparent that they did not belong to it. Wells had no marvels or terrors for those who had been in the war, it was clear that Galsworthy did not understand the younger generation as he had understood the older, Bennett's *Pretty Lady* seemed absurdly timid, and no one was going to learn the ropes of Conrad's ships. Moreover whatever the quality of their fiction they had made no innovation in technique, and this to a day in which all forms of literature were being radically overhauled was enough to condemn them.

Among the minor Edwardian novelists Maurice Hewlett occupies a high place; in fact at one time he promised to be a major novelist when his romances of the middle ages *The Forest Lovers* (1898) and *Richard Yea and Nay* (1900) were the literary sensations of their day. His reputation fell, however, when he attempted novels of contemporary life, and though his later Norse romances were good, they did not wholly fulfil the promise of his beginnings. Another disappointment was Gilbert Cannan whose social novels from 1910 to 1915 showed great distinction. A mental breakdown at the end of the war forced him to give up writing, although his books continued to be published until 1924. Robert Hichens enjoyed a decade of great popularity beginning with the tremendous success of *The Garden of Allah* (1904) and sustained by *Bella Donna* (1909) and *The Fruitful Vine* (1911). His vogue, however, passed with the war and the twenty-odd novels that he wrote between 1919 and 1942 commanded little attention. Ford Maddox Hueffer (who changed his last name to Ford) began as an historical romancer but turned for his later material to contemporary life. Early in his career he was Joseph Conrad's collaborator in *The Inheritors* and *Romance*. A meticulous stylist with French rather than English standards of fiction, he was a technician rather than a creator and served literature less by his own writings than by his introduction of new authors in the *English Review* and the *transatlantic Review* which he edited before and after the war. Leonard Merrick and Oliver Onions were debarred from great success simply by their failure to please the public. The delightful comedy of Merrick's books bordered disturbingly on tragedy in a way that disappointed equally those who wanted a "pleasant" and those who wanted a "strong" story. Onions was a vigorous writer with a wholly negative attitude; he showed his readers a despicable world in which he had nothing to offer but his anger. J. C. Snaith, E. F. Benson, and the eccentric and exuberant M. P. Shiel were without durable substance. The catalogue of unfulfilled promise may be completed with Eden Phillpotts who appeared in the later nineties as a regional novelist of Devon. He had undoubted talent but as his writing was the whole interest of his life he produced too much—more than a hundred novels besides plays and short stories.

The most curious story in Edwardian letters is that of William De Morgan, a retired manufacturer of art pottery who in 1906 astonished readers and critics by producing a remarkably successful first novel, *Joseph Vance,* at the age of sixty-seven. Had De Morgan discovered his talent sooner he would probably have held a high place among his contemporaries: as it was he established a solid reputation with half a dozen excellent, if somewhat old-fashioned, novels before he died of influenza in 1917.

The lighter novelists were led by William J. Locke, who captivated the public with the delicate gaiety of *The Morals of Marcus Ordeyne* (1905) and *The Beloved Vagabond* (1906). Archibald Marshall wrote quiet, humorous stories of the county families, the best being *The Eldest Son* (1911) and *The Honour of the Clintons* (1913); and "George A. Birmingham" farcical stories of Irish life. "Elizabeth" wrote with a more subdued humor her stories of life in Prussia, the fruits of a trying first marriage. "C N and A M Williamson" exploited the new interest in motoring in *The Lightning Conductor* (1902) and with a series of light, clever stories that were half touring guides, won a popularity that lasted until the novelty of the sport, as it was then considered, had worn away. Adventure seekers were entertained by E. Phillips Oppenheim's novels of international intrigue and secret diplomacy, or the exploits of Baroness Orczy's Sir Percy Blakeney (*The Scarlet Pimpernel*).

An isolated event of great importance was the publication in 1903 of *The Way of All Flesh* a year after the death of its author. Written between 1872 and 1884 it was the work of the eccentric genius Samuel Butler (1835-1902), who authorized its publication on his death bed. Largely autobiographical, it is a bitter attack on old-fashioned piety and the narrow tyranny of the Victorian household. Its influence which became even greater after the war, when it appealed to the general spirit of revolt, can be traced in the work of Somerset Maugham and others.

In the field of the short story, though there was no one to compete with the now veteran Kipling, the Edwardian years developed a number of able writers. Most of the novelists mentioned produced one or more volumes in the genre, Wells, Galsworthy, Hewlett, and Locke being the more skillful. W. W. Jacobs could be counted on for an annual volume, collected from *The Strand Magazine*, of his tales of comic seafaring men or the incredible rustics who gathered at the Cauliflower Inn. Much more skillful and sophisticated, "Saki" recounted the social flippancies of irresponsible young men in a vein that P. G. Wodehouse was later to make more popular. Horace Annesley Vachel, of little account as a novelist, wrote some exceedingly clever and amusing stories, especially the three volumes about Quinney's antique shop, and Algernon Blackwood gave a new flavor to the occult. For a few years Richard Middleton contributed to magazines delicate, fantastic stories that after his tragic death filled a couple of volumes. One of these, *The Ghost Ship*, has a deserved reputation as a masterpiece of fantasy but has never received the credit due it as an early, subtle, and artistically successful experiment in the stream-of-consciousness. Another master of the fantastic, impossible to classify, is Arthur Machen whose tales of diabolism, long and short, are neither novels nor short stories. In spite of the remarkable skill with which he could evoke the horror and evil of an ancient pagan world he was little read and had only a transient popularity when his work was "discovered" in the nineteen-twenties.

Edwardian fiction will be remembered chiefly for the splendid picture it preserves of England in the early twentieth century. It was intensely contemporaneous; at no time in the nineteenth century were so few good historical stories written. But if its writers were concerned with their own world, their attitude toward it was on the whole conservative. Of the major novelists only Galsworthy and Wells were actively critical of society. Bennett was keenly aware of social injustice but inclined to accept it with a shrug, and Galsworthy was an evangelist calling to repentance rather than a reformer. Wells alone went to the roots of social organization with constructive, if impractical, criticism. The attitude of novelists toward religion and politics, though not always complacent, had not changed noticeably since the eighties and nineties. The problems created by the changing position of women were discussed in many novels, such as *Ann Veronica* and *The Man of Property,* but the experience of Hardy and Moore had made writers shy of attempting any frank treatment of sex. The old prudishness died hard, and D. H. Lawrence, the first of the younger men to come out and fight it during the war, was severely punished by the suppression of *The Rainbow* and the refusal of all publishers to handle *Women in Love.*

Conservatism was as marked in the form as in the content of fiction. The Edwardians were much occupied with questions of technique but too well satisfied with the study of Flaubert, Turgeniev, and Henry James to make any experiments of their own. Bennett in the Clayhanger novels and Galsworthy in *The Forsyte Saga* made use of the trilogy to get the sustained effect of the old three-volume novel without its inconveniences, but there was no marked technical change until 1920.

The absence of women writers in these years is noticeable and at first surprising. After Mrs. Ward and Marie Corelli there were few new names except May Sinclair whose reputation was made by *The Divine Fire* (1904). There was presumably no lack of talent, but the best feminine minds were politically focused on the struggle for the vote and the movement for higher education that accompanied it. After the war, when these issues had been settled, women became as prominent as men in nearly all branches of literature.

When **Joseph Conrad (1857-1924)** began to write English fiction he had already lived two lives as different from each other as both were from the new one on which he was entering. He was born near Kiev in the Ukraine and christened Teodor Josef Konrad Korzeniowski. In his early childhood he shared with his parents political exile in Vologda, the punishment for his father's nationalistic activities.

His mother died under the hardship; his father survived his release by one year. Left an orphan in 1869 at the age of twelve, Conrad was brought up by his maternal uncle. The Bobrowskis, his mother's family, were landholders in the Ukraine, and expected him to follow the tradition of Polish gentlemen. To their consternation, at the age of fifteen, he announced his intention of becoming a merchant seaman.

JOSEPH CONRAD

Conrad's father had been a highly cultivated man, a poet and the translator of Shakespeare into Polish. He had introduced his son to English letters, and it was by the sea stories of Frederick Marryat and of Fenimore Cooper (so little regarded now) that Conrad's imagination was turned toward the sea. Promises, dissuasions, travel with a tutor could not divert him, nor would he consent to go to the Imperial Naval Academy at Pola and become an officer in the Austrian service. He would be a merchant seaman and in English ships. At length in desperation the family consigned him to friends in Marseilles who would take him in hand while he served his apprenticeship to a pilot of the port. Experience of hardship it was thought would cure him. Nothing of the sort. He learned his trade, while Marseilles of the 'seventies educated him in the world. His great moment came when one night in the pilot's boat he touched the side of a veritable English ship.

Conrad's second life began with his first deep-water voyage to the West Indies. Seasoned by two or three such he went

to England and began his service in her ships. To understand the years that followed one should read *The Mirror
of the Sea,* the most revelatory of all his books, defining, as
he says "the terms of my relation to the sea." And more, for
there in half a dozen significant statements one will find the
keys to his art: "To see! To see!—this is the craving of the
sailor, as of the rest of blind humanity." "Ships are all right;
it's the men who are in 'em." To return, he passed for master
in 1880, held command, and became a British subject in
1886. He had achieved what he set out to do. Then he was
led into the adventure that put an end to his seafaring. He
tells in *A Personal Record* how at the age of nine he put his
finger on a blank space in the map of Africa and said, "When
I grow up I shall go *there.*" In 1889 he went, commanding
a river steamer for a Belgian development company, and it
was then that the first seven chapters of *Almayer's Folly*
were written. The adventure ended in West Coast fever that
sent him home a very sick man. After a stay ashore and a
visit to Poland, he shipped again, this time as first mate of
the *Torrens,* a crack passenger-carrying clipper in the Australian trade. Not long after his impaired health obliged him
to go ashore for good, and the novel at which he had been
working for five years was completed.

With the publication of *Almayer's Folly* in 1895 Conrad
began his career as an English author. Galsworthy and
Edward Garnett, who had recommended its publication,
introduced him to a brilliant literary circle including Henry
James, Stephen Crane, W. H. Hudson, Cunninghame-
Graham, and Ford M. Hueffer * his collaborator. Among
these he won an almost immediate *succes d'estime,* but for
years the public was dishearteningly indifferent to his work
The way to popular success in the first decade of the century
was through the magazine serial and Conrad's books, con-

* Later Ford Maddox Ford.

ceived in total effect, were wholly lacking in "serial quality."
He was a laborious writer, each book causing him fresh
agonies, and his eighteen years of struggle against poverty
and obscurity were bitter. Only a Civil List pension and the
help of his literary agent J. B. Pinker enabled him to weather
the worst of them. Yet during these years he did nearly all
of his enduring work. His wife, Jessie George Conrad, whom
he married in 1896, has left an indiscreetly candid record of
the stress of their domestic life in this trying time. When
popular recognition came at length in 1913 it was for
Chance, not one of his greatest books. Thereafter he enjoyed
roughly a decade of literary celebrity, culminating in his
visit to the United States in 1923. He died in the following
year and was buried in the Catholic cemetery in Canterbury,
in the county he loved and had made his home. After the
funeral Cunninghame-Graham wrote an eloquent final tribute in his essay *Inveni Portum.*

Conrad never became English except in allegiance. Short
and square, with a high-cheeked, sallow oriental face and
pointed beard, his restless tension expressed in quick Latin
gestures, he was a foreigner at sight. The language that he
wrote so beautifully, he spoke with a harsh Cockney accent
acquired at sea. His manner was simple yet with a high-bred,
foreign courtesy. "Something there was about him both of
the Court and of the quarterdeck."

Conrad disliked being called a "sea writer" because his
intention was wholly different from that of the artless yarn
spinners to whom the term is usually applied. To see, and
to make others see, the significances of human character in
motive and action, and to estimate the values accurately, was
his whole purpose as an artist and to this the setting in
Costaguana or Malaya, in the bark *Judea* or the S. S. *Nan-
Shan* was purely incidental. So far he was justified, yet the
label is not only inevitable but true.

The world that Conrad spiritually inhabited, and that

haunted like a recurring memory scenes farthest removed
from it, was the world of seamen in the sailing ships that
even then were disappearing from the sea. The sea was something hostile to be overcome, a challenge to youth and fortitude; it was also a mirror reflecting pitilessly the true image
of man. The ship constrained her crew within a narrow circle
of duty, requiring of them the extreme of professional skill
and devotion. The essentially masculine ideals of the received tradition of seamen are expressed in every page he
wrote.

Twice, in minor works, *Youth* and *Typhoon,* Conrad
wrote of man triumphant over the sea, but neither the
second mate of the *Judea* nor Captain McWhirr approaches
the power of his greater characters. These take their stature
not from triumphant strength but from the tragic flaw of
character that betrays it and robs it of its victory. Lord Jim
deserts his duty and jumps from the sinking ship to save his
skin, Nostromo destroys his integrity by stealing the silver,
Tom Lingard leaves Kassim and Immada to their fate in his
infatuation for Mrs. Travers, Almayer allows the poison of
the East to rob him of his pride of Western civilization. The
mirror has shown the flaw in the image, always the image of
man. It is a world in which women have subordinate roles,
and when, in *The Arrow of Gold,* Conrad tries to create a
woman comparable to his tragic heroes he is not notably
successful. Rita is voluble rather than brilliant, strange
rather than subtle. Her creator's labor seems to be a desperate incantation in which the operative word of the spell is
wanting. She will not come to life.

It was a romantic passion that sent Conrad to sea, a passion that, he says, survived every disillusion of experience. It
is to be found in a title, *The Rescue: A Romance of the
Shallows*—without the final phrase it would be ordinary, but
there it is, three notes of music evoking a whole scene remote
and dangerous. In his intense feeling for scene and in his

power to convey it Conrad is always an undefeated romantic. But there is nothing shoddy about Conrad's romanticism, it is never used to cast glamor over inferior work; he would abate no detail of truth to attain it. His descriptions are essential to the unfolding of the story: the stricken vessel in the loneliness of oceanic space, the sinister coast of *The Heart of Darkness,* the superbly realized Golfo Placido are the places in which alone these things could happen as they have been conceived and these men achieve their destiny in the fullest possible expression of their strength and weakness. Such romance may fall, as it has, out of fashion, but it is durable art.

Conrad's stories are either novels or shorter pieces which he called "tales" since they are not technically short stories. The difference is in the scale of events and characters. Of the former he thought *Nostromo* and *The Nigger of the "Narcissus"* his best; the first choice is sure, the second questionable. *The Heart of Darkness, Lord Jim,* and *The Rescue* stand high in the list. Of the tales, *Youth* and *Typhoon,* already mentioned, are among the best. Of the major Edwardian novelists he is the purest artist, the only one without any sort of propagandist axe to grind. "It had to be done," he said of *Nostromo.* He wrote under the artist's compulsion to express his vision "with the ineradicable hope—of ultimately, some day, at some moment, making myself understood."

COLLECTED WORKS: Canterbury Edition (1924), Memorial Edition (1925), Malay Edition (1927). FICTION: *Almayer's Folly* (1895), *An Outcast of the Islands* (1896), *The Nigger of the "Narcissus,"* [*The Children of the Sea*] (1897), *Tales of Unrest* (1898), *Lord Jim* (1900), *The Inheritors,* with F. M. Hueffer (1901), *Typhoon* (1902), *Youth* (1902), *Romance,* with F. M. Hueffer (1903), *Typhoon and Other Stories* (1903), *Nostromo* (1904), *The Secret Agent* (1907), *A Set of Six* (1908), *Under Western Eyes* (1911), *'Twixt Land and Sea* (1912), *Chance* (1913), *Victory* (1915), *Within the Tides* (1916), *The Shadow Line* (1917), *The Arrow of Gold* (1919), *The Rescue*

(1920), *The Rover* (1923), *Suspense* (unfinished) (1925), *Tales of Hearsay* (1925), *The Sisters* (1928), *The Complete Short Stories of Joseph Conrad* (1933). PLAYS: *One Day More* (1919), *The Secret Agent* (1921), *Laughing Anne* (1923), *Three Plays* (1934). ESSAYS: *The Mirror of the Sea* (1906), *Some Reminiscences [A Personal Record]* (1912), *Notes on Life and Letters* (1921), *Notes on My Books* (1921), *Last Essays* (1926), *Conrad's Prefaces to His Works* (1937). LETTERS: *Joseph Conrad's Letters to His Wife* (1927), *Conrad to a Friend: 150 Selected Letters from Joseph Conrad to Richard Curle* (1928), also pub. as *Letters of Joseph Conrad to Richard Curle* (1928), *Letters from Joseph Conrad, 1895-1924* (1928), *Lettres françaises* (Paris, 1930), *Letters from Joseph Conrad to Marguerite Poradowska* (1940).

Thomas J. Wise, *A Bibliography of the Writings of Joseph Conrad* (1920); "Bibliographies of Modern Authors, Joseph Conrad," *London Mercury*, II (1920), 476-477; George Jean-Aubry, *Joseph Conrad: Life and Letters* (1927); Jessie Conrad, *Personal Recollections of Joseph Conrad* (1924); Richard Curle, *Joseph Conrad* (1914), *Joseph Conrad: The History of His Books* (1924), *The Personality of Joseph Conrad* (1925), *The Last Twelve Years of Joseph Conrad* (1928), "Joseph Conrad: Ten Years After," *Virginia Quar. Rev.*, X (1934), 420-435; F. M. Ford, "Working with Conrad," *Yale Rev.*, XVIII (1929), 699-715, "Conrad and the Sea," in *Portraits From Life* (1937); Gustav Morf, *The Polish Heritage of Joseph Conrad* (1930); Albert Guerard, Jr., "Joseph Conrad," in *Direction One* (1947); Hugh Walpole, *Joseph Conrad* (1925); W. J. Cross, "Joseph Conrad," in *Four Contemporary Novelists* (1930); E. K. Brown, "James and Conrad," *Yale Rev.*, XXXV (1945-46), 265-285; F. M. Stowell, "Conrad," *Essays and Studies*, VI (1920), 88-112; Edward Garnett, "Joseph Conrad," *Century*, CXV (1928), 385-392, 593-600; C. K. Allen, "Joseph Conrad," *Contemp. Rev.*, CXXV (1924), 54-62; Cornelius Weygandt, "The Art of Joseph Conrad," *Schelling Anniversary Papers* (Phila., 1923); R. L. Megroz, *Joseph Conrad's Mind and Method* (1931); W. W. Bancroft, *Joseph Conrad: His Philosophy of Life* (Boston, 1933); A. R. Thompson, "The Humanism of Joseph Conrad," *Sewanee Rev.*, XXXVII, 204-220; H. P. Austin, "Joseph Conrad and the Ironic Attitude," *Fortnightly Rev.*, CXXX (1928), 376-388; R. G. Lillard, "Irony in Hardy and Conrad," *PMLA*, L (1935), 316-322; Morton D. Zabel, "Joseph Conrad: Chance and Recognition," *Sewanee Rev.*, LIII (1945), 1-22; James V. Fletcher, "Ethical Symbolism in Conrad," *College*

English, II (1940), 19-26; H. T. Webster, "Joseph Conrad: A Re-interpretation of Five Novels," *College English,* VII (1945-46), 125-134; John D. Gordon, "The Rajah Brooke and Joseph Conrad," *Studies in Philology,* XXXV (1938), 613-634; Arthur Symons, *Notes on Joseph Conrad* (1925); Oliver Warner, *Joseph Conrad* (1950).

The career of **Herbert George Wells (1866-1946)** may be divided conveniently into two periods, the first, to 1900, of escape from the narrow conditions of his childhood, the second, to his death, of search for a better world and a more rational society. To this search his work as a literary artist is incidental.

HERBERT GEORGE WELLS

He was born in a cramped little house in Bromley, Kent, behind a crockery shop which his father, a gardener and cricketer, ran helplessly into bankruptcy. His mother, a former ladies' maid, worked hard to raise her children and, when the shop failed, went back into service as a housekeeper to support them. She was anxious to see her sons placed in respectable trades, and so at the age of fourteen, after a very sketchy schooling, Wells was sent "on trial" to a draper's in Windsor. This was the first of six starts in life that he has recorded. To follow him through them all, as pupil-teacher, chemist's assistant and again at a draper's, would be tedious, and for such details the reader is referred to *Experiment in Autobiography* (1934) of which they make the most interesting part.

At length in 1884 by hard reading he won a scholarship at

the Normal School of Science in London and spent his first
year there in T. H. Huxley's course in Elementary Biology.
Huxley's inspiring teaching gave him a love for science that
he never lost, but subsequent courses were dull, he neglected
his work for other interests, and in 1887 lost his scholarship.
After two more experiences of school teaching he took his
B.Sc. degree in London University in 1890.

For the next three years Wells was employed as biology
instructor in a correspondence school preparing candidates
for the London University examinations. For this school he
wrote his first published work, a *Textbook of Biology*. In
1893 he gave up teaching for journalism, writing at first for
the *Fortnightly Review* and the *Saturday Review* and later
for the *Pall Mall Gazette*. In 1893 *The Yellow Book* published his story *A Slip Under the Microscope*. By 1896 he
was making over £1,000 a year: he had reached independence and completely liberated himself from his origins.

In 1891 Wells had married his cousin, Isabella Mary
Wells, but they proved temperamentally unsuited to each
other. They were separated at the end of 1892 and divorced
three years later. In January 1893 he went to live in Morn-
ington Place with Amy Catherine Robbins, a science student
with whom he had fallen in love. Neither then believed in
marriage but social pressure forced them to marry immediately after his divorce in 1895. The first Mrs. Wells remarried
and lived until 1931, the second lived until 1927.

Wells' literary career dates virtually from his second marriage; what he did before that was largely prentice work.
The Time Machine appeared in 1895, *The Island of Dr.
Moreau* in 1896, and *The Invisible Man* in 1897. These,
which made his reputation, and other stories he wrote in this
period exploit the "marvelous" aspects of science in fantasies—"violent visions" Chesterton called them—which have
still a power over the popular imagination. *The Time
Machine* is the first projection of the four dimensional con-

tinuum in fiction and *The Island of Dr. Moreau* a horrible
dramatization of biological evolution. Down to 1905 Wells
was known almost exclusively for work of this kind.

His second phase as a realistic novelist began in 1900 with
Love and Mr. Lewisham, the story of a schoolmaster, containing some autobiographical matter. *Kipps* appeared in
1905 and *Ann Veronica* and *Tono Bungay* both in 1909—
Wells' *annus mirabilis.* The last is unquestionably his
masterpiece, a satiric contrast of two false ideals, that of the
feudal aristocracy of Bladesover, and that of the modern
business world in which Uncle Ponderevo achieves wealth by
fraudulent advertising. Wells hated both of them; the first
he knew intimately from Up Park where his mother had
been housekeeper, the second only from general but shrewd
observation. Between them they seemed to possess the world
of that day. If modern society was to escape complete de-
civilization, it seemed to Wells that it must find other ideals
to which the scientist and the educator could best point the
way. More and more social ideas developed in dialogue
usurped the place of character and action in his novels, to
the detriment of their literary art. During World War I his
sturdy unbelief yielded temporarily to the mysticism that
affected many of the older generation and he wrote *Mr.
Britling Sees It Through* (1916) and *The Soul of a Bishop*
(1917). With *Joan and Peter* (1918) and *The Undying Fire*
(1919) the second phase of his literary work ended.

Perhaps the most important act of Wells' youth was his
reading of Plato's *Republic.* It disclosed to him the possibility of a rational and ordered society that his scientific
mind thoroughly approved. Confirmed in socialism by experience and further reading, he joined the Fabian Society
and soon going beyond its rather academic policies began
to plan a socialized world of his own. In 1900 he published
in the *Fortnightly Review* the series of far-seeing articles on
population and society which became *Anticipations,* and

two years later a second series, *Mankind in the Making. A Modern Utopia* (1906) is his manifesto for the organization of the new world and is in effect a free adaptation to modern conditions of the leading ideas of Plato. It places the direction of the state in the hands of an elite order, the "Samurai," for which Wells later found parallels in the Russian Communist party and the Italian Fascists. Following its publication he tried to "capture" the Fabian Society, as a means of making its principles effective and, failing, resigned. Thereafter he thought and worked alone.

For some years Wells' propaganda for a planned society ran side by side with his literary work, but in time it absorbed the best part of his thought and effort. World War I, weakening whatever it did not overthrow of the old order, seemed to him a unique opportunity for a new beginning. The confusion of public and private thought during the peace negotiations brought home to him the necessity of educating an entire generation to new political concepts and he began his series of world surveys, *The Outline of History* (1920), *The Science of Life,* with Julian Huxley and G. P. Wells (1929), and *The Work, Wealth and Happiness of Mankind* (1932). The indifference of England's first Labor Government (1923) disappointed but did not discourage him. He now had a world-wide audience and the popularity of his later books revived interest in his earlier ones. But as the world marched toward another world war, and neither his "educative" nor his political works produced any appreciable effect Wells became increasingly despondent. *The Anatomy of Frustration: A Modern Synthesis* (1936), *The Fate of Man* (1939) and *The New World Order* (1940) mark the decline of his effort and influence.

Though a Socialist, Wells was vehemently anti-Marxian and repudiated the whole doctrine of the class war. On the other hand although many of his doctrines, and especially his conception of the "Samurai," had totalitarian tendencies, he equally abhorred the ultimate developments of fascism. His teachings, at least temporarily, suffered the fate of all rational programs when the world is moving toward a crisis along emotional paths.

Whether the world gained when Wells sacrificed his undoubtedly great powers as a novelist to his preoccupation with the world-state each reader may decide for himself. His *Experiment in Autobiography* makes it perfectly clear that for Wells nothing else was possible. The novel as an art form failed to satisfy him: he needed a more elastic and more dramatic vehicle for his ideas. His fiction developed, as he says, more and more toward the dialogue and therefore always farther from the symbolism through which alone the novel can convey ideas. It was inevitable that his scientific mind with its passion for completeness and precision should ultimately prefer direct exposition. But though it was more satisfactory to Wells, his work of this sort has shown no clear superiority to an equal amount of fiction of the quality of *Tono Bungay*.

Like Bennett, Wells was a self-made man of the people, ambitious, confident, and Philistine. His artistic impulse was as genuine as Bennett's but not nearly so strong. In the arts other than literature he seems to have had little interest. He wanted to be known less as a creator of beauty than as a shaper of destiny, but it was when his thought was quickened by his art that it was most influential. At the end he felt that he had failed.

COLLECTED WORKS: Atlantic Edition (1924). AUTOBIOGRAPHY: *An Experiment in Autobiography* (1934). FICTION: *The Time Machine* (1895), *The Wonderful Visit* (1895), *The Stolen Bacillus* (1896), *The Island of Doctor Moreau* (1896), *The Wheels of Chance* (1896), *The Red Room* (1896), *The Invisible Man* (1897), *Thirty Strange Stories* (1897), *The Plattner Story* (1897), *The War of the Worlds* (1898), *When the Sleeper Wakes* (1899), *A Cure For Love* (1899), *Tales of Space and Time* (1899), *The Vacant Country* (1899), *Love and Mr. Lewisham* (1899), *The First Men in the*

Moon (1901), *The Sea Lady* (1902), *Twelve Stories and a Dream* (1903), *The Food of the Gods* (1904), *Kipps* (1905), *A Modern Utopia* (1905), *In the Days of the Comet* (1906), *The War in the Air* (1908), *Ann Veronica* (1909), *Tono Bungay* (1909), *The History of Mr. Polly* (1909), *The New Machiavelli* (1911), *The Country of the Blind* (1911), *Marriage* (1912), *The Passionate Friends* (1913), *The World Set Free* (1914), *The Wife of Sir Isaac Harman* (1914), *Bealby* (1915), *The Research Magnificent* (1915), *Mr. Britling Sees It Through* (1916), *The Soul of a Bishop* (1916), *Joan and Peter* (1917), *The Undying Fire* (1919), *The Secret Places of the Heart* (1922), *Men Like Gods* (1923), *The Dream* (1924), *Christina Alberta's Father* (1925), *The Adventures of Tommy* (1925), *The World of William Clissold* (1926), *Meanwhile* (1927), *Mr. Blettsworthy on Rampole Island* (1928), *The King Who Was a King* (1929), *The Autocracy of Mr. Parham* (1930), *The Bulpington of Blup* (1933), *The Shape of Things To Come* (1933), *The Man Who Could Work Miracles* (1936), *The Croquet Player* (1936), *Brynhild* (1937), *The Camford Visitation* (1937), *Star Begotten* (1937), *The Brothers* (1938), *Apropos of Dolores* (1938), *The Dictator* (1939), *The Holy Terror* (1939), *Babes in the Darkling Wood* (1940), *All Aboard For Ararat* (1940), *You Can't Be Too Careful* (1941). NON-FICTION: *Select Conversations With an Uncle* (1895), *Certain Personal Matters* (1898), *The Discovery of the Future* (1902), *Mankind in the Making* (1903), *New Worlds For Old* (1908), *First and Last Things* (1908), *The Great State* [*Socialism and the Great State*] (1912), *An Englishman Looks at the World* [*Social Forces in England and America*] (1914), *God, the Invisible King* (1917), *The Outline of History* (1920), *The Salvaging of Civilization* (1921), *Socialism and the Scientific Motive* (1923), *After Democracy* (1929), *The Way to World Peace* (1930), *The Work, Wealth and Happiness of Mankind* (1931), *The Science of Life* (1931), *The Anatomy of Frustration* (1936), *World Brain* (1938), *The Enlarged and Revised Outline of History* (1940), *The New World Order* (1940), *The Common Sense of War and Peace* (1940), *The Conquest of Time* (1942), *Mind at the End of Its Tether* (1946).

Geoffrey H. Wells, *The Works of H. G. Wells, 1887-1925: A Bibliography, Dictionary, and Subject Index* (1926), *H. G. Wells: A Sketch for a Portrait* (1930); Georges A. Connes, *A Dictionary of Characters and Scenes in the Novels, Romances, and Short Stories of H. G. Wells* (Dijon, 1926), "L'Autobiographie de H. G. Wells," *Rev. Anglo-Americaine*, XIII (1936), 311-325; Henry Arthur Jones,

My Dear Wells (1921); R. T. Hopkins, *H. G. Wells* (1922); Ivor
Brown, *H. G. Wells* (1925); Sidney Dark, *The Outline of H. G.
Wells* (1922); W. T. Cross, "H. G. Wells," in *Four Contemporary
Novelists* (1930); Helene Richter, "Herbert George Wells," *Anglia,*
XLVI (1922), 97-136; F. M. Ford, "H. G. Wells" in *Portraits From
Life* (1937); J. B. Priestley, "H. G. Wells," *English Jour.,* XIV
(1925), 89-97; Andre Maurois, "Wells" in *Prophets and Poets*
(1935); F. H. Doughty, *H. G. Wells, Educationist* (1926); Stuart
P. Sherman, "H. G. Wells and the Victorians," *Amer. Bookman,*
LXXIV (1931), 230-237; E. K. Brown, "Two Formulas for Fiction:
Henry James and H. G. Wells," *College English,* VIII (1946-47),
7-17; Stanley Kauffman, "Wells and the New Generation," *College
English,* I (1939-40), 573-582; W. J. Sykes, "Is Wells Also Among
the Prophets," *Queen's Quarterly,* XLIX (1942), 233-245.

John Galsworthy (1867-1933) was the son of John Galsworthy, attorney, of Kingston, Surrey, descendant of a solid
line of Devonshire yeomen. Of his farmer ancestry, close to
the soil of England, secure in the worth of their station,
Galsworthy in his later years was very proud.

He was schooled at Bournemouth and Harrow, where he
proved good at football and track, and then entered New
College, Oxford. At the university he was a typical upper-
middle-class undergraduate, a good student, lazily interested
in sport, socially conventional, somewhat reserved. He had
no especial inclination to literature. He read for honors in
law, in which he took only a Second, and was called to the
bar in 1890. As he did not need to work immediately, Galsworthy read law for the next four years and completed his
education by travel. For this he chose regions off the beaten
track, Russia, the Canadian Northwest, the South Seas. Returning from the last journey in 1893, he sailed as passenger
from Adelaide to Cape Town in the ship *Torrens,* of which
Joseph Conrad was first mate. The two quickly became
friends.

It was his future wife who made Galsworthy a writer.
When they met after his return to England she was unhap-

pily married to his cousin, Arthur Galsworthy. She was a woman of exceptional character and charm and they were rapidly and irresistibly drawn to one another, though it was to be ten years before they could marry. One day in 1895 as he was boarding a train at the Gare du Nord in Paris, she said, "Why don't you write? You're just the person." Her complete confidence gave him the courage to persevere in an intention that had been growing ever since his meeting with Conrad.

JOHN GALSWORTHY

Since his university days Galsworthy had read widely and especially admired the work of Turgenev and Flaubert. But he had no preparation for writing fiction and had to develop a technique by sheer hard work. It was not until 1897 that he published his first volume *From the Four Winds*. This was followed by *Jocelyn, Villa Rubein,* and *A Man of Devon*. All of these were issued under the pseudonym John Sinjohn. At this time Galsworthy seemed to his contemporaries a literary amateur, a man about town who saw life through a club window.

It was partly maturity, partly the influence of Turgenev, but mostly the knowledge of suffering gained from learning of the unhappiness of Ada Galsworthy and from appearing as co-respondent in a divorce suit that changed his character as a writer. He turned against the smug conventionality of his own class and became the champion of the artist, the rebel, and the underdog. *The Island Pharisees* (1904) marks the beginning of this revolt.

In 1905, Arthur Galsworthy having obtained his divorce, John and Ada Galsworthy were married. It was from first to last a happy and successful marriage. They made their home at Manaton in Devon, and after 1918 at Grove Lodge, Hampstead. *The Man of Property*, published the year following their marriage, is the first of Galsworthy's really mature works, the beginning of the *Forsyte Saga* (1922). From then on his literary career was one of continued success, but it was not until after World War I that the remaining novels of the *Saga* appeared, *In Chancery* (1920) and *To Let* (1921). The theme of the *Saga* is "the impingement of Beauty and the claims of Freedom on a possessive world" represented by the Forsytes, admittedly a portrait gallery of Galsworthy's own family. It is also a superb period study of the upper middle class in the last Victorian generation. "Here it rests, preserved in its own juice: The Sense of Property."

The younger Forsytes in England of the nineteen-twenties were studied in a second trilogy *A Modern Comedy* (1929) which includes *The White Monkey* (1924), *The Silver Spoon* (1926) and *Swan Song* (1929). This was less successful, for though Galsworthy worked on these novels with equal care, he did not understand the postwar generation as he had the elder Forsytes, and all that he had to say about their class had been fully presented in the *Saga*.

The novels that appeared between *The Man of Property* and the rest of the *Saga*—*The Country House, Fraternity, The Patrician, The Dark Flower, The Freelands, Beyond,* and *Saint's Progress*—deal largely with the same class in the same understanding but unsympathetic way. His three last novels—*Maid in Waiting* (1931), *Flowering Wilderness* (1932) and *One More River* (1933)—formed a third trilogy, *End of the Chapter* (1934). They were more hastily done than his earlier work and show a marked decline in interest and power.

Galsworthy's first play, *The Silver Box,* appeared in the same year as *The Man of Property.* It was followed by *Strife* (1909) and *Justice* (1910), all three being bitter protests against social injustice, more effective as propaganda than as art. Protest and fantasy alternated as the types of his early plays. Of the later plays *The Skin Game* (1920), *Loyalties* (1922), and *Old English* (1924) are dramatically better and have had popular success. In all he wrote twenty-eight plays, published during his lifetime in eight volumes, but his determined sacrifice of story and character to didactic purpose is a blemish in his work that has kept it below the first rate. His plays have not the durable quality of the *Saga.*

Galsworthy wrote about a dozen volumes each of short stories and essays. The stories, though generally too sentimental, are touching and sometimes poignant treatments of obscure tragedy or twisted, sad ironies. A few are amusing. The best of them are, after the *Saga,* the best of Galsworthy's writing. The essays deal for the most part with national affairs, humane causes, and the problems of the artist in a Philistine society. There are also, fantasies aside, a number of pieces that partake of both genres and can be only arbitrarily classified. They are narrative in form, but character and incident are used, not as in the plays for direct propaganda, but more subtly for the enhancement of a mood or sentiment in the fashion of the essay. Generally Galsworthy preferred to dramatize his ideas rather than expound them.

No reader of Galsworthy can fail to be reminded frequently of Thackeray. The Forsytes are the Osbornes and Sedleys of a later day and, like them, could have been portrayed only by a man who was of their world however he might have rebelled against its standards. In both cases the rebellion was of the heart and had its origin in sobering experiences. But Galsworthy is far more open than Thackeray to the charge of allowing his heart to rule his head and manipulating the behavior of his characters into conformity with his sentiments. His zeal for causes often gets the better of his intelligence and even of his sense of humor. He knew this and scanned his books closely for "the soft touch." To the cautious reader, his best situations, his most dramatic moments are often suspect. But the largeness of the offending heart that has compassion for all sorts of unfortunate men and helpless animals compels sympathy if not assent. His books were, as he said, a criticism of one half of himself by the other.

It is doubtful whether the qualities of the man may be allowed to affect one's judgment of the artist but in the case of Galsworthy this is inescapable. He was a fine gentleman in the best sense of that phrase, and that fact informed everything he did or wrote. The consideration that postponed his marriage that no scandal might distress his father's last years, his unostentatious patriotism, his courageous indifference to conventions, his rarely failing fairness pervade his work with the soundness of character that is the basis of all wholly satisfying friendships.

Galsworthy's career reached its zenith at the close of the nineteen-twenties. Of the major Edwardian writers he had the widest appeal and had won the greatest popularity. Though he had refused a knighthood after World War I (considering a title incompatible with the principles embodied in his work), he accepted the Order of Merit in 1929. Thereafter he presided in Paris at the dinner of the PEN Club. In 1932 he received the Nobel Prize for literature. With these in addition to the usual public recognitions and honorary degrees of a literary man, he approached his death in 1933 full of the honors of eminent achievement.

That his reputation has greatly sunk since then is not surprising. He had been overesteemed, and later critical dispraise had its effect. But the *Forsyte Saga* is secure and there is enough other good work to assure his place among the greater of his contemporaries.

Collected Works: Manaton Edition (1922), Grove Edition (1932).
Fiction: As John Sinjohn: *From the Four Winds* (1897), *Jocelyn*
(1898), *Villa Rubein* (1900), *A Man of Devon* (1901). As John
Galsworthy: *The Island Pharisees* (1904), *Th Man of Property*
(1906), *The Country House* (1907), *Fraternity* (1909), *The Patrician*
(1911), *The Dark Flower* (1913), *The Freelands* (1915), *Beyond*
(1917), *Five Tales* (1918), *Saint's Progress* (1919), *In Chancery*
(1920), *Tatterdemalion* (1920), *Awakening* (1920), *To Let* (1921),
The Forsyte Saga (1922), *Captures* (1923), *The White Monkey*
(1924), *Caravan* (1925), *The Silver Spoon* (1926), *Swan Song* (1928),
A Modern Comedy (1929), *Maid in Waiting* (1931), *Flowering
Wilderness* (1932), *Over the River* [*One More River*] (1934), *The
Apple Tree* (1934), *The End of the Chapter* (1934). Plays: *Plays
(The Silver Box, Joy, Strife)* (1909), *Plays, Second Series (The
Eldest Son, The Little Dream, Justice)* (1912), *Plays, Third Series
(The Fugitive, The Pigeon, The Mob)* (1914), *Plays, Fourth Series
(A Bit o' Love, The Foundations, The Skin Game)* (1920), *Six
Short Plays (First and Last, The Little Man, Hall Marked, Defeat,
The Sun, Punch and Go)* (1921), *Plays, Fifth Series (A Family Man,
Loyalties, Windows)* (1923), *Plays, Sixth Series (The Forest, Old
English, The Show)* (1926), *Plays, Seventh Series (Escape, Exiled,
The Roof)* (1930), *The Winter Garden* (1935). Essays: *A Commen-
tary* (1908), *A Motley* (1910), *The Inn of Tranquillity* (1912), *The
Little Man and Other Satires* (1915), *A Sheaf* (1916); *The Land*
(1918), *Another Sheaf* (1919), *The Burning Spear* (1919), *Castles
in Spain* (1927), *Candelabra* (1932).

H. V. Marrot, *A Bibliography of the Works of John Galsworthy*
(1928), *The Life and Letters of John Galsworthy* (1936); G. H.
Fabes, *John Galsworthy, His First Editions* (1932); Leon Schalit
(E. E. Coe and T. Harbury translators), *John Galsworthy: A Survey*
(1929); Sheila Kaye Smith, *John Galsworthy* (1916); Natalie Cro-
man, *John Galsworthy* (1933); M. E. Reynolds, *Memories of John
Galsworthy* (n.d.); Joseph Conrad, *John Galsworthy: An Appreciation* (1922); Wilbur T. Cross, "John Galsworthy" in *Four Contemporary Novelists* (1930); F. M. Ford, "Galsworthy" in *Portraits
From Life* (1937); F. C. Steinmayer, "Der Werdegang von John
Galsworthy's Welt-und-Kunstanschauung," *Anglia*, N.F., XXXVII
(1925), 97-152, 244-266, 304-344, and N.F., XXXVIII (1926), 245-
286; Dorothy Martin, "Mr. Galsworthy as Artist and Reformer,"
Yale Rev., XIV (1929), 126-139; R. H. Coats, *John Galsworthy as
a Dramatic Artist* (1926); V. Dupont, *John Galsworthy the Dra-*

matic Artist (Paris, 1942); W. H. Trumbauer, *Gerhart Hauptmann and John Galsworthy: A Parallel* (Phila., 1917); Edouard Guyot, "Diagnostique du Forsytisme," *Rev. Anglo-Americaine,* X (1933), 290-300; F. T. Grove, "Morality in the Forsyte Saga," *Univ. Toronto Quar.,* XV (1945-46), 54-64; Erika Leimert, *Victorianismus bei Galsworthy* (Marburg, 1930); O. Funke, "Zur erlebten Rede bei Galsworthy," *Englische Studien,* LXIV (1929), 450-474; Henry Mark, *Die Verwendung der Mundart und des Slang in den Werken von John Galsworthy* (Breslau, 1936).

Arnold Bennett (1867-1931), a pushing Philistine and a sensitive artist, a puritan and a sybarite, is very hard to judge fairly. Though he is the most straightforward of writers and though he has written of himself more candidly than any of his contemporaries, both the man and his work are curiously elusive, almost impossible to comprehend in a statement that will adequately present at once their surprising strength and equally surprising weakness.

ARNOLD BENNETT

He came to London in 1888 at the age of twenty-one (he was Enoch Arnold Bennett then) to try his luck, but principally to escape his father's domination and his native town of Hanley, where he had passed his youth in the ugly, puritanical atmosphere of the Staffordshire potteries. He had behind him an average schooling, some knowledge of the law, gained in his father's office, and a taste of journalism as a contributor to a local paper. His self-confidence was unbounded.

Bennett's first twelve years in London (1888-1900) were a period of apprenticeship and discovery of his own powers.

He began as cost clerk to a law firm at twenty-five shillings a week, but though he did his work well, he was irresistibly drawn toward letters. In 1891 he went to live in Chelsea among artists, and under the influence of his new friends began to work at free lance journalism, though without much success. In 1893 he won a competition in *Tit Bits* and in the same year became, not, he says, by merit but by influence, assistant editor of *Woman,* a "smart" weekly. Two years later his story *A Letter Home* was published in *The Yellow Book* (July, 1895). When his chief retired shortly after, Bennett succeeded him and held the job for four years (1896-1900). During his connection with the paper Bennett not only learned the business of journalism, as he did everything else quickly and thoroughly, but found his feet as a writer. His first novel, *A Man from the North,* was published by Lane in 1898; he sold a number of serials to newspaper syndicates, and comedies to theatrical producers; he became dramatic critic to the *Academy* and principal reader to a publishing house. At thirty-three, satisfied that he could do well in any profitable branch of literature, he retired from journalism and from London, settling in Bedfordshire to follow his true vocation as a novelist.

In the years between this hegira and World War I, Bennett produced most of his best and a great deal of his worst fiction. *Anna of the Five Towns, Sacred and Profane Love, The Old Wives' Tale, Clayhanger, The Card,* and *Hilda Lessways,* established him unshakeably.

These, although the action often takes place in London or abroad, are regional stories of the Five Towns of Staffordshire. The characters are Bennett's own people, rebels in one way or another against the drab atmosphere that oppressed his youth. He writes of them with a shrewd, humorous understanding that gave him the reputation of being able to make the dullest people interesting. They are by no means all equally good—*Clayhanger,* containing a large element of autobiography, is the best—but taken all together, they constitute an impressive achievement in naturalistic fiction.

At the same time—just as poets write detective stories to pay their way—he was turning out light fiction of an entirely different sort. The *Grand Babylon Hotel, The Gates of Wrath, The Loot of Cities, The City of Pleasure,* and others are thrillers, set in an atmosphere of sham splendor and weighed down with all the claptrap of melodrama—frank pot-boilers. From them he made an excellent income, an important matter to a man who always frankly regarded literature as a business, his journal showing that he received £1200 for 375,000 words in 1907 and £16,000 for 160,000 words by 1912.

During these years Bedfordshire failed to hold Bennett, as all things did once the novelty had worn off. France drew him more and more. In 1903 he began to live in Paris: four years later he married there and made Fontainebleau his home until 1912, when he took a country house in Essex. During the First World War he was active on many civilian committees and was appointed by Lord Beaverbrook director of British propaganda in France. In 1916 he published *These Twain,* completing the Clayhanger trilogy (*Clayhanger, Hilda Lessways*), and two years later *The Pretty Lady,* the pathetic story of a French prostitute in London during the war.

In the years between the war and his death Bennett had ceased to write about the Five Towns. His later novels, *Lillian, Mr. Prohack, Riceyman Steps, Lord Raingo, Imperial Palace* deal mostly with London and reflect Bennett's enlarged experience, compensating in scope and variety for the intimate knowledge that distinguished his earlier work. *Riceyman Steps,* the grim tragedy of a miserly bookseller, and *Imperial Palace,* the prose epic of a great hotel, are easily the best. The latter is especially characteristic, embodying as it does Bennett's lifelong interest in superlative catering and efficient organization. Aside from these two, there is nothing really distinguished among his later books and on the whole they sustained rather than increased the reputation he had made by 1912.

Though he will be remembered chiefly as a novelist, Bennett was as versatile as he was prolific. His bibliography includes thirty-seven novels, seven volumes of short stories, fourteen volumes of essays and travels, ten of his popular "philosophies" (*The Human Machine, How to Live on Twenty-Four Hours a Day,* etc.) seventeen plays, to say nothing of his autobiographical writing (*The Truth About an Author, Journals*) and a mass of uncollected contributions to the press. In none of these was he a failure, though his plays are far below the level of his fiction. He was at his best as a critic, at his worst as an essayist because outside of literature he had few general ideas, only an intense interest in specific things. As "Jacob Tonson" in the *New Age* (1908-11) he made a reputation that gave him wide popular authority. His standard was high, though he was willing to recognize the public taste, he was honest, his perception, if uneven was acute, and his style vigorous, clear and often amusing. At the last he shared with Gosse, the critic, the power to assure the popular acceptance of a new book or author.

"I began as a journalist," Bennett wrote in *The Savour of Life* (1928), "and I have never ceased to be a journalist." And further—"I write for money. I write for as much money as I can get." This commercial attitude toward the business of authorship he insisted upon throughout his life. It was not a pose: it was part of a thoroughly sincere materialism, an absorbing interest in things, a desire to own them, to know about them. In his novels plot and character are in constant danger of being lost in details of milieu, especially of ways of earning a living. His people "get on" or are desperately trying to, and how they do it is as important to him as to them. He held that "the evidence of the superficies is valuable" and his works are pre-eminently a document of the superficies of the Edwardian world. If the artist in him had not been of real magnitude he might have been no more than a writer of first rate "features."

Artistically Bennett was formed abroad. Until he was mature his knowledge of the English classics was astonishingly imperfect; many of them he never esteemed. He felt at home in France, and Gallic culture and thought came easily to him. Flaubert, the Goncourts, Zola, and Dostoievsky were his literary models. He acquired the French passion for form and discipline of style. As with George Moore, the acquisition of a foreign culture totally unconnected with his native tradition, left a part of him, the cocky provincial, isolated and unmodified and thus often betrayed him into appalling lapses of style and taste. He despised English puritanism for its artistic timidity, yet whenever he attempted a Gallic truth of naturalism his early puritanism made him recoil from his own audacities, leaving them ineffectual and sometimes silly. France refined to fastidiousness his natural love of excellence, but his English provincialism too often interpreted it in terms of shops, trains, and hotels. He never resolved this conflict.

Throughout life Bennett had the superb self-confidence of genius. The young man of thirty-three who wrote a book about his career was certain of his success. He succeeded in the world beyond question: in art his complete success is not so clear. He will probably be considered third among the major Edwardian novelists.

FICTION: *A Man From the North* (1898), *The Grand Babylon Hotel* (1902), *Anna of the Five Towns* (1902), *Leonora* (1903), *The Gates of Wrath* (1903), *A Great Man* (1904); *Teresa of Watling Street* (1904), *The Loot of Cities* (1905), *Sacred and Profane Love* (1905), re-published as *The Book of Carlotta* (1911), *Tales of the Five Towns* (1905), *Whom God Hath Joined* (1906), *Hugo* (1906), *The Grim Smile of the Five Towns* (1907), *The City of Pleasure* (1907),

The Ghost (1907), *The Old Wives' Tale* (1908), *Buried Alive*
(1908), *The Glimpse* (1909), *Clayhanger* (1910), *Helen With the
High Hand* (1910), *The Card* [*Denry the Audacious*] (1911), *Hilda
Lessways* (1911), *The Matador of the Five Towns* (1912), *The
Regent* [*The Old Adam*] (1913), *The Price of Love* (1914), *These
Twain* (1915), *The Lion's Share* (1916), *The Pretty Lady* (1918),
The Roll Call (1918), *Lillian* (1922), *Mr. Prohack* (1922), *Ricey-
man Steps* (1923), *Elsie and the Child* (1924), *Lord Raingo* (1924),
The Woman Who Stole Everything (1927), *Accident* (1928), *The
Strange Vanguard* [*The Vanguard*] (1928), *Imperial Palace* (1930).
PLAYS: *Cupid and Common Sense* (1908), *What the Public Wants*
(1910), *The Honeymoon* (1911), *The Great Adventure* (1913), *The
Title* (1918), *Sacred and Profane Love* (1919), *Judith* (1919), *Body
and Soul* (1921), *The Love Match* (1922), *Don Juan de Marana*
(1923), *The Bright Island* (1924). MISCELLANEOUS: *The Truth
About an Author* (1903), *Things That Interested Me* (1906), *The
Reasonable Life* (1907), *The Human Machine* (1908), *How to Live
on Twenty-four Hours a Day* (1908), *Literary Taste* (1909), *Those
United States* [*Your United States*] (1912), *Paris Nights* (1913),
From the Log of the Velsa (1914), *The Author's Craft* (1914),
Books and Persons (1917), *Self and Self-Management* (1918),
Things that Have Interested Me (1921, Second Series 1923, Third
Series 1926), *The Savour of Life* (1928), *The Journals of Arnold
Bennett* (1932-33).

George Lafourcade, *Arnold Bennett: A Study* (1939); F. J. Darton,
Arnold Bennett (1915); Marguerite Bennett, *Arnold Bennett*
(1925), *My Arnold Bennett* (1931); L. G. Johnson, *Arnold Bennett
of the Five Towns* (1924); Rebecca West, *Arnold Bennett Himself*
(1931); Dorothy C. Bennett, *Arnold Bennett* (1935); "Geoffrey
West" (Geoffrey H. Wells), *The Problem of Arnold Bennett* (1932);
E. Massoulard, "Die Romantische Elemente in Arnold Bennett,"
Bonner Studien, XXXIV (1938), 1-86; W. T. Cross, "Arnold Ben-
nett" in *Four Contemporary Novelists* (1930); Virginia Woolf, *Mr.
Bennett and Mrs. Brown* (1924); J. B. Simons, *Arnold Bennett and
His Novels* (Oxford, 1936); B. W. Downs, "Arnold Bennett," *No.
Amer. Rev.*, CCXIX (1924), 71-78; J. B. Priestley, "Mr. Arnold
Bennett," *London Mercury*, IX (1924), 394-406; Louis Tellier,
"Arnold Bennett, ou de la mutilation voluntaire," *Rev. Anglo-
Americaine*, XI (1933-34), 313-321; Paul Dottin, "Arnold Bennett,"
Revue de France, XIe An, 4 (1931), 176-184; Orlo Williams, "The
Old Wives' Tale," *National Rev.*, XCIX (1932), 387-397.

George Moore (1852-1933) was the eldest son of George Henry Moore, M.P., of Moore Hall, County Mayo. The Moores were an old family in the tradition of Anglo-Irish squires and it was a disap-
pointment to his parents when the heir failed to develop the character needed to carry on that tradition. A "slow boy" at Oscott, the English school to which he was sent, he showed none of the qualities of the soldier or the country gentleman to compensate for his lack of scholarship. Consequently he drifted into ado-
lescence with a feeling of in-
feriority, of being an ugly duckling for whom there was no place in the family's scheme of things. His father left him

GEORGE MOORE

largely to himself to pick up a knowledge of the world from the tenantry and the grooms of the racing stable. He read indiscriminately and blundered into the discovery of Shelley, whose spell remained upon him for life.

In 1869, when Moore was seventeen, the family moved to London to be near the House of Commons. It was there, through the influence of a cousin, that Moore first became interested in art and for a while took lessons at the South Kensington Museum school. He continued to be an avid reader of the poetry to which Shelley had led him, though his statement that he had read most of the English poets before he was twenty-one is probably inaccurate. In 1870 his father died and three years later at his majority he became master of the heavily mortgaged estate of 12,500 acres that gave him an income of about £500 a year. On this he went to Paris to study art. Three years in the ateliers convinced him that he could never be a painter and he turned, rather feebly and affectedly at first, to literature. Though his work of these days is negligible—two plays and two volumes of immature and derivative verse—Paris gave him his vision of the world of culture and the acquaintance of artists and writers, especially Manet and Zola. Admiration of Balzac followed. The café Nouvelle Athènes in the Place Pigalle was his not wholly adequate substitute for the formal education he never had.

When the Irish Land League troubles of 1879 cut off his income from the estate, he returned to London to write seriously for a living, taking chambers in the Temple. After a period of art criticism and reviewing, he published his first novel, *A Modern Lover,* in 1883. In 1894 he published *Esther Waters,* an unsparingly realistic story of a betrayed servant girl. By this time he was the author of eight novels, none of them except the last remarkable, all in the tradition of French naturalism. *Esther Waters* is a work of considerable power, but the fact that it shared the moral censure of Hardy's last novels had much to do with making the reputation of the book and its author. *Celibates,* a volume of short stories and *Evelyn Innes,* a novel inferior to *Esther Waters,* complete his fiction of this period.

In London Moore had seen much of W. B. Yeats, who in 1899 carried him off to Dublin to help in the literary revival going forward there. Moore was not reluctant, his French culture made him contemptuous of English art, and he hated the brash jingoism of the Boer War period. He was full of enthusiasm for the Celtic Revival, but before long he found Ireland bigoted and unsympathetic. He renounced Catholicism and called himself a Protestant. After 1906 his discontent grew steadily and in 1911 he left Ireland for good. In one view this time was unproductive; he published *The Untilled Field,* a volume of short stories, in 1903, *The*

Lake, a novel, in 1905, *Reminiscences of the Impressionist Painters* and *Memoirs of My Dead Life* in 1906, and nothing further until he went to England. But Ireland gave him abundant material, and in the sterile years, 1906-1911, he conceived or began much that appeared later.

Upon his return to London, Moore took his well-known house in Ebury Street, where he spent the rest of his days. Here he produced the first fruits of his Irish sojourn, the trilogy *Hail and Farewell (Ave,* 1911, *Salve,* 1912, *Vale,* 1914). This Shandean mixture of inaccurate autobiography, malicious gossip, and prejudiced criticism is, in spite of a hundred faults of taste and style, a work of unmistakable genius. So too *Avowals* (1919) and *Conversations in Ebury Street* (1924), books of much the same sort. His novels of this period show a completely new manner of treating historic romance with antique simplicity. *The Brook Kerith* (1916) and *Heloise and Abelard* (1921), which Moore called the only prose epics in English, are his finest work. The deceptive naturalness of their manner effectively conceals the heavy labors of research and the discipline of a new style that went to their making. After *Ulick and Soracha* (1926) he wrote nothing of any note.

Moore's plays of which he wrote eight, from the early *Worldliness* (1874?) to the amusing Shakespearean burlesque *The Making of an Immortal* (1937), add little if anything to his reputation: he himself had a poor opinion of some of them. Their theatrical history is unimportant.

It has been said of Moore that he "conducted his education in public"; certainly his books, and it is part of their interest, show more than any other major writer's his gropings toward artistic maturity. Many of his faults remained undisciplined to the end, but it is remarkable that he should have formed upon his unadmirable character, pretentious, untrustworthy, and somewhat vulgar, an artist of great variety and subtlety of expression and, though inconstantly, of power and conscientiousness. All but his worst lapses are redeemed by a passionate love of beauty in which few English writers have exceeded him.

COLLECTED WORKS: Collected Works of George Moore. The Carra Edition. Printed for subscribers only (1922), *The Works of George Moore* (1927-30). FICTION: *A Modern Lover* (1883), *A Mummer's Wife* (1885), *A Drama in Muslin* (1886), *A Mere Accident* (1887), *Spring Days* (1888), *Mike Fletcher* (1889), *Vain Fortune* (1892), *Esther Waters* (1894), *Celibates* (1895), *Evelyn Innes* (1898), *Sister Teresa* (1901), *The Untilled Field* (1903), *The Lake* (1905), *Muslin,* revision of *A Drama in Muslin* (1915), *The Brook Kerith* (1916), *Lewis Seymour and Some Women,* based on *A Modern Lover* (1917), *A Story Teller's Holiday* (1918), *Héloise and Abelard* (1921), *Fragments from Héloise and Abelard,* additions and corrections (1921), *In Single Strictness* (1922), *Ulick and Soracha* (1926), *Peronnick the Fool* (1926), *Celibate Lives,* revision of *In Single Strictness* (1927), *Aphrodite in Aulis* (1930), *The Talking Pine* (1930), *A Flood* (1930). PLAYS: *Worldliness* (1874), *Martin Luther,* with Bernard Lopez (1879), *The Strike at Arlingford* (1893), *The Bending of the Bough* (1900), *The Apostle* (1911), *Esther Waters* (1913), *Elizabeth Cooper* (1913), *The Coming of Gabrielle* (1920), *The Making of an Immortal* (1927), *The Passing of the Essenes* (1930). MISCELLANEOUS: *Flowers of Passion* (1878), *Pagan Poems* (1881), *Literature at Nurse* (1885), *Parnell and His Island* (1887), *Confessions of a Young Man* (1888), *Impressions and Opinions* (1891), *Modern Painting* (1893), *The Royal Academy, 1895* (1895), *Reminiscences of the Impressionist Painters* (1906), *Memoirs of My Dead Life* (1906), *Hail and Farewell* (1911-14), *Avowals* (1919), *Conversations in Ebury Street* (1924), *Pure Poetry: An Anthology,* [*An Anthology of Pure Poetry*] (1924), *The Pastoral Loves of Daphnis and Chloe* (1924,) *A Communication to My Friends* (1933). LETTERS: *Letters from George Moore to Ed. Dujardin, 1886-1922* (1929), *Letters of George Moore, with an Introduction by John Eglinton* (1942).

"Bibliographies of Modern Authors, George Moore," *London Mercury,* III (1921), 660-661; Joseph Hone, *The Life of George Moore* (1936); Charles Morgan, *Epitaph on George Moore* (1935); W. B. Yeats, *Autobiographies* (1938); John Freeman, *A Portrait of George Moore in a Study of His Work* (1922); B. H. Clark, "George Moore At Work," *Amer. Mercury,* IV (1925), 202-209;

Daniel Halevy, "George Moore," *Rev. de Paris*, XXIXᵉ An, 5 (1922), 763-770; R. P. Sechler, *George Moore: A Disciple of Walter Pater* (Phila., 1931); W. D. Ferguson, *The Influence of a Flaubert on George Moore* (Phila., 1934); S. M. Steward, "J. K. Huysmans and George Moore," *Retrospective Rev.*, XXV (1934),197-206; Douglas Cooper, "George Moore and Modern Art," *Horizon*, II (1945), 113-130; J. Middleton Murry, *Wrap Me Up In My Aubusson Carpet* (1924); Geraint Goodwin, *Conversations With George Moore* (1929).

George Gissing (1857-1903) was one of the most pathetically tragic figures of modern letters, afflicted all his life with ill health, poverty, and troubles largely of his own making. The son of a provincial chemist, he showed as a boy promise of a brilliant scholarly career until he was expelled from college in Manchester for stealing from his fellow students in order to help a prostitute whom he wanted to marry and reform. He went to jail for his thefts and thereafter was helped by friends to a passage to the United States, where he spent a year in vain attempts to support himself at whatever work he could get. At twenty he returned to England and

GEORGE GISSING

married the girl for whose sake he had lost his chances. She was now thoroughly dissolute and for the ten years until her death made his life a burden. A second marriage was almost equally unhappy.

From the time of his marriage Gissing supported himself —meagerly at all times—by fiction, journalism, and tutor-

ing. His first novel, *Workers in the Dawn* was published
at his own cost in 1880, but recognition did not come to
him until he had written *Demos* six years later. *New Grub
Street* (1891), embodying some of his experiences in America, has been one of his most popular books. In all he wrote
twenty-two novels besides works of travel and criticism. The
moderate success of these relieved him of the hardest pressure of poverty, but to write them he had to drive a tired
mind and body relentlessly. At forty-six he died of pneu-
monia in the south of France.

Dickens was Gissing's literary model, and it was in the
world of Dickens, the world of the poor and the shabby
genteel, that Gissing passed his whole life—for him there
was no happy escape into prosperity and fame. Consequently
he wrote of that world without the humor and easy optimism of Dickens, though too often with his melodrama.
His novels are sincere, workmanlike studies of the lives of
the unfortunate and submerged, "the ignobly decent," often
showing real strength of characterization and local color,
but not very moving, because he had no real temperamental
identification with his subjects; it was only tragic accident
that had thrown him among them. His true world, as
Veranilda and *By the Ionian Sea* sufficiently show, was the
world of classic Rome, leisured, intellectual, aristocratic.
The need of money made him the bitter chronicler of his
social purgatory. Except for the pseudo-autobiographical
The Private Papers of Henry Ryecroft (1903) Gissing has
become a neglected author. Standing between the Victorians
and the modern realists, he followed the old-fashioned technique of the older school and dared not carry the candor of
his social explorations so far as did the following generation. But like many an outmoded writer he showed a way
to those who were to surpass him; his influence went far
in the shaping of the socially-conscious novel in Edwardian
and early Georgian fiction.

FICTION: *Workers in the Dawn* (1880), *The Unclassed* (1884), *Isabel Clarendon* (1886), *Demos* (1886), *Thyrza* (1887), *A Life's Morning* (1888), *The Nether World* (1889), *The Emancipated* (1890), *New Grub Street* (1891), *Denzil Quarrier* (1892), *Born in Exile* (1892), *The Odd Women* (1893), *In the Year of Jubilee* (1894), *Eve's Ransom* (1895), *The Paying Guest* (1895), *Sleeping Fires* (1895), *The Whirlpool* (1897), *Human Odds and Ends* (1898), *The Town Traveller* (1898), *The Crown of Life* (1899), *Our Friend the Charlatan* (1901), *Veranilda* (1904), *Will Warburton* (1905), *The House of Cobwebs* (1906). MISCELLANEOUS: *Charles Dickens: A Critical Study* (1898), *By the Ionian Sea* (1901), *The Private Papers of Henry Ryecroft* (1903). LETTERS: *Letters of George Gissing to Members of his Family,* ed. A. and E. Gissing (1927).

Frank Swinnerton, *George Gissing: A Critical Study* (1912); R. C. McKay, *George Gissing and His Critic Frank Swinnerton* (Phila., 1933); May Yates, *George Gissing: An Appreciation* (Manchester, England, 1933); Anton Weber, *George Gissing und die Soziale Frage* (Leipzig, 1932); S. V. Gapp, *George Gissing, Classicist* (Phila., 1936).

Mrs. Humphrey Ward (1851-1920) was born Mary Augusta Arnold, a granddaughter of Dr. Arnold of Rugby and a niece of Matthew Arnold. She was educated in England to which her father, Thomas Arnold, a fervent but unstable religious thinker, had removed his family from Australia where his daughter was born. When she was nineteen she met among the intellectual company who frequented her father's house at Oxford, T. Humphrey Ward, a don of Brasenose College. They were married in 1872. Ward, of course, forfeited his Fellowship by marriage and he and Mrs. Ward both turned to journalism for their support.

In 1884 Mrs. Ward published her first novel, *Miss Bretherton.* Four years later *Robert Elsmere* startled the whole English-speaking world with its challenge of accepted religious standards. For the next twenty years her books were avidly read and discussed, although critics found her talent didactic and critical rather than creative. *The Testing of*

Diana Mallory (1908) was her last widely popular book and thereafter the number of her readers rapidly declined. In her later years, after 1913, she wrote far too much. During the First World War her veteran talents and the prestige of her name were employed in propaganda to arouse American sympathy for England. She died in the spring of 1920 in London where she had lived ever since her marriage.

Mrs. Ward's work has fallen into almost complete oblivion, the common fate of fiction that is intensely concerned with issues of the day that lose all controversial interest once they have become history. It takes the genius of Dickens or Disraeli to arouse our interest in the problems that vexed our great-grandfathers. And Mrs. Ward with all her candor and keen intelligence in discussion had not the creative power to animate her work beyond her own time. Moreover many of her views have been discredited: tireless and generous in social work, she was no democrat; one of the most intelligent and independent Englishwomen of her day, she was bitterly opposed to women's suffrage. Her novels now have chiefly a reference interest for those who want to understand the social order that passed away during the First World War.

Mrs. Ward's sister, Julia, married Leonard Huxley, so that Julian and Aldous Huxley are her nephews.

COLLECTED EDITION: *The Writings of Mrs. Humphrey Ward* (1909-12). AUTOBIOGRAPHY: *A Writer's Recollections* (1918). NOVELS: *Miss Bretherton* (1884), *Robert Elsmere* (1888), *The History of David Grieve* (1892), *Marcella* (1894), *The Story of Bessie Costrell* (1895), *Sir George Tressady* (1896), *Hilbeck of Bannisdale* (1898), *Eleanor* (1900), *Lady Rose's Daughter* (1903), *The Marriage of William Ashe* (1905), *Fenwick's Career* (1906), *The Testing of Diana Mallory* (1908), *Marriage a la Mode* (1909), *Canadian Born* (1910), *The Case of Richard Meynell* (1911), *The Compton Family* (1913), *The Mating of Lydia* (1913), *Delia Blancheflower* (1914), *Eltham House* (1915), *A Great Success* (1916), *Lady Connie* (1916), *"Missing"* (1917), *The War and Elizabeth* [*Elizabeth's Campaign*] (1918),

Cousin Philip (1919), *Helena* (1919), *Harvest* (1920). MISCELLA-
NEOUS: *William Thomas Arnold,* with C. E. Montague (Manchester, England, 1906), *L'effort de l'Angleterre* [*England's Effort*]
(1916), *Toward the Goal* (1917), *Fields of Victory* (1919).

Janet Penrose Trevelyan, *The Life of Mrs. Humphrey Ward*
(1923); D. H. Davies, *Beiträge zur Stilistik Mrs. Humphrey Wards*
(Marburg, Germany, 1907); Firmin Roz, "Mme. Humphrey Ward"
in *Le Roman anglais contemporain* (Paris, 1912).

Maurice (Henry) Hewlett (1861-1923) was born at Wey-
bridge, Surrey, the son of Henry Gay Hewlett, Keeper of
the Land Revenue Records. He left school at eighteen and
entered the study of law at Gray's Inn without attending a
university. In 1888 he married before completing his studies
and when called to the Bar at the age of thirty he did not
practice but turned to literature as a profession.

The cult of Italy created by Browning, Ruskin, and Pater
was then at its height, and to Italy Hewlett went to find
material and inspiration for his work. His early writing,
Earthwork Out of Tuscany (1895), *The Masque of Dead
Florentines* (1895) and *Little Novels of Italy* (1899) is of
the precious, ivory-tower school of the nineties, though better than most work of its kind. Artificial and derivative as
it is, it shows a writer with real power of style.

Hewlett found his true metier in *The Forest Lovers*
(1898), a romance of the Middle Ages which enjoyed a
great popularity. Then for two years he succeeded his father
as Keeper of the Land Revenue Records. *Richard Yea-and-
Nay* (1900), with Richard Coeur de Lion for its hero, and
The Queen's Quair (1904) thoroughly established his reputation as an historical novelist. *The Queen's Quair* was his
own favorite and that of the critics but the public has always preferred *Richard Yea-and-Nay* for its adventurous
and romantic appeal.

Hewlett next produced a trilogy of contemporary life—
Halfway House (1908), *Open Country* (1909), and *Rest Har-*

row (1910)—which was disappointing to both readers and reviewers. Hewlett's mind was scholarly and retrospective, perfectly suited for historical fiction but not for the portrayal of his own society. It was now apparent that he had no great power of handling character unsupported by the glamor of historic setting, and he prudently looked around for new historical material. This he found in the Icelandic Sagas from which the best of his later novels are drawn. These tales such as *Frey and His Wife* (1916), *Thorgils* (1917), *Gudrid the Fair* (1918) and *The Outlaw* (1919) have, naturally, less picturesqueness than his early books but are much better stories.

Besides his novels he wrote a number of short stories, the best probably those in *The New Canterbury Tales* (1901), several volumes of verse and several more of essays. His verse, even the much admired *Song of the Plow* (1916), is of minor importance. His later essays are probably the best work he did, mature and balanced, easy and natural in style, and enriched with a deep knowledge and appreciation of country life.

In the years of his popularity, Hewlett made a handsome fortune—reputed to have been £80,000—from his writing. His wife, a Victorian parson's daughter, made another of her own by building airplanes for the government during the First World War. Neither seems to have cared much for money, however, and by lavish generosity they parted with most of it, living simply and contentedly in the country. Hewlett's last years were spent in a cottage in Wiltshire where he wrote his last four volumes of essays.

Hewlett has suffered, like many of his contemporaries, an undeserved neglect through the repudiation of everything Edwardian by the post-war generation. Unfortunately his early novels were occasionally blemished by the "Wardour Street" theatricality that is found so abundantly in Scott and by the time his saga tales appeared public attention had shifted to the work of younger writers produced by the war. Yet his merit deserves continued reading. There is no better historical novelist between Stevenson and Robert Graves, and, within his field, no better essayist of the nineteen-twenties.

FICTION: *The Forest Lovers* (1898), *Little Novels of Italy* (1899), *The Life and Death of Richard Yea-and-Nay* (1900), *New Canterbury Tales* (1901), *The Queen's Quair* (1904), *The Fool Errant* (1905), *Fond Adventures* (1905), *The Stooping Lady* (1907), *Halfway House* (1908), *The Spanish Jade* (1908), *Open Country* (1909), *The Ruinous Face* (1909), *Rest Harrow* (1910), *Letters to Sanchia* (1910), *Brazenhead the Great* (1911), *The Song of Renny* (1911), *The Birth of Roland* (1911), *Mrs. Lancelot* (1912), *Lore of Proserpine* (1913), *Bendish* (1913), *A Lover's Tale* (1914), *The Little Iliad* (1915), *Frey and His Wife* (1916), *Love and Lucy* (1916), *Thorgils of Treadholt [Thorgils]* (1917), *Gugrid the Fair* (1918), *The Outlaw* (1919), *The Light Heart* (1920), *Manwaring* (1920). ESSAYS: *Earthwork Out of Tuscany* (1895), *Saint Gervase of Plessy* (1900), *The Road in Tuscany* (1904), *In a Green Shade* (1920), *Wiltshire Essays* (1921), *Extemporary Essays* (1922), *Last Essays* (1924).

P. H. Muir, "A Bibliography of the First Editions of Books by Maurice Henry Hewlett (1868-1923)," Suppl., *Bookman's Jour.* (1927), "A Short Life of Maurice Hewlett with a Bibliographical List of his Writings," *Wiltshire Historical Magazine,* XLII (1923), 374-377; "Bibliographies of Modern Authors, Maurice Hewlett," *London Mercury,* I (1920), 625-626; A. B. Sutherland, *Maurice Hewlett: Historical Romancer* (1938); J. B. Priestley, "Maurice Hewlett's Later Verse and Prose," *London Mercury,* VIII (1923), 368-379, reprinted in *Figures in Modern Literature* (1924); Stephen Gwynn, "Maurice Hewlett," *Edinburgh Rev.,* CCXXXIX (1924), 61-72; W. H. Graham, "Maurice Hewlett," *Fortnightly Rev.,* CXVIII (1925), 47-63.

As the creator of Sherlock Holmes, **Arthur Conan Doyle (1859-1930)** occupies a unique position in modern letters. To the reader of modern detective fiction the famous stories do not seem, in spite of the praise of devotees, supremely clever in either plot or atmosphere, nor Holmes himself remarkable except for his encyclopedic knowledge. That is because Doyle took the detective story where Wilkie Collins had left it and brought it almost at once to its high modern development. Thus Sherlock Holmes as the archetype of almost all fictional detectives since his day has become a legend, the most famous character in English letters, known even to the illiterate and preserved by the screen and radio into another age.

Doyle was born in Edinburgh, the son of an unsuccessful civil servant and grandson of the famous Irish cartoonist, John Doyle. As the family were pious Catholics Doyle was educated in Jesuit schools in England and Austria. In 1876 he entered the medical school at the University of Edinburgh and five years later began the practice of medicine. After going to sea as surgeon, first in a whaler and then in a West African passenger liner, he established an office and awaited a practice. It was the failure of the latter to support him that drove him to writing.

The character of Holmes was built largely upon recollections of Joseph Bell, a lecturer in anatomy at Edinburgh. Holmes made his first appearance in 1887 in a full-length novel, *A Study in Scarlet,* with a background of London and early Utah. Three years later appeared *The Sign of the Four*. Both of these were revenge plots in which the story behind the crime shared the interest with the process of detection. But it was not until the adventures began to appear as short stories in the *Strand Magazine* that the great popularity of Holmes began. Thereafter Doyle stuck with one exception to the episodic story which threw all the emphasis on the achievements of Holmes. The exception was the best, and probably the most popular, of all the series, *The Hound of the Baskervilles* (1902), a novel that combined the full excitement of detection with an atmosphere of authentically "gothick" terror. The Holmes cycle proper ended with *His Last Bow* (1917); *The Case Book of Sherlock*

Holmes (1927) was a not completely successful attempt to revive it.

But though Sherlock Holmes made his fortune, it was as an historical romancer that Doyle wished to be known. In 1888 he wrote *Micah Clarke,* a really fine story of Monmouth's rebellion, and two years later *The White Company,* his far better known picture of the days of Edward III. *Rodney Stone* dealt with the sporting world of the Regency, the "Gerard" books with Napoleon's campaigns, and *Sir Nigel* (1906) again with the Hundred Years' War. These show a real gift of narration and an ability to create absorbing plot and atmosphere but not character. The best of them, *The White Company,* owes a good deal to Reade's *The Cloister and the Hearth.* They are stories of exciting action, singularly weak in "romantic" interest or entirely without it. Inevitably, they have become schoolboy reading, the better reading of the better schoolboy, like the novels of Marrayat, and like those capable of being enjoyed again in middle age—but they are fatally immature. He must be put among the great yarn spinners, to whom, regrettably, literary appraisals can never do justice in proportion to the pleasure they give us.

In 1912 he began to weave tales of adventure in a new vein about the leonine figure of Professor Challenger and in 1915 wrote his only detective story outside the Holmes cycle, *The Valley of Fear,* based on the history of the "Molly Maguires," a gang who terrorized the coal regions of Pennsylvania. In all Conan Doyle wrote some fifty volumes of fiction. With literary success Doyle abandoned medicine for good. He soon attained affluence and public recognition. In 1902 he was knighted and appointed Deputy-Lieutenant of Surrey—but for political rather than literary services. He was twice married, in 1885 and in 1907.

The death of his son during World War I was a turning point in Doyle's life. He had left the Catholic church many years before, and now the desire to communicate with the dead led him, with many of his generation, to spiritualism. Thereafter, with Sir Oliver Lodge, he devoted himself to psychical research and to propaganda for his belief. What he then wrote, however interesting, was of no importance as literature, and in any case the quality of his work had fallen off steadily since about 1910.

AUTOBIOGRAPHY: *Memories and Adventures* (1924). FICTION: *A Study in Scarlet* (1887), *Micah Clarke* (1889), *The Sign of the Four* (1890), *The White Company* (1891), *The Adventures of Sherlock Holmes* (1892), *The Great Shadow* (1893), *The Memoires of Sherlock Holmes* (1894), *Round the Red Lamp* (1894), *The Stark Munro Letters* (1895), *Rodney Stone* (1896), *The Exploits of Brigadier Gerard* (1896), *Uncle Bernac* (1897), *The Hound of the Baskervilles* (1902), *The Adventures of Gerard* (1903), *The Return of Sherlock Holmes* (1905), *Sir Nigel* (1906), *The Last Galley* (1911), *The Lost World* (1912), *The Valley of Fear* (1914), *His Last Bow* (1917), *The Great Keinplatz Experiment* (1919), *The Last of the Legions* (1922), *The Black Doctor* (1925), *The Case Book of Sherlock Holmes* (1927), *The Maracot Deep* (1929).

John Dickson Carr, *The Life of Sir Arthur Conan Doyle* (1948); Coulson Kernahan, "Personal Memories of Sherlock Holmes," *London Quar.*, CLIX (1934), 449-460.

"Saki." (Hector Hugh Munro, 1870-1916) was born at Akyab, Burma, where his father was inspector-general of police. "The Munro clan," writes E. H. Munro, his sister, "has always been composed of fighters and writers. Our grandfather [was] a colonel in the Indian Army. My mother's mother . . . .belonged to the Macnab clan. So Hector was Celtic on both sides of his family." At the age of two he was brought home to England with his elder brother and sister, and left in the care of two maiden aunts near Barnstaple, North Devon. The aunts, to judge from Miss Munro's account of them, were singularly unamiable women whose government of their charges was a spiteful tyranny. Unhap-

piness is often the lot of Anglo-Indian children, and Hector
Munro endured it stoically, but it left a deep impression
on him as his work shows. He attended school at Exmouth
and Bedford until he was
seventeen, and then for two
years was taught by his father
with whom he travelled widely
on the continent. In 1893
Munro left England to join
his father's service, the Burma
Military Police, in which his
elder brother had preceded
him. A year of Burma broke
his health completely and he
returned to Devon to recover.

HECTOR HUGH MUNRO

Those who know only the
Saki of the stories are often
unaware that Munro was a
journalist first of all. In 1896,
having recovered from his Burmese experience, he went to
London where be began by writing satires for the *Westminster Gazette*. In 1902 he became foreign correspondent
for the *Morning Post* and for the next six years represented
it in the Balkans, in Warsaw, in St. Petersburg (whence he
reported the Red Sunday of 1905), and in Paris. In 1908,
after his father's death, he settled in London, writing for
several journals, publishing his only novel, *The Unbearable
Bassington* (1912), and the Saki stories. He was still known
chiefly as a political writer and satirist.

Although he was forty-four when war in 1914 broke out,
Munro enlisted early in the 22d Royal Fusiliers, refused a
commission, and went out to France as a corporal. He was
from all testimony an excellent soldier. He was killed by
a sniper at Beaumont-Hamel in November, 1916.

The stories for which Munro is gratefully remembered

were collected in a series of volumes beginning with *Reginald* (1904) and ending with *The Square Egg and Other Sketches* (1924). Most of them recount with remarkable swiftness and economy the adventures of those insouciant young men Reginald and Clovis. Readers will recognize them as the literary ancestors of Bertie Wooster, but as often with the ancestors of aristocratic nincompoops superior in character and attainments to their notorious descendant. They are "nuts," but highly intelligent "nuts," purposeful and consistent in their devastating raids upon stupidity and convention, suave and subtle in their methods. It is not hard to trace them to Saki's boyhood and to the child's desire for revenge upon the adult world. All that is complacent, tiresome, or pretentious in maturity is fair game for them, and the child in the reader enters delightedly into a game that gives its instinctive derision of grown-up ways the fullest satisfaction.

The world of Reginald and Clovis shows the lighter side of Saki but he was not all of one mood. "Both aunts," says Miss Munro, "were guilty of mental cruelty: we often longed for revenge with an intensity I suspect we inherited from our Highland ancestry." The revenge that Saki took in "The Lumber Room" is merely amusing and might have belonged to the childhood of Clovis, but in "Srendi Vashtar" there is a rather horrible, if understandable, cruelty. In several other stories, such as "The Music on The Hill" and "The Wolves of Cernogratz" the sombre side of the Celtic imagination is very effectively at work. "Esme" is a perfect fusion of the macabre and the comic. In these as in his lighter stories Saki is a master of swift effect, creating a situation in two or three sentences and touching even his climaxes so lightly that only the alert will appreciate them at once. It is this delicacy and sureness of touch, rather than his impish humor, that gives his work its durability.

Though the sketches collected in *The Square Egg* were

written from the Western Front, the tales of Saki belong to the prewar years of the century and often require a knowledge of that lost, untroubled time for their full relish. Nevertheless the omnibus edition of them published in the United States in 1930 ran through ten printings in thirteen years. Whatever may be topical in Saki, there is enough of the perennial human comedy to assure him a high place among the writers of the short story.

STORIES AND SKETCHES: *Reginald* (1904), *Reginald in Russia* (1910), *The Chronicles of Clovis* (1912), *Beasts and Super Beasts* (1914), *The Toys of Peace and Other Papers* (1919), *The Square Egg and Other Sketches* (1924), *The Complete Short Stories of Saki* (1930). NOVEL: *The Unbearable Bassington* (1912).

Biography by E. H. Munro in *The Complete Short Stories of Saki* (1930).

One of the most popular short story writers before the First World War was **William Wymark Jacobs (1863-1943)**, whose yarns cleverly illustrated by Will Owen were for years a regular feature of the *Strand Magazine.* He was born in Wapping (H. M. Tomlinson's "shipping parish") where his father managed the South Devon Wharf. From school he entered the Post Office as a Civil Service clerk, remaining there until he had turned a taste for writing into professional success. In 1899 with three books published, he resigned and for the next twenty years held his public with a steady flow of amusing but monotonously similar stories.

Arnold Bennett found Jacobs lacking in the curiosity that broadens and matures the mind. It is true; his last books are exactly like his first; his rare fertility in the invention of incident seldom rose above the schoolboyish hoax or practical joke set forth with all the obviousness of a cartoon. The fun, though, was undeniably funny of its kind and he could achieve shrewd touches of characterization though never sustained character. In tales of horror, of which he wrote a few, he had a small mastery. "The Monkey's Paw" is a classic in its field, often reprinted. But generally he is a supreme comic-strip artist in prose, repeating endlessly the ludicrous blunders and infantile revenges of impossible sailors and rustics.

FICTION: *Many Cargoes* (1896), *The Skipper's Wooing* (1897), *More Cargoes* (1898), *A Master of Craft* (1900), *Light Freights* (1901), *The Lady of the Barge* (1902), *At Sunwich Port* (1902), *Odd Craft* (1903), *Dialstone Lane* (1904), *Captains All* (1905), *Short Cruises* (1907), *Salthaven* (1908), *Sailors' Knots* (1909), *Ship's Company* (1911), *Night Watches* (1914), *The Castaway* (1917), *Deep Waters* (1919), *Sea Whispers* (1926), *Snug Harbor* (1931).

Arnold Bennett, "W. W. Jacobs and Aristophanes," in *Books and Persons* (1917); J. B. Priestley, "W. W. Jacobs," in *Figures in Modern Literature* (1924).

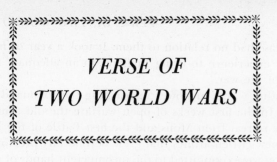

VERSE OF TWO WORLD WARS

THE FIRST WAR: 1914-1918

George V, 1910-1936

THE FIRST WORLD WAR differed radically from the Second in that neither soldiers nor civilians really knew what they were going into. Despite the lessons of the Boer War and Haldane's reforms the British army was utterly inadequate in numbers and equipment. The nation had not seen war close at hand for a hundred years and a short decisive campaign was generally expected. Everywhere in the fall of 1914 well-informed people were saying that the war could not last beyond six months because men could not be made to face modern artillery and machinegun fire for longer and because the cost in lives and money would be too heavy for even the great powers to bear. They tragically underestimated human endurance of these things.

The response of the nation was better than some of the politicians expected but was not altogether admirable. There was a great deal of cheap, rhetorical patriotism that vented itself in the hounding of anyone suspected of slacking by those whose lives were undisturbed. "Business as usual" with its bluff suggestion of an imperturbable people was too often a cover for profiteering or pleasure-seeking. The national church failed lamentably to understand or meet the needs of the fighting men. In the first months a gulf widened between soldiers and civilians that caused men on leave to feel themselves in an alien world whose gaiety and ease had no relation to them. It took a year or more of bitter experience to bring England to an adequate realization of the war.

Reality was even slower in reaching the command in the field. In the first weeks of open warfare the old army died in the retreat from Mons and the first Battle of the Marne. The new citizen armies that grew beyond any previous conception were committed to the incompetent hands of cavalry generals, veterans of South Africa, with no adequate idea of trench warfare on this vast new scale. The war settled into the long horror of the Western Front. Neuve Chapelle, Loos, Ypres, the Somme, Passchendaele brought appalling— and unnecessary—casualty lists but nothing that looked like victory or even substantial gain. More and more guns pounded Flanders into a sea of mud across which no army could advance to a decision. Again and again the command sent its divisions forward to break in agony against the machineguns and wire of the enemy. The war lengthened to two years, then three of dogged endurance under bombardment that shattered men's minds and bodies, with the constant horror of gas in the hideous desolation of a ruined land. The men who looked out of their waterlogged trenches at the shell holes and the limp bodies on the wire were not averse to fighting—that is recorded in the battle honors of their regiments—but they had hoped to fight for victory, and as the third year passed it seemed that there could be no victory but only a release by wounds or death from the endless attack and counterattack that led to nothing.

Never have troops been subjected to a more terrible ordeal than the infantry of that war. As it moved inexorably toward a stalemate, the war itself became the enemy of the men who felt they had been betrayed to its imbecile Moloch-machinery. There was no failure of courage, but apathy and bitterness clogged the collective will. After the effort

of 1917 had failed and the depleted armies were left to meet
the new power, released by the collapse of Russia, of the
German attack of 1918, the British effort was spent. It was
under the command of Foch and with the weight of American divisions beside them that they at last moved forward
over the old enemy lines.

The British army of 1918 was no longer recognizable as
the force that had entered France four years before: in its
oldest battalions perhaps ten per cent of the men survived.
It was composed of conscripts who had come from a different
England, and it numbered its units by divisions instead of by
regiments. It had developed a fighting air force from a mere
toy and had acquired uncouth weapons: tanks, trench mor-
tars, grenades, and all the apparatus of chemical warfare.
But it had discarded *Tipperary, There's a Long, Long Trail,*
and *Keep the Home Fires Burning,* and sang of *Made-
moiselle from Armentières* or mournfully, as the regulars
had done before it:

> Old soldiers never die
> They just fade away.

To England the Western Front was the war. Africa, Palestine, the fiasco of Gallipoli, T. E. Lawrence's picturesque
desert campaign, however important, were "side shows." At
sea the navy had the arduous but unspectacular duties of
blockade and convoy—Jellicoe's battle of Jutland its one
dubious claim to victory. In the scores of thousands who died
in Flanders were the best of a whole generation, the men
who had answered Kitchener's early call for volunteers.
They were an incalculable loss to the nation, but in the
surviving fraction there was enough of mind and genius
to preserve for the future the memory of what they had
done and suffered. Men with literary gifts as a rule served
in the infantry, having neither the influential connections
nor the technical training to be more fortunately placed.

Most of them were captains or subalterns in the line—Ford
M. Ford, Robert Graves, and Siegfried Sassoon in the Welsh
Fusiliers; C. E. Montague in the Royal Fusiliers; Edmund
Blunden in the Sussex Regiment, Alec Waugh in the Dorset
Regiment; R. H. Mottram in the Norfolk Regiment, Osbert
and Sacheverel Sitwell in the Grenadier Guards, to name
only a few of the more prominent. During the next ten years
they created, in verse, in fiction, and in memoirs a record
of the reality of warfare until then unapproached in English
literature.

In that record, almost as much as in the war itself, lies
the clue to the difference in attitude between the generation
of, say, 1890 and those of 1920 and after. The readers of this
page will not have known a world free of the fear of war,
and even those who did, find that lost innocence hard to
recover. Yet it is a fact that until 1914 the Englishman and
the American at least, lived in such a world. Whatever
statesmen and journalists and soldiers may have known, ordinary men of good will thoroughly believed in peace, not
as an ideal only but as the actual condition in which an industrial age would go forward equably, prosperous and pacific. That belief died hard amid pathetic idealisms like
Henry Ford's peace ship expedition that was to settle the
war by reasonable argument. By the time the Armistice was
signed, it was among the lost illusions. The men who had
fought might be desperately resolved that such things as
they had seen should never happen again, but their very
testimony made those things no longer unthinkable as once
they had been. The "war books" are the epitaph of an age
too foolishly simple to survive.

To civilian England the war after 1915 brought radical
changes, familiar now from repetition but then new to English life and contrary to all its ingrained traditions. In 1915,
Asquith's Liberal cabinet, in office when the war began,
was obliged to accept a coalition of Unionist and Labor

members. In 1916, Asquith was replaced by the fiery little Welshman, David Lloyd George, who remained Prime Minister for the duration. With each change came an increase in the official machinery for the direction of the war and Englishmen, who have never liked their bureaucrats, now found personal liberty curtailed in every direction by the Defense of the Realm Act, the detestable DORA that has replaced Victorian Mrs. Grundy as the embodiment of the killjoy. But they accepted these things as they accepted the even more detestable conscription because they had learned two new fears: invasion from the Zeppelin raids, and starvation from the submarine campaign. In 1917 came legislation that changed the whole political character of the kingdom: The Representation of the People Act enfranchised all those men excluded hitherto and at the same time gave the vote to women. England was, in political form at least, at last democratic.

The war had brought the inevitable ruptures in social and economic life. The accolade of the commission brought thousands of men into circles they could never have entered before and thousands of others rose to wealth and authority in war industries and civil administration. War marriages made wide breaches in the barriers of class, a process favored by the unprecedented activity of women in war services and war industries. These latter were changing the whole pattern of industrial England, and to meet efficiently their financial needs in 1917 the hundreds of private banks in the country were absorbed into five large institutions. The era of personal relations between the manufacturer or merchant and his banker, both local men whose families had perhaps worked together for generations, was over and the way open for the impersonal methods of modern corporations. In England, where personal relations have always counted for a great deal in all walks of life, this was a radical change.

War industries again strongly affected labor which for the first time had become of major political importance. In spite of spreading government controls, there was a scandalous amount of war profiteering, and as the war dragged on labor became increasingly restive until in 1918 there was a really serious outbreak of strikes. Most shocking to many people was the strike in London of the Metropolitan Police. It was on the whole good-natured and short, being settled in twenty-four hours, but the mere possibility of such a thing seemed to open a crevasse in the solid earth. If the reinforcement of the Allies by the AEF had not turned the tide of the war in its blackest hour after the German breakthrough of March 1918, there is no saying what might have happened in England. As it was, the nation was seriously divided within, while across the Channel in Flanders the armies had acquired a corporate feeling apart from and largely hostile to all who had been at home, out of the fighting. England was in far more danger at the end of the war than at the beginning.

PREMIERS

Herbert Asquith (Liberal), *1914-1915*
Herbert Asquith (Coalition), *1915-1916*
David Lloyd George (Coalition), *1916-1918*

THE SECOND WAR: 1939-1945

George VI, 1936-1952

THE SECOND WAR had been generally forseen from the time of Hitler's rise to power in the middle thirties and though there was a brief interval after Chamberlain's appeasement of Germany at Munich when many believed war had been averted, the outbreak when it came carried nothing like the shock of 1914. But at the outset England and her allies

LONDON IN THE BLITZ: WORLD WAR II

fatally underestimated the enemy. When after an exasperating year of the "phony war" the German power was fully exerted, France collapsed like a card house and England lost her last effective army in the disaster of Dunkirk. Then the nation buckled down to the grim defense of home and empire that reached its crisis in the Battle of Britain in 1941 and its most serious blow in the loss of Singapore in 1942. The next year, with American aid, began the process of reconquest culminating in the invasion of Normandy and the final defeat of Germany in 1945.

The literary aspects of the Second War were as different from those of the First as the military. Much of the soldier's fundamental experience had been made familiar by the older generation: since there were few illusions there was none of the bitterness of reaction that inspired Sassoon and Owen. Nor was there a scene of action that represented the tragedy of a generation as did the Western Front. In the wide-flung theaters of the Second War the symbolic value of experience was often lost in the local and particular. Moreover the soldier could no longer feel himself so utterly separated in his world of danger and suffering from the civilian. In England the poignancy of wartime tragedy was as immediately known to ruined evacuees or to the fire fighters of the London blitz as to the men at any of the fronts in the quickly changing aspects of mechanized war. Thoughtful writers were consequently less interested in the soldier's plight than in the moral problems of his situation: loyalty, the responsibilities of command, or the implications of social guilt in the mass bombing of enemy cities. These, and especially the last, were a province equally open to civilian writers, a fact which led to the increasing penetration of the purely military frontier of war literature. It is expressive of the difference of twenty-five years that the best English war poems of the nineteen-forties were written by Edith Sitwell, a woman and a civilian.

General statements about the literature of the Second War at the present are, necessarily, incautious, since it is still in the making. It took ten years to get the best books of the First War written, it may be that we are still awaiting the best of the Second.

PREMIERS

Chamberlain (Liberal), *1937-1940*
Churchill (Coalition), *1940-1945*

WAR VERSE

Out of the two wars of the twentieth century there has come a considerable amount of verse. Its volume and range can be seen in such collections as E. B. Osborne's *The Muse in Arms* (1919), Edmund Blunden's *Anthology of War Poems* (1930), G. H. Clark's *The New Treasury of War Poetry* (1943), and Oscar Williams's *The War Poets* (1945). Some of it belongs to the main stream of patriotic verse; some it deals with individual tragedy; and a large part of it deals in a bitter and graphic way with the futility and horror of war as a means of purging the world of its political and economic ills. It is commendable that so little of it was devoted to attacks on the enemy. Name-calling and mud-slinging were evidently considered beneath the poet's calling. The bitterness was directed more against slackers and those who held high-paying jobs, officialdom, and war itself than against Germany and Japan. In his poem "To Germany," Charles Hamilton Sorley, who was killed in action in the First War, expressed the sentiment of many of the soldier-poets of both wars when he exclaimed: "You are blind like us." Although E. B. Osborne in the introductory note to *The Muse in Arms* states that the poetry of the First War illustrates the soldiers' "singular capacity for remembering the splendour and forgetting the squalor of the

dreadful vocation in which they were suddenly engaged—
a capacity at the root of that infinite cheerfulness which
was such a priceless military asset in the early days of disillusion and disaster," the horrors and futility of war were
by no means ignored. In fact, the note of futility was frequent and insistent, and was doubly effective in that it came
as something new and not altogether desirable to zealous
nationalists. By the time the Second War broke out, the
theme of futility was generally recognized by most of the
young men who turned their thoughts to verse; and without going back to flag-waving and nationalistic sentiment,
they accepted their lot with a sort of grim resignation. Some
of them, including the versatile John Gawsworth (Terence
Fytton Armstrong), deliberately sought and found themes
which were detached from war without losing sight of its
menacing glow. In many of the poems which came out of
the last war, there is not so much a feeling that war is tragic
and futile, but that life itself, of which war is a part, is
a grim business.

During the First War, the older poets including Hardy,
Kipling, Masefield, Binyon, and Noyes contributed much
to the stream of war verse. Hardy's "The Pity of It" and
"A Christmas Ghost Story" are forceful expressions by the
master of irony; Kipling's "A Nativity" and "My Boy Jack"
are among his finest poetic achievements; and Noyes's "The
Wine Press" and "The Victory Dance" are bitterly effective
treatments of the tragedy of war. It was among the younger
men, however, some of whom had been in the thick of the
struggle, that war for a time became the chief source of
poetic inspiration. Many of these poets in time turned to
other themes to do their finest and most distinctive work;
but in spite of the fact that Siegfried Sassoon, Robert Graves,
W. W. Gibson, and Edmund Blunden widened their scope
in the postwar decades and produced their most character-

istic and mature work in fields other than war poetry, they are still often associated with the poems which came out of their experiences in the trenches. Rupert Brooke, remembered chiefly for "The Soldier," stands somewhat apart from the young men of his generation, although it is not unlikely, as has been suggested by some of his friends, that had he lived, he too would have added his voice to those which cried out against war. "We may remind ourselves," wrote Robert Graves, "of one or two facts usually overlooked: That Rupert Brooke saw many warlike scenes but no actual fighting, that Robert Nichols, with the best of intentions, only saw three weeks' service in France and this on a quiet sector with the artillery: that of the other poets with reputations as War-poets not more than four or five (including Siegfried Sassoon, Wilfred Owen who was killed just before the Armistice, Isaac Rosenberg, Edmund Blunden and Herbert Read) bore the heat and burden of the War: and that only Siegfried Sassoon published his verse while the War was still on." There were others, including W. W. Gibson, who although not bearing "the heat and burden of the War" felt enough of it to view it realistically.

Although Lascelles Abercrombie said that Brooke's sonnets in *1914* are "among the few supreme utterances of English patriotism," the star of **Rupert Brooke (1887-1915)** has almost waned. During the First World War and through the early twenties, he was enshrined as a national hero, and his verses were read by many to whom poetry was a rare diet. The significance which was attached to his name and his poetry was in part the result of his untimely death in the ill-fated Gallipoli campaign. Even during the War, however, a few of his soldier-poet contemporaries were unsympathetic to his romantic conception of war and soldiers. Charles Hamilton Sorley, killed in battle at the age of twenty, observed at the time of Brooke's enlistment: "Rupert Brooke

is far too obsessed with his own sacrifice, regarding the going to war of himself (and others) as a highly intense, remarkable, and sacrificial exploit, whereas it is merely the

RUPERT BROOKE

conduct demanded of him
(and others) by the turn of
circumstances, where noncom-
pliance with this demand
would have made life intoler-
able. He has clothed his attitude in fine words: but his is,
nevertheless, the sentimental
attitude." This feeling of Sorley's came to be shared by an
increasing number of young
men who without fanfare
did their long turn in the
trenches; and after the War,

with the romantic conception of militarism attacked on all
sides, Brooke and his war poems began to descend from the
lofty plane to which they were thrust at the time of his
death. In spite of what Sorley called the "sentimental attitude," however, Brooke was a very talented poet and a
great spirit.

He was born at Rugby in 1887, the son of William Brooke,
assistant master at Rugby. Since his boyhood was spent in
the cultural atmosphere of academic surroundings, it was
not remarkable for him to write poetry at an early age, and
to win a prize for his poem "The Bastille" when he was
only eighteen. While at King's College, Cambridge, he read
widely in the poets, especially those of the seventeenth century; and he contributed verses to the *Gownsman* and the
Cambridge Review. After graduating from the University,
he travelled much on the Continent, to take up residence in
1910 at the University of Munich. Back in England, he contributed poetry to the *Westminster Gazette* and the *Eng-*

lish Review, much of which was commended highly by even the sterner critics. In 1913 he travelled in America before going to Hawaii, Samoa, and Tahiti. Soon after the outbreak of the War, Brooke volunteered for service in France. He was commissioned and sent to Belgium, but at the evacuation of Antwerp, he was recalled to go into training for the Dardanelles campaign. On his way to the Aegean, he suffered a sunstroke from which he apparently recovered, although his resistance was weakened by the experience. A virulent blood poisoning set in as the result of an abrasion while his ship was lying off the coast of Asia Minor. It was on a French hospital ship which was anchored off the island of Scyros that Brooke died on April 23, 1915, at the age of twenty-seven.

Although only two small volumes of verse were published during his lifetime, there is more variety in Brooke's poetry than is commonly supposed. In addition to the well-known patriotic poems in *1914,* including "The Soldier," there are scores of love poems in which there is a wide range of theme and sentiment. At times he is the youthful cynic in his contemplation of love; and again, in such a fine poem as "The Call," he is youth, responsive to love's beauty. In this poem there is something of Byron's strength with something of Shelley's lyric quality. Although not a love poem in the strictest sense, "The Great Lover" is a fine expression of Brooke's zest for life. The sonnets in *1914,* despite the quality which has been called romanticized patriotism, are lofty in theme and manner, and it is only the determined realist who is not moved by them. It is idle to try to determine what Brooke might have written had he been granted more time, but he was possessed of talents which tempt one to believe that he would have become a great poet.

VERSE: *Poems* (1911), *1914, Five Sonnets* (1915), *1914 and Other Poems* (1915), *Collected Poems* (1915), *The Old Vicarage, Grantchester* (1916), *Selected Poems* (1917), *Complete Poems* (1932).

MISCELLANEOUS: *Lithuania, a Drama in One Act* (1915), *John Webster and the Elizabethan Drama* (1916), *Letters From America* (1916), *Fragments Now First Collected, Some Being Hitherto Unpublished* (1925).

Arthur Stringer, *Red Wine of Youth: A Biography of Rupert Brooke* (1948); Edward Marsh, *Rupert Brooke: A Memoir* (1918); Maurice Browne, *Recollections of Rupert Brooke* (Chicago, 1927); Stanley Casson, *Rupert Brooke and Scyros* (1921); John Drinkwater, *Rupert Brooke: An Essay* (1916); H. W. Garrod, "Rupert Brooke" in *The Profession of Poetry* (1929); E. A. McCourt, "Rupert Brooke: A Reappraisal," *Dalhousie Rev.*, XXIV (1944), 148-156.

Siegfried Sassoon (1886-   ) was one of the war poets who saw much action at the front. He was in Palestine and France, won the Military Cross as a Captain in the Royal

SIEGFRIED SASSOON

Welsh Fusiliers for bravery beyond the line of duty, and was wounded in battle. "Before the War," said Robert Nichols, "poetry was for him just something for private and particular enjoyment— like a ride alone before breakfast." After the War, however, Sassoon was ready to say to Nichols: "War has made me. I think I am a man as well as a poet. . . . It's dangerous even to speak of how here and there the individual may gain some hardship of soul by it. For war is hell and those who institute it are criminals. Were there anything to say for it, it should not be said, for its spiritual disasters far outweigh any of its advantages."

Siegfried Sassoon was born in 1886, the son of a well-to-do country gentleman of Persian-Jewish ancestry who had married the sister of the sculptor Thornycroft. The boy was reared in an atmosphere which suggests none of the grimness of his war verse. There were books, piano lessons, tennis, and fox-hunting in an environment of peace and refinement. He was sent to Marlborough School and later to Christ Church, Oxford. His ambition from the age of eight was to become a poet. As early as 1911, when he was twenty-five, he had published privately *Twelve Sonnets,* and the following year, *Melodies, An Ode for Music,* and *Hyacinth.* His reading of Hardy and Masefield led him in time to forsake mere prettiness of theme and line; but the most powerful force which led him away from conventional and derivative verse was his experience in the First World War. He was in the thick of it—in the trenches, in battle, and in base hospitals. Whereas most of the young men who saw action were not to express themselves in verse until the War was over, Sassoon had some of his verses printed while the din of battle was still in his ears. Since 1918, he has explored many fields in both prose and verse. His fictional prose pieces, in which there is a considerable amount of autobiographical revelation, and the three volumes of autobiography, not only disclose much of the man and the poet, but also a stylist of engaging literary manners. He continues to write poetry, and recently he finished an intensive study, *George Meredith* (1949).

Robert Nichols divided Sassoon's poetry in 1918 in two classes: the idyllic and the satiric, or "the paradise poems and the suffering world poems." To Nichols's classification now must be added a third tendency which appears in *The Heart's Journey* (1927) and *Vigils* (1934) in which he is neither idealist nor satirist, but the poet seeking to reconcile life's ill and good. In contrast to the earlier poems, the poems which represent this tendency are reflective and ab-

stract. Of the early poems in which there is detachment from
the suffering world, none is finer than "The Old Huntsman." It takes on the form of a monologue in which the
old man whose life has been bound up with hounds and
jumpers, reflects on the changes which time has wrought
in both custom and himself. The same volume which contained "The Old Huntsman," the poem which gave the
collection its title, contained a series of short poems in
which Sassoon's enraged response to the horrors of war
found its earliest expression. It was in the poems in *Counter-
Attack* (1918), however, that his bitterness is most pronounced. There is nothing of Brooke's glorification of the
soldier's lot, and nothing of Binyon's willingness to see some
good in the conflict. There are "Lines of gray, muttering
faces, masked with fear" moving up for the attack; and the
mud, the stenches, the cries of the wounded, and the futility
of it all come to the reader in staccato lines. He made no
effort to disguise his wrath at the thought of those who instituted war and of the officials who sat far behind the
lines, "Gulping and guzzling in the best hotels, reading
the Roll of Honour . . ." In his later work, notably in *Vigils*
(1934), the poet's anger has subsided, but the effect of war
has not been entirely forgotten. Many of these later poems
show the poet in his maturity, recognizing the world's inability to profit by its experiences, but recognizing at the
same time man's ability to find comfort and strength in the
search for the ultimate good.

VERSE: *Twelve Sonnets* (1912), *Hyacinth* (1912), *Melodies* (1912),
Discoveries (1915), *Morning Glory* (1916), *The Old Huntsman and
Other Poems* (1917), *Counter-Attack and Other Poems* (1918), *War
Poems* (1919), *Picture Show* (1919), *Satirical Poems* (1926), *The
Heart's Journey* (1927), *Vigils* (1934), *Rimed Ruminations* (1940),
Poems Newly Selected (1940), *Collected Poems* (1948). PROSE: *The
Memoirs of a Fox-Hunting Man* (1928), *The Memoirs of an In-
fantry Officer* (1930), *Sherston's Progress* (1936). AUTOBIOGRAPHY:

The Old Century and Seven More Years (1939), *The Weald of Youth* (1942), *Siegfried's Journey* (1945).

F. J. H. Darton, *From Surtees to Sassoon* (1931), 81-121; Edmund Blunden, "Siegfried Sassoon's Poetry," *London Mercury*, XX (1929), 156-166.

Only a relatively small part of the poetry of **W. W. Gibson** (**1878-**   ) deals with war themes. He has been called the poet of tenement and trench, but these are only two of his many backgrounds. He is pro-
lific and versatile, with a range of theme almost comparable to Masefield's, and with a be-wildering variety of manners. The portrait gallery in his poems is exceptionally wide, with characters ranging from the strong, young savage who is a slave of the Queen of Babylon in *Akra the Slave* (1910) to the shepherds in *Daily Bread* (1910) and the miners in *Fuel* (1934). There are occasional poems, dedica-tory verses, and epigrams; nar-

W. W. GIBSON

rative, dramatic, and lyric poetry; and verse in traditional patterns and in irregular, modernistic schemes. In some of his early work, there is a resemblance to Tennyson; in the dramatic monologues, he suggests Browning; and in the poems in *Daily Bread, Fires* (1912), and *Livelihood* (1917) there is something of both Hardy and Masefield. His war verse, too, is varied in theme and spirit, although it inclines more toward the tone of Sassoon than that of Brooke.

Wilfrid Wilson Gibson (he has dropped the "Wilson" in signing his more recent works) was born in Hexham, Northumberland, in 1878, the son of a pharmacist. The atmosphere of the North Country was part of his birthright, and the shepherds and lowly folk of whom he was later to write were part of his early environment. The boy had scant formal schooling, although he was never without good books. His older sister had married an Oxford professor who encouraged him with his reading and his early efforts to write verse. When his father died, Gibson was left with a modest inheritance, and with the small income that the legacy provided he decided to devote his time to writing. It was not until the publication of *Stonefolds* in 1907 that his name began to attract attention. More than thirty volumes of verse have come from his pen, and until the middle thirties his creative energy showed little diminution.

Gibson's poetry is so varied in theme and manner that simple classification is impossible; but it is in the war poems, the dramatic episodes in verse, and the brief reflective lyrics that he has done his most representative work. The war poems are to be found chiefly in the collection entitled *Battle and Other Poems* (1916). It is important to note that these poems appeared before he saw action in France. Furthermore, Gibson's war verse is more of an illustration of his ability to project himself into the feelings of the soldier in the trenches than an illumination of his own experiences. He was in his middle thirties during the war years, but most of the poems express the sentiments of a homesick boy who has been taken from scenes of rustic quiet into the tumult of battle. Such poems as "The Reek," "Raining," and "The Question" are unadorned expressions of a farm boy's longing for familiar scenes, made poignant by their simplicity. Gibson is especially successful in catching the flitting thoughts and streams-of-consciousness which are part of the soldier's experience as the grimness of war advances and recedes in turn. "Before Action" and "The Dancers" are effective translations of the subconscious and semiconscious musings of the war-weary boy to whom battle is an awful dream and home the only reality. In "The Bayonet" there is something of Sassoon's bitterness, and "Back" reiterates forcefully the futility of the struggle. It is this theme of futility which stands out in Gibson's later war verse in which he expresses, out of his own experiences viewed in retrospect, the sentiment which must oppress most soldiers after the long ordeal is over.

The dramatic episodes in *Stonefolds, Daily Bread, Fires,* and *Livelihood* deal with lowly folk who are often poor and afflicted. Shepherds (for whom Gibson had a particular liking), miners, stonecutters, and ferrymen are the protagonists who struggle against the obstacles of poverty and circumstance. The minor characters, especially the gossiping women who at times perform a sort of chorus function, recall figures out of Hardy's novels. A certain drabness and sense of tragedy hang over the episodes, and yet the author is neither ironic nor bitter. There is no soul-stirring lament for things as they are. The simple folk in these dramatic episodes are not strongly individualized: they are rather types who illustrate through their struggles the universal plight of man. Read singly, these stories reveal plainly the lack of individuality in the characters; but if one reads a half-dozen or more of them at one sitting—and they are short enough to permit this—one is conscious not of particular men and women, but of humanity at large. These episodes are usually cast into the form of versified dialogue in which the diction and verse are rough and irregular in keeping with the characters and their backgrounds. After 1920, Gibson employed the dialogue vehicle less frequently: his dramatic episodes were cast into a more direct and compact narrative form. The poem "The Stone" in *Fires* (1912), and the pieces in *Fuel* (1934) are illustrative of his power in the compact narrative form.

As a lyric and reflective poet, Gibson has shown competence in form, but there is little which is outstanding in melody and imagery. When he no longer has a narrative theme to develop, he has too often sought inspiration in subjects which are more casual than poetic. His dedicatory verses, many of which appear in *Friends* (1916) are tasteful tributes in which there is sincere feeling expressed with restraint. "To Rupert Brooke" in *Friends* and "Reunion" in *Hazards* are fine expressions of his pleasure and gratitude in having friends of noble aim and rich human sympathy. "Poet, Beware!" and "A Poet" in *Hazards* are illuminations of Gibson's creed. He is neither of "the art-for-art's-sake" school, nor is he of the race of poets who seek out a solution to the problems of man's ills through social and spiritual agencies. His talents are directed primarily at a recognition of the varied aspects of life, and although there is much in his work that is drab and prosaic, there are poems, especially among the dramatic episodes, which have insight and power.

Urlyn the Harper and Other Songs (1902), *Akra the Slave* (1910), *Daily Bread* (1910), *Fires* (1912), *Borderlands and Thoroughfares* (1915), *Battle and Other Poems* (1916), *Friends* (1916), *Krindlesyke* (1922), *Kestrel Edge and Other Plays* (1924), *Collected Poems, 1905-1925* (1926), *Hazards* (1930), *Islands, Poems, 1930-1932* (1932), *Fuel* (1934), *Coming and Going* (1938), *The Alert* (1942), *The Outpost* (1944).

John Gawsworth, "W. W. Gibson" in *Ten Contemporaries: Notes Toward Their Definitive Bibliographies* (First Series, 1932); Geraldine P. Dilla, "The Development of Wilfrid Gibson's Poetic Art," *Sewanee Rev.*, XXX (1922), 39-57; J. H. Holmes, "W. W. Gibson: Poet of Tenement and Trench," *Survey*, XXXVII (1917), 409-411; John Freeman, "Wilfrid Gibson, Poet," *Bookman* (London), LXXV (1928), 172-174.

Edmund Blunden (1896-   ), like many of the young poets who saw action in France during the First War, wrote a considerable amount of war verse, and one of the most powerful of the prose works which came out of the conflict, *Undertones of War* (1928). Although he had written much poetry before he turned his talent to war themes, it was through *Undertones of War* and such poems as "Third Ypres" that he gained wide recognition, and as a result, he has often been associated with war and its aftermath. A thorough reading of his works, however, indicates that his occupation with war was only a phase of his writing, and in volume at least, a comparatively small phase. By far the larger number of his poems deal with English country and village life to which his temperament and talent were singularly attuned. Even in his war verse, there is something of the pastoral poet showing through.

Edmund Charles Blunden was born at Yalding, Kent, in 1896. From his poems one can readily gather that from early childhood he was attached to scenes of rustic simplicity and that he showed some of the inclinations of a naturalist. While at Queen's College, Oxford, he wrote verse; and as early as 1916, he issued three slender volumes of pastoral verse which was later collected into one volume *The Waggoner and Other Poems* (1920). Soon after the outbreak of the War, he enlisted in the army to serve as a lieutenant in the Royal Sussex Regiment. Unlike Sassoon and the other young men who wrote verse while the heat of battle was still on them, Blunden had little to say about the War until the middle twenties. After the Armistice, he contributed to the literary periodicals, and for a time was assistant editor of the *Athenaeum*. With the publication of *The Shepherd* in 1922, he received the Hawthornden Prize, a distinction which bore out the judgments of some of the reviewers that he was one of the most promising of the younger poets. From 1924 to 1927 he was a professor of English Literature at the Imperial University in Tokyo. Back in England he issued some of his verse including *Retreat* (1928) and his fine prose work *Undertones of War* (1928). He continues to write poetry, and for his many critical biographies he has come to be recognized as an authority in literary history.

The poems which deal with war were apparently written long after the struggle was over. Time, however, instead of relieving the wound which war had caused only deepened the poet's sense of sorrow and futility. In "Third Ypres" he asks:

> But who with what command can now relieve
> The dead men from that chaos, or my soul?

In "Reunion in War," his bitterness bursts into flame in the last stanza, but generally the tone of his war verse is expressed in the line: "Tired with dull grief, grown old beyond my day." The poems in *After the Bombing* (1945) written during the Second World War are likewise subdued in tone.

The state of mind which led Blunden during the First War and in the years immediately following to find his chief source of inspiration in pastoral themes was shared by some of his contemporaries, but with Blunden the return to nature was a natural development of his interests and personality. There is so much that is vital in his nature poetry that one is inclined to believe that he would have gravitated to pastoral themes regardless of the circumstances which beset him and his generation. In his use of specific detail, there is something of the naturalist's manner, for his observations are vivid and precise. He is not directly concerned with a philosophy of nature; generally he is content to record his observations and reflections, many of which suggest the sere days of autumn rather than the green of spring. The contemplative quality of the poems and their way of provoking a mood keep them from becoming merely good reporting. Blunden's later verse is less sinewy, but it has not lost strength. His many prose studies in literary criticism show searching judgments and a consistently agreeable style.

VERSE: *Poems* (1914), *The Barn* (1916), *The Harbingers, Poems* (1916), *Pastorals* (1916), *The Waggoner and Other Poems* (1920), *The Shepherd and Other Poems of Peace and War* (1922), *To Nature, New Poems* (1923), *English Poems* (1925), *Far East* (1925), *Masks of Time: A New Collection of Poems, Principally Meditative* (1925), *Japanese Garland* (1928), *Retreat* (1928), *Near and Far, New Poems* (1929), *Collected Poems, 1914-1930* (1930), *Halfway House: A Miscellany of New Poems* (1932), *Choice or Chance, New Poems* (1934), *An Elegy and Other Poems* (1937), *Shells by a Stream: New Poems* (1944). PROSE: *Undertones of War* (1928), *Leigh Hunt and His Circle* (1930), *Charles Lamb and His Contemporaries* (1932), *The Face of England* (1932), *Votive Tablets: Studies Chiefly Appreciative of English Authors and Books* (1932), *The Mind's Eye* (1934), *Edward Gibbon and His Age* (1935), *Thomas Hardy* (1942), *Shelley: a Life Story* (1946).

A. S. Gasworth and Jacob Schwartz, *A Bibliography of Edmund Blunden: With Preface and Copious Notes by Edmund Blunden* (1931); W. H. Dunn, "Edmund Blunden and his Poetry," *Lond. Quar. Rev.*, LXVII (1928), 74-82; A. W. Fox, "Edmund Blunden," *Manchester Quar.*, XIV (1923), 115-122.

Robert Nichols (1893-   ), who wrote the Preface to Siegfried Sassoon's *Counter-Attack*, drew themes for much of his verse from his war experience which was brief in actual time, but intense and lasting in effect. His attitude was similar to Sassoon's. "Were there anything to say for war," said Sassoon, "it should not be said; for its spiritual disasters far outweigh any of its advantages." To which Nichols added: "For myself, this is the truth. War does not ennoble, it degrades." Although some of his war poems including the well-known "Assault" cannot be identified with Nichols's own experience, for he was in France for only three weeks, he was sufficiently aware of the horrors of war to give his work power and conviction. *Ardours and Endurances* (1917) provides a sequence which carries the soldier through all of the stages. It is divided into the Summons, Farewell to Places of Comfort, the Approach, Battle, the Dead, and the Aftermath. The verse in these sections is descriptive and narrative, and profits by being read as a sequence. There is bitterness in the poem, but it rarely takes on the sharpness of Sassoon's phrases, and for all the bold short lines, it lacks Sassoon's vigor. The imagery is less concrete and the diction less forceful. In spite of the fact that in the years immediately following the Armistice Nichols was considered one of the most spirited spokesmen among the verse writers who condemned war, his poems have not stood up well with the passing of time, possibly by reason of the inevitable comparison between his work and that of Sassoon. Nichols's later poems in *The Budded Branch* (1918), the *Sonnets to Aurelia* (1919) in the Elizabethan manner, and the satirical *Fisbo* (1934) show him in a variety of moods of which those in the verses in the Aurelia group are most clearly poetic. The interestingly conceived drama, *Wings Over Europe* (1928) written with Maurice Browne, is representative of Nichols's more ambitious work in prose.

WILFRED OWEN

Of the young poets who were killed in action in the First War, Wilfred Owen, Isaac Rosenberg, and Charles Hamilton Sorley are outstanding. **Wilfred Owen (1893-1918)** was killed on November 4, 1918, a week before the Armistice. The verses which he wrote during his long experience at the front were unrevised and it was not until 1920 that Siegfried Sassoon collected and edited them under the title *Poems*. Had Owen lived, it is probable that he could have given the verses more structural finish and greater clarity. Some of the lines are obscure, as if Owen had jotted them down out of a fragmentary impression to be expanded and clarified at a less pressing time. The themes range from such a patriotic sentiment as that in his fine lyric "Greater Love" to the bitterness and sorrow expressed in "Apologia Pro Poemate Meo" and "Anthem for Doomed Youth." In "Dulce Et Decorum Est . . ." there are a Sassoon-like vigor and harshness of phrase. In his notes which were possibly intended to form the substance of a preface to a volume of poems, he wrote: "Above all, I am not concerned with poetry . . . my subject is War and the Pity of War . . . the Poetry is in the Pity." And later he added: "All a poet can do today is to warn." Although it would seem from such observations that Owen considered poetry only as a means to an end, time has judged his works favorably, not as forceful propaganda, but as poetry which can take its place with the finest in war verse.

Edmund Blunden, Introduction, *The Poems of Wilfred Owen* (1931); I. M. Parsons, "The Poems of Wilfred Owen," *New Criterion*, X, (1931), 658-699.

Isaac Rosenberg (1890-1918), although of delicate health from childhood, enlisted for service in France early in 1915, and after much suffering at the front was killed in action on April 1, 1918. His schooling had been scanty, at least when it is compared with that of Owen and Sorley, but even in his mid-teens he had determined to become a poet. *Night and Day* (1912) and *Youth* (1915) show the characteristics of his early manner: fervent feeling, and unconventional imagery and rhythms mark these pieces in which there is occasional strength. *Moses* (1916), with its sharp censure in the poem "The Jew," is a cry from the heart, somewhat disfigured in its expression by its strain on the medium which never seems to be completely mastered. His later work, collected and edited by Gordon Bottomley and Denys Harding, along with the early volumes, under the title *The Collected Works of Isaac Rosenberg* (1937) includes the poems which deal with the poet's attitude toward war. "Dead Man's Dump," the best-known of his poems, is a forcefully impelled expression of his response to the havoc of war in which the irregular lines are well adapted to the theme. "The Dead Heroes," which follows a conventional rime scheme in its glorification of the sacrifice which his comrades have made in order to give England her power, is more subdued in theme and manner, but with no perceptible loss of strength. Perhaps justifiably, Rosenberg's verse has been more widely discussed in recent years than that of most of the poets of the First War. There is no doubt that it is sincere in feeling, and that it shows both originality and strength in presentation.

Charles Hamilton Sorley (1895-1915) was the first of the soldier poets, and the youngest, to give his life for his country. He was killed in action near Hulluch a few months after he had turned twenty. Outwardly his life was somewhat similar to Rupert Brooke's: he was the son of a Cambridge University professor, he was widely read in the classics at the Marlborough School and at University College, Oxford, where he was elected to a scholarship; and he had much of Brooke's personal charm and zest for life. After leaving Oxford, he spent six months in Germany, to return to England at the outbreak of the War. He attained the rank of captain in the Seventh Service Battalion of the Suffolk Regiment, which saw prompt action in France. While at school, he had written poetry, and the muse stayed with him to the end. Much of his verse was unrevised, and after he had joined the forces and the suggestion was made to him to get his poems ready for printing, according to his father, he put the proposal aside as premature. "This is no time for olive yards and vineyards," he said, "more especially of the small-hold-

ings type. For three years, or the duration of the war, let be."
The year after his death, his father, W. R. Sorley, collected
his verse and some of his prose which seemed to illuminate
the poet's mind and art, and issued the slender volume under
the title *Marlborough and Other Poems* (1916). Very few of
the poems in the book deal with war, and when they do,
there is a sort of quiet exaltation rather than a vehement
bitterness. In spite of the fact that he recognized that "there
is no such thing as a just war," he was not concerned with
war's injustices, or with its grimness. Nor are the German
soldiers arch-fiends who are responsible for all the suffering.
In his poem "To Germany" he says: "And in each other's
dearest ways we stand and hiss and hate. And the blind fight
the blind." Sorley's best known poem, "The Song of the
Ungirt Runners," shows a fine zest for life and the struggle,
although its application need not be narrowed to the conflict of war. All of his verse indicates that Sorley was undoubtedly a poet of great promise.

Julian Grenfell (1892-1915), who died in May, 1915 of
wounds received in battle, wrote relatively little, but his
poem "Into Battle" is of outstanding power in its insistence
on the nobility of the soldiers' sacrifice. Although war may
be futile, and the soldiers' role that of a pawn in the hands
of politicians and profiteers,

> All the bright company of Heaven
> Hold him in their high comradeship.

It was of this poem that Rudyard Kipling said: "His lips
must have been touched." Maurice Baring's "In Memoriam,
A.H.," which has been called one of the great elegies in the
language, and John McCrae's "In Flanders' Fields," which
has become the unofficial poem of Armistice Day celebra-
tions, are well-known poems which have justifiably survived;
and Richard Aldington's collection *Images of War* (1919),
some of the verses of Herbert Read in *Songs of Chaos* (1915)

and *Naked Warriors* (1919), and Robert Graves' "It's a Queer Time" and "Escape" are further examples of the poetic expression of war themes. Grenfell, Baring, and McCrae belong essentially to the old order in their attitude toward war and in their manner of expression, whereas Aldington, Read, and Graves are of the school of disillusionment and their manner is modernistic. It is idle to try to conclude which attitude and manner have the more permanent poetic worth, but one is tempted to reflect in the light of the recent war that the poetry which came out of the first struggle and dealt with the futility and horror of war proved to be an ineffectual deterrent.

It is too early to attempt even a relatively complete survey of the poetry which grew out of the Second World War and to undertake an estimate of its worth. It is probable, as was the case in 1918, that much is still to be written. The anthologies compiled by George Herbert Clark, *The New Treasury of War Poetry* (1943), and especially Oscar Williams, *The War Poets* (1945) indicate in some measure the scope, and the tendencies and characteristics of the verse that has appeared thus far. Many of the names which appear in these collections will appear infrequently under the titles of poems in the future, for in spite of the fact that some of the contributors have expressed the idea that "war poetry" is an inept label for their work, their creative urge seems to have been exhausted with the coming of peace. It is true that very few of the recent war poems deal with actual fighting. There is little which suggests Sassoon's bitter outcries, but, on the other hand, there is little which belongs to Brooke's theme or manner. It would seem that the ills of humanity at large, rather than the particular affliction of war, are the most frequently recurrent theme, with a lament that man has not learned his lesson. War, although uppermost as an evil, is only a part of the havoc man has brought upon himself by his unwillingness to be fair with his fellows. After reading scores of poems written by those who saw action, one comes away with the impression that the poets were more largely concerned with the causes of war than with the actual results.

Of the writers who were in the forces who illustrate the major tendencies in war verse, Roy Fuller, Henry Treece, Vernon Watkins, Julian Symons, Alun Lewis, John Pudney, and John Gawsworth may be considered fairly representative. **Roy Fuller** (1912-   ), who saw service in both the British Navy and the RAF, will probably continue to find sources of inspiration for his talent in themes other than war. He has written several small volumes of verse, of which *A Lost Season* (1940) is indicative of his attitude toward the struggle into which his generation was thrust. In "What is Terrible," he says that besides his fear, his misspent time, his love, hurt and postponed, war brought to him the realization that the obvious organization of life is terrible. **Henry Treece** (1912-   ), often considered the leader of the apocalyptic school of poetry, saw active service as a flight lieutenant in the RAF, and was co-editor of the collection *Air-Force Poetry*. Although in his poem "In the Third Year of the War," he sees no end to man's plight, a nostalgic note comes into some of his verse: peace, as opposed to war, at least permits some hope and joy. **Vernon Watkins** (1907-   ), a Welshman, was a sergeant in the RAF to whom poetry was a vocation long before he heard the call to arms. "No poet is made by war," he said. . . . "The truest statements about war are made under one's breath. . . . Bad art and false gods motivate war as much as national greed." He is sensitive to the ugliness which grows out of prejudice and hatred among nations, but he finds no capitalist system as the root of the evil. **Julian Symons** (1912-   ), on the other hand, found the social structure of the world to blame. Even the prospects of victory for Britain did not lessen his concern for what to him is the essential trouble: "The rich still sliding in their

limousines, Churchill returning with his oranges. . . ." The
apathy of a decaying empire, the greed of the "American
paw," the unwillingness of man to see where the fault lies,
these are the targets for Symons' essentially satirical talent.
Alun Lewis (1915-1944), a Welsh poet who lost his life in the
Burma Campaign, was not directly concerned with social
revolution. In the sonnet "Infantry," and especially in
"Troopship in the Tropics," there are fine descriptive passages which are unburdened by any message of reform. The
posthumously issued *Ha! Ha! Among the Trumpets* (1945) is
representative of Lewis's promise as a poet. **John Pudney
(1909-   )**, author of a considerable amount of verse during
the thirties, including the widely varied poems in *Spring
Encounter* (1934) and *Open the Sky* (1935), wrote war verse
out of his experience in the RAF. In the poems in *Flight
Above Cloud* (1944), no flags are waved, nor does he attempt
to trace either the reasons for war or the results. His province
is largely the air and its men. He never ceases to wonder at
the marvel of flight, although his manner is often that of the
deliberately casual airman about to take off on a mission.
The tribute "To American Airmen" is a sincere expression
of regard, and the four sonnets entitled "The Dead" show a
fine talent for making articulate his feeling of the heroic
spirit which belongs to airmen, not only British, but all
who fly.

The most versatile and prolific of the younger poets
who contributed to the stream of war verse is **"John Gawsworth" (Terence Armstrong 1912-   )**. Although only
twenty-seven years old at the outbreak of the War, he had
issued more than ten small volumes of verse, edited a half-
dozen anthologies, and distinguished himself as a biblio-
grapher and critic. He was awarded the Benson Medal for
poetry in 1939, and many of the older poets spoke highly of
his work. Masefield named him "one of the most beautiful
and promising of our younger writers." During the War he

saw service as a sergeant in the RAF in Tunisia, Italy, and India. Out of this experience he drew some of his themes for the verse in *Snow and Sand: Poems From the Mediterranean, 1924-44* (1945) and *Blow No Bugles: Poems from Two Wars, 1942-45* (1945). Such poems as "Anniversary of the Death of a Pilot," "Convalescence," and "On V-J Day" have war themes; but even here, as with the others, there is no attempt to explain the cause and effect of war. War exists; and its menacing glow is present in the heavens, and "the guns are complaining in the hills." To Gawsworth, however, war is largely a background for sentiments which belong to the undulating life of man. The poems are never hortatory, and rarely does satire enter. He finds themes for poems apparently everywhere, and with a natural fluency, he turns these themes into verse which is at times more facile than consummate.

Sidney Keyes (1922-1943), killed in action in the Tunisian campaign, was probably the most promising of the younger poets. Born in Dartford, Kent, schooled at Tonbridge and Queen's College, Oxford, he wrote verse of distinctive quality and merit before the outbreak of the war. It was the war, however, which heightened his poetic sensibility and gave direction to his talent. From Oxford in 1941, he announced in a preface to a collection of poems, written by himself and seven other students: "We seem to share a horror at the world's predicament, together with the feeling that we cannot save ourselves without some kind of spiritual readjustment...." If the war gave direction to his thought and feeling, his reading in Yeats, Rilke, and Jung influenced his manner. *Collected Poems* (1945) contains the verse which appeared in *The Iron Laurel* (1942) and *The Cruel Solstice* (1944). Of the longer poems, "The Foreign Gate," influenced perceptibly by Rilke, although inconclusive in the development of theme, is richly lyrical; and "The Wilderness," with passages which recall Eliot's "The Waste Land" shows the poet's rare ability in the use of symbols. Of the shorter poems which deal with war, "Two Offices of a Sentry," "Ulster Soldier," and "War Poet" indicate plainly Keyes' great poetic promise, if not complete fulfillment.

For a more complete consideration of the verse of the Second World War, see Stephen Spender's *Poetry Since 1939* (1946), and the anthologies of Keidrych Rhys, *Poems from the Forces* (1942), *More Poems from the Forces* (1943); Julian Symons, *An Anthology of War Poetry* (1943); and M. J. Tambimuttu, *Poetry in Wartime* (1942).

POETRY & FICTION
1918—1950

George V, 1910-1936
Edward VIII (uncrowned, 1936)
George VI, 1936-1952
Elizabeth II, 1952-

ENGLAND BETWEEN WARS

When the noisy celebration of Armistice Night in November, 1918, was over, England entered a difficult year of re-adjustment in which she seemed to some of her people dangerously near to revolution. Many if not most of the troops returned in a mutinous temper that was not mollified when they found the "land fit for heroes to live in" promised them by Lloyd George wholly unprepared for their return. Demobilized officers slept on park benches or sold their clothes to buy food; their men often fared worse. Parliament could produce for their relief nothing better than a series of improvised and partial measures that were far from satis-factory. There was much discontent and some suffering but no violence; and as 1919 focused attention on the peace negotiations at Versailles, the surrendering and scuttling of the German fleet at Scapa Flow, and the appearance of Lady Astor, the first woman member in the House of Commons, England passed safely into the postwar twenties.

Lloyd George's coalition government, formed in the crisis of 1916, was given a mandate to conclude the peace in the "khaki election" shortly after the Armistice and remained in power for four difficult years. At the end of that time, unable to fulfil the promises he had made in the enthusiasm of the war, the Prime Minister resigned. He was succeeded by the Conservative Stanley Baldwin. The fall of Lloyd George marks the virtual disappearance from English politics of the Liberal party: for the next quarter century the Conservatives under Baldwin were to alternate in office with the Labor party under Ramsay MacDonald. They had the same problems of adjusting the enormous war debts owed to and by England, of rehabilitating industry in the face of ruinous foreign competition, and of devising measures of relief for the alarming spread of unemployment. The Conservatives, always the better financiers, were handicapped by the desperate condition of major industries, such as mining and shipping: Labor's plans for social amelioration were made ineffective by the party's dependence on what remained of the Liberals for a parliamentary majority. Both were haunted by bolshevism, the bogey man of the world since 1917. Exhaustion and frustration characterize the politics of the whole period.

The new opposition of parties and the appearance of the first Labor Government (which lasted only ten months) in 1924, showed how profoundly ten years had changed English society. By its manifest ineptitude during the war the governing class had lost a great deal of its prestige and by economic process a great deal of its wealth. Owners recovering estates lent to the government for the duration found them too costly to maintain and, renting them to Americans or profiteers, removed themselves to apartments in London where life was gayer. Titled men and women in business, or playing at it, became quite usual; genteel insolvency received the cachet of smartness. Aristocracy thus cut off from its tradition yielded easily to the desire pervading all classes to forget the war and began to cultivate the cynical hedonism of the jazz age. The new rich, on the other hand, had no real desire for the standards and manners of the class they had partially supplanted, although as accessories to their new titles and properties they might affect them. What remained of the old aristocratic life in the twenties was a highly artificial survival. It was the day of the flapper, of shingled hair and short skirts, of American night clubs and cocktails, and of a desperately asserted sophistication.

A by-product of this situation was the enhanced value of the Old School Tie. Properly its colors denoted one of the seven "public" schools—Eton, Harrow, Winchester, Rugby, Westminster, Charterhouse, and Shrewsbury—but since 1900 a large number of other establishments had been pretending to public school status and tradition. With all other criteria of position badly confused, community of education at one of the old exclusive schools became the most trustworthy bond of the higher snobbery. At the same time the public school system, both its genuine and bogus varieties, was pitilessly attacked by most of the literary men who had been through its mill. Its narrow classicism, its contempt for intellect, its brutalizing discipline and archaic traditions were ridiculed and denounced with a bitterness that in Dickens' day would have been final, but that appears to have had little, if any, effect. The public school had become a social rather than an educational institution. The universities, on the other hand, were in a better state than ever. Their curricula had been extended and modernized and there was an increase of serious, hard work among dons and undergraduates. But their social value had declined. Oxford and Cambridge, except in certain colleges, were felt to be contaminated by women, Rhodes scholars, colonials, and exservicemen, while the rapid modern growth of the London and the provincial universities—Liverpool, Leeds, Bristol, Durham, and Wales—had withdrawn from the mere possession of a degree its former distinction.

Below the fashionable strata the new poverty meant a less

amusing privation. The middle class found living dearer, the professions crowded, little businesses crushed by big ones, and a decent position harder and harder to maintain. For working people—when they had work—life was fish and chips, bread and marge, and beer that always got weaker. But many of them were on the dole (Unemployment Insurance), and none of the often proposed schemes of public works, housing, or increased relief materialized in real betterment. The diversions of the pub and the cinema, of betting on football pools or dog races (there were hardly any others) were open only to those on regular wages. In all industrial towns idle men, empty pipes in their mouths, hands in empty pockets, loafed on street corners, having nowhere else to go. There was irony rather than reassurance in the imposing display of the British Empire Exhibition at Wembley in 1924.

A better symbol of the spirit of the nation was to be seen in the new monuments, from the Cenotaph in Whitehall to unpretentious village memorial tablets, commemorating the war dead. In public and in private life the nation was suffering more than it would admit the loss of its best young manhood. Many, like Mrs. Viveash of Aldous Huxley's *Antic Hay,* tried to escape their memories in frantic distraction, but as many searched hungrily for consolation and assurance. Sir A. Conan Doyle and Sir Oliver Lodge believed that they had established psychic contact with their dead sons and published their experiences. For some years a passionate belief in spiritualism was widespread and brought comfort to thousands until skepticism, exposure of imposters, and mere lapse of time put an end to it. It lasted long enough, however, to emphasize unpleasantly the declining authority of the Church of England. Institutional and ritualistic, it had failed to establish any real spiritual contact with the armies during the war; now it failed to sustain the survivors who needed it as badly. As a body (there were, naturally, many individual and local exceptions) it moved away from the life of the people and relapsed into the merely official thing it had been in the eighteenth century.

In 1926 there was a new alarm of revolution when the withdrawal of a state subsidy from the coal mines precipitated a general strike of union labor. It lasted for nine days and was broken by volunteers from the upper and middle classes who turned out and maintained the essential utilities and services. The strike and its failure alarmed both management and labor and brought them to a more co-operative attitude. From this time dates an increasing trend to the left in the politics of the middle class, especially in the intellectual portion of it. This was well under way when the depression of the thirties brought severe economic distress. There was now a class of the permanently unemployed and in some communities virtually all were on the dole. At the worst they numbered 3,000,000. Laborers throughout England were still living in airless "back-to-back" houses in courts and alleys unchanged since mid-Victorian days. Loss of faith in the Labor party and a new attachment to socialism or communism was an inevitable result.

Radicalism is the natural atmosphere of the arts, breathed by Thackeray and George Eliot no less than by Morris and Shaw. But the younger Georgians were more aggressive in their political radicalism than any generation since the French Revolution: doctrinaire communism supplemented their artistic aims exactly as doctrinaire republicanism had those of the Romantic Movement. The arts were again in a period of new making when tradition was being ruthlessly jettisoned. Letters had broken through the old reticences and with the aid of psychology were developing new means of expression. Dadaism and Picasso had given a new direction to painting. Londoners gaped at Epstein's *Rima* in horror or mirth, but in either case with incomprehension. Long before the public had accepted these novelties or even become aware of them, they were outmoded by abstractionism and surrealism. Functional architecture with its appropriate decor arrived from Germany, and jazz with its disclosure of new rhythms and startling effects of stridency from America. Once again defiance of academic tradition required defiance of the whole order of which it was the expression, either from consistency of principle or because it was all part of the fun. The appearance of book clubs with the labels of Left, Right, Conservative, and Liberal stressed the political preoccupations of writers and readers.

Far more disturbing to the average man than this ferment in the arts, which hardly affected him at all, was the increasing influence of America, which affected his daily life a good deal. The United States was not popular in England during the postwar decades; the large share claimed by Americans in the winning of the war, their insistence upon the payment of the war debt, their repudiation of the League of Nations, and their easy acquisition of art treasures that Englishmen could no longer afford to keep, all provoked a natural resentment. Yet year by year Americanism, if it did not enter the fabric, was more apparent on the surface of English life. It was not all new. Before 1914 Woolworth stores, Ford cars, and Hollywood films were quite usual, and American methods in journalism and big business were beginning to have their effect. But now the pace of the invasion was accelerated. Cocktails, imported dancebands, and the Charleston furnished the same entertainment to night club patrons in London as in New York. The "talkies" brought into every town the transatlantic accent and idiom, which began to be echoed in the speech of the young. American pulp magazines eclipsed their British competitors in supplying fiction for the adolescent, and among the educated more American books were read and American plays seen. The BBC kept the radio ("wireless" as they prefer to call it) thoroughly national but could not countervail a taste for crooners and the music of Tin Pan Alley.

In London the tendency was evident in such new buildings as Bush House, Adelaide House in rebuilt Regent Street, and the apartment blocks of the West End, in the displays of the larger stores and in advertising. Here it became part of a process of the time by which the city was losing much of its distinctive color. Its historical monuments were still intact and traditional pageantry could be seen at the Palace and the Tower, but its streets had lost their distinctive vehicles and a large proportion of their picturesque vendors and beggars. At times, to be sure, there were processions of unemployed Welsh miners, grimly tramping the streets throughout the day, singing their noble, melancholy songs—but they were of a new and solemn portentousness. The slums were not so horrible and the West End not so smart as they had been; pedestrians pushed faster along the sidewalks in the felt-hatted, business-suited indistinction of modern city crowds everywhere. There was a loss of character and of the impalpable atmosphere of intimacy that central London had managed to retain through all the rapid expansion of the nineteenth century. In 1935 it seemed to Max Beerbohm, who had loved it in his Victorian youth, "a bright, cheerful, salubrious Hell."

By this time, the middle thirties, England had weathered the depression, and enjoyed a brief relaxation of the strain of postwar years, during which it was appropriate to celebrate the King's Silver Jubilee in May, 1935. In the following autumn a General Election put an end to Ramsay MacDonald's "National Government," in office since 1929, and returned Baldwin and the Conservatives in spite of the new strength of the Socialist Party which was so diffused that it failed to elect candidates. At the New Year of 1936 King George died at the height of a popularity he had earned, despite his lack of personal force, by twenty-five years of undeviating attention to duty.

The Prince of Wales who succeeded to the throne as Edward VIII was a very different sort of man from his father. He was of the generation that had fought the war and bitterly resented having been denied any real part in it. He shared the impatience of his contemporaries with the conventions and the institutional ceremony of the old order. If, like his grandfather, Edward VII, he had been a conspicuous playboy in his youth, it was largely because he was allowed nothing very serious to do. When he was given the job of touring the world as a kind of supersalesman of empire trade he did it well. He began his reign by disquieting officialdom with changes in the routine and etiquette of his household that showed he had no intention of sustaining all the traditions of the royal family begun by Victoria. As the time of his coronation drew near, rumors, carefully withheld from the press, began to circulate of his friendship with Mrs. Wallis Simpson, a twice-divorced American, and when these were at length confirmed by the king's avowal of his intention to marry her the shock to the nation was profound. Popular feeling widely supported the king, but the upper classes and the whole official world of church and state were against him. On December 10, 1936, he was forced to abdicate in favor of his brother, the Duke of York, who was crowned as George VI. Edward, now Duke of Windsor, went into virtual exile.

To the average man the abdication was a violent shock: the English had once killed their king, and talk of abolishing the Crown had been common of late, but that the king should walk out on the people was unthinkable. It seriously impaired the attachment to the Royal Family which had been maintained for four generations. To the classes which had brought it about it was even more serious, a death warrant from which there could be only the appearance of a reprieve. Everything was done in the elaborate pageantry of the coronation to make it appear that nothing serious had happened, but the fact was patent: the abdication marked the end of English aristocracy as an effective social order. An inauspicious new day had dawned.

Like his father, George V, the new king began his reign in years of tension and conflict that were the prelude to war. Fascists and Communists aggressively dividing Europe into two great political camps were creating a situation in which people like the English, instinctively averse to all political extremes and ideological systems, could only be bewildered. Liberal idealists served in the International Brigade in Spain against Franco, often to be disillusioned long before they were defeated; their opposites joined Sir Oswald Moseley's British Union of Fascists and were noisy and truculent but no more than a nuisance. In general the spirit of the country was thoroughly pacific; the people had no large sympathy for either party and no desire for war on any terms. But through the expressions of pacifism there had been audible for some years a note of anxiety that deepened to alarm as of those who know uneasily that they are whistling in the dark. The warnings and pleas of a generation of writers had been without effect. The Peace Pledge Union founded in 1935 had enrolled within two years 130,000 members pledged to renounce war utterly, but when the threat of Fascist war became immediate, it grew no farther. The Oxford Group movement, widely publicised in the thirties, and the new interest in oriental mysticism, both expressions of a sincere belief that the world could be saved by the regeneration of the individual, had reached only a few. These and other moral resources had failed, material resources were not at hand. The navy was in good condition but principle and economy had both kept the army below efficient strength, while conservatism had kept it obsolete. Organization had not been brought up to date, mechanized equipment of all kinds was lacking, and the RAF was far below parity with the German Luftwaffe.

In this state of things England could only remain a non-intervening spectator of the occupation of the Rhineland, the Spanish war, the "Anschluss," Russia's attack on Finland —all the aggressions that were leading inexorably, step by step, to world war. Against Italy in the Abyssinian war of 1935-36 she invoked the economic sanctions of the League of Nations, but the action only emphasized the impotence of all that was moderate and peaceable in Europe. At last in 1938 Neville Chamberlain's hopeless "appeasement" of Nazi Germany at Munich made war inevitable, though at the time it was widely believed to have averted it.

The approach of war, 1937-39, brought distress and bewilderment to many intellectual groups. To the leftist-pacifists it presented a dilemma: Fascism must be stopped at any cost, yet war must be avoided at any cost. Either way it meant a sacrifice of principle that was made by all but a few who persisted in the intellectual muddle they had begun with. To others the certainty of war meant the certain end of European culture and all that to them was worth working for. Some of these emigrated to the United States where they felt the arts, and artists, had a chance of surviving. To still others it brought the apathy of despair. Propaganda, which had been penetrating the arts rapidly for ten years, now very nearly monopolized them and a widespread paralysis of the creative impulse lasted until the first stages of the war had clarified many issues and engendered a new spirit.

In the last months though press and public tried to remain optimistic almost everyone must have known what was coming. Issue of gas masks, preparation of shelters, organization of air-raid protection left little doubt of the virtual certainty. At the War Ministry, Sir Leslie Hore-Belisha had been rapidly overhauling the army and now its units were brought to established strength. Conscription during peace was for the first time put into effect. Pacifist sentiment, though not extinct, began to fade before the immediate danger, and there was a cessation of talk about "imperialist wars" as well as about Chamberlain's diplomatic triumph. England was not wholly unprepared for the declaration of war that followed upon the invasion of Poland, September 3, 1939. For the second time the lights of Europe went out.

On a Christmas eve during the war some fifty children, exiled to Nassau for their safety, were gathered for a party in the gardens of the Royal Victoria Hotel. After the refreshments and games and presents, a piano struck up a familiar carol and the children were urged to sing. They stood listlessly holding song sheets: a few timid voices began but without support soon died away as if oppressed by the heavy air and the rustle of the palms that had no relevance to English homes. Another carol and another obtained only a pathetic effort of politeness. Then the pianist launched into "Tipperary" and in an instant all those youngsters were with him, rollicking through the tinny old music-hall number, eager for more. In the next half hour they sang them all—"There's a Long, Long Trail," "Pack up Your Troubles," "Keep the Home Fires Burning"—the songs of their fathers' war, and their shrill, breathless voices carried no consciousness of tragic implication. That made it almost unbearable. Nearby at Government House the Duke of Windsor, an exile of an older lost generation, kept the season with official entertainment.

The years following the war were most discouraging for English writers. Victory had been won at the price of economic ruin; and in the new reign of "austerity" many authors found they could not live without an editorial, academic, or civil service post to support them and could not do their best work if they gave their time and effort honestly to these. There was also a marked decline, almost to the vanishing point, in the number of literary periodicals that were the principal publishers of poetry, essays, and short stories. Consequently while there was still a good market for popular and useful works, in the more serious kinds of literature only writers of established reputation and assured sales could maintain their position. Young men of talent turned to other careers than writing, and some who had begun well withdrew. Philip Toynbee, a young novelist of great promise, felt that it was not worth while to write in such times; Henry Green turned successfully to manufacturing, and though he has not ceased to write, the quality of his later work has declined.

The one conspicuous triumph over the adversity of the times was that of the dramatist **Christopher Fry (1907-   )**. After some years as a successful director and a period of army service, he was "discovered" as a dramatic writer in 1946 by John Gielgud who produced *The Lady's Not For Burning* with brilliant success. In 1950 four of his plays were on the London stage concurrently. Fry is a poet whose fables affirming the triumph of youth and life over age and death are clothed in an Elizabethan exuberance of language and lightness of wit. His success has been principally in comedy, but his early tragedy *The First Born* (1946) and, recently, *A Sleep of Prisoners* show his competence in handling more serious themes. He has brought more life to the poetic drama in England than anyone else in modern times, not excepting T. S. Eliot.[1]

Fry's career is one of the few bright notes in a generally sombre picture. The century that began with the splendid energy of the Edwardians shows at its mid-point a faltering in English letters due to no failure of talent but to conditions more inimical to English writers than any they have had to face since the Wars of the Roses. The death of Shaw

[1] Fry's other plays are: *A Boy With a Cart* (1937), *A Phoenix Too Frequent* (1946), *Thor With Angels* (1948), *Venus Observed* (1949). See Derek Stanford, *Christopher Fry, An Appreciation* (1951).

no less than the death of Queen Victoria marked the end of an era, an era for which we have as yet no name.

PREMIERS

Lloyd George (Coalition), *1918-1923*
Stanley Baldwin (Conservative), *1923-1924*
Ramsay MacDonald (Labor), *1924*, (*10 Months*)
Stanley Baldwin (Conservative), *1924-1929*
Ramsay MacDonald ("National Government"), *1929-1935*
Stanley Baldwin (Conservative), *1935-1937*
Neville Chamberlain (Conservative), *1937-1939*

THE MODERNIST POETS

It was in the interval between the wars that the aims and standards of the established order in poetry were challenged by an increasing number of young writers whose literary ideals were at variance with those of the traditionalists, and especially those of the Georgians. The two world wars were not responsible for everything which has been indiscriminately attributed to them, but there is no doubt that much of the spirit of revolt in recent literature can be traced to the shifting political and social standards which appeared during the First War and its aftermath. The old avenues which for long had been accepted as the only means to the highest civilization and culture began to be regarded with mistrust, and much which had heretofore been considered the only media for expression in the arts, especially in painting and poetry, began to appear conventionalized and restricted. In both subject-matter and form, poetry sought to widen its scope by breaking away from what the practitioners of the new art considered artificial and confining.

The theories and principles of the so-called new poets had their roots in many soils, and there are scores of instances in which some of the principles of the modernists were employed with varying degrees of conviction and skill long before the turn of the century. It has even been pointed out that the free rhythms and irregular metrical patterns of the modernists are more truly in line with the Biblical and Anglo-Saxon traditions than all of the stylized metrics of Swinburne and Tennyson. Although there are fundamental similarities between the old traditions and the manner of the modernists, the new poets are often plainly experimentalists. New media and modifications of the old have been attempted in order to try to make articulate the themes which have grown out of the marked changes of the times. Writers who were impressionable to the influence of two great wars, progressive political ideologies, the rapid strides of the machine age, and the psychological precepts of Jung and Freud sought new forms which, they felt, were more appropriate to their themes than the strictly patterned manner of the traditionalists. Although some of the changes of the past thirty years were only a natural reaction against Victorian standards, the revolt of the modernists has its chief roots in the spirit of the times.

Groups and cults have sprung up, often ephemeral and without organization, which have been at cross purposes not only with the traditionalists but with one another as well, which bear on their standards such names as imagists, futurists, dadaists, surrealists, and apocalyptics. Among them there have been the leftists and the rightists, the Marxists and the conservative laborites. Concise differentiation among the various groups is impossible, for there has been an exasperating overlapping in the aims and works of most of the exponents of these schools. There are some who hold to familiar stanzaic patterns and regularity of line but who avoid conventional poetic themes and diction. Others retain poetic themes and diction but insist on complete freedom in matters compositional, including design of line, logical sequence, and even syntax. And there are instances in which a poet has started out zealously in one camp and ended up in another, or even back with the traditionalists.

In a general sense, however, modernist poetry has shown the characteristics indicated by Selden Rodman in *A New Anthology of Modern Poetry* (1938):

imagery patterned on everyday speech.

absence of inversions, stilted apostrophes, conventional end-rhymes, "poetic" language generally, except where used deliberately for incantatory effect.

freedom from the ordinary logic of sequence, jumping from one image to the next by association rather than by the usual cause-effect method.

emphasis on the ordinary, in reaction against the traditional poetic emphasis on the cosmic.

concern with the naked consciousness and the newly identified "unconscious" as against the "soul."

concern with the common man, almost to the exclusion of the "hero" or the extraordinary man.

concern with the social order as against "heaven" and "nature" *

Although concern with the social order, especially that which derived from Russian communism, has declined sharply with the increasing concern with man as an individual who must work out his destiny independent of social agencies, most of the modernists continue to view skeptically the old pathways of nature and religion in which the traditionalists have found guidance and inspiration.

A notable exception in this respect is **T. S. Eliot (1888-   )** who as early as 1928 stated that he was "an Anglo-Catholic in religion, a classicist in literature, and a royalist in politics." The skeptical and cynical Eliot of "The Hippopotamus" has indicated after his sojourn in the wasteland a profound desire for the emotional and spiritual security of religion in the *Quartets* (1943). The emptiness which he had

* Reprinted with the permission of Random House.

outlined so insistently in *The Waste Land* (1922) was a near approach to nihilism; and with a temperament and background such as his it was almost inevitable that he should try to find something in traditional religion as a way to spiritual calm.

T. S. ELIOT

Thomas Stearns Eliot was born in St. Louis, Missouri, in 1888. His paternal grandfather, after graduating from Harvard College, established the first Unitarian Church in St. Louis, and was Chancellor of Washington University which he had helped to found. Eliot's father was a successful businessman with some reputation as a bookman. After preparing for college at the local schools, Eliot entered Harvard in 1906, there to earn both his bachelor's and master's degrees. While at Harvard he wrote poetry, some of which appeared in the *Harvard Advocate,* of which he was the editor. His interest in languages and literature led him to continue his education at the Sorbonne, where he amassed much of his store of information about French literature. Upon his return to America he resumed his work at Harvard and for a time was an assistant in the department of philosophy. After being awarded a traveling scholarship, he went to Europe again, to study in Germany for a time before settling down at Merton College, Oxford. During the First World War he taught school near London for a year before becoming associated with Lloyds Bank. Before the end of the war, however, he gave up his work with the banking firm to become assistant editor of *The Egoist.* Since 1920, he has devoted his time exclusively to editing periodicals, including *The Criterion,* lecturing on literature, and writing critical essays and poetry. Although he has spent considerable time in his native America, he has adopted England as his home. He married an Englishwoman, Miss Vivienne Haigh, in 1915, became a member of the Anglican Church, and in 1927 became a subject of the Crown. He has had the Order of Merit conferred on him, and in 1948, he won the Nobel Prize for poetry.

As early as 1917, Eliot impressed a small audience with a sample of his extraordinary talent in "The Love Song of J. Alfred Prufrock." In the development of the theme of a sensitive man's sense of futility in the stratum of society to which he belongs, there is nothing of the usual logic of sequence; and the images, many of which are susceptible to different levels of interpretation, are thrust into the irregular lines with little by way of transition. The poet's remarkable talent for attaining effects with words and images of totally different pitch appears at times in "Prufrock," but its poetic force is more fully realized in the well-unified "Portrait of a Lady," and in the shorter poems such as "Sweeney among the Nightingales"—a title in itself rich in suggestion of the sharp contrasts which may be expected. *The Waste Land* (1922), if not "a center for the poetic achievement of the first quarter of the present century," has created more discussion and exercized a wider influence than any recent literary work. The five parts are related rather than connected by the prevailing mood suggested in the title. The spiritual and moral emptiness of the present generation and of the trend of civilization is the background out of which the theme emerges. Miss Jessie L. Weston's *From Ritual to Romance* provides a key to the plan of the poem, but many of the passages depend for satisfactory explication on a familiarity with a wide field of culture-history including mythology, Oriental literature and religion, Dante's *Divine Comedy,* and Frazer's *The Golden*

Bough. Although probably the most notable poem of the twentieth century, replete with passages which can be recognized at once as poetic, *The Waste Land* falls short of greatness by reason of its lack of self-sufficiency.

Eliot's negative approach in *The Waste Land* began to give way to a somewhat more positive attitude in the so-called "Ariel Poems," but it was not until "Ash Wednesday" (1930) appeared that he indicated a path away from desolation in what in his Essay on Dante he called "a coherent traditional system of dogma and morals." The positive assertion emerges only after a long conflict in which the poet prays that he can forget:

> These matters that with myself I too much discuss
> Too much explain...*

The four long poems which make up *Quartets* (1943) are in a sense a continuation of the assertion, although these poems have much in them which is not directly concerned with the necessity for an abiding religion. "The Dry Salvages" and "Little Gidding" are not so full of arresting and ingeniously contrived images as the early poems, nor are the contrasts in association and tonal quality so pronounced. They have some of the subdued and flowing tone of meditative poetry in which at times a mystical element is part of the mood. In fact, it has been aptly observed that "the poet who was regarded as the spokesman of a disillusioned generation has become the poet of Christian mysticism."

The plays *The Rock* (1934), *Murder in the Cathedral* (1935), *The Family Reunion* (1939), and *The Cocktail Party* (1949) have themes and characters which lend themselves to dramatic rendering, but Eliot's dramaturgy, like his versification, is not confined to the more conventional patterns. Although his people attain an adequate reality, they are essentially symbolic: Becket, for example, in *Mur-*

* T. S. Eliot, *Ash Wednesday*. Reprinted with permission of Harcourt, Brace and Company.

der in the Cathedral is memorable more as a symbol of conflict than as a biographical portrait. These plays have been successfully produced, but their real power is not in dramatic situation, suspense, and climax, but in the frequently recurrent poetry of the lines.

Eliot's critical essays are erudite and provocative. In *For Lancelot Andrewes* (1929), *Selected Essays, 1917-1932* (1932), *Essays Ancient and Modern* (1936), and *Notes Toward the Definition of Culture* (1948), there is an indication that some sort of system of aesthetics is evolving, although as yet there is no clearly defined pattern. His familiarity with many literatures, even the more obscure phases of them, is plain in the wide variety of his subjects and in his occasional comparative approach. He is at constant pains to define his terms in order to clarify his judgments, most of which are provocative and searching. His forthrightness in modifying some of the statements in his earlier essays in more recent works has supported rather than impaired his reputation as a discerning critic. Among his finest achievements are his essays "The Metaphysical Poets" (1921), "Religion and Literature" (1935), and especially "Dante" (1929), all of which appear in the new edition of *Selected Essays* (1950). His precepts are widely discussed and quoted, and many of the essays possess a stylistic merit which makes his criticism in itself a form of creation.

VERSE: *Prufrock and Other Observations* (1917), *Poems* (1919), *Ara Vos Prec* (1920), *The Waste Land* (1922), *Poems, 1909-1925* (1925), *Journey of the Magi* (1927), *A Song for Simeon* (1928), *Animula* (1929), *Ash Wednesday* (1930), *Marina* (1930), *Triumphal March* (1931), *Sweeney Agonistes: Fragments of an Aristophanic Melodrama* (1932), *Collected Poems: 1909-1935* (1936), *Old Possum's Book of Practical Cats* (1939), *Four Quartets* (1943), includes "Burnt Norton," "East Coker," "The Dry Salvages," and "Little Gidding." PLAYS: *The Rock: A Pageant Play* (1934), *Murder in the Cathedral* (1935), *The Family Reunion* (1939), *The Cocktail Party*, produced in Edinburgh (1949). PROSE: *The Sacred Wood* (1920),

Homage to John Dryden (1924), *For Lancelot Andrewes: Essays on Style and Order* (1928), *Selected Essays, 1917-1932* (1932), *The Use of Poetry and the Use of Criticism* (1933), *After Strange Gods: A Primer of Modern Heresy* (1934), *Elizabethan Essays* (1934), *Essays Ancient and Modern* (1936), *Points of View* (1941), *Notes Toward the Definition of Culture* (1948), *Selected Essays* (1950), *Poetry and Drama* (1951).

Donald C. Gallup, *A Bibliographical Check-list of the Writings of T. S. Eliot* (New Haven, 1947); F. O. Mathiessen, *The Achievement of T. S. Eliot* (Boston, 1935); George Williamson, *The Talent of T. S. Eliot* (Seattle, 1930); Thomas McGreevy, *Thomas Stearns Eliot: A Study* (1931); Elizabeth Drew, *T. S. Eliot: The Design of his Poetry* (1949); H. L. Gardner, *The Art of T. S. Eliot* (1950); Leonard Unger, ed., *T. S. Eliot: A Selected Critique* (1948); Richard March and Tambimuttu, eds., *T. S. Eliot: A Symposium* (1948); Genevieve M. Foster, "The Archetypal Imagery in T. S. Eliot," *PMLA*, LX (1945), 567-587; C. L. Barber, "T. S. Eliot After Strange Gods," *Southern Rev.*, VI (1940), 387-416; William Blisset, "The Argument of T. S. Eliot's *Four Quartets*," *Univ. of Toronto Quar.* XV (1946), 115-126; Raymond Preston, *"Four Quartets" Rehearsed* (1946); Ben Ray Redman, "T. S. Eliot: In Sight of Posterity," *Sat. Rev. Lit.*, XXXII (March 12, 1949), 9-11.

In spite of the small grain of truth in F. R. Leavis's comment that "the Sitwells belong more to the history of publicity than to the history of poetry," **Edith, Osbert,** and **Sacheverell Sitwell** are interesting figures in recent literature. They are the talented offspring of Sir George Sitwell who traced his ancestry back to the Angevin kings, and who felt that strict conventionality was the proper environment for his family. He was the sort of Englishman who "would appear for dinner even in a sordid wayside *trattoria* dressed in white tie and tails." To his daughter Edith he once remarked that the best kind of Englishwoman was one who should be bad at nothing and good at nothing. The young Sitwells obviously found much in the old order which was stifling, and once started on their career of rejection of the old, they gloried in their new freedom.

Of the three, **Edith Sitwell (1887-   )** is best known and the most prolific poet. As a child she startled her parents by the pronouncement that she wanted to be a genius. She wrote verse in her teens, but it was not until she made her residence in London and began to edit the progressive periodical-anthology *Wheels* in 1916 that her talent took shape. *The Mother and Other Poems* (1915) had failed to attract much notice; it was with *Clowns' Houses* (1918) and *The Wooden Pegasus* (1920) that she attracted an increasingly wide and curious audience; and by the time *Façade* (1922) was presented at the Aeolian Hall in London, "Sitwellism" became a part of the vocabulary of the literati. Four small volumes appeared between 1922 and *Gold Coast Customs* (1929), to be followed by an interval in which she devoted her time to prose studies of which *Alexander Pope* (1930) and *The English Eccentrics* (1933) are representative. She returned to verse during and after the Second War to produce some of her best work.

EDITH SITWELL

There are essentially two Edith Sitwells, the early and the late. In her early work there is a considerable amount of toying with verse patterns and tonal effects, and what seems at least on the surface to be nonsense verse, although it is not unlikely that she would resent such a term. It is unfortunate that the virtuosity of the poet blinds some readers to the fact that in the earlier pieces including *Façade* she is doing little more than playing with tonal patterns and ingenious imagery. It is scarcely possible that Miss Sitwell had anything important to say in such dexterously turned pieces as "Hornpipe" and "Fox Trot." She has said that she dislikes simplicity, but such a statement should not mislead anyone into the notion that her word-playing is always the medium for portents and profound readings of life. Although she herself has given support to the conclusion that *Gold Coast Customs,* written as early as 1929, was a definite prophecy of the imminence of the Second World War, the verses which appeared in the collection are more noteworthy for their rhythms than for any clear demonstration of prescience. Among the earlier volumes, however, there are poems which are not always exercises in verbal and tonal virtuosity, for there is much in *The Sleeping Beauty* (1924) and *Troy Park* (1925) which shows emotional depth. In the latter collection, "Colonel Fantock," with its nostalgic note and the implication that the times are out of joint, maintains a high poetic level. Of the shorter poems, "The King of China's Daughter" and "Panope" have more genuine feeling and authentic poetic phrase than the much-anthologized "Aubade." As an example of shifting of sense-impressions "Aubade" has interest, for "light creaks," "flowers cluck," and the light which "creaks" also "whines." In another verse-exercise, "Trio for Two Cats and a Trombone," "light is braying like an ass."

In her later work, although she has not forsaken artifice entirely, she is less the virtuoso and more the poet. She herself has observed that by the forties, her "time of experiments was done." *The Song of the Cold* (1945), *Green Song* (1946) and *The Shadow of Cain* (1947) show a perceptible deepening of feeling which can be traced probably to her consciousness of the tragedy of war. The awfulness of the atomic bomb, and the penalty man is paying for his unwillingness to try to cultivate what is good in his own nature and nature at large, have become themes to which she responds with profound feeling. The title-poem of her most recent collection, *The Canticle of the Rose* (1949) reaffirms her belief in the existence of elements of good in man if he will recognize them and follow them. There is a softening of tone in these poems, with a frequent use of a long line which eliminates the abrupt, staccato effects in much of her early verse. The symbols, although still arresting, are more plainly integrated in the fabric of the theme, and their recurrent use in different contexts is limited to recognizable poetic ends. Without losing her deftness in the manipulation of images and tones, Miss Sitwell has demonstrated in her later work far more than the sheen of virtuosity.

Osbert Sitwell (1892-   ), now Sir Osbert, chief publicist for his sister and younger brother, and an author of varied talents, was born in London with the advantages that belong to an aristocratic heritage. He was educated by private tutors until he entered Eton. In one of his volumes of memoirs, *The Scarlet Tree,* he reported that he liked Eton, except for the work and the games, and for the boys and the masters. During the First World War he saw service in France as an officer in the Grenadier Guards, out of which he emerged with some of Sassoon's bitterness toward war and its instigators. Such pieces as "Babel" and "Tears," written out of his wartime experience, are as forceful as anything he has done in verse. Although marked for a public career, since his late twenties he has devoted his chief time to writing. He contributed verse to *Wheels,* and later issued small volumes of poems under the titles *Argonaut and Juggernaut* (1920) and *Out of the Flame* (1923). The prevailing tone of the verse in these collections is satiric. Although his manner shows many of the characteristics of the modernists, in his verse he was never particularly concerned with form. He is generally more compressed and comprehensible than his sister; in fact, by comparison, his verse makes for easy reading. His later work has been done chiefly in prose, in which he works with considerable felicity. The four volumes of memoirs—*Left Hand, Right Hand* (1944), *The Scarlet Tree* (1946), *Great Morning!* (1947), and *Laughter in the Next Room* (1948)— are engaging illuminations of his heritage and the environment in which he was reared. Sir George Sitwell, the father of the triumvirate, for all of the satirical thrusts of the author, emerges, if not the hero of the memoirs, a very personable and likeable figure. Besides being a persuasive account of the Sitwells, these memoirs are a well-mellowed record of Edwardian England.

Sacheverell Sitwell (1897-   ), the youngest of the trio, and the Peregrine of *Colonel Fantock*, has shown a striking versatility in interests and talents. Like Osbert, he was sent to Eton, and later he attended Balliol College, Oxford. After the First World War in which he served as an officer in the Grenadier Guards, he submitted verse to the literary *Wheels* on which his sister and others of the new schools were riding. The verse in *The People's Palace* (1918), *The One Hundred and One Harlequins* (1922), and *The Thirteenth Caesar* (1924) seems plainly experimental. There is a conscious and at times clever use of image and tonal effect in which dissonance is frequent, but there is no real depth of theme, nor are there any really memorable lines. "Doctor Donne and Gargantua," which the reader is led to believe is to be a poem of serious intent has some of the design of a great poem, but the final result is fragmentary and disappointing. The poems in *The Cyder Feast* (1927), although without loftiness of purpose or design, present their themes more simply and directly. His more recent work has been done largely in prose in which he employs a lucid and engaging style in treating a wide variety of subjects in the arts, especially architecture and music.

EDITH SITWELL: VERSE: *Clowns' Houses* (1918), *The Wooden Pegasus* (1920), *Façade* (1922), *The Sleeping Beauty* (1924), *Troy Park* (1925), *Rustic Elegies* (1927), *Gold Coast Customs* (1929), *Collected Poems* (1930), *Poems Old and New* (1940), *Street Songs* (1943), *The Song of the Cold* (1945), *Green Song* (1946), *The Shadow of Cain* (1947), *The Canticle of thè Rose: Poems 1917-1949* (1949). PROSE: *Poetry and Criticism* (1925), *Alexander Pope* (1930), *Bath* (1932), *The English Eccentrics* (1933), *Aspects of Poetry* (1934), *Victoria of England* (1936), *Trio: Dissertations on Some Aspects of National Genius*, with Osbert and Sacheverell (1938), *I Live Under a Black Sun, A Novel* (1938), *A Poet's Notebook* (1944), *Fanfare for Elizabeth* (1946).

SIR OSBERT SITWELL: VERSE: *Argonaut and Juggernaut* (1919), *Out of the Flame* (1923), *England Reclaimed* (1927), *Collected Poems and Satires* (1931), *Penny Foolish* (1935). PROSE: *Before the Bombardment* (1926), *The Man Who Lost Himself* (1929), *Miracle on Sinai* (1933), *Left Hand, Right Hand* (1944), *The Scarlet Tree* (1946), *Great Morning!* (1947), *Laughter in the Next Room* (1948), *Noble Essences* (1950).

SACHEVERELL SITWELL: VERSE: *The People's Palace* (1918). *The One Hundred and One Harlequins* (1922), *The Thirteenth Caesar* (1924), *The Cyder Feast* (1927), *Doctor Donne and Gargantua* (1930), *Collected Poems* (1936), *Selected Poems* (1948). PROSE: *Southern Baroque Art* (1924), *German Baroque Art* (1927), *The Gothick North* (1929), *Spanish Baroque Art* (1931), *Mozart* (1932), *Liszt* (1934), *The Hunters and the Hunted* (1947), *Morning Noon and Night in London* (1947).

Thomas Balston, *Sitwelliana, 1915-1927* (1928), a check-list of the Sitwells' works; R. L. Megroz, *The Three Sitwells* (1927); Sherard Vines, *The Sitwells* (1928); Osbert Burdett, "The Sitwells," *London Mercury*, XV (1927), 515-525; Horace Gregory, "The 'Vita Nuova' of Baroque Art in the Recent Poetry of Edith Sitwell," *Poetry*, LXVI (1945), 148-156; C. M. Bowra, *Edith Sitwell* (1947); José Garcia Villa, ed., *A Celebration for Edith Sitwell* (1948), articles by Stephen Spender, Maurice Bowra, Horace Gregory, Gordon Bottomely, Richard Church, and others.

Harold Monro (1879-1932) was a modernist more in theory than in practice. As the editor of *Poetry and Drama*, he tried to make plain to his readers that he and his contributors were striking out into new and unexplored fields of poetic expression, but by far the larger part of his verse has an easily recognized attachment to the established order. There are elements in his verse which are definitely modernistic, to be sure, especially in such poems as "London Interior" and "Bitter Sanctuary," in which the measures are irregular and the imagery and diction are drawn from everyday speech; but these elements are not frequent or pronounced in his work at large. They seem to be rather well-deliberated devices which are employed to give his verse additional latitude, and to demonstrate the author's feeling of necessity for escape from the conventional manner. Certainly "Everything," "The Earth for Sale," and "Midnight Lamentation," among many others, belong essentially to the main current of English poetry. A careful reading of his prose criticism and his verse would seem to indicate that he was convinced of some of the principles of the modernists, but that he was unable to cut completely free from the traditionalists.

Harold Edward Monro was born in Brussels, Belgium, the son of a well-to-do civil engineer of Scotch descent. The boy was schooled in England, chiefly at Radley, before matriculating at Caius College, Cambridge, where he received his degree in 1901. While at Cambridge he was known as an assiduous poetry reader and a dilettante in the arts. After his graduation, he studied law for a short time before becoming engaged in a variety of occupations which included selling real estate and operating a poultry farm. Such occupations were evidently not to his liking, for his interests had long been literary, and finally he turned to literature as a profession. He was later to describe himself as an "author, publisher, editor, and book-seller," in all of which roles he became well known in London. As early as 1908, he had issued a small sheaf of verse entitled *Judas*. The Samurai Press, his first venture in publishing, had only an ephemeral existence; and his *Poetry Review,* founded in order to consider "poetry in its relation to life," was also short-lived. But in 1912, with the founding of the Poetry Bookshop and the quarterly *Poetry and Drama,* Monro became a London institution. Many of the younger poets carried their wares to him for publication, and the room above his bookshop became a gathering place for the more progressive of the literati where verse was read and judged. The First World War interrupted Monro's efforts, but upon his return, after serving in the War Office and as an officer in the antiaircraft corps, he reopened the Bookshop and launched a new periodical, *The Chapbook,* in which much of the spirit of *Poetry and Drama* was preserved. In 1920, he married Alida Klemantaski, herself a poet, who assisted him as both bookseller and editor. The same year he issued his concise and at times oversevere critical analysis of some of his contemporaries under the title *Some Contemporary Poets,* and in 1929 he brought out *Twentieth Century Poetry,* an anthology in which his tastes are clearly indicated. From 1908 until 1928, he wrote verse, much of which appeared in his periodicals and in chapbooks. His death in 1932 left a void for many of the younger poets who had found him and his Bookshop a source of encouragement and inspiration.

Although Monro has been called "a drab poet," and a "poet by intention" rather than "a singer by intuition," there is a considerable body of his verse in which he has handled worth-while and unusual poetic themes in a skilful and beautiful way. Furthermore, the song quality which in his defense of the modernists he insisted was unnecessary appears again and again in his verse. "Solitude," "The Nightingale Near the House," and "Midnight Lamentation" are rich in melody and tonal effect. The last-named poem, for all of its artful manipulation of pronouns in the closing lines of the early stanzas, cannot be dismissed as mere rhetoric. Pieces such as "The Dog" have wide appeal, but they are not great poetry in either theme or manner, nor is the graphic "Bitter Sanctuary" of lasting quality. The poems which make up *Real Property* are uneven, some of them lacking in poetic substance; and in Part I especially, there is little that the reader wishes to retain. His finest and most characteristic theme is that which appears in many of the poems: a sort of mystic relationship between the poet and inanimate objects which he recognizes as a part of him. His feeling of association with the furnishings of his room, especially those which have served him well, becomes almost an expression of obligation. Thus a candle, the bed, an old copper basin all have "little cries," and become animated with the poet's sensitive response to their presence. In "Everything," and in many of the stanzas in *Strange Meetings,* this relationship finds its choicest expression. Although definitely a minor poet, and one who profits greatly by selection, Harold Monro is nonetheless a true poet in a considerable part of his work.

VERSE: *Judas* (1908), *Before Dawn* (1911), *Children of Love* (1914), *Trees* (1915), *Strange Meetings* (1917), *Real Property* (1922), The *Earth for Sale* (1928), *Collected Poems* (1933). PROSE: *Some Contemporary Poets* (1920).

There is no sustained biographical or critical treatment of Harold Monro. T. S. Eliot's critical note which appears in the Introduction to *The Collected Poems of Harold Monro* (1933) and Frank Flint's note in the Introduction to the same volume are useful but inadequate. The treatment in Herbert Palmer's *Post-Victorian Poetry* (1938) is well considered.

In 1915 Harold Monro issued from his Poetry Bookshop a small volume entitled *Images Old and New* by **Richard Aldington (1892-   )**. At the time of the publication of these poems the school of modernistic verse known as Imagist had already attracted considerable attention. Vividness of image, conciseness and compression, suggestion rather than explicit expression, and freedom from conventional verse patterns are the most pronounced features of Imagist poetry. Richard Aldington's most characteristic verse shows all of these features. He has refused to be too strictly identified with any group or movement in his more recent work, and his fine ear for rhythms and tonal effects has always kept him from dealing with only verbal polychromes.

Richard Aldington, although he has spent much time in the United States, was born in England in 1892, and after studying at Dover College, matriculated at London University. Here he laid an excellent foundation in the classical languages and literatures which was later to be utilized in his translations of the Greek and Roman poets. It has been suggested that Aldington's particular form of pictorial image is the result of his familiarity with Greek literature. As early as 1909, before he was twenty, Aldington had verses published in London, but it was not until he came under the influence of Ezra Pound between 1910 and 1912 that his work took on a distinctive Imagist quality. It was in 1912 that "Choricos" appeared in the second number of the American periodical *Poetry,* a poem considered by the more zealous Imagists as "one of the finest death songs in the language—of a beauty pure and sculpturesque, whitely carved in marble." It was with this poem and those which appeared in *Images Old and New* (1915) that Aldington became known as the leader of the Imagist movement in England. During the First World War, in which he served at the front, his themes changed perceptibly. *Images of War* (1919) is a bitter indictment of war, and *A Fool in the Forest* (1925), with its dissonances and implications of despair, suggests something of T. S. Eliot's *Waste Land.* Following the war, Aldington married the American Hilda Doolittle, known by her initials H.D., one of the outstanding American Imagists. He has written novels, including *Death of a Hero* (1929) and more recently he has done a considerable amount of excellent translating from the Greek, Roman, and French poets, all of which is in the poetic spirit. The autobiographical *Life for Life's Sake* (1941) is an engaging and illuminating record of his artistic development, and especially of his association with the literary movements of his generation.

Although Imagism as a cult is no longer active, it must be observed that a sort of Imagism appears in much great poetry, and that Aldington's application of the Imagist principles led him not only to a distinctive but to a genuinely poetic expression. His metaphors, fresh and original, are drawn from a sensitive response to a wide variety of sensory experiences, chiefly pictorial. There is no apparent labor in these parallels although they give the impression of being finely wrought. The music in the lines is almost always submissive to the pictorial element, but the free verse in which the images are drawn is a felicitous and often melodious medium. Such poems as "Lesbia," "The Poplar," and the series of six poems entitled "Images" show not only fine workmanship but emotional range and depth as well.

VERSE: *Choricos* (1912), *Images* (1915), [*Images Old and New*] (1916); *The Love Poems of Myrrhine and Konallis: A Cycle of Prose Poems Written after the Greek Manner* (1917), expanded and issued as *The Love of Myrrhine and Konallis* (1926), *Reverie: A Little Book of Poems for H.D.* (1917), *Images of War* (1919), *Images of Desire* (1919), *War and Love* (1919), *Exile and Other Poems* (1923), *A Fool in the Forest: A Phantasmagoria* (1925), *Collected Poems* (1928), *Hark the Herald* (1928), *The Eaten Heart* (1929), *A Dream in the Luxembourg* (1930), [*Love and the Luxembourg*] (1930), *Poems* (1934), *Complete Poems* (1949). PROSE: *Death of a Hero: A Novel* (1929), *The Colonel's Daughter: A Novel* (1931), *All Men are Enemies: A Romance* (1933), *Women Must Work* (1934), *At All Costs* (1930), *Last Straws* (1930), *Two Stories: Deserter and The Lads of the Village* (1930), *A War Story* (1930), *Stepping Heavenward* (1931), *Soft Answers* (1932). STUDIES: *The Poet and His Age* (1922), *Literary Studies and Reviews*

(1924), *French Studies and Reviews* (1926), *Remy de Gourmont: A Modern Man of Letters* (1927), *D. H. Lawrence: An Indiscretion* (1927). MEMOIRS: *Life for Life's Sake* (1941).

Thomas McGreevy, *Richard Aldington, an Englishman* (1931); Glenn Hughes, *Imagism and the Imagists* (1931); May Sinclair, "Richard Aldington's Images," *English Rev.,* XXXII (1921), 397-404; "Imagists as a Group," ns., *Nation,* CXII (1925), 20-22.

The year 1915 saw not only the publication of Aldington's *Images* and the beginning of Amy Lowell's anthologies *Some Imagist Poets,* but also the appearance of the most distinctive verse of **Frank Flint (1885-**) whose work in *Cadences* is definitely in the Imagist manner. Later in the same year his "History of Imagism" was printed in the May issue of *The Egoist* in which there was a justification of what the Imagists were trying to do, and an expository note on the verse in *Cadences.* Although his early work *In the Net of the Stars* (1909) was far removed from the content and style of the traditionalists, it is in *Cadences* and *Otherworld* (1920) that the characteristics of Imagism are most clearly illustrated. In the unrimed, irregular lines there are richly suggestive images which appeal to the mind rather than to the senses and the emotions. Richard Aldington has judged much of Flint's poetry aptly in his review of *Otherworld:* "Melancholy, sometimes a little bitter, sometimes mellowed by reflection; an eager love of beauty which is often thwarted and disappointed; an essential sweetness, loneliness, and good sense; above all, an instinctive gusto for ordinary human life in spite of the weakness and folly and sordidness."

W. H. Auden (1907-) is one of the most productive and versatile of the younger poets. He has been a more vigorous propagandist than his literary associates, Day Lewis, MacNeice, and Spender; and it is possibly for this reason that the reviewers have attributed qualities of leadership to him. His shifting views and individual idiom, however, have disqualified him for maintaining a consistent leadership in any faction, and for essentially the same reasons, he is in no sense a follower. His work has come

W. H. AUDEN

to represent a cloth of many colors, in which as yet no pronounced design is discernible. For a time he was no doubt sincere in his belief that man's salvation lay in the proper application of communism, but more recently he has placed the responsibility on the individual. His manner ranges from the very serious to the breezy and from the highly elliptical to the diffuse. Often he is dynamic and eloquent, and again, overingenious and labored.

Wystan Hugh Auden was born in 1907 into an environment that suggested little of what he was later to consider the plight of those of his class. His grandfathers on both sides were Church of England clergymen, and his father was a physician who held the post of medical officer at the University of Birmingham. The boy attended Gresham's School where he followed an early interest in biology; and it is reported that he was widely read in many fields before he matriculated at Christ Church, Oxford, where he was known as a young man of independent intellect and radical views. After leaving Oxford, he spent some time in Germany before settling down temporarily to the profession of teaching in boys' schools. These early stages in the poet's development he traces in Part IV of his "Letter to Lord Byron" from which can be gathered his feelings concerning

English boys' schools, the teachers in such institutions, and the influences which determined his career as a poet. He states explicitly that his early attachment for the poetry of Edward Thomas, Rupert Brooke, and Thomas Hardy, and the critical canons of Matthew Arnold he rejected in favor of the "gasworks and dried tubers" of T. S. Eliot and the verdicts of *The Criterion*. He traces the influences of John Layard, the anthropologist, Homer Lane, the psychologist, and D. H. Lawrence, the poet, on his development during the time immediately following his leaving Oxford. His experiences and impressions after 1935 have not been recorded in the same autobiographical fashion, but they all found expression in his works. During the Spanish Civil War, he drove an ambulance at the front and turned his pen to a zealous support of the Loyalists. In 1936 he accompanied his fellow-poet Louis MacNeice to Iceland, out of which the *Letters from Iceland* (1937) developed. In 1938 he went with Christopher Isherwood to China where they gathered materials for *Journey to a War* (1939) and discussed joint projects for the future. Before the outbreak of the Second World War, Auden came to the United States which he has decided to adopt as his home. Here he has held guest professorships at the University of Michigan, Swarthmore College, and Bennington College. For his long poem *The Age of Anxiety* (1946) he was awarded the Pulitzer Prize. Recently he has done a considerable amount of reviewing.

Until Auden came to America, his most distinctive work was included in the fairly sizable volume *Poems* (1934). It contains "Paid on Both Sides," a short verse play which he calls a charade and which has much of the puzzling quality of a charade; "The Orators, an English Study" which is a medley of prose, jingles, and odes in three books, with prologue and epilogue; and the short verse play "The Dance of Death" in which a leftist theme is presented through a medium which suggests a Chinese drama. The most forceful pieces in the collection are the short poems, especially Number 22 with the first line, "Get there if you can and see the land you once were proud to own" in which there is a vigorous preachment against the blindness of those who failed to recognize the urgent need for social change. To the theme of the emptiness and disintegration of his particular class in England, he went again and again, with the frequent insistence and prediction that unless changes were made immediately, utter destruction would result. In many of these poems the implicit remedy for man's ills is communism. The themes would seem to indicate that Auden sought to reach a wide audience, but his manner often thrusts a formidable obstacle in the way of the reader who seeks ready comprehensibility. An idiom of sharp ellipsis, irregular syntax, and often conflicting images impairs the effect of some of these earlier poems.

His more recent verse which has appeared under the titles *Another Time* (1940), *The Double Man* (1941), *For the Time Being* (1945), and his most ambitious recent effort *The Age of Anxiety* (1946), show both a widening and deepening of theme, and a style less given to individual mannerisms. Although he is still concerned with the confusion and frustration which beset the present generation as illustrated in *The Age of Anxiety,* with his English background receding and his ideal of communism crumbling, he no longer has a particular class to warn or a specific solution to offer for improving conditions. In these later poems there are hints that religion may be the answer, and that man's loneliness and sense of futility may drive him to realize the necessity of love for one another. Disillusioned with the poet's attempt to create a Utopian society by dispensing propaganda, he has become concerned with the eternal verities which are in keeping with the poet's art.

Verse: *Poems* (1930), *The Orators: An English Study* (1932), *The Dance of Death* (1933), *Poems* (1934), *Look, Stranger* (1936), *[On This Island]* (1937), *Spain* (1937), *Letters from Iceland,* with Louis MacNeice (1937), *Journey to a War,* with Christopher Isherwood (1939), *Another time* (1940), *Some Poems* (1940), *New Year Letter [The Double Man]* (1941), *For the Time Being* (1945), *The Age of Anxiety* (1946), *Nones* (1951). Plays, with Christopher Isherwood: *The Dog Beneath the Skin* (1935), *Ascent of F 6* (1936), *On the Frontier* (1938).

Francis Scarfe, *Auden and After* (1942); Richard Hoggart, *W. H. Auden* (1951); Stephen Spender, "The Importance of W. H. Auden," *London Mercury,* XXXIX (1939), 613-619; J. G. Southworth, "Wystan Hugh Auden," *Sewanee Rev.,* XLVI (1938), 189-205; Randall Jarrell, "Freud to Paul: Stages in Auden's Ideology," *Partisan Rev.* (1945), 437-457; Malcolm Cowley, "Auden and Spender," *New Republic,* LXXX (1934), 189-190; J. W. Beach, "The Poems of Auden and the Prose Diathesis," *Virginia Quar. Rev.,* XXV (1949), 365-383; Maurice Cranston, "Poet's Retreat," *John O'London's Weekly,* LVII (Feb. 6, 1948), 1.

Although the name of **C. Day Lewis (1904-   )** is often linked with that of Auden by reason of their Oxford association and their common interest in leftist verse in the thirties, the similarities as personalities and poets are superficial. Less given to extremes than the youger poet, Day Lewis is nonetheless a positive personality; and where Auden's utterance is at times prosaic, Day Lewis is essentially lyrical. He himself sees no continuous line in his poetic development, but rather a series of fresh starts to each of which he has brought a well-disciplined talent.

Cecil Day Lewis was born at Ballintubber, Queen's County, Ireland, the only son of an English clergyman and a mother who was a descendant of Oliver Goldsmith. The family moved to England when he was three. He was a precocious child, for he has observed that his verse-writing habit goes back to the age of six. At the Sherborne School in Dorset where he went on a scholarship he won many distinctions, including the Poetry Prize in two successive years. He matriculated at Wadham College, Oxford in 1923 to pursue an already lively interest in the Roman poets and to take an active part in the literary groups. While at the University he issued some of his verse, *Beechen Vigil and Other Poems* (1925), and was co-editor with Auden of *Oxford Poetry* in 1927. Until 1935 he was a teacher at Helensburgh near Glasgow and Cheltenham College, and in order to supplement his income he wrote detective fiction under the name Nicholas Blake, children's stories, and novels. During the war, he was engaged at the Ministry of Information and with his translation in verse of Virgil's *Georgics,* and more recently he has been working on a translation of the *Aeneid.* His well-considered and lucid essays in *A Hope for Poetry* (1934) and *The Poetic Image* (1947), the Clark Lectures delivered at Cambridge in 1946, and the considerable body of his creative work in poetry have given him a high place in contemporary literature. Recently he has been appointed Professor of Poetry at Oxford and has been suggested as the next laureate.

Day Lewis, although identified with the leftist group and "cause poetry" in the thirties, has at the earlier and later extremities of his work demonstrated that his interest in the social order was only an interlude or a passing phase of his verse. His espousal of the cause—"the road these times should take"—was not the result of poetic whim, much less the result of an eagerness to be identified with a group or creed, for there is no doubt that he was sincere when he exclaimed: "It is now or never . . . the break with the past." During and since the war, however, he, like most of the leftist writers, has forsaken the theme of social revolt for less limited sources of inspiration. In *Poems in Wartime* (1940) he found a temporary though compelling theme susceptible to a variety of moods; and in *Short is the Time: Poems 1936-1943* (1943), and *Poems, 1943-1947* (1948), he has shown an increasing range and depth. Always a careful technician and craftman, his verse is disciplined without losing animation and gives proof of his line:

> The poet's inward pride, the certainty of power.

VERSE: *Beechen Vigil and Other Poems* (1925), *Country Comet* (1928), *Transitional Poem* (1929), *From Feathers to Iron* (1931), *The Magnetic Mountain* (1933), *A Time to Dance and Other Poems* (1935), *Overtures to Death and Other Poems* (1938), *Poems in Wartime* (1940), *Word Over All* (1943), *Short is the Time: Poems 1936-1943* (1943), *Poems 1943-1947* (1948). PROSE: *A Hope for Poetry* (1934), *The Poetic Image* (1947). Of the detective stories, *A Question of Proof* (1935) is representative.

Francis Scarfe, "The Development of Day Lewis" in *Auden and After* (1942); Stanley J. Kunitz, "Between Two Worlds," *Poetry*, XLVII (1935), 158-162; James G. Southworth, "Cecil Day Lewis," *Sewanee Rev.*, XLV (1937), 469-484; Campbell Nairne, "The New Professor of Poetry," *John O'London's Weekly*, LX (March 16, 1951), 1-2.

Louis MacNeice (1907-   ) belongs to the group of younger poets who were concerned with social revolt in the thirties and who rejected in large measure the themes and manner of the traditionalists. Although lacking the experimental daring of Auden and the intensity of Spender, he has written much which reflects the tendencies in recent verse. His most characteristic themes deal with contemporary issues, although of late, he, like the others, has become more interested in the individual than in political ideologies; and his manner, although deliberately down to earth, shows an inclination to vary the basic rhythms of standard versification rather than to reject them altogether. He has said that his own preference is for "poetry that is musical, but that the characteristics of this music are not superficial prettiness or smoothness." In his effort to avoid mere prettiness and smoothness, he has often produced lines which, at least to the traditionalist ear, are not only prose-like but also possessed of the flatness which often accompanies an off-hand reference to a commonplace topic. Once accustomed to his casual manner, the reader can often see in MacNeice's work a sincere feeling seeking and at times finding a poetic expression.

Frederick Louis MacNeice was born in Belfast in 1907, the son of a clergyman who had been Bishop of Down, Connor, and Dromore. From an early age, he tells us, he was fascinated by the cadences and imagery of the Bible. Of his Ulster background he wrote: "I cannot be anyone else than what this land engendered me." At the age of fourteen he was sent to the Marlborough School where he read romantic poetry lazily, but he was evidently sufficiently interested in verse to keep a "case-book" of reflections about the poetry that interested him. This collection of notes he continued after his matriculation at Oxford in 1926; and after reading James Joyce's *Ulysses,* T. S. Eliot's *The Waste Land,* and the novels of D. H. Lawrence—from which he says that his Oxford ideology was built—and talking about poetry with his contemporaries, chiefly Auden, he found much to commit to his "case-book." Poetry and Greek became his chief interests at college. After leaving Oxford, he married and settled for five years as professor of classical literature at the University of Birmingham, later to go to London to lecture on Greek at London University. In 1941 he visited the United States where for a time he held a guest lectureship at Cornell University. During the greater part of the War, he was a script writer for the BBC, and more recently, along with his writing of poetry, he has devoted much of his time and talent to radio drama.

His most characteristic poetry thus far shows him confused about the present and uneasy about the future. This bewilderment of mind and spirit—certainly a legitimate theme for modern verse—is sufficiently intense and recurrent to lead him to seek its expression in various ways. "An Eclogue for Christmas," written in dialogue form which is an excellent vehicle for his conversational tone, is a sort of *Waste Land* in miniature: although there is an occasional note of regret that the old order no longer suffices, that the "so ephemeral things" cannot be permanent, the regret gives way to a feeling of desolation and impending cataclysm. Those who have nothing by way of tradition, who have no dreams, will fare best, for they have nothing to lose in the upheaval. Apparently there is no way to prepare for it, much less escape it. Early in the thirties, MacNeice mistrusted communism as a way out; and since the War he has put aside any concern with Marxist principles. Without losing sight of the perplexities which beset humanity, he is more occupied with man's relationship to man than with man's integration in a social pattern. In such verses as "Birmingham," "The British Museum Reading Room," and "Refugees" he is both imagist and impressionist; and in the poems in his recent volume *Holes in the Sky* (1948) there is much which suggests a compromise in both theme and manner with the traditionalists.

VERSE: *Blind Fireworks* (1929), *Poems* (1935), *Poems* (1937), *The Earth Compels* (1938), *Poems: 1925-1940* (1941), *Plant and Phantom* (1941), *Springboard: Poems 1941-1944* (1944), *Holes in the Sky* (1948), *The Dark Tower and Other Radio Scripts* (1948). PROSE: *Modern Poetry: A Personal Essay* (1938), *The Poetry of W. B. Yeats* (1941).

Francis Scarfe, "Louis MacNeice: Poetry and Common Sense," in *Auden and After* (1942); Delmore Schwartz, "Adroitly Naïve," *Poetry,* XLVIII (1936), 115-118; Julian Symons, "Louis MacNeice: the Poet as Everyman," *Poetry,* LVI (1940), 86-95; T. G. Wilson, "One of the Best," *Poetry,* VI (1938), 339-344; Stuart G. Brown, "Some Poems of Louis MacNeice," *Sewanee Rev.,* LI (1943), 62-72.

Of the new voices which sounded during the early thirties, none showed more promise of high poetic attainment than that of **Stephen Spender (1909-   )**. The reviews which followed the publication of his *Poems* in 1933 were generally enthusiastic: in some sources he was compared to Shelley as a rebel-lyrist. This promise has in some measure been fulfilled, although there are aspects of his craftmanship which are still somewhat removed from consummate artistry. Like many of the poets of his generation, he recognized the need for social change; but like most of them, he, too, has become disillusioned about the efficacy of the communist system as the road to man's salvation. He is still acutely sensitive to man's plight, but in the poems of his recent volumes, *Poems of Dedication* (1947) and *The Edge of Being* (1949) his approach to his themes is so highly subjective that there is little room for suggestions of means by which mankind at large can be relieved of distress.

STEPHEN SPENDER

Stephen Harold Spender was born in London in 1909, the son of Harold Spender, a journalist of considerable note. In his youth he showed a talent for painting, but he never considered it as a career. From his poems and autobiography, one can gather that his boyhood was sheltered, and that he regarded with mingled envy and fear the young rowdies who moved about his neighborhood. Even before he entered University College, Oxford, in 1927, he recognized the greatness of the poet's calling and had written verse, some of which was published as *Nine Experiments* (1928). Although sensitive and retiring, at Oxford he became familiar with some of the young poets who were in attendance, among whom Auden was the dominating figure.

Even before Oxford, he was well aware of prevalent social injustices and need for change, but it is likely that his associations at the University did much to help him crystallize the sentiment in the poem, "No man shall hunger: Man shall be man." After leaving Oxford, he travelled on the continent, chiefly in Germany where he became intimate with Christopher Isherwood who had taken up residence in Berlin; and in 1937 he attended the International Writers' Conference in Spain where he was attentive to the preachments of André Malraux, the French antifascist author. Back in London he devoted much of his talent to writing pieces which were largely propaganda and to helping Cyril Connolly edit the progressive magazine *Horizon*. During the war, in an official capacity he helped to preserve morale on the home front. Since 1945, he sojourned for a time in Germany, according to his own report "to inquire into the lives and ideas of the German intellectuals, with a particular view of discovering any surviving talent in German literature." The result was *European Witness* (1946), a series of travel essays in which a political note predominates. In the autumn of 1946 he came to the United States, but as yet the result of his observations of the American scene has not appeared. He has held a guest professorship at Sarah Lawrence College and has lectured at many of the colleges in the east.

In spite of the fact that Spender's work is probably far from finished, and that it is too early to try to offer an inclusive estimate of his place in contemporary poetry, his work thus far shows seriousness of purpose and unmistakable talent. Even in his earlier volumes, his best if not his most distinctive work is that in which his search for greatness and beauty leads him away from the theme of man's inhumanity to man. Such poems as the one which begins, "I think continually of those who were truly great," the three stanzas of "Statistics," and the imagist poem "Winter

Landscape" have in them more genuine poetic feeling than all the verses in *Vienna*. Number 42, the last piece in *Poems* (1933), however, shows both propagandist and poet at work with neither role suffering greatly at the expense of the other. In the later poems which appear in *Poems of Dedication* (1947) and *The Edge of Being* (1949) the element of romanticism which is not always perceptible in the earlier poems often appears. "Elegy for Margaret" and the sonnet "You were born, must die; were loved, must love" in the volume of 1947 are not only unburdened by any cause but also rich in feeling and lyric tone. Most of the poems in *The Edge of Being* show a heightening intensity in expressing feelings that are individual to the poet. At forty, Spender's craftsmanship retains some of its early unevenness, but he has become many voices, all vibrant, and some genuinely poetic.

VERSE: *Nine Experiments* (1928), *Twenty Poems* (1930), *Poems* (1933), *Vienna* (1935), *The Still Center* (1939), *Poems of Dedication* (1947), *Returning to Vienna* (1947), *The Edge of Being* (1949). PROSE: *The Destructive Element* (1935), *Forward From Liberalism* (1937), *The New Realism* (1939), *European Witness* (1946), *World Within World* (1951), an autobiography.

Francis Scarfe, "Stephen Spender: A Sensitive" in *Auden and After* (1942); Malcolm Cowley, "Auden and Spender," *New Republic*, LXXX (1934), 180-190; James G. Southworth, "Stephen Spender," *Sewanee Rev.*, XLV (1937), 272-284; F. Cudworth Flint, "New Leaders in English Poetry," *Virginia Quar. Rev.*, XIV (1938), 502-518; Paul Engle, "New English Poets," *English Jour.*, XXVII (1938), 98-101; C. I. Glicksberg, "Poetry and Social Revolution," *Dalhousie Rev.*, XVII (1938), 493-503.

Of the younger poets who revolted against the leftist theme and intellectualized manner of Auden and his Oxford contemporaries, the Welshman **Dylan Thomas (1914-   )** is the most difficult to classify—and to understand. As yet he has not convinced all of his readers that he is a poet: Spender has said that "he is a poet of whom, at times, we can use the word 'genius' "; whereas the usually discerning Julian Symons has called Thomas a fake. His verse schemes generally conform to easily recognized patterns, but his riotous imagery has led Louis MacNeice to observe: "He is like a drunk man speaking wildly but rhythmically, pouring out a series of nonsense images, the cumulative effect of which is usually vital and sometimes even seems to have a message . . ."

Born in Wales, Dylan Thomas attended the Swansea Grammar School where he was known as a precocious but difficult student. In his late teens he wrote prose and verse, and in his early twenties he worked as a journalist. Much of his youth is illuminated in *The Portrait of the Artist as a Young Dog* (1940) in which such stories as "The Peaches" and "One Warm Saturday" are especially revealing and well told. His first volume of verse, *18 Poems* (1934), was largely written before he had turned twenty, to be followed by *25 Poems* (1936). These earlier verses and those in *The Map of Love* (1939) were included in *The World I Breathe* (1939). Although this early work attracted attention, in 1938 the American periodical *Poetry* carried in its "London Letter" the notice that Thomas had not as yet reached the stage of being an "accepted writer." With *New Poems* (1943) and *Deaths and Entrances* (1946) he gained a wider audience, and at present he is recognized in many places as a poet who has fulfilled some of his promise.

His prose tales such as "The Burning Baby," "The Orchards," and "A Prospect of the Sea," less profuse in imagery than his verse, have a strange beauty. Possibly in Welsh folklore there is something of their tone, but they have no antecedents or parallels in English narrative. His poetry is highly subjective in that it reveals an acute consciousness of self which takes on an expression more of self-deliverance than an effort to share his emotions with the reader. It is, as he himself has said, "the record of an individual struggle from darkness towards some measure of light. My poetry is, or should be useful to others for its individual recording of that same struggle with which they are necessarily acquainted." In much of the early verse it is apparent that some sort of conflict is going on, but the reader, confronted by an seemingly inexhausible procession of strange and at times contradictory symbols, often has difficulty in correlating the poet's struggle with his own. There are instances in which the images have a beauty independent of the line, stanza, or poem as a whole; but it is in such a piece as "Poem in October" in which the imagery is integrated with the theme and mood that Thomas has done his finest work.

VERSE: *18 Poems* (1934), *25 Poems* (1936), *The Map of Love* (1939), *The World I Breathe* (1939), *New Poems* (1943), *Deaths and Entrances* (1946), *Selected Writings* (1936), *In Country Sleep* (1952). PROSE: *Portrait of the Artist as a Young Dog* (1940). Some prose is included in *The World I Breathe* and *Selected Writings*.

Henry Treece, *Dylan Thomas* (1949); Francis Scarfe, "Dylan Thomas: A Pioneer" in *Auden and After* (1942); M. W. Stearn, "Unsex the Skeleton: Notes on the Poetry of Dylan Thomas," *Sewanee Rev.*, LII (1944), 424-440; Robert Horan, "In Defense of Dylan Thomas," *Kenyon Rev.*, VII (1945), 304-310; John L. Sweeney, Introduction, *Selected Writings of Dylan Thomas* (1946).

"Hugh MacDiarmid," (Christopher M. Grieve 1892-), has been described as "the father of the Scottish Renaissance and Scotland's leading living poet." Although he has given up the openly communistic theme so clearly expressed in his "Second Hymn to Lenin," he is still far from the traditionalist fold in either content or manner. Of late, however, he has been less of the experimenter in measures and diction, and less of the poet of political and social reform. In the verse in *The Present Age* (1940) a transition is apparent, for without losing any of his vigor, he has effected a partial compromise between the old order and his inclination to be a law unto himself. He was born in Scotland in 1892, educated at the local schools and the

University of Edinburgh, and since 1925 has held literature
as a profession. Already as a student at the University, he
was active in the Fabian Society; and with the spread of
communism, he subscribed zealously to its principles. It
has been reported that he was expelled from the Communist
party for insisting on Scottish autonomy, a stand which
would indicate that he was a rebel even among radicals. In
1937 he lived in comparative isolation on one of the Shet-
land Islands, apparently unwilling to be a disciple of any
faction. Among his pleasures he has listed Anglo-phobia!
In his verse, the Scotch heritage and background come out
again and again, not only in his use of the Scots vernacular,
or "Lallans" as most of the contemporary Scotch poets prefer
to call it, but also in his peculiar brand of satire. With a few
exceptions such as that in the poem "With the Lifting of the
Head," his themes would seem to indicate that he is a zealous
patriot. He wrote the preface to Benn's *Anthology of Scottish Poets* which strikes a far more sympathetic note than
that in his robust satiric verses entitled "On the Oxford
Book of Victorian Verse," in which collection he detects
more chaff than wheat. His best if not his most characteristic
work is that in a minor key in which he blends a reflective
idea or mood which is unburdened by any political axe-
grinding with measures which in spite of their irregularity
of quantity and stress are melodic. Such poems as "Audh and
Cunaide" and "In the Glen of Silence" which appeared in
Life and Letters in November, 1947, indicate that Mac-
Diarmid's voice can be not only strong, but also poetic.

VERSE: *Sangschaw* (1925), *Penny Wheep* (1926), *To Circumjack
Cencrastus or The Curly Snake* (1930), *Penny Wheep to Stony
Limits and Other Poems* (1934), *The Present Age* (1940), *A Kist
of Whistles* (1947). PROSE: *Lucky Poet*, autobiography (1938).

Alexander Scott, "Scots Since 'Sangschaw,' " *Life and Letters*, LV
(1947), 102-108; J. G. Southworth, "Hugh MacDiarmid," *Sewanee
Rev.*, XLVIII (1940), 105-118.

FICTION

The peace brought into prominence several novelists whose early work before the war had been overshadowed by the established Edwardian writers. Frank Swinnerton made his mark in 1917 with *Nocturne,* a unique little work whose perfection he never approached again. His studies of middle-class London were carefully realistic but unimaginative, and after a few years his readers found them monotonous. If Swinnerton was not sufficiently versatile, Compton Mackenzie, a fine writer at his best, energetic and provocative, was too much so. By being unpredictable he alienated the large class of critics and readers who attach themselves to an author whose character and ideas they think they know. J. D. Beresford had solid unspectacular merit: Stephen McKenna wrote brilliantly but rather superficially of smart political society. The dismal collapse of Sir Hugh Walpole's reputation before his death made it clear that he owed it more to his social talents and skilful journalism than to his literary merit. He was far too prolific and swamped a few good novels like *The Cathedral* (1922) in a mass of inferior work. William McFee began vigorously in the tradition of Conrad with *Aliens* (1914) and *Casuals of the Sea* (1916) and wrote some admirable novels until he left the sea and settled in the United States in 1923, after which his work became verbose and mannered.

In contrast to these men whose reputations, high in the twenties, dwindled steadily in the next decade is Somerset Maugham. After twenty years of steady effort he was first considered seriously in 1915 when *Of Human Bondage* revealed a new depth and scope in his work. Never as good as the best of the others at their best, he rose for the next thirty years in popularity, if not in critical estimation, to attain one of the most remarkable reputations made by a writer who was a great craftsman but not a great artist. Belated recog-

nition of another order came to E. M. Forster with the publication of *A Passage to India* in 1924. He alone of those
named has held a place among the first-rate novelists, though
he has written no further novels for more than twenty years.
His perceptive social criticism, his genuinely liberal philosophy, and the authenticity and clear realization of his characters show him to be a genius who in his earlier work was
a generation ahead of his time.

It was inevitable that severe criticism of the old social and
moral standards should be the dominant note of the newer
fiction and in this the leader was D. H. Lawrence. He had
begun his protest before the war, but the suppression by
authority of *The Rainbow* (1915) and *Women in Love*
(1920) had postponed the impact of his work to a more re-
ceptive time. Disgusted with idealism and intellectualism,
Lawrence believed that he had found in "the dark wisdom
of the blood" the key to a more natural and more fully
expressive life. His paganism and the mystical value he attached to primitive sexuality effectively concealed his fundamental puritanism and created a widespread cult among a
generation that was violently antipuritanical. It was only
when the Fascist tendencies of his later novels became suspect that he lost credit as the prophet of a new morality. A
decade after his early death in 1930 he was more correctly
appreciated as a remarkable but very imperfect artist. A far
more dangerous, because genuinely pagan, attack upon accepted morals was Norman Douglas's *South Wind* (1917).
Learned, mature, witty, and urbane, it was the antithesis of
the violence and seriousness of Lawrence.

A younger man than either of these, Aldous Huxley belonged wholly to the postwar literary movement. *Crome
Yellow* (1921) was the first of a series of novels that under
the brilliance of their satire were detached and pitiless clini-
cal studies of a dislocated society. By the end of the twenties
disgust and then despair succeeded to the detachment until

at last Huxley turned to mysticism as a means of social regeneration, and the mantle of satire descended to Evelyn
Waugh. Less subtle and penetrating than Huxley's, Waugh's
novels are still exquisitely witty satires on the amoral, insol-
vent smart people of the thirties. Rose Macaulay, highly
praised in 1920 for *Potterism,* had all the qualifications of an
excellent social satirist except strong convictions. Without
these her gifts were dissipated in urbane derision, enjoyable
but insignificant.

Complementary to the objectivism of the satirists was the
new subjectivism of another group. As early as 1915 Dorothy
M. Richardson had quietly begun the series of novels collectively called *Pilgrimage,* of which five had appeared by
1920 when they began to attract general attention. Her
impressionistic technique was not wholly new; variants of
it had been used by Sterne, by Eduard Dujardin, and by
others, but it was now spoken of as the "stream-of-consciousness" and its development became the most important technical advance of modern fiction. Miss Richardson carried the
sensations and perceptions of a single character through a
dozen novels. Virginia Woolf applied the method more
subtly in a variety of new patterns, prolonging a single consciousness unbroken through several generations, or exhausting the sensational content of successive moments of
being. May Sinclair, once widely known as the author of
The Divine Fire (1904), also belongs in her later writing to
this school. The farthest development of the stream-of-consciousness to the present is, of course, in Joyce's *Ulysses*
(1922) and *Finnegan's Wake* (1939), the latter requiring a
new handling of language to express simultaneous consciousness at different levels. Closely related to these are such
experiments with time as are found in Rumer Godden's
Take Three Tenses (1945) and the dream sequences and
dream symbolism of Mervin Peake's *Titus Groan* (1946).
The work of most novelists since 1925 shows the occasional

influence of this technique. The whole group are indebted to Proust, to William James, to Freud and Jung. Going beyond the practical and intuitive knowledge of psychology on which novelists have always relied, they have availed themselves of the modern science and have tried to translate its discoveries into literary terms.

Regional fiction after the war was more abundant than ever. Francis Brett Young and Mary Webb wrote of the West Midlands; Phyllis Bentley and Storm Jameson of Yorkshire. R. H. Mottram explored the rich past of his native city of Norwich. Sheila Kaye-Smith continued the tradition of Hardy in her studies of country life in Sussex. Scotland was represented by Neill Gunn, A. J. Cronin, and George Blake; Wales by Richard Llewellyn and (unsympathetically) by Caradoc Evans. They produced, on the whole, a body of very good work with some outstanding books, such as Mary Webb's *Precious Bane* (1924), Sheila Kaye-Smith's *Joanna Godden* (1921), and Richard Llewellyn's *How Green Was My Valley* (1939).

The closely related type, the family chronicle novel, was represented—aside of course from Galsworthy's long-a-making *Forsyte Saga* (1922)—by such books as G. B. Stern's *The Matriarch* (1924) and its successors, by Clemence Dane's *Broome Stages* (1931) and Victoria Sackville-West's *Family History* (1932).

Historical fiction remained weak, the twenties having little to show beyond the romances of "E. Barrington" (Mrs. L. Adams Beck). In 1934 Robert Graves, the poet, appeared in a new role with *I, Claudius,* a scholarly classical novel. This was followed by others of the same sort, then by two good stories of the American Revolution, a new version of the voyage of the *Argo,* and the rather disappointing *King Jesus* (1946). He is now England's best historical novelist. On a somewhat more popular level C. S. Forester has written stirring military and naval stories, chiefly of the Napoleonic wars, the best known being the Captain Horatio Hornblower series. There have also been isolated works like F. Tennyson Jesse's excellent *Lacquer Lady* (1929).

In 1918 appeared the first of the war novels *The Return of the Soldier* by Rebecca West, a study of a shell-shocked veteran. For fifteen years they appeared steadily, forming at best a fairly large group, most of them centering in realistic accounts of battle experience, with few touches of the lighter side of war to relieve their tragedy and bitter disillusionment. Probably the best was R. H. Mottram's *Spanish Farm* trilogy (1924); C. E. Montague's *Rough Justice* (1926), Richard Aldington's *The Death of a Hero* (1929) and C. S. Forester's *The General* (1936) are noteworthy in this group.

Violence and crime have been ingredients of popular fiction from its beginnings and in the discord of the postwar years they regained the prominence they had in the ballads and lost after the Elizabethan dramatists. Though in 1930 Priestley seemed about to revive the jolly popular novel with a strong flavor of Dickens and though the perennial supply of saccharine romances has never failed, the most vigorous popular writing of the past quarter-century has gone into tales of secret service and detection. During the war John Buchan stepped suddenly into popularity with *The Thirty-Nine Steps* (1915) and *Greenmantle* (1916), and until his death in 1940 continued to write thrillers of international intrigue and espionage, mostly of high quality. Nearly as good were the similar tales of "Francis Beeding," collaborations by two members of the League of Nations Secretariat. Since 1930 Graham Greene has raised the estimation of this sort of work by giving a new importance to its psychological aspects. In the detective field, though a great deal of trash has been written, the work of Dorothy Sayres, Margery Allingham, Agatha Christie, Freeman Wills Crofts, and R. A. J. Walling is generally of reliable goodness. The field has been occasionally invaded by such writers as A. A. Milne,

Father Ronald Knox, the poet C. Day Lewis (under the pseudonym Nicholas Blake), the economist G. D. H. Cole and his wife, C. M. Cole.

As reading for escape the detective story has completely replaced the romance of far away and has relegated other rivals to unimportance. In its frankly artificial world the reader finds a keen excitement free of serious moral connotations that no other sort of fiction can provide. Daphne Du Maurier has had considerable success with the old-fashioned terrors of the Gothic school but the appeal of the terrible and fantastic seems to have waned. Particularly curious in view of the widespread belief in spiritualism after the war, is the decline of interest in the supernatural. Indicative of the new direction that fantasy has taken is Richard Hughes' *A High Wind in Jamaica* (in the American edition *The Innocent Voyage*), really a rather grim study of the imperviousness of innocence in a world of violence. A different direction, reminiscent of Rider Haggard, is represented by the pseudo-mystical escapism of James Hilton's *Lost Horizon*.

In five years, between 1919 and 1925, the technique of the short story was radically changed by the work of Katherine Mansfield. Her method, employing suggestions rather than statements and replacing the well-contrived incident with a subtly created atmosphere, has influenced nearly all writers in the field, and has rendered the traditional type of short story hopelessly old fashioned. In spite of the decline of the literary periodicals that have always been its principal vehicle, the short story because of this refreshment of its technique has more than held its own in recent years. Among the best writers since 1920 have been Elizabeth Bowen, Virginia Woolf, *Monday or Tuesday* (1921), Rosamund Lehmann, *The Gypsy's Baby* (1946), E. M. Forster, *The Eternal Moment* (1921), C. E. Montague, *Fiery Particles* (1923), and Osbert Sitwell, *Open The Door* (1941). Of these only Miss Bowen is known chiefly for her work in this field, in which she is perhaps second only to Miss Mansfield. D. H. Lawrence and Aldous Huxley were less successful in their short stories than in their novels. Somerset Maugham's attractive blend of Kipling and Conrad has given his stories, like his novels, a sustained popularity. The fantasies of A. E. Coppard kept alive by their poetic freshness a type that generally declined after the war. In 1916 Thomas Burke recalled attention to the East End with his *Limehouse Nights.*

A significant feature of this period is that it has not produced any of those "great novelists" that have hitherto appeared in every generation since Richardson. Genius has not been wanting but in the wide diffusion of talent no single author has achieved the old pre-eminence among many who are thoroughly good. Not only has the general level of fiction risen but the temper of the period has been averse to making national institutions of its authors or to encouraging monumental collected works. Even the recognition accorded such writers as Lawrence, Huxley, Joyce, and Virginia Woolf, while it has given them a high position has given them a different sort of position from the solid emplacements of the leading Edwardians. To the many of varying degrees of talent and competence a short review can do no sort of justice—even in several cases the bare justice of mention—nor pause for such ephemeral reputations as those of Ronald Firbank and Michael Arlen. The assignment of authors to schools and groups, always a somewhat arbitrary business, has become, owing to the multiplicity of new patterns—structural, thematic, and stylistic—in the novel, more highly artificial than ever. Nothing, therefore, has been attempted here beyond the indication of characteristic movements and tendencies.

From these one generalisation may be made: that the changes in the character of fiction advocated and begun by Meredith have been almost wholly realized in our time. Meredith, himself an indifferent story teller, regretted the dominance of narrative in the novel, which he felt could become mature only by becoming a vehicle for ideas. This we have seen. Since 1920 there has been a general and sharp decline in story-telling and plot throughout fiction: in many of the best novels these elements are negligible. At the same time, not merely through discussion and analysis, but by a new use of symbolism borrowed from poetry, music, and painting, a higher degree of significance has been achieved than ever before. If, say, *Clayhanger* and *Nostromo* are compared with *Mrs. Dalloway* and *The Ballad and The Source,* there can be no doubt that the latter make a greater demand upon the intellect and proceed from a wholly different conception of the function of the novel. They are immeasurably inferior as stories. Which are the better is a pointless question: the difference is not specific but generic. Unfortunately since about 1935 the intellectual tendency in fiction has become involved with the propagandist tendency in all the arts so that many novels, especially toward the left, are avowed vehicles of "ideologies." Those who believe that this is merely a transient fashion may turn for comfort to the beginning of the last century when Charles Lamb was reproved for his political indifference and Walter Scott was accused by Hazlitt of writing to bolster up a decaying society.

(William) Somerset Maugham (1874-   ) spent his early childhood in Paris, where he was born. His mother died when he was eight years old, his father, who was solicitor to the British Embassy, two years later. An orphan of ten, Maugham was taken into the household of a clerical uncle at Whistable on the coast of Kent. England was virtually a foreign country to the child and as he grew older he found the atmosphere of narrow social and religious orthodoxy in which he was reared unbearable. King's School, Canterbury, which he entered at thirteen, meant little to him one way or the other, and he used his health—he had inherited tubercular weakness from his mother—as an excuse to escape from it to private tutors in Hyeres and later in Heidelberg.

Returning from Germany at eighteen, he rejected the career in the Church his uncle had chosen for him, and indifferently agreed to study medicine in which he had no interest. At least this would enable him to live in London alone. In 1892 he entered St. Thomas' Hospital and studied there for five years with increasing interest but without abandoning his already formed resolution to be a writer. His first novel, *Liza of Lambeth* (1897) was the product of his visits to patients in the worst of the London slums.

Maugham had to wait ten years for assurance of literary success. As soon as he had qualified in medicine at the age of twenty-three he went abroad and for some years lived in Spain and France. He wrote two further novels and had a play produced by the Stage Society, but until the appearance, in 1907, of *Lady Frederick* at the Court Theatre he was struggling against discouragement. Then four of his plays were produced within a year, and he knew he had arrived. He still has an audience on the screen.

Until 1915 he was known chiefly as a playright but *Of Human Bondage* caused a complete revaluation of his work. The scope and unshirking realism of this largely autobiographical book showed Maugham to be a potential major novelist. He has never achieved its power again, but for now more than thirty years he has held his own as a highly popular novelist with such books as *The Moon and Sixpence* (1919), *Cakes and Ale* (1930), *The Narrow Corner* (1932), *Theatre* (1937), and *The Razor's Edge* (1944), as well as several volumes of short stories. *The Trembling of a Leaf* 1921) contained his most popular story *Miss Thompson*, now known as *Rain*. Though his plays have taken a secondary place they have not been neglected, and his three most successful, *The Circle* (1921), *Our Betters* (1923), and *The*

Letter (1927) belong to these years. Like Charles Reade, Maugham sometimes produced "convertible" works, novels to be dramatized or vice versa.

Today Maugham is, in the United States at least, the most popular living English author despite a steady flow of critical depreciation. And both public and critics are right, the public in insisting on his splendid capability as a story teller, the honesty of his realism, and his clear independent judgment; the critics in denying him the rank of artist in the serious meaning of the term. "I have a clear and logical brain," he says of himself, "but not a very subtle nor a very powerful one." That is it. The whole of that really remarkable book *The Summing Up* (1938) increases the reader's admiration for a mind that one feels would recognize and estimate correctly the whole content of a situation but would rarely apprehend anything beyond it—which is what the artist must do. Maugham's position in the literature of our day appears to be rather like that of Anthony Trollope and Charles Reade among the Victorians—admirable writers who could often beat their betters but who could not jointly or severally have produced *Bleak House.*

Maugham is sentimentally attached to England but has never felt completely at home among English people. He has lived in many parts of the world and, like Kipling, is a master of local atmosphere that gives his work an air of cosmopolitan sophistication. During both World Wars he was employed by the British government on secret missions: his secret service story *Ashenden* (1928), based on his earlier experiences, was made required reading for agents of the secret service. His travel books, *The Land of the Blessed Virgin* (1905) and *The Gentleman in the Parlor* (1930), are among his pleasantest writings.

Maugham suffered in childhood from a severe stammer and throughout life from tubercular weakness. The first by subjecting him to ridicule at a most sensitive age gave him a feeling of separateness from his fellows that he has always retained, the second his passionate love of life. Both may be held to account for the caustic wit that often makes him seem cruelly indifferent to the feelings of others and that has antagonized many fellow writers.

Maugham's marriage to Lady Wellcome in 1915 ended in a divorce seven years later.

FICTION: *Liza of Lambeth* (1897), *The Making of a Saint* (1898), *Orientations* (1899), *The Hero* (1901), *Mrs. Craddock* (1902), *The Merry-go-round* (1904), *The Bishop's Apron* (1906), *The Explorer* (1907), *The Magician* (1908), *Of Human Bondage* (1915), *The Moon and Sixpence* (1919), *The Trembling of a Leaf*, also pub. as *Rain and Other Stories* (1921), *The Painted Veil* (1925), *The Casuarina Tree* (1926), Reprinted as *The Letter* (1929), *Ashenden* (1928), *Cakes and Ale* (1930), *Six Stories Written in the First Person Singular* (1931), *The Narrow Corner* (1932), *Ah King* (1933), *Altogether,* [*East and West*] (1934), *Don Fernando* (1935), *Cosmopolitans* (1936), *Theatre* (1937), *Creatures of Circumstance* (1937), *Princess September and the Nightingale* (1939), *Christmas Holiday* (1939), *The Mixture as Before* (1940), *Up at the Villa* (1941), *The Horn Before the Dawn* (1942), *The Unconquered* (1944), *The Razor's Edge* (1944), *Then and Now* (1946), *Catalina* (1948). PLAYS: *A Man of Honour* (1903), *Penelope* (1907), *The Explorer* (1909), *Mrs. Dot* (1912), *Lady Frederick* (1912), *Jack Straw* (1912), *The Tenth Man* (1913), *Landed Gentry* (1913), *The Land of Promise* (1913), *The Unknown* (1920), *The Circle* (1921), *East of Suez* (1922), *Caesar's Wife* (1922), *Home and Beauty* (1923), *Our Betters* (1923), *The Unattainable* (1923), *Loaves and Fishes* (1924), *The Letter* (1925), *The Constant Wife* (1926), *The Sacred Flame* (1928), *The Bread Winner* (1930), *Plays* (1931), *For Services Rendered* (1932), *Sheppey* (1933). MISCELLANEOUS: *The Gentleman in the Parlor* (1930), *The Summing Up* (1938).

F. T. Bason, *A Bibliography of the Writings of William Somerset Maugham* (1931); Percy H. Muir, "William Somerset Maugham: Some Bibliographical Observations," *Book Collector's Quar.,* IX (1933), 72-84, X (1933), 19-26; Paul Dottin, *W. Somerset Maugham et ses romans* (1928); Claude S. McIver, *William Somerset Maugham* (Phila., 1936); R. H. Ward, *William Somerset Maugham*

(1937); R. A. Cordell, *William Somerset Maugham* (1937);
N. W. Sawyer, *The Comedy of Manners from Sheridan to
Maugham* (1931); C. M. Montague, "William Somerset Maugham
—Dramatist," *Poet Lore,* XLVII (1941), 40-55; Theodore Spencer
"Somerset Maugham," *College English,* II (1940), 1-10; W. O.
Ross, "W. Somerset Maugham: Theme and Variations," *College
English,* VIII (1946-47), 113-122.

Frank (Arthur) Swinnerton (1884-   ) was born in London, into a home increasingly depressed by poverty. His
father, of old Staffordshire stock, was an unsuccessful copper-
plate engraver, thrown out of work for long periods by the
decline of his art. Only the cheerfulness and courage of his
Scottish mother kept the family going. Prolonged illness and
the virtual starvation produced by a family income of ten to
fifteen shillings a week made his childhood a hard one and
sent him to work as soon as he was capable of earning a
wage. At the age of fourteen he became office boy to *The
Scottish Cyclist* at six shillings a week.

This was the beginning of a long association with publishing. Two years later, after a brief interval in a shipping
office, he entered the employ of J. M. Dent and Co., the
publishers of *Everyman's Library,* where he did well but was
unhappy. After six years, at the age of twenty-two, he left
them to go to Chatto and Windus, with whom he remained
until the early nineteen-twenties. There he soon became a
publisher's reader and proved himself an excellent critic
with a sure sense of the commercial value of a book. He is
very proud of having discovered *The Young Visiters* for his
firm. In the course of years he gained a thorough knowledge
of the business of literary production and a wide acquaintance, both of which make his autobiography as well as his
survey, *The Georgian Literary Scene* (1934), and his excellent Dent Lecture, *The Reviewing and Criticism of Books*
(1939), interesting references for the literary life of his day.

Swinnerton's start as a novelist came about three years

after his going to Chatto's. He had been writing a novel in
the evenings and, when it failed to win a competitive prize,
submitted it to his firm, who decided to publish it. *The
Merry Heart* (1909) is a pleasant, improbable story, immature but buoyed up by an infectious good nature. It brought
him no great notice but gave him the confidence to continue.
During the next seven years he produced five novels, slowly
making a reputation, but without conspicuous success. Then
in 1917 *Nocturne* won a sudden and deserved popularity.
For fifteen years thereafter he was widely read on both sides
of the Atlantic and by many readers and critics very highly
esteemed. In the thirties, however, his audience declined and
he does not seem today as important in modern fiction as he
once promised to be.

Swinnerton is a realist dealing with the ordinary lives of
the lower middle class. Until success brought him money and
leisure his experience was severely limited and since that
time he has chosen to remain, artistically, in a rather restricted world. Within its limits his novels have all that keen
perception, a deep sympathetic understanding of his characters, ironic humor, and artistic conscientiousness can give
them. They show the kind of imagination that enables a
novelist to give life to his characters but in general they are
seriously deficient in the kind that gives color and charm to
a story. Swinnerton has described himself as "cold," and his
novels, while they command attention, fail to evoke any
warmth of response in the reader. When he attempts to
heighten their action, it may merely spill over, as in *The
Georgian House*, into unrestrained melodrama. He is not a
storyteller; his forte is analysis.

His best work, by general consent, is *Nocturne* (1917), a
cockney idyll, perfect in its kind. It is a short work recording
the events of a single night in which two girls of the working
class, sisters of contrasted temperaments—dutiful and daring

—find each the love suited to her character. It is the least pretentious and most imaginative of his books. *Coquette* (1917) and *September* (1921) divide honors for second place. In addition to his novels Swinnerton wrote an unsympathetic but valuable critical study of Stevenson and a moderately sympathetic one of Gissing. From 1912 on he did a great deal of reviewing and a well-known series of literary articles in the *Bookman*.

A childhood gift of Louisa Alcott's *Little Women* and *Good Wives* provided, Swinnerton says, his "real introduction to and preparation for the novelist's craft." Later he was drawn to George Gissing's work by their common ill fortune and love of books, and the influence of Gissing can be traced in many of his novels, in one of which Gissing appears as a character. But it was his friend Arnold Bennett who more than anyone else influenced Swinnerton's mature work. Bennett's wide knowledge of men and occupations, his confidence, his precise realism, were increasingly reflected in Swinnerton's novels. Only Bennett's cosmopolitanism eluded him; he has always been intensely a Londoner.

AUTOBIOGRAPHY: *Swinnerton: An Autobiography* (1936). NOVELS: *The Merry Heart* (1909), *The Casement* (1911), *The Happy Family* (1912), *On the Staircase* (1914), *The Chaste Wife* (1916), *Nocturne* (1917), *Shops and Houses* (1918), *September* (1919), *Coquette* (1921), *The Three Lovers* (1922), *The Young Idea* (1922), *Young Felix* (1923), *The Elder Sister* (1925), *Summer Storm* (1926), *A Brood of Ducklings* (1928), *Sketch of a Sinner* (1929), *The Georgian House* (1932), *Elizabeth* (1934), *Harvest Comedy* (1937), *The Two Wives* (1939), *The Fortunate Lady* (1941), *Thankless Child* (1942), *A Woman in Sunshine* (1945). MISCELLANEOUS: *George Gissing: A Critical Study* (1912), *R. L. Stevenson: A Critical Study* (1914), *The Georgian Scene* (1934).

R. C. McKay, *George Gissing and His Critic Frank Swinnerton* (Phila., 1933); Thomas Beer, "Frank Swinnerton," *Bookman,* LVIII (1923-24), 404-409.

Compton Mackenzie (1882-   ) comes of American and
Scottish ancestry that included a number of actors and
writers. He was educated at St. Paul's School and Oxford,
taking honors in history at the latter. He served in the First
World War in the Mediterranean area, winning a number
of decorations for his outstanding Intelligence work. He has
since received political and academic distinctions.

His first novel, *The Passionate Elopement,* appeared in
1911, but his reputation really dates from *Sinister Street*
three years later. During the war and for ten years after, he
had a large following of readers and a good share of critical
appreciation. In 1919 *Sylvia and Michael* and *Poor Relations* brought his best work before the public. They were
excellent novels, realistic, well constructed, witty, and the
latter cleverly satiric. By the end of the twenties, however,
Mackenzie lost many of his readers, largely because of the
increasingly propagandist character of his novels. He is a
man of strong and often eccentric opinions that he has
allowed to pervade his work at the cost of its artistic merit.
He has continued producing novels into the nineteen-forties.

Since his undergraduate days Mackenzie has been active
in literary journalism. He has also had four plays produced
and has written a variety of books on literature, history, and
religion. His war memoirs, *Aegean Memories* (1940), a revision of an earlier work suppressed for its disclosure of
official secrets, contains some of his best writing.

Mackenzie was received into the Catholic Church in 1914.
He has lived for many years on romantic islands, Capri,
Jethoh, one of the minor Channel Islands, and later Barra
in the Outer Hebrides.

Fiction: *The Passionate Elopement* (1911), *Carnival* (1912), *Sinister Street,* [*Youth's Encounter*] (1913), *Guy and Pauline,*
[*Plasher's Mead*] (1915), *The Early Life and Adventures of
Sylvia Scarlett* (1918), *Poor Relations* (1919), *Sylvia and Michael*
(1919), *The Vanity Girl* (1920), *Rich Relatives* (1921), *The Altar*

Steps (1922), *The Seven Ages of Woman* (1922), *The Parson's Progress* (1923), *The Heavenly Ladder* (1924), *The Old Men of the Sea* (1924), *Coral* (1925), *Fairy Gold* (1926), *Vestal Fire* (1927), *Rogues and Vagabonds* (1927), *Extremes Meet* (1928), *Extraordinary Women* (1928), *The Three Couriers* (1929), *April Fools* (1930), *Buttercups and Daisies,* [*For Sale*] (1931), *Our Street* (1931), *Water on the Brain* (1933), *The Darkening Green* (1934), *Figure of Eight* (1936), *The East Wind of Love* (1937), *The South Wind of Love* (1937), *The West Wind of Love* (1940), *West to North* (1940), *The North Wind of Love* (1945), *Again to the North* (1946). MISCELLANEOUS: *Gallipoli Memories* (1929), *First Athenian Memories* (1931), *Greek Memories* (1932), *Literature in My Time* (1933), *Marathon and Salamis* (1934), *Pericles* (1937), *Aegean Memories* (1940).

John Freeman, "The Novels of Mr. Compton Mackenzie," *London Mercury,* I (1919-20), 448-457; Mary Bateman, "Compton Mackenzie," *Catholic World,* CXV (1922), 733-745; Sheila Kaye-Smith, "Compton Mackenzie and His Work," *Bookman,* LXII (391-395).

Sir Hugh Walpole (1884-1941) was born in Auckland, N. Z., the son of an English clergyman who afterward became Bishop of Edinburgh. He was educated in England at King's School, Canterbury (where Somerset Maugham had been earlier) and Oxford. After graduating he taught school for a while before going to London to make his way as a writer. He began by reviewing for *The Evening Standard* and published his first novel, written while he was still an undergraduate, in 1909. Thereafter he published a novel a year, but it was not until the fifth, *Fortitude* (1913), that he was rewarded by public recognition.

During the war he served with the Red Cross in Russia and was decorated for courage. This experience gave him some valuable material for his later books. He did not allow the war to interrupt his literary production but with one exception (1918) continued to produce at least one novel a year until his death.

Walpole disavowed any theory of the novel as an art form

or of fictional technique, and except in their regularity of appearance his own are bewilderingly various in character and of all degrees of quality from very good to very bad. He could at will write realistically of modern society, wallow in the romantic adventures of the *Herries* series, or sentimentalize childhood in *Jeremy*. He seems to have judged it better for his career to keep himself constantly before the public than to appear only at his best. And though as a consequence he has never had a sure position in critical estimation, he was an eminently successful popular novelist. His title and other honors were earned largely by his social adroitness in promoting the public relations of literature and especially, as reviewer and lecturer, improving the American market for British authors.

Yet if he deserved in some measure the caricature Somerset Maugham has drawn of him in *Cakes and Ale,* Walpole also wrote some good books. Besides *Fortitude* (1913), *The Cathedral* (1922), *The Duchess of Wrexe* (1914) and *Portrait of a Man With Red Hair* (1925), show that at his best he was something more than a competent writer.

COLLECTED WORKS: *The Cumberland Edition of the Novels* (1934). FICTION: *The Wooden Horse* (1909), *Maradick At Forty* (1910), *Mr. Perrin and Mr. Traill* [*The Gods and Mr. Perrin*] (1911), *The Prelude to Adventure* (1912), *Fortitude* (1913), *The Duchess of Wrexe* (1914), *The Gooden Scarecrow* (1915), *The Dark Forest* (1916), *The Green Mirror* (1917), *Jeremy* (1919), *The Secret City* (1919), *The Captives* (1920), *The Young Enchanted* (1921), *The Thirteen Travelers* (1921), *The Cathedral* (1922), *Jeremy and Hamlet* (1923), *The Old Ladies* (1924), *Portrait of a Man With Red Hair* (1925), *Harmer John* (1926), *Jeremy at Crale* (1927), *Wintersmoon* (1928), *The Silver Thorn* (1928), *Hans Frost* (1929), *Farthing Hall,* with J. B. Priestley (1929), *Rogue Herries* (1930), *Above the Dark Circus* [*Above the Dark Tumult*] (1931), *Judith Paris* (1931), *The Fortress* (1932), *Vanessa* (1933), *All Souls' Night* (1933), *Captain Nicholas* (1934), *Cathedral Service* (1934), *The Inquisitor* (1935), *A Prayer For My Son* (1936), *John Cornelius* (1937), *The Joyful Delaneys* (1938), *Head in Green Bronze* (1938),

The Sea Tower (1939), *The Bright Pavilions* (1940), *The Blind Man's House* (1941), *The Killer and the Slain* (1942), *Katherine Christian* (1943).

Clemence Dane, *Tradition and Hugh Walpole* (1929); J. B. Priestley, "Hugh Walpole," *English Jour.*, XVII (1928), 529-536; Irene Marinoff, "Hugh Walpole," *Anglia*, LVI (1932), 104-107, Rupert Hart-Davis, *Hugh Walpole* (1952).

William McFee (1881-   ) was born at sea in the ship *Erin's Isle* commanded by his father, a Canadian shipbuilder and shipmaster who soon after left the sea to become a ship's husband (marine superintendent) in London. Before his father's death in 1891, McFee was initiated into the seafaring world, but thereafter the atmosphere of his youth was that of suburban London, and when he completed his schooling at seventeen he became an articled apprentice to a London engineering firm. Here for three years he learned his profession in a severely practical way, continuing his studies at night. After completing his apprenticeship he worked for some time in the office of a consulting engineer. He read widely and made friends among the writers and artists of Chelsea. Then rather suddenly he decided to go to sea, and through an uncle obtained an engineer's berth in the S. S. *Rotherfield*, a tramp steamer.

McFee spent the next four years at sea in various ships, becoming at last chief engineer of the S. S. *Fernfield*. In 1908 he published his first book, *Letters from an Ocean Tramp*, and began a novel. Then in 1911 he made a second important decision and came to the United States. Here he entered the employ of the United Fruit Company, with which he remained until 1922 except for an interval of war service as an engineer officer in the British Navy. His seafaring has taken him to all parts of the world, but the Mediterranean and the Caribbean are the seas he knows best.

In New York after the war McFee was drawn by Christopher Morley into the group of writers that frequented

Frank Shay's bookshop on Christopher Street. A friend in
this group was the literary Captain David Bone * of the old
Anchor Line, and for a short while after leaving the sea,
McFee ran "The High Seas Bookshop" aboard Captain
Bone's ship the *Tuscania*. He later became a United States
citizen and settled permanently in Westport, Conn. He has
been twice married.

McFee's earlier novels, *Aliens* (1914), *Casuals of the Sea*
(1916), *Captain Macedoine's Daughter* (1920), and *Command*
(1922) were written at sea or in the intervals of voyages. His
characters were around him, and ideas came at such moments as when he was clearing bilge suctions in a gale off
Hatteras. They made the reader familiar with people
whose business is with ships, lives seen intimately and realistically by the writer. His later novels, however, while they
gain in sophistication, lose in immediacy through being put
into the mouth of his long-winded narrator Mr. Spenlove.
This garrulous chief engineer of passenger ships recalls
rather than presents the world of his characters; the effect of
both story and atmosphere are weakened. Like Conrad,
McFee moves in a cosmopolitan world of Englishmen and
Scots, Creoles and New Yorkers, Levantines and Latin
Americans, focusing attention on the characters of seafaring
men as they are developed by the discipline of their calling
and their usually unfortunate entanglements ashore.

In addition to his novels and his volumes of short stories
such as *Pilgrims of Adversity* (1928) and *Sailors of Fortune*
(1929), McFee has written a great deal of excellent general
prose. *Harbors of Memory* (1916), *Swallowing the Anchor*
(1925), and *More Harbors of Memory* (1934) are volumes of
essays of wide range of subject, including reminiscences,
comment on marine disasters, criticism of literature and of
the American scene. *The Watch Below* (1940) and *In the*

* Author of *The Brassbounder, Broken Stowage, Merchantmen at
War,* etc.

First Watch (1946) are expositions, with a slight disguise of narrative, of life in British tramp steamers in the early years of the century. They are the only authentic literary record of the age at sea that followed the age of Conrad's wind-jammers, and for those who remember it or want to understand it the best sort of reading. *Sunlight in New Granada* (1925) is a travel study of Colombia, and *Life of Sir Martin Frobisher,* a sound biography.

Despite his Canadian ancestry, his United States citizenship, and his long residence in this country, McFee is essentially a British writer. His formative years were passed in London and in British ships, and when he came to America his standards were formed. Honesty, an insistence upon soundness and precision, is at the core of them. He has been a candid and unsparing, but never unfair, critic of American ways, disliking our slackness, our approximations, our emotionalism, but as readily appreciating the compensations that determined his choice of a home. As an artist he has never emigrated; though the greater part of his writing has been done on this side of the Atlantic he has never written a book with a really American flavor. Possibly he would not care to.

Comparison between McFee and Conrad, the foremost modern writers of the sea, is nearly inevitable, and in fiction all to Conrad's advantage. McFee is neither so keen a psychologist, nor so delicate a stylist. He has created no characters so durable as Tom Lingard or Lord Jim; he has no descriptions approaching Conrad's best. As expositors of the conditions and traditions of their calling they are more nearly equal; many things in McFee's essays are comparable to *Notes on Life and Letters.* In all McFee's work there is a solid competence in grasp and execution; and he has successfully recorded the values of the life he knew and chose to express.

FICTION: *Letters From an Ocean Tramp* (1908), re-issued as *An Ocean Tramp* (1921), *Aliens* (1914), *Casuals of the Sea* (1916),

Captain Macedoine's Daughter (1920), *Command* (1922), *Race* (1924), *Pilgrims of Adversity* (1928), *Sailors of Fortune* (1929), *North of Suez* (1930), *The Harbourmaster* (1931), *No Castle in Spain* (1933), *The Beachcomber* (1935), *Sailor's Bane* (1936), *Derelicts* (1938), *Spenlove in Arcady* (1941), *Ship to Shore* (1944). MISCELLANEOUS: *Harbous of Memory* (1921), *More Harbours of Memory* (1934), *Watch Below* (1940), *In the First Watch* (1946).

Harry E. Maule, *William McFee* (1923).

Ralph Hale Mottram (1883-   ) was born in Norwich to a family of Quaker tradition, but lately Unitarian. Three generations of Mottrams before him had been highly trusted employees of Gurney's Bank of that city and when he had finished school, he followed them. In 1914 he joined the Norfolk Regiment and served the entire war in France, chiefly in staff assignments. Upon leaving the service he married and returned to the bank, now merged into the greater Barclay's.

Although he had published two volumes of verse before the war under the pseudonym "J. Marjoram," it was not until 1924 that Mottram published a novel based on his war experience, largely through the encouragement of John Galsworthy, whom he had known for many years. The success of *The Spanish Farm* led him to expand it into a trilogy during the next two years, and in 1927, at forty-four, he retired from banking to start a new career in literature. Since then he has been known as a regional novelist of his native city and county, though he has also written a variety of short stories, essays, and biographical studies as well as histories of financial speculation and of the East India Company.

With his background it is natural that Mottram should be conservative in tastes and outlook, and this inherited tendency was strengthened by the deep impression made upon his youth by Norwich, the most conservative city of East Anglia and the richest in historical monuments. *Auto-*

biography With a Difference (1938), really a series of essays, shows to what extent the richness of the past affected him. Tradition and the continuity of life are his constant themes. He writes of local character and local ways with an understanding and affection that may be compared in kind, though not in quality, to Hardy's feeling for Dorset. Though he has never again reached the high level of *The Spanish Farm Trilogy,* the best English fiction of the First World War, his Norwich stories are among the finest regional writing since that time. Especially *Our Mr. Dormer* (1927), which follows closely the history of his own family, exhibits the love of sound, unhurrying progress and the feeling for local color that are characteristic of his work. He is commonly considered of the school of Galsworthy but he has escaped Galsworthy's social evangelism and his worse sentimentality.

FICTION: *The Spanish Farm* (1924), *Sixty-four, ninety-four* (1925), *The Crime at Vanderlynden's* (1926), *The Spanish Farm Trilogy* (1927), *Our Mr. Dormer* (1927), *The English Miss* (1928), *The Boroughmonger* (1929), *Europa's Beast* [*A Rich Man's Daughter*] (1930), *The New Providence* (1930), *Castle Island* (1931), *The Headless Hound and Other Stories* (1931), *The Lost Christmas Presents* (1931), *Home for the Holidays* (1932), *Dazzle* (1932), *The Lame Dog* [*At the Sign of the Lame Dog*] (1933), *A Good Old-Fashioned Christmas* (1933), *Bumphrey's* (1934), *Strawberry Time and The Banquet* (1934), *Early Morning* (1935), *Flower Pot End* (1935), *Time To Be Going* (1937), *There Was a Jolly Miller* (1938), *You Can't Have It Back* (1939), *Miss Lavington* (1939), *The Ghost and the Maiden* (1940), *The World Turns Slowly Round* (1942), *The Corbells at War* (1943), *Visit of the Princess* (1946), *Buxton the Liberator* (1946).

H. G. Fabes, *The First Editions of Ralph Hale Mottram* (1934).

Though not a prolific or widely popular writer, **Charles Edward Montague (1867-1928)** has been highly esteemed. His father, Francis Montague, was an Irish priest who left the Church, married, and moved to England to raise his family. The household was a happy one devoted to plain living and high thinking. The young Montagues were encouraged in generous enthusiasms tempered by sound judgment and, as the family means were straitened, were urged to get all the education they could by their own efforts. Upon completing his course at the City of London School in 1885, Charles Edward received an exhibition (scholarship) to Balliol College, Oxford, where he took a first in classics in 1887, and two years later a second in humane letters.

While still an undergraduate Montague was noticed by C. P. Scott of the *Manchester Guardian,* under his editorship one of the world's great papers and the best school of English journalism. Scott offered Montague a job and he passed directly from Oxford to the *Guardian,* where he remained until 1925, becoming Scott's son-in-law and chief assistant.

Montague's first book, aside from his contribution to a collaborative volume on the Manchester stage, *A Hind Let Loose* (1910), was a clever satire, setting forth the adventures of a brilliant Irish journalist who writes political articles for rival papers, and in spite of detection, gets away with it because the incapable editors can not do without him. It was followed by the less successful *The Morning's War* in 1913.

In 1914 although he was overage for service, Montague dyed his gray hair and enlisted in the Royal Fusiliers. But though he could disguise his age he could not change it, and despite his gallantry and courage his health broke under the strain of the Western Front. He was sent home, commissioned, and reassigned to Intelligence in which he served the rest of the war. His military record was excellent.

Two more novels followed the war, *Rough Justice* (1926) and *Right off the Map* (1927), and two volumes of short stories, *Fiery Particles* (1923) and *Action* (1928). The novels are bitter indictments of militarism. The first shows up the romantic weakling who intoxicates himself and others with rhetoric against the realities of war, the second exposes the betrayal of the people, and especially the soldiers, by the politicians and intellectuals who have brought on a war between imaginary states. The short stories are less serious. "Honours Easy" (in *Fiery Particles*) is an exquisitely witty and true satire on military honors and decorations.

In the field of nonfiction Montague's finest work is *Disenchantment* (1922), one of the very best books to come out of the First World War. Its theme is the betrayal of patriotic idealism by the professional militarists, but many of its most memorable passages are in the incidental descriptions of the Western Front. In these the sombre beauty of Montague's prose places him high among modern stylists.

Of his three volumes of essays, the first, *Dramatic Values* (1911), embodies the best of his criticism for the *Guardian*, and the third, *A Writer's Notes on His Trade* (1930), his sound if not always very original observations on the craft of letters, posthumously published. Between these lies *The Right Place* (1924), a series of essays on the spirit of place and the true enjoyment of it that show Montague to be a thorough master of the essay form.

From these few books, showing command of form but rather narrow range, Montague emerges not only as a writer of very high competence but an attractive and often impressive character. From his Irish parents he inherited a romanticism, deep rather than exuberant. To balance it he was endowed with a clear, realistic vision that penetrated all pretensions and left the disenchanted romantic sometimes jeering sometimes bitter. But when not in conflict these qualities could produce, as in *The Right Place*, a mellow Montaigne-like wisdom completely winning in its tolerance and catholicity. An athlete in college, later an enthusiastic mountain climber, Montague combined a thorough physical enjoyment of life, especially out of doors, with his knowledge of men and books. Probably it was this all-aroundness of life that preserved his spontaneity and freshness, so that, though actually older than Belloc or Chesterton, for example, he seems often nearer to writers and readers of the following generation. He was a fastidious craftsman, and though most of his life's effort was given to the *Guardian,* in the small but distinguished body of permanent work that he left there is nothing shabby or shoddy. He would have liked that to be final.

NOVELS: *A Hind Let Loose* (1910), *The Morning's War* (1913), *Rough Justice* (1926), *Right Off the Map* (1927). SHORT STORIES: *Fiery Particles* (1923), *Action* (1928). MEMOIRS AND ESSAYS: *William Thomas Arnold,* with Mrs. H. Ward (1907), *Dramatic Values* (1911), *The Front Line* (1917), *The Western Front* (1917), *The Calais Ban* (1918), *Disenchantment* (1922), *The Right Place* (1924), *A Writer's Notes on His Trade* (1930).

Oliver Elton, *C. E. Montague* (1929); Dixon Scott, "C. E. Montague," in *Men of Letters* (1916); J. B. Priestley, "C. E. Montague," *London Mercury,* XVIII (1928), 381-390; D. N. Dalglish, "The Author of Disenchantment," *Adelphi,* IV (1926), 214-225.

Ford Maddox Ford (1873-1939) was born Ford Maddox Hueffer. His father was a German editor working in London, his mother the daughter of Maddox Brown, the Pre-Raphaelite painter, and a sister-in-law of William Rossetti. Reared in a highly intellectual atmosphere, he began to write at seventeen and at twenty-five was invited to collaborate with Conrad. In 1908 he founded *The English Review,* the most brilliant literary periodical of Edwardian days, in which he "discovered" D. H. Lawrence. At the same time he was making his name as an author of historical fiction. In 1914 he entered the service and served the war as an officer in the Welsh Fusiliers.

After the war he changed his name to Ford. Always Gallic in his personal tastes and literary standards, he lived mostly in France, and as editor of *the transatlantic review* was prominent in the Paris circle that included Joyce and Ezra

Pound. His principal work at the time was a series of war novels—*No More Parades* (1925), *A Man Could Stand Up* (1926), *The Last Post* (1928). These have been reissued in 1951. In his later years he lectured at Olivet College, Michigan. He died in France.

It is hard to say why Ford does not occupy a higher place in English fiction than he does except that with objectivity, conscientious technique, and a fastidious sense of style he is somewhat dull. His voluminous critical work is rather narrow in its exclusive admiration of what derives from France, but it is as the discoverer and appreciator of the genius of others rather than for his creative work that he will be remembered. He is a delightful and malicious but wholly untrustworthy literary gossip.

FICTION: *The Shifting of the Fire* (1892), *The Inheritors,* With *Joseph Conrad* (1901), *Romance*, with Joseph Conrad (1903), *Benefactor* (1905), *The Fifth Queen* (1906), *An English Girl* (1907), *Privy Seal* (1907), *The Fifth Queen Crowned* (1908), *Mr. Apollo* (1908), *The "Half-Moon"* (1909), *A Call* (1910), *The Portrait* (1910), *Ladies Whose Bright Eyes* (1911), *The Panel* [*Ring For Nancy*] (1912), *Mr. Fleight* (1913), *The Young Lovell* (1913), *The Good Soldier* (1915), *The Marsden Case* (1923), *Some Do Not* (1924), *No More Parades* (1925), *A Man Could Stand Up* (1926), *A Little Less Than Gods* (1928), *The Last Post* (1928), *When the Wicked Man* (1931), *The Rash Act* (1933), *Henry For Hugh* (1934), *Vive le Roi* (1936). MISCELLANEOUS: *Joseph Conrad, a personal remembrance* (1924), *Mightier Than the Sword* (1938). VERSE: *Collected Poems* (1916, reissued 1936).

Douglas Goldring, *South Lodge* (1943); Lawrence Price, "Ford Maddox Ford," *Univ. of California Chronicle,* XXVII (1925), 346-365; John Peale Bishop, "The Poems of Ford Maddox Ford," *Poetry,* L (1937), 336-341; Ezra Pound, "Ford Maddox (Hueffer) Ford; Obit," *Nineteenth Century,* CXXVI (1939), 178-181.

The son of a London architect, **Edward Morgan Forster** (**1879-**   ) was educated at Tonbridge School and Cambridge. He entered Kings College at the latter in 1897, took his degree in classics in 1900, and remained a further year reading history. After the university he spent a year (1901-2) travelling in Italy and Greece, an experience that seasoned

his mind and has meant a great deal to him throughout his life.

He began writing in 1903 for *The Independent Review,* a liberal periodical of anti-imperialist politics, founded by some of his Cambridge teachers. Two years later, at the age of twenty-six, he published his first novel *Where Angels Fear to Tread.* Three more novels, all of distinction, followed within five years—

EDWARD MORGAN FORSTER

The Longest Journey (1907), *A Room With A View* (1908), and *Howards End* (1910). Then there was a sudden slackening, and though he projected two novels and completed a play which was not produced, he published nothing further before the First World War, except a volume of short stories, *The Celestial Omnibus* (1911). In 1912 he travelled to India in company with his former Cambridge tutor and friend, G. Lowes Dickinson, gathering impressions that twelve years later were embodied in the most popular of his novels.

The war made the same gap in Forster's life as in those of all his generation and broke his literary career into sharply divided sections. For three years, 1915-18, he was in Egypt, working as a civilian for the British Government. After the war he returned to London where he followed literary journalism and became identified with the Bloomsbury circle of Virginia Woolf. In 1922 he went again to India.

The work of Forster's second period is highly diversified. First were two Egyptian books, *Alexandria: A History And*

A Guide (1922) and *Pharos and Pharillon* (1923), a volume of historical essays. Then in 1924 appeared his best known and to the present his latest novel, *A Passage to India,* begun before the war and resumed with the fresh impressions of his second visit to India. In 1927 he was made an honorary fellow of his college and delivered the Clark Lectures in literature which were published as *Aspects of the Novel.* Another volume of short stories, *The Eternal Moment,* appeared in 1928. He published nothing further of importance until 1934, which was marked by his rather dull biography, *Goldsworthy Lowes Dickinson,* and *Abinger Harvest,* a collection of his essays up to that time. Since then he has written only a pageant, *England's Pleasant Land* (1940), and a few essays published in pamphlet form.

Forster is a slight, shy, gentle-humored man. His uneventful later years have been passed at Abinger in Meredith's part of Surrey. His work has been recognized by a number of academic honors and literary distinctions and prizes.

Forster presents a nice problem in placing. Chronologically nearly all his fiction, the most important part of his work, was done before 1912. Yet not merely by virtue of belated discovery, but by the essential temper and feeling of his work he is virtually a contemporary author. That is because what he has to say is more pertinent to the present generation than it was to the last. In a world increasingly regimented by authority he protests as a genuine liberal, not the advocate of some new regimentation. He distrusts all those official persons—soldiers, clergymen, teachers—whose business it is to direct others' lives, and looks for the salvation of humanity to the good will and decency of its unorganized individuals. It is a hard faith to hold now, let alone to propagate, but its assertion is a timely commentary and challenge. As Forster sees it, the bar to the effective utilization of general decency is "the uneducated heart." The phrase has no sentimental implications; it refers to the insensitivity and arrogance that keep men apart when the tyranny of the community standard fosters the will to conformity. Therefore he sets friendship above patriotism, and though (or perhaps because) his mother's people were of the famous Clapham Sect of evangelicals, will have no truck with puritanism. For him insensitive and conventional people are impaired personalities; in a way, they do not really exist.

Ideas, of which this is the leading one, are the essence of Forster's novels. His early books especially show a strong discipleship to Meredith, relying on character and the discussion of ideas rather than on plot. That is not to say that they are plotless; on the contrary the stories are good, but the conflict of the real people, vital and sincere, and the sham ones, smug and bound by shibboleths, and the contrast of their ideals is of greater significance. Fortunately the influence of Meredith does not extend to style; Forster's prose is simple and natural.

Howards End, though not so well known as *A Passage to India,* is Forster's best novel. It deals with the relations of two cultivated young women, the English-born daughters of a self-exiled German liberal, with a typical well-to-do family of the practical and conventional English middle class. It is an analysis of the failure of those relations and through them of the tragedy of failure in all human relations, rather depressing in its implication that such failure is unavoidable in our society, but absorbing, and distinguished by finely realized characters. The theme of *A Passage to India* is the power of convention in keeping apart individuals and peoples as shown in the relations of English and Indians. The good will of individuals capable of reconciling east and west is frustrated by narrow exclusiveness, and without the feeling of inevitability of the earlier book, there is in the ending a mere inconclusiveness that points to no solution of Indian race relations. Forster's short stories are less impressive than his novels probably because he is less adept in statement and suggestion than in the ampler development of his theme that a longer work allows.

Forster's essays are never dull and show a generous culture and a wide range of interest. He is best when dealing with character, weakest as a critic. He has the gift, priceless in an essayist, of establishing ease and intimacy with the reader, and one sometimes overlooks in the charming frankness and ease of his monologue that his mood toward his material is not wholly satisfactory or that a responsibility has been shirked. However, these failures are not frequent or very serious and against them one may set his unpretentious wisdom and the pleasure in good expression that is the justification of belles lettres.

NOVELS: *Where Angels Fear to Tread* (1905), *The Longest Journey* (1907), *A Room With A View* (1908), *Howards End* (1910), *A Passage to India* (1924). SHORT STORIES: *The Celestial Omnibus* (1911), *The Eternal Moment* (1928). MISCELLANEOUS: *Alexandria: A History and a Guide* (1922), *Pharos and Pharillon* (1923), *Aspects of the Novel* (1927), *A Letter to Madan Blanchard* (1931), *Goldsworthy Lowes Dickinson* (1934), *Abinger Harvest* (1936), *What I Believe* (1939), *Virginia Woolf* (1942).

Lionel Trilling, *E. M. Forster* (Norfolk, Conn., 1943); F. R. Leavis, "E. M. Forster," *Scrutiny*, VII (1938), 185-202; Edward Shanks, "Mr. E. M. Forster," *London Mercury*, XVI (1927), 265-274; Peter Burra, "The Novels of E. M. Forster," *New Century*, CXVI (1934), 581-594; Howard N. Doughty, "The Novels of E. M. Forster," *Bookman*, LXXV (1932), 542-549; E. K. Brown, "E. M. Forster and the Contemplative Novel," *Univ. Toronto Quar.*, III (1934), 349-361; M. Belgion, "The Diabolism of Mr. Forster," *Criterion*, XIV (1934), 54-73; Austin Warren, "The Novels of E. M. Forster, *Amer. Rev.*, IX (1937), 226-252; H. M. McLuhan, "Kipling and Forster," *Sewanee Rev.*, LII (1944), 332-343.

One of the most brilliant and tragically ineffectual figures of his time was **(George) Norman Douglas (1868-1951)**. Born in Austria of Scottish and German ancestry, he was educated at Uppingham in England and the Karlsruhe Gymnasium in Germany. At twenty-five he entered the diplomatic service in which he was, officially, active for only three and a half years, being for most of that time attached to the embassy at St. Petersburg (Petrograd). He then went to Italy, where, at Naples and Capri, he lived with intervals until the First World War. He has travelled widely in Syria, Tunisia, and India. His later home was in France, from which he escaped with difficulty after the German invasion of 1940.

Interested from childhood in natural history, Douglas began while still at the Gymnasium (1886) to publish zoological monographs, and these were his only writings down to 1895. His first venture into fiction was *Unprofessional Tales* (1901—under pseudonym Normyx), which was so poorly received that he did not make another attempt until *South Wind* (1917). This unique novel, a satiric study of a group of expatriated English in the island of Nepenthe (Capri), is Douglas' one worthy achievement as an artist. In it all his powers, his philosophy, his scholarship, his humor, his wide knowledge of men, find adequate expression and the result is a masterpiece of satire, one of the fine and utterly enjoyable novels of the language. His later works of fiction fail dismally to show anything of its quality and charm.

Douglas' most consistent writing is to be found in his books of travel and topography. Most of these deal with the south of Italy and especially the vicinity of Naples. The best, and best known, are *Siren Land* (1911) and *Old Calabria* (1915). Between 1904 and 1915 Douglas published a series of studies of the history and topography of Capri which were collected in 1930 as *Capri: Materials for a Description of the Island*. He has also written a number of essays and a diverting autobiography, *Looking Back* (1933).

Douglas belongs to that line of gifted and adventurous

Scots that from the time of Duns Scotus have compelled the admiration of Europe. Everything written by or about him attests his strong and genial character and his accomplishments as naturalist, linguist, archaeologist, and civilized cosmopolitan. Why he did not make those gifts more effective has never been adequately explained. He was not a literary dilettante. In spite of the distinction of his family, he was for much of his life a poor man, glad to earn money by his writing and finding it hard to do so. A clue may be found in his method of writing his autobiography by picking up at random the visiting cards that have accumulated for years and tracing their associations. He had the antiquarian's interest in the traces of the past, the human story behind the document or the artifact. It is an interest rich in gratification, but unprofitable. Douglas could not easily write the picturesque travel book that would sell to tourists. When he wrote *South Wind* he was forty-nine; it exhausted the creative observation of half a life time and left him nothing more to say. For many men *Old Calabria* and *South Wind* would be a sufficient achievement, but for Douglas it seems inadequate.

AUTOBIOGRAPHY: *Looking Back* (1933). FICTION: *Unprofessional Tales* (1901), *South Wind* (1917), *They Went* (1920), *In the Beginning* (1927), *The Angel of Manfredonia* (1929), *Nerinda* (1901), reprinted 1929. TRAVEL: *Siren Land* (1911), *Fountains in the Sand* (1912), *Old Calabria* (1915), *Alone* (1921), *Together* (1923), *One Day* (1929), *Summer Islands, Ischia and Ponza* (1931), *Capri: Materials for a Description of the Island* (1930). MISCELLANEOUS: *London Street Games* (1916), *D. H. Lawrence and Maurice Magnus* (1924), *Experiments* (1925), *Birds and Beasts of the Greek Anthology* (1927), *Good Bye to Western Culture* (1930).

E. D. MacDonald, *Bibliography of the Writings of Norman Douglas* (Phila., 1927); H. M. Tomlinson, *Norman Douglas* (1931); G. and L. Clements, "Norman Douglas," *Rev. Anglo-Americaine* (1931), 29-40; Richard McGillivray, *Norman Douglas* (1933); Robert Lynd, "Mr. Norman Douglas' Dislikes" in *Books and Authors* (1923).

The boyhood of **David Herbert Lawrence (1885-1930)** was darkened by poverty and by the drunkenness of his father, a Nottinghamshire coal miner. With the help and encourage-

DAVID HERBERT
LAWRENCE

ment of his mother, a former teacher, he passed through the high school and later the University College of Nottingham and became himself a school teacher at Croydon. But this was merely a way of escape from the mining country and the fate of his parents; he had written verse from early days and his ambition was literary. The publication in 1911 of his first novel, *The White Peacock,* though it brought him little money, decided his career. During the next two years he brought out his first volume of poems and two further

novels, of which the second, *Sons and Lovers,* first drew general attention. It has always been, partly because of its large autobiographical element, a favorite with Lawrence's readers.

In the summer of 1912 Lawrence fell in love and eloped with the wife of Professor Weekley of Nottingham. They spent most of the next two years on the continent until the professor obtained his divorce, when they returned to England and were married on the eve of the First World War. Mrs. Lawrence was a German, born Frieda von Richthofen, daughter of the governor of Metz and cousin of Germany's most famous military flier. Her connections and Lawrence's unconcealed distaste for the war made them objects of police surveillance and some petty persecution. Then in 1915 the authorities suppressed his fourth novel, *The Rainbow,* seriously damaging his reputation and reducing his already narrow means. England had become unbearable to Lawrence; he had projected to J. M. Murry a scheme for a community in Florida (reminiscent of Coleridge's and Southey's pantisocracy), and when the war was over he left the country —save for short visits—for good.

The years 1919 to 1922 were spent mostly in Italy and Sicily. *Women in Love,* his best work, a continuation of *The Rainbow,* written during the war and refused by English publishers who were then afraid to handle his work, appeared in New York. An invitation from Mabel Dodge Luhan to come to Taos, New Mexico, revived Lawrence's thoughts of an American community and started him on his world travels. The first stage took him via Ceylon to Australia, where he wrote *Kangaroo,* the second via New Zealand, Tahiti, and San Francisco to Taos. Except for one short visit to England, the next three years were spent at Del Monte ranch which Mrs. Luhan gave him, with winters in Mexico (1923 and 1924) for his health. From Mexico he drew the imperfect but remarkable *The Plumed Serpent.*

The end of 1925 took him back to Europe and the remaining years were spent near Florence (1926-28), in Switzerland, and on the Riviera. Lawrence's genius was now recognized and he was widely acknowledged the most important contemporary English writer, but his success had not made him rich and he still had trouble with the police. *Lady Chatterley's Lover* (1928) was suppressed on both sides of the Atlantic, and in the feeling over it the exhibition of his paintings in London was closed as obscene. Anger at this renewal of public hostility may have helped to shorten his life. Lawrence's physical history was much like Stevenson's: he had been subject to tuberculosis since early childhood and had travelled to seek milder climates for his health's sake. He died at the age of 44 in Vence in the south of France.

In Lawrence's life the typically masculine influences: his father, the police, war, and commercialism had all been hostile; and the feminine: his mother, his wife, his many women admirers, friendly. But as a man he bitterly resented his dependence upon women, and rebelled against the modern intellectual-idealistic society in which women dominate. Hence the mystical importance he attached to sex and his tiresome insistence on the "maleness" of his heroes. Because his wife was his social superior (as his mother had been his father's) and her children were her first husband's, he subjects his women to coarse, physically powerful men, strong in the dark, pagan "wisdom of the blood," the ultimate expression of this being the utter abandonment of the aristocratic Lady Chatterley to the embraces of a gamekeeper.

The atmosphere of his novels and stories is one of physical and emotional violence: his characters love and hate (especially hate) immediately and intensely; they seem never to know those moderate feelings that make up the greater experience of most of humanity. As a result they are often unbelievable, and even the best of them inconsistent. They are true to their creator: Lawrence's married life was a perpetual Donnybrook of the most frightful rows and his friendships a history of tragic partings and revulsions due to his immoderate demands for spiritual support and acquiescence. His frustrated will to realize a fuller life found its symbol in ruthless leadership, so that in *Kangaroo* there is political violence in the making and in *The Plumed Serpent* a full dress Fascist revolution in Mexico. He knew that the Kingdom of Heaven is not to be taken by arms, but being what he was, he could not help trying, nor could he think sustainedly of men and women without an exasperation that utterly confounded his judgment.

Only in his travel books and the descriptive parts of his novels does Lawrence appear happy and poised. Wherever he was a spectator or transient, free of the friction of personal relationships, his marvelous eye and quick sympathy recorded the scene accurately and vividly. In *The Plumed Serpent,* for example, the unforgettable pictures of a Mexican town are of a quality irreconcilable with its downright silly political melodrama. The observant, reflective Lawrence of *Sea and Sardinia* or *Etruscan Places* is a much saner person than his angry, creative alter ego—a contrast that may be noted in Milton, Carlyle, and other puritans.

Puritanism (traceable to the relation of his parents?) expresses the self-betrayal of Lawrence's art. The earliest and best influence on his writing was that of Hardy, but it did not last. His most enduring novels are the early pair *The Rainbow* and *Women in Love,* which tell the decline and fall of the Brangwyns, yeomen long attached to their land but marrying away from it to become lost in the third generation. Between the beginning of the first, which is pure Hardy, and the end of the second, the waning of the influence is clear. Lawrence had neither Hardy's humor nor his patience; his obsessive, puritanical will to power for his ideas drove him, with Shaw and Wells, down the road of Fascist ideology. But Lawrence, though he was emotionally unstable, was neither a sex-ridden pagan nor a warped puritan. He often made the common mistake of treating morals and society, which are materials of art, as ends; but except in his worst moments he was sufficiently an artist to save himself from disaster.

Lawrence is among those few eminent prose men who also demand serious consideration as poets. His verse is in the first place a highly important commentary on his life and thought. From the early poems of love and nature in Nottinghamshire, one can trace biographically every crisis of his life, his mother's death, his union with Frieda, the war, as well as every contact with a new environment in Bavaria, Italy, or Mexico, and his response to it. But beyond this documentary interest the best of it is poetry of high quality. Beginning as a traditionalist in the timid early

Georgian years, Lawrence could rise above the general contemporary level to the splendid vigor of "The Wild Common." Thereafter the influences of the imagists and of
Whitman liberated his technique and from "Look We Have
Come Through" (1917) he has a command of rhythms exquisitely responsive to every mood and subject. A comparison of the delicate mobility of "Fishes" or "Bat" with the
sustained sombreness of "The Ship of Death" will show
his power in this, as their subjects his range of interest. His
weakness is to write too often on the impulse of momentary
irritation so that the emotion—not "recollected in tran-
quility"—comes out raw, a metrical footnote to his biography and not always a good one. Whether Lawrence is a
lesser major poet or a greater minor one is hard to say—
probably the former.

FICTION: *The White Peacock* (1911), *The Trespasser* (1912), *Sons
and Lovers* (1913), *The Prussian Officer* (1914), *The Rainbow*
(1915), *The Lost Girl* (1920), *Women in Love* (1920), *England,
My England* (1922), *Aaron's Rod* (1922), *The Ladybird,* [*The
Captain's Doll*] (1923), *Kangaroo* (1923), *The Boy in the
Bush,* with M. L. Skinner (1924), *St. Mawr* (1925), *The Plumed
Serpent* (1926), *Glad Ghosts* (1926), *The Woman Who Rode
Away* (1928), *Rawdon's Roof* (1928), *Lady Chatterley's Lover*
(1928), *Love Among the Haystacks* (1930), *The Virgin and the
Gipsy* (1930), *The Escaped Cock* (1930), [*The Man Who Died*]
(1931), *The Lovely Lady* (1930), *A Modern Lover* (1934),
The Tales of D. H. Lawrence (1934), *The First Lady Chatterley*
(1944). VERSE: *Love Poems and Others* (1913), *Amores* (1916),
Look We Have Come Through (1917), *New Poems* (1918), *Bay*
(1919), *Tortoises* (1921), *Birds, Beasts and Flowers* (1923), *The
Collected Poems of D. H. Lawrence* (1928), *Pansies* (1929), *Nettles*
(1930), *The Triumph of the Machine* (1930), *Last Poems* (1932),
The Ship of Death (1933), *Poems* (1939). PLAYS: *The Widowing of
Mrs. Holroyd* (1914), *Touch and Go* (1920), *David* (1926), *The
Plays of D. H. Lawrence* (1936). MISCELLANEOUS: *Twilight in
Italy* (1916), *Sea and Sardinia* (1921), *Psychoanalysis and the
Unconscious* (1921), *Movements in European History* (1921),
Fantasia of the Unconscious (1922), *Studies in Classic American*

Literature (1923), *Reflections on the Death of a Porcupine* (1925), *Mornings in Mexico* (1927), *The Paintings of D. H. Lawrence* (1929), *Pornography and Obscenity* (1929), *My Skirmish With Jolly Roger* (1929), *Apropos of Lady Chatterley's Lover* (1930), *Assorted Articles* (1930), *Etruscan Places* (1932), *Apocalypse* (1932), *We Need One Another* (1933), *Phoenix* (1936), *D. H. Lawrence's Unpublished Foreword to Lady Chatterley's Lover* (1936). LETTERS: *Letters of D. H. Lawrence* (1932), *D. H. Lawrence: Reminiscences and Correspondence*, ed. E. and A. Brewster (1934).

Edward MacDonald, *A Bibliography of the Writings of D. H. Lawrence* (1925); L. C. Powell, *The Manuscripts of D. H. Lawrence* (Los Angeles Public Library 1937); Frieda Lawrence, *Not I But the Wind* (1934); Ada Lawrence, *Young Lorenzo* (Florence, 1931); J. Middleton Murry, *D. H. Lawrence, Two Essays* (1930), *Son of Woman* (1931), *Reminiscences of D. H. Lawrence* (1933); E. T., *D. H. Lawrence: A Personal Record* (1935); Catherine Carswell, *Savage Pilgrimage* (1935); Mabel D. Luhan, *Lorenzo in Taos* (1933); Dorothy Brett, *Lawrence and Brett* (1933); F. R. Leavis, *D. H. Lawrence* (1930); Rebecca West, *D. H. Lawrence* (1931); Stephen Potter, *D. H. Lawrence: A First Study* (1930); Hugh Kingsmill, *Life of D. H. Lawrence* (1938); W. Y. Tyndall, *D. H. Lawrence and His Cow Susan* (1939); Horace Gregory, *Pilgrim of the Apocalypse: A Critical Study of D. H. Lawrence* (1933); Anaïs Nin, *D. H. Lawrence* (Paris, 1932); H. J. Seligman, *D. H. Lawrence: An American Interpretation* (1924); Lionel Trilling, "D. H. Lawrence," *Symposium* I (1930), 361-371; F. M. Ford, "D. H. Lawrence," *Amer. Mercury*, XXXVIII (1936), 167-179, reprinted in *Portraits From Life* (1937); André Maurois, "D. H. Lawrence," in *Prophets and Poets* (1935); Robert Tunstill, "D. H. Lawrence," *London Mercury*, XXI (1930), 538-545; Dayton Kobler, "D. H. Lawrence," *Sewanee Rev.*, XXXIX (1931), 25-38; Maurice Lanoire, "D. H. Lawrence," *Rev. de Paris*, XXXIX (1932), 909-925; Edward Garnett, "D. H. Lawrence: His Posthumous Papers," *London Mercury*, XXXV (1937), 152-160; Louis Cazamian, "D. H. Lawrence and Katherine Mansfield As Letter Writers," *Univ. Toronto Quar.*, III (1934), 436-453; Max Wildi, "The Birth of Expressionism in the Work of D. H. Lawrence," *Eng. Studies*, XIX (1937), 241-259; A. W. Harrison, "The Philosophy of D. H. Lawrence," *Hibbert Jour.*, XXXII (1934), 554-563; Elisco Vivas, "Lawrence's Problems," *Kenyon Rev.*, III (1941), 83-94; T. M. Pearce, "The Unpublished 'Lady Chatterley's Lover,'"

New Mexico Quar., VIII (1938), 171-179; Margaret Gardiner, "Meeting the Master," *Horizon,* II (1940), 184-191; Rhys Davies, "D. H. Lawrence in Bandol," *ibid,* 191-208; D. H. Lawrence number, *Adelphi,* N. S., III (1930), 241-321; Anthony P. West, *D. H. Lawrence* (1950).

Aldous (Leonard) Huxley (1894-   ) was born to science and letters. His father, Leonard Huxley, was the son of T. H. Huxley the biologist; his mother was a niece of Mat-

ALDOUS HUXLEY

thew Arnold, and sister of Mrs. Humphrey Ward. A schoolboy at Eton, Aldous Huxley had begun to follow his elder brother Julian in the study of biology, intending to become a doctor, when at eighteen he became almost completely blind. Though he slowly recovered his sight, the weakness of his eyes remained a constant handicap to him. This put an end to his pursuit of science.

At Oxford he took full advantage of undergraduate liberty to study English letters in his own way and to exercise his gift for verse. His early volumes *The Burning Wheel* (1916) and *The Defeat of Youth* (1918) placed him well among the young poets of the war years and gave promise of the quality of his mature work in *Leda* (1920) and *The Cicadas* (1931). Thoughtful and graceful as the verse is in all of these, however, Huxley has never become more than an interesting minor poet.

After graduation and a short—apparently painful—experience of teaching, Huxley married and turned to journalism for a livelihood. To the brilliant *Athenaeum* under Middleton Murry's editorship in 1919-20, Huxley contributed criticism and essays over the signature "Autolycus," and at the same time wrote for the *Westminster Gazette,* the *London Mercury* and *Vanity Fair,* overworking himself severely. These early essays include travel impressions and criticism of a wide range of subject matter, letters, painting, music, and architecture.

Though he published a volume of short stories, *Limbo,* in 1920, it was not until the following year upon the appearance of *Crome Yellow* that Huxley's importance in fiction was recognized. *Antic Hay* (1923), *Those Barren Leaves* (1925), and *Point Counter Point* (1928) put him within the decade among the foremost novelists of his generation. These four books are his finest achievement. Satirical studies of a decadent society they are essentially novels of ideas in the tradition of Peacock and Meredith. There is a minimum of narrative in all of them—indeed Huxley treats his beginnings and endings quite cavalierly—and the characters are static, less interesting for what they are or do than for what they say. Each novel becomes a series of conversation pieces that delight equally with their wit and their unsparing disesteem of humanity.

In *Brave New World* (1932), dealing with advanced technological civilization, a change appears in Huxley's fiction. His explorations as a "natural historian of society" have led to disgust and horror, and his work declines in *After Many a Summer Dies the Swan* (1940) to almost savage buffoonery. *Time Must Have a Stop* (1944) and *Ape and Essence* (1948) show a partial recovery but none of these have the quality of his earlier novels. The machinery is unpleasantly evident and the ideas seem imposed upon, not generated by, the characters.

Huxley's four volumes of short stories contain some excellent work such as *The Gioconda Smile,* but the medium is not wholly suited to him and in spite of their cleverness these must be considered a minor part of his fiction.

His later essays, *Proper Studies* (1927), *Do What You Will* (1929), and *Ends and Means* (1937), are a serious examination of the ethics of society and of the individual. In them as in his single biographical work, *Grey Eminence* (1941) there is an increasing despair of the modern world and concern for the salvation of the individual soul. Finally *The Perennial Philosophy* (1944) develops the faith common to the mystics of all great religions through an illuminating selection from their writings with Huxley's running commentary and exposition. Here mysticism is offered as the only possible salvation for mankind.

Throughout his progress from the sophisticated novelist of the twenties to the mystic of the forties one can perceive a perfectly consistent personality running throughout Huxley's work. He has practiced his and Lawrence's creed of living with the whole of one's being, and as he has matured, new aspects of his character have found their expression. He is both more consistent and less versatile than he appears. In spite of the variety of literary forms he has employed Huxley has always been an essayist; everything in the world without finds its correspondent in the mind and provokes discussion. And though Huxley, like most men who live amid the play of ideas, has been widely influenced by the thoughts of others, he has been on the whole successful in assimilating what he has received and subordinating it to the original bent of his own mind. He is often edifying and seldom dull.

On the solid basis of his inheritance and training Huxley has built a cosmopolitan experience. From his first success he lived much of the time in Italy and France and travelled in the East Indies and Central America. Then, because of a treatment that proved of great help to his eyes, he came to the United States. For several years he has lived in California. He has seen a good deal of the material and social worlds, but his important life has been intellectual.

FICTION: *Limbo* (1920), *Crome Yellow* (1922), *Mortal Coils* (1922), *Antic Hay* (1923), *Little Mexican and Other Stories* [*Young Archimedes*] (1924), *Those Barren Leaves* (1925), *Two or Three Graces* (1926), *Point Counter Point* (1928), *Brief Candles* (1930), *Brave New World* (1932), *Eyeless in Gaza* (1936), *After Many a Summer Dies the Swan* (1939), *Time Must Have a Stop* (1944), *Ape and Essence* (1948). MISCELLANEOUS: *On the Margin* (1923), *Along the Road* (1925), *Essays New and Old* (1926), *Jesting Pilate* (1926), *Proper Studies* (1927), *Do What You Will* (1929), *Holy Face and Other Essays* (1929), *Music at Night* (1931), *Texts and Pretexts* (1932), *Beyond the Mexique Bay* (1934), *The Olive Tree* (1936), *Ends and Means* (1937), *Grey Eminence* (1941), *The Perennial Philosophy* (1945), *Science, Liberty and Peace* (1946).

H. R. Duval, *Aldous Huxley: A Bibliography* (1939); Alexander Henderson, *Aldous Huxley* (1936); André Maurois, "Aldous Huxley," in *Poets and Prophets* (1935); John Freeman, "Aldous Huxley," *Mercury*, XV (1927), 391-400; Henry Alexander, "Lawrence and Huxley," *Queen's Quar.*, XLII (1935), 96-108; J. H. Roberts, "Huxley and Lawrence," *Virginia Quar. Rev.*, XIII (1937), 546-557; William Y. Tindall, "The Trouble With Aldous Huxley," *American Scholar*, XI (1942), 452-464; F. T. Hoffman, "Aldous Huxley and the Novel of Ideas," *College English*, VIII (1946-47), 129-137; H. T. Webster, "Aldous Huxley: Notes on a Moral Evolution," *So. Atlantic Quar.*, XLV (1946), 372-383; Reinhold Hoops, "Die Weltanschauung Aldous Huxleys," *Englische Studien*, LXXII (1937), 73-92; M. M. Kirkwood, "The Thought of Aldous Huxley," *Univ. Toronto Quar.*, VI (1937), 189-194; M. D. Petre, "Bolshevist Ideals and the 'Brave New World,'" *Hibbert Jour.*, XXXI (1932), 61-71; Doris N. Dalglish, "Aldous Huxley's Poetry," *London Mercury*, XXXVIII (1938), 437-444; D. S. Savage, "Aldous Huxley and the Dissociation of Personality," *Sat. Rev. Lit.*, V (1947), 537-568.

Rose Macaulay was born, probably toward the end of the eighties, in Cambridge, where her father was a university lecturer in English literature. Accustomed to an intellectual environment from childhood and educated largely

abroad, she grew naturally into a "good European," sophisticated and intelligent. Before she had entered Newnham
College, Oxford, she had written her first novel, *Abbot's
Verney* which was published in 1906. During the next fourteen years she wrote five more without becoming very well
known, but in 1920 *Potterism* brought her sudden reputation. Its cold scorn of the second rate and its pitiless exposure of the inadequacies of the postwar generation made
it one of the most widely discussed books of the year. For
the next ten years everything she wrote was well received
and she was considered second only to Aldous Huxley
among contemporary satirists. Then, like many authors
highly esteemed in the twenties, she suffered a decline of
popularity. Her wit belonged wholly to that decade of irresponsible mockery, and as the thirties became more serious,
she could not adjust herself to the new feeling of the times.
What had seemed so clever when *Told By An Idiot* (1923)
and *Crewe Train* (1926) first appeared, no longer appealed,
and dispraise, as always, retroactive in effect, did serious
injustice to her earlier reputation. What she wrote in the
twenties is as good as ever, and that is very good. But it
is also true that she had little of new importance to say.

Rose Macaulay's is a type of culture that belonged to the
eighteenth century. In the society of Lord Chesterfield and
Horace Walpole she would have been perfectly at her ease.
Intellectual, cosmopolitan, urbane, she is contemptuous of
all inferiorities and of all easy softness of mind or character. Her wit is deadly to false pretensions, but she distrusts
earnestness and enthusiasm. Her deep-seated sense of futility
keeps her aloof from causes. In a world increasingly perplexed and anxious her intellectual detachment could only
seem heartless and shallow. Yet her attitude is a highly
civilized one and her work, its intelligent entertainment
aside, an excellent physic for those prone to generous but
uncritical partisanship.

Abbot's Verney (1906); *The Furnace* (1907); *The Valley Captives* (1911); *The Lee Shore* (1912); *The Making of a Bigot* (1914); *What Not* (1919); *Potterism* (1920); *Dangerous Ages* (1921); *Mystery at Geneva* (1922); *Told By An Idiot* (1923); *Orphan Island* (1924); *Crewe Train* (1926); *Daisy and Daphne* (1928); *Staying With Relations* (1930); *The Shadow Flies* (1932); *Going Abroad* (1934); *I Would Be Private* (1937); *And No Man's Wit* (1940); *They Went to Portugal* (1946).

Alec (Alexander Raban) Waugh (1898-   ) and Evelyn Waugh (1903-   ) are the sons of Arthur Waugh, a well-known publisher, for several years head of the historic firm of Chapman and Hall. Alec Waugh made a sensational debut in letters at the age of nineteen with the publication of *The Loom of Youth* (1918), a savage attack upon the English public schools and especially Sherburne, which he had only recently left. While the book was still a literary sensation he was commissioned in the army and served the last year of the war on the Western Front and in a German prison camp. This experience he used in his second novel *The Prisoners of Mainz,* published in 1919. Thereafter he continued to write novels and travel books of good, unspectacular quality. His position for some years has been among those middling authors who never achieve great popular or critical success. He is married and has three children. He served again in the army during the Second World War.

Evelyn Waugh, still in school in 1918, proceeded to Hertford College, Oxford, where he was Senior History Scholar, and where he became known for his brilliance and his pose of fashionable playboy. Short periods of art study and journalism followed college before he settled down to authorship. His first, uncharacteristic book, a study of Rossetti, was published in 1928. In the same year he turned to satiric fiction, drawing his material from the raffish society of the younger set in postwar London, which he studied in order to exploit. These satires, *Decline and Fall* (1928), *Vile Bodies* (1930), and *Black Mischief* (1932), are astonishingly clever and amusing, without the intellectual richness of Aldous Huxley's early novels, but with a breadth and robustness that lift them far above the trivial impertinences of Ronald Firbank, which, superficially, they resemble. *A Handful of Dust* (1934) and *Brideshead Revisited* (1945) show Waugh's ability to handle more serious themes effectively; there is good characterization in both, and the grimly ironic ending of the former is masterly. Except in these, however, he has continued his earlier vein of sophisticated satire, but with an increasing moral implication that steadies his work even in its most hilarious moments. Since 1930 he has been a Catholic, and his religious opinions color both *Brideshead Revisited* and his study of Edmund Campion (1935). Not a satirist of the first rank—one places him with Disraeli rather than with Thackeray—Waugh is one of the most intelligent and witty commentators on the weakness of our time.

In private life Waugh is a conservative English gentleman living in a Georgian country house in Gloucestershire. His first marriage ended, after two years, in a divorce. In 1937 he married Laura Herbert, his present wife, by whom he has three children. He served in the Second War in the Royal Marines.

ALEC WAUGH. Fiction: *The Loom of Youth* (1918), *Pleasure* (1921), *Roland Wheetely* (1922), *Card Castle* (1925), *Kept* (1925), *Love In These Days* (1926), *Nor Many Waters* (1928), *Portrait of a Celibate* (1929), *Three Score and Ten* (1929), *"Sir, she said"* (1930), *So Lovers Dream* (1931), *Thirteen Such Years* (1932), *Tropic Seed* (1932), *Leap Before You Look* (1933), *Wheels Within Wheels* [*The Golden Ripple*] (1933), *Pages in a Woman's Life* (1934), *The Balliols* (1934), *Jill Somerset* (1936), *Eight Short Stories* (1937), *Going Their Own Ways* (1938), *No Truce With Time* (1941). Miscellaneous: *The Prisoners of Mainz* (1919), *Public School Life* (1922), *Myself When Young* (1924), *On Doing*

What One Likes (1926), *The Colored Countries* [*Hot Countries*] (1930), *Most Women——* (1931), *The American Woman* (1932).

EVELYN WAUGH. Fiction: *Decline and Fall* (1928), *Vile Bodies* (1930), *Black Mischief* (1932), *A Handful of Dust* (1934), *Mr. Loveday's Little Outing and Other Sad Stories* (1936), *Scoop* (1938), *Put Out More Flags* (1942), *Brideshead Revisited* (1945), *Scott-King's Modern Europe* (1947, Am. ed. 1949), *The Loved One* (1948), *Work Suspended* (1949), *Helena* (1950). Miscellaneous: *Rossetti, his life and works* (1928), *Labels* [*A Bachelor Abroad*] (1930), *Remote People* (1931), [*They Were Still Dancing*] (1932), *Ninety-two Days* (1934), *Edmund Campion* (1935), *Waugh in Abyssinia* (1936), *Robbery Under Law* [*Mexico: An Object Lesson*] (1939), *When the Going Was Good* (1947).

Rose Macaulay, "Evelyn Waugh," *Horizon*, XIV (1946), 360-377.

The early life of **Dorothy M. Richardson (1882-   )** may have been something like that of her heroine Miriam Henderson, for the breakup of her home forced her to go to work at eighteen as a teacher and later as a clerk. In 1908 she began writing for *The Saturday Review*. By 1914 she had published a history of the Quakers and translated some vegetarian tracts from French and German: she had also made a start on the work of fiction that was to occupy her for twenty-four years. Otherwise her life appears to have been uneventful. She is the wife of Alan Odle, an artist, and divides her life between her writing and her home.

Miss Richardson is known for the series of novels collectively called *Pilgrimage,* written at intervals between 1914 and 1938. These books, or "chapters" as Miss Richardson calls them, twelve in all, develop the life of Miriam Henderson, a middle-class London girl, who becomes self-supporting when her father loses his money. In successive books she is seen as a young teacher, as a governess, as a secretary, living in a Bloomsbury boarding house, escaping for brief holidays with old friends. Nothing critical or exciting happens: the reader merely follows the routine of

Miriam's day, on bus tops, in streets, at the dentist's office where she works, and back to her room. It is a world as restricted and eventless as that of Jane Austen, and continued through twelve volumes should be dull. That it is not is due to Miss Richardson's uncanny skill in appreciating and communicating the subjective value of Miriam's ordinary experiences and her relations with others. Even if Miss Richardson does not succeed in rescuing all of these from triviality, she gives a remarkably clear analysis of the significance of the private experience of the average person.

The character of *Pilgrimage* took shape in the making. *Pointed Roofs* (1915), the first "chapter," set out to be an ordinary novel, but with each succeeding volume the subjective and minutely analytical character of the work grew. Though not quite the first example of stream-of-consciousness technique in modern English fiction, *Pilgrimage* was the first important work to be recognized as such. It at once attracted the attention of Edward Garnett and J. D. Beresford and soon exerted a wide influence on younger writers of fiction. It has been Miss Richardson's misfortune that the technique was so soon more highly developed by Virginia Woolf, Joyce, and others, so that long before her series was completed it seemed a little out of date. Comparatively few readers have taken the trouble to complete the reading of *Pilgrimage* in order to receive the total effect of the work as Miss Richardson intended. It is a good deal to ask of the average reader that he wait twenty-three years to read twelve books entirely about a single character, and it is easy to understand that *Pilgrimage* has not been popular. None the less its importance in the development of modern fiction has been great.

Fiction: "Chapter Novels" of *Pilgrimage: Pointed Roofs* (1915), *Backwater* (1916), *Honeycomb* (1917), *The Tunnel* (1919), *Interim* (1919), *Deadlock* (1921), *Revolving Lights* (1923), *The Trap* (1925), *Oberland* (1928), *Dawn's Left Hand* (1931), *Clear Horizon*

(1935), *Dimple Hill* (1938), *Pilgrimage,* 4 v. (1938). Miscellaneous: *Gleanings from the Works of George Fox* (N. D.), *The Quakers Past and Present* (1914), *John Austen and the Inseparables* (1930).

John Cowper Powys, *Dorothy M. Richardson* (1931); Louise Morgan, *Dorothy M. Richardson* (c. 1932); May Sinclair, Introduction to *Pointed Roofs* (1919); Lawrence Hyde, "The Work of Dorothy Richardson," *Adelphi,* II (1924), 508-517; Harvey Eagleson, "Pedestal For Statue," *Sewanee Rev.,* XLII (1934), 42-53.

Virginia Woolf (1882-1941) was the daughter of Leslie Stephen by his second wife, Julia Duckworth. (Harriet Thackeray was Stephen's first wife; Mrs. Woolf was not, therefore, as has been stated, Thackeray's granddaughter). Leslie Stephen, a former Cambridge don, became well known as essayist and editor of *The Cornhill Magazine* and later of *The Dictionary of National Biography.* His house was a center of literary associations and his daughter's life must have been much like that of Katherine Hilbery in her novel *Night and Day.* Hardy, Stevenson, Ruskin, and Meredith were visitors to the household; James Russell Lowell

VIRGINIA WOOLF

was her godfather. A delicate child, she was educated at home, largely self-educated in her father's library, especially complete in its collection of eighteenth-century authors. Holidays were spent in Cornwall. Her intellectual environment was of the highest quality, but her youth, without experience of school or travel, was outwardly uneventful. About the time of her father's death in 1904 she began reviewing for *The Times Literary Supplement* and two years later wrote her first novel, which remained for some years unpublished.

In 1912 she married Leonard Woolf, a former colonial civil servant who had resigned to devote himself to history and journalism. After her marriage she reworked the manuscript of her novel, *The Voyage Out*. It was published in 1915 but because of the war attracted less attention than it deserved. The following year Mrs. Woolf suffered a mental breakdown, and upon her recovery she and her husband started the Hogarth Press, at first a hobby for which they did all the printing themselves, but before long a full-fledged publishing enterprise which brought to notice such writers as Katherine Mansfield, T. S. Eliot, and E. M. Forster. In 1919 she published her second novel, *Night and Day,* a long, laborious work and a comparative failure. A volume of short stories, *Monday or Tuesday* (1921), showed a marked increase of power. This was followed by three distinguished novels, *Jacob's Room* (1922), *Mrs. Dalloway* (1925), and *To the Lighthouse* (1927). These placed Mrs. Woolf unquestionably among the best of modern novelists.

In 1928 appeared the most unusual of Mrs. Woolf's books, *Orlando.* Called a biography and dedicated to her friend Victoria Sackville-West, it traces an unbroken individual consciousness through all the generations of ancestors who contributed to the making of Miss Sackville-West's poem *The Land.* The life of Orlando, a boy in the reign of Queen Elizabeth who becomes a woman at Constantinople at the end of the seventeenth century and is still a young woman in modern England, is a literary pageant of three centuries, developing its theme unostentatiously in episodes of great vigor and beauty. *Orlando* was followed by *The Waves* (1931) and *The Years* (1937). In addition to her novels she published two volumes of literary essays, *The Common Reader* (1925) and *The Second Common Reader* (1932), and two volumes, *A Room of One's Own* (1929) and *Three Guineas* (1938), in advocacy of women's rights. In 1941 experiencing a recurrence of the symptoms of her earlier breakdown, and fearing permanent madness, she drowned herself. A further volume of essays, *The Death of the Moth*, containing some of her best work, was published in 1942.

Since *The Voyage Out*, which was largely traditional in its technique, Mrs. Woolf has been identified with the experimental school of psychological novelists. Perhaps because of her limited experience she preferred to treat the life of the mind rather than that of the body. Hardly to be called a follower of Joyce and Proust, she has explored the modes of consciousness, especially the "moment of being." Her way of developing its significance can best be studied in her essays *The Mark on The Wall* and *The Death of the Moth*. The impact of experience on her characters may be compressed within a day as in *Mrs. Dalloway* or extended over a lifetime as in *The Waves*. The essential "moments of being" are carried upon as light a structure of narrative as possible. Moreover Mrs. Woolf believes that the full implications of a character are to be found only in their extension into other characters. These may be as, again, in *Mrs. Dalloway* all the persons surrounding the central character at a given time or, as in *Orlando,* a series of progenitors whose qualities are focussed in the last of the line. Her novels are studies rather than stories.

The world of Mrs. Woolf's novels is a very narrow one, in many ways like that of Jane Austen except that it is metropolitan instead of provincial. She restricts herself almost entirely to the English scene and to the intellectual middle class that she knew. She takes her people largely for granted and passes few moral judgments. Like Jane Austen she knows only two unforgivable sins, stupidity and vulgarity. The resemblance is not accidental; both minds were formed by the literature of the eighteenth century and saw their own impassioned times in the light of that more reasonable and realistic age.

The eighteenth-century quality of Mrs. Woolf's mind becomes even more salient when one turns to her literary criticism. The two *Common Reader* volumes and *The Death of the Moth* show her to have been, almost uniquely among her contemporaries, a critic without a "system." She read a book to extract its essential quality and passed judgment on what she found. She could therefore take apparently incompatible positions and make contradictory statements. But under this superficial inconsistency one soon discovers a sound sense, a firm grasp of the uncodified rules of good taste, and an unshakable belief in the supremacy of the intellect. Her view, expressed in *A Room of One's Own,* that economic independence and leisure are necessary for women (men already have them) if they are to make the best of their minds is certainly an eighteenth-century view rather than a modern one. However ruthlessly in her fiction and experimental essays she may have discarded traditional apparatus, her fundamental views are all traditional and her exploration of consciousness is derived from Sterne rather than from Freud.

In her essays Mrs. Woolf wrote firm, lucid prose, beautifully suited to the conveyance of critical ideas. In her subjective experiments and increasingly in her novels her style was elaborate, delicately, sometimes too self-consciously wrought. Sometimes the reader's attention is fixed upon some minute object—a snail on the wall, the cold feet of insects, a dying moth—that serves to focus a moment of experience, at others a succession of symbols make a kaleidoscopic pattern. It is a technique that sometimes involves her in the common fault of English prose stylists, that of trespassing upon the ground of poetry. But she was trying to express difficult things in a new way, and her style shows the energy of an original creative mind.

Mrs. Woolf's influence on her contemporaries was intense rather than broad. Her house was the center of a coterie, the Bloomsbury group—Lytton Strachey, the Bells, Roger Fry, and the authors published by the Hogarth Press. They were a distinguished but rather exclusive and self-centered circle. Mrs. Woolf did not, like Strachey, found a popular school of writing, nor did she leave great promise of work undone. Indeed it seems as if when she ended her life she had said about all she had to say. But she had done a great deal in applying the methods of the Imagists to the novel and in developing the technique of the stream-of-consciousness. She will be praised by discriminating critics and will occupy an important place in the historical development of English fiction.

NOVELS: *The Voyage Out* (1915), *Night and Day* (1919), *Jacob's Room* (1922), *Mrs. Dalloway* (1925), *To the Lighthouse* (1927), *Orlando* (1928), *The Waves* (1931), *The Years* (1937), *Between the Acts* (1941). SHORT STORIES: *Two Stories*, with Leonard Woolf (1917), *Kew Gardens* (1919), *The Mark on the Wall* (1919), *Monday or Tuesday* (1921). MISCELLANEOUS: *Mr. Bennett and Mrs. Brown* (1924), *The Common Reader* (1925), *A Room of One's Own* (1929), *On Being Ill* (1930), *Beau Brummell* (1930), *Street Haunting* (1930), *The Common Reader: Second Series*, [*The Second Common Reader*] (1932), *A Letter to a Young Poet* (1932), *Flush: A Biography* (1933), *Walter Sichert: A Conversation* (1934), *Three Guineas* (1938), *Roger Fry: A Biography* (1940), *The Death of the Moth* (1942), *The Leaning Tower* (1947), *The Moment* (1947).

Winifred Holtby, *Virginia Woolf* (1932); David Daiches, *Virginia Woolf* (1942); E. M. Forster, *Virginia Woolf* (1942); Joan Bennett, *Virginia Woolf* (1945); Deborah Newton, *Virginia Woolf* (Melbourne, 1946); P. C. Quennell, *A Letter to Mrs. Virginia Woolf* (1932); Robert Peel, "Virginia Woolf," *Criterion,* XIII (1933), 78-96; Joseph W. Beach, "Virginia Woolf," *English Jour.,* XXVI (1937), 603-612; Peter Burra, "Virginia Woolf," *New Century,* CXV (1934), 112-125; J. A. E. Smart, "Virginia Woolf," *Dalhousie Review,* XXI (1941-42), 37-50; Solomon Fishman, "Virginia Woolf on the Novel," *Sewanee Rev.,* LI (1943), 321-340; J. H.

Roberts, "Toward Virginia Woolf," *Virginia Quar. Rev.*, X (1934), 587-602; "Vision and Design in Virginia Woolf," *PMLA*, LXI (1946), 835-847; Floris Delattre, *Le Roman Psychologique de Virginia Woolf* (Paris, 1932), "Le nouveau roman de Virginia Woolf," *Etudes Anglaises* (1937), 239-296, "La durée bergsonienne dans le roman de Virginia Woolf," *Rev. Anglo-Americaine*, IX (1931), 97-108; H. E. Monroe, "The Inception of Mrs. Woolf's Art," *College English*, II (1940), 216-250; James S. Wilson, "Time and Virginia Woolf," *Virginia Quar. Rev.* XVIII (1942), 267-276;

John Lehmann, "Virginia Woolf," *Writers of Today*, II (1948); Desmond Pacey, "Virginia Woolf as a Literary Critic," *Univ. Toronto Quar.*, XVII (1947-48), 234-245; William Troy, "Virginia Woolf: The Poetic Method," *Symposium*, III (1932), 53-64; "Virginia Woolf: The Poetic Style," *ibid.*, 153-167.

James (Augustine Aloysius) Joyce (1882-1941) was born to middle class parents of declining fortunes in a suburb of Dublin. His father, John Stanislas Joyce, an easy-going,

JAMES JOYCE

convivial man, lost first his capital and then a post in municipal politics, letting his family sink to the sordid low-water mark of shabby gentility. The one exception to his general neglect of their affairs was the education of his eldest son. At the age of six James was placed in Clongowes Wood College where he stayed for three years (1888-1891); later he attended Belvedere College (1894-1897) and University College, Dublin (1898-1902). All these were Jesuit schools, and there is no better education, within its limits, than that given by the Order. Joyce received from them, besides his A.B., a remarkably thorough grounding in letters, philosophy, and languages, to which he was rapidly adding a wider culture of his own acquiring.

In 1902 Dublin offered excellent prospects to young Joyce. His character and abilities had impressed his teachers from his early school days, assuring his career as a Jesuit scholar if he chose to join the order. He once considered it, encouraged by his mother's piety, but he distrusted the priests, who had, he felt, betrayed Parnell and would always sacrifice the interests of the people to those of the Church. Alternatively his abilities could not fail of distinction in the Irish literary revival then in full swung, but to Joyce the narrow emphasis upon its national character seemed a betrayal of culture to political ends. He wanted to develop his genius, of which he felt sure, free of priests and politicians, and to him that did not seem possible at home.

In the fall of 1902 Joyce went to Paris to study medicine, but was too poor to pay his tuition and for six months lived grimly on the edge of starvation. In the spring he was called home by his mother's last illness and spent the next year in various "digs" around Dublin—including the Martello tower of *Ulysses*—supporting himself by teaching. After his marriage in the fall of 1904 to Norah Barnacle he went abroad for the second time.

Familiar with several modern languages, Joyce obtained through an agency a post with the Berlitz School in Zurich. Arriving there he found the agency was a fraud and that he had no job. The Berlitz people, however, placed him in Trieste where he lived for the next ten years and where his children were born. Up to this time Joyce had earned nothing by literature. As a young collegian he had put forth a critique of Ibsen and a pamphlet attacking the national theater: his early verse, *Chamber Music* (1907), had been published but brought him nothing, and *Dubliners* (written 1904-5), offensive to Irish patriotism and too strong a brew for English taste, could not find a publisher. He was working out a new technique in a spiritual record of his youth, *A Portrait of the Artist as a Young Man,* the outgrowth of an earlier and abandoned manuscript called *Stephen Hero* (posthumously published, 1944). In the meantime he kept his family on his Berlitz salary of £80 a year, meagerly supplemented by private effort.

In 1914 the First World War drove Joyce from Trieste, then an Austrian city, back to Zurich, where work as correspondent in a bank and a small grant from the English government continued him in poverty. Ezra Pound, who was to be a loyal and helpful friend to Joyce, serialized *Portrait of the Artist* in *The Egoist,* the organ of the Anglo-American literary exiles in Paris, and the book was published in New York in 1916.

After the war Joyce returned to Trieste for a year and then removed to Paris, which was his home for his remaining twenty years. Here in 1921 he completed *Ulysses,* which overlapping *Portrait of the Artist,* had been in the making since he first conceived it as an episode for *Dubliners.* The first edition was published in Paris, 1922, by "Shakespeare and Co." (Sylvia Beach) and was followed by a prolonged and disheartening struggle to legalize its circulation in England and the United States, in both of which it was banned. The first "legal" American edition appeared in 1933, following a favorable decision in a U. S. District Court. In 1927 Joyce published *Pomes Penyeach,* his second volume of verse, and in the magazine *transition* a curious prose experiment *Haveth Childers Everywhere,* the first of several instalments of *Work in Progress,* which when completed became *Finnegan's Wake* (1939).

Once again war drove Joyce to Switzerland, in 1940. He was still poor, worried over family troubles, and ill. Following an operation he died in Zurich in 1941.

Joyce's life was a disheartening struggle sustained with the utmost courage. He was a teacher and writer, dependent upon his eyes; yet these gave him constant pain and anxiety. In spite of repeated operations he was for long periods nearly blind, and during his latter years always wrote with difficulty. Like D. H. Lawrence he had to fight bitter public hostility. His first three important books were published only after heartbreaking and ruinous delays, and when *Finnegan's Wake* at last appeared without hindrance the public was contemptuous or apathetic. By mortally offending his fellow Irishmen and the Catholic Church he had cut himself off completely from home. Only a strong character and a just estimate of his own genius could have sustained him.

Joyce is the terrible *homo unius libri;* his verse and single play aside, all that he wrote is virtually a single book unfolding from *Stephen Hero* to *Finnegan's Wake* with the organic wholeness and inevitability of a strong, slow-growing plant. *Stephen Hero* tentatively and *Portrait of the Artist as a Young Man* consummately present youth's quest of integrity. Stephen Daedalus (Joyce) come to manhood, examines the forces that have shaped him from infancy—family, community, church—and considers the claims of each to his loyalty. In pain his character is born: he frees himself of them all and stands alone, self-realized. His hero brought to birth, Joyce in *Dubliners* explores his environment, the historic, vulgar Dublin he loved and despised. In *Ulysses* he brings them together again in a new relation. Stephen (no longer Joyce but the protomartyr) goes about his affairs in Dublin on 16 June, 1904: elsewhere in the city Leopold Bloom, advertising solicitor, goes about his. Eventually their paths join, each being the complement of the other in the father and son relationship of the spirit. Between them in the course of the day and in the microcosm of the city they have surveyed human life from birth to death. Each is the eternal wanderer in the maze of experience, repeating the endless martyrdom, each, being temporal, is incomplete and seeking his complementary link (Ulysses-Telemachus) in the chain of being. *Ulysses* traces the stream-of-consciousness in the individual's waking life, touching only at points the world of dreams. *Finnegan's Wake* is the dream of life in which the whole race is involved. In the dream of a single night the martyrdom is repeated again and again, the last words of the book linking to the first to make it an endlessly recurring cycle. With its characters of multiple identity, appearing now as one person, now another, yet always themselves, and its subtle idiom in which a word or phrase may have a like multiplicity of meaning, it is the expression of the many in one and the hardest work of fiction in any language to read and understand. It completes the synthesis of Joyce's epic of man from the unfolding of the individual to the cosmic history of the race.

Not since Milton has an English writer brought so much scholarship to a work of imagination as Joyce, or made such demands upon his reader. Theology, philosophy, psychology, history, a dozen languages, and the classics of as many literatures form the background for the appreciation of *Ulysses* and *Finnegan's Wake*. It was incomprehension from incapacity or malevolence that caused most of the moral denunciation of the former. In these books Joyce shows unsparingly the coarseness of physical life just as Swift did, but they are in no sense pornographic. And the reader who does not bring his whole mind and education to bear at every moment in penetrating the circumstance to get at the meaning will have wasted his time. It may be noted here, parenthetically, that the reader should not rely implicitly on the "keys" to these books: each interpreter emphasizes the elements that interest him, makes his mistakes, and leaves many things untouched.

Finally Joyce is one of the great modern masters of English style. The gradually unfolding maturity of expression in the *Portrait of the Artist* as Stephen grows and develops,

the historical evolution of the Holles Street chapter of
Ulysses, the voices that break out in *Finnegan's Wake* as
from some cosmic radio, show his perfect control of word
and cadence. He achieved at length the most original idiom
of his time for the expression of the deeper levels of the
subconscious and the extra-temporal elements in human nature and experience. It is the antithesis of the subjectivism
of Gertrude Stein, as objective as a mathematical demonstration, and uncouth and outrageous as it may at first
appear, it will prove on consideration curiously traditional.
Joyce had a cosmopolitanism of intellect rare since the best
minds of the seventeenth and eighteenth centuries, and he
used all his resources. It will be hard to estimate his contribution to the resources of the language until a successor
of equal gifts appears.

FICTION: *Dubliners* (1914), *A Portrait of the Artist as a Young
Man* (1916), *Ulysses* (1922), *Finnegan's Wake* (1939). PLAY: *Exiles*
(1918). VERSE: *Chamber Music* (1907), *Pomes Penyeach* (1927),
Collected Poems (1937).

Herbert S. Gorman, *James Joyce* (1939); Harry Levin, *James
Joyce* (Norfolk, Conn., 1941); Louis Goldring, *James Joyce* (1933);
Valery Larbaud, "James Joyce," *Nouvelle Rev. Française,* N. S.,
IXᵉ An (1922), 385-409; Edmund Wilson, "James Joyce," *New
Republic,* LXI (1929), 84-93; E. R. Curtius, "James Joyce," *Die
Literatur,* XXXI (1929), 121-128; Paul Elmer More, "James
Joyce," *Amer. Rev.,* V, 129-157; Gilbert Stuart, *James Joyce's
"Ulysses": A Study* (1931); "The Latin Background of James
Joyce's Art," *Horizon,* X (1944), 178-189; R. M. Kain, *The Fabu-
lous Voyager* (Chicago, 1947); Frank Budgen, *James Joyce and
the Making of Ulysses* (1934); "James Joyce," *Horizon,* III (1940),
104-109; "Joyce's Chapters of Going Forth By Day," *Horizon,* IV
(1941), 172-191; R. F. Roberts, "Bibliographical Notes on James
Joyce's 'Ulysses,' " *Colophon* (Spring, 1936), 565-579; P. J. Smith,
A Key to the "Ulysses" of James Joyce (Chicago, 1927); T. S.
Eliot, "Ulysses, Order and Myth," *Dial,* LXXV (1923), 480-483;
Bernhard Fehr, "James Joyce's 'Ulysses,' " *Englische Studien,* LX
(1925-26), 180-205; D. G. Van der Vat, "Paternity in 'Ulysses,' "
English Studies, XIX (1937), 145-158; J. Baake, "Das Riesen-

scherzbuch Ulysses," *Bonner Studien,* XXXII (1937); Edouard
Dujardin, *Le Monologue interieur: son apparition, ses origines,
sa place dans l'oeuvre de James Joyce* (Paris, 1931); Eugene Jolas
and others, *Our Exagmination round his Factification for In-
camination of Work in Progress* (Paris, 1921), reprinted as *An
Exagmination of James Joyce* (Norfolk, Conn., 1939); Carola
Giedeon-Welcker, "Work in Progress," *Neue Schweizer Rund-
schau,* XXII (1929), 660-671; J. Campbell and H. M. Robinson,
A Skeleton Key to Finnegan's Wake (1946); Charles Duff, *James
Joyce and the Plain Reader* (1932); Irene Hendry, "Joyce's Epiph-
anies," *Sat. Rev. Lit.,* IV (1946), 449-467; Michael Stuart, "Mr.
Joyce's Word Creatures," *Symposium,* II (1931), 459-467; Alec
Brown, "Joyce's 'Ulysses' and the Novel," *Dublin Mag.,* N.S., IX
(1934), 41-50; Cyril Connolly, "The Position of Joyce," *Life and
Letters,* V (1929), reprinted in *The Condemned Playground*
(1945); A. M. Petit Jean, "Signification de Joyce," *Études An-
glaises,* I (1937), 405-417; L. A. G. Strong, "James Joyce and the
New Fiction," *Amer. Mercury,* XXXV (1935), 433-437; "James
Joyce and Vocal Music," *Essays and Studies,* XXXI (1946), 95-106;
E. R. Curtius, "Technik und Thematik von James Joyce," *Neue
Schweizer Rundschau,* XXII (1929), 47-68; B. J. Morse, "Mr. Joyce
and Shakespeare," *Englische Studien,* LXV (1931), 367-381; Padraic Colum and others, "Homage to James Joyce," *transition,* 21
(1932), 256-273; John Eglinton, "The Beginnings of James Joyce,"
Life and Letters, VIII (1932), 400-414; Ernest Boyd, "Joyce and
the New Irish Writers," *Current History,* XXXIX (1934), 699-704.

Francis Brett Young (1884-   ) was born at Hales Owen,
Worcestershire, the son of a physician. At twenty-two he
took his degree in medicine at Birmingham and in 1907
entered practice at Brixham, Devon, where he remained,
except for a voyage as ship's surgeon, until 1915. He married in 1908. Young's war service (1915-18) took him to
East Africa as a Major in the Royal Army Medical Corps.
Of this experience *Marching On Tanga* (1918) gives a vivid
account. After the war he made his home for some years in
Capri, where he met D. H. Lawrence, Compton Mackenzie,
and Norman Douglas. Since 1933 he has lived again in his
native Worcestershire.

Young's first novel, *Undergrowth* (1913), was written in collaboration with his brother Eric and was a not very successful experiment. However, in its presentation of the effect of the spirit of place upon man it struck at once the significant note of his later work. Known today chiefly as a regional novelist of the West Midlands, Young differs from most writers of this kind in caring less for local character and dialect than for landscape and the feel of the country. He is at his best in his wonderfully evocative descriptive passages, and his most interesting book is *Portrait of a Village* (1938), in which he abandons story and character completely for a delicate and imaginative study of locality. Though he is known chiefly for novels of the English country, *Cold Harbor* (1924), *Jim Redlake* (1930), *The House Under the Water* (1932), and *White Ladies* (1935), Young has drawn upon his seagoing days, in *Sea Horses* (1925), and upon Africa, which he visited for a second time in 1922, for some of his material. *Woodsmoke* (1924) recalls his army days in East Africa; *They Seek a Country* (1941) is a fine story of the great Boer trek.

A lover of music since his schooldays, Young has written verse, not generally with great success, his real poetry being found in his prose descriptions of nature. He published volumes of verse in 1917 and 1918 and in 1941 *The Island,* a sequence of patriotic poems and dramatic scenes reminiscent of Hardy and Kipling.

With great sensitiveness to beauty and to romantic suggestion, real though limited gifts, and with considerable technical ability, Young has failed to become more than a competent novelist because of diffuseness and a frequent sentimentality in the handling of his characters.

FICTION: *Undergrowth,* with E. Brett Young (1913), *Deep Sea* (1914), *The Dark Tower* (1915), *The Iron Age* (1916), *The Crescent Moon* (1918), *The Young Physician* (1919), *The Tragic Bride* (1920), *The Black Diamond* (1921), *The Red Knight* (1922), *Pil-*

grim's Rest (1922), *Cold Harbor (*1924*)*, *Woodsmoke* (1924), *Sea Horses* (1925), *Portrait of Clare,* [*Love Is Enough*] (1927), *The Key of Life* (1928), *My Brother Jonathan* (1928), *Black Roses* (1929), *Jim Redlake,* [*The Redlakes*] (1930), *Mr. and Mrs. Pennington* (1931), *The House Under the Water* (1932), *Blood Oranges* (1932), *The Cage Bird and Other Stories* (1933), *This Little World* (1934), *White Ladies* (1935), *The Forest* (1936), *They Seek a Country* (1937), *Portrait of a Village* (1937), *Dr. Bradley Remembers* (1938), *The City of Gold* (1939), *The Ship's Surgeon's Yarn,* [*Cotswold Honey*] (1940), *Mr. Lucton's Freedom,* [*The Happy Highway*] (1940), *A Man About the House* (1942).

Eric G. Twitchett, *Francis Brett Young* (1936).

Sheila Kaye-Smith (1888-   ) was born at St. Leonards-on-Sea, Sussex, where her father was a physician. Factual detail of her early life is meagre, except that she began writing in early childhood. Her first novel, *The Tramping Methodist,* published when she was twenty, dealt with the rural life of her native county, as have all her subsequent books. By the end of the First World War she was a well-known regional novelist of the school of Hardy with nine novels to her credit. Her best work appeared immediately afterward, *Joanna Godden* (1921), showing a creative power that she never equalled again.

In 1924 Miss Kaye-Smith married the Rev. T. Penrose Fry, an Anglican clergyman and five years later was received with her husband into the Catholic Church. The novels that she wrote after her marriage show a decline in quality and in interest, though in *Susan Spray* (1931) she returned successfully to her first theme of rural Methodism. During the Second World War the Frys farmed their land in Sussex and sheltered evacuees.

Sheila Kaye-Smith has been hampered by the self-imposed restriction of her regionalism. It is not too hard for a novelist to follow Dickens and to find ample new material in the variety of cities, but to follow Hardy where the simplicity and conservatism of country life severely limit the possibilities of character and situation is another matter— especially as in Sheila Kaye-Smith's case Sussex is the eastern frontier of Hardy's country and offers none of the differences in racial stock, occupation, and environment that would be found in, say, Staffordshire or Westmoreland. Consequently as her work progressed, the monotony of her themes became more evident along with a straining to distinguish character by peculiarity or quaintness. Possibly like Jane Austen, whom she admires, she has been afraid to venture beyond what she knows well (How long, by the way, could Jane Austen have gone on writing novels about her little world?), but possibly also her talents would have developed more fully with greater scope. Joanna Godden and Susan Spray are both memorable characters and the novels have real warmth of local color and a passionate feeling for the land.

FICTION: *The Tramping Methodist* (1908), *Starbrace* (1909), *Spell Land* (1910), *Isle of Thorns* (1913), *Three Against the World*, [*The Three Furlongers* (1914), *Sussex Gorse* (1916), *Little England*, [*The Four Roads*] (1918), *The Challenge to Sirius* (1918), *Tamarisk Town* (1919), *Green Apple Harvest* (1920), *Joanna Godden* (1922), *The End of the House of Alard* (1923), *The George and the Crown* (1925), *Joanna Godden Married and Other Stories* (1926), *Iron and Smoke* (1928), *A Wedding Morn* (1928), *The Village Doctor* (1929), *Shepherds in Sackcloth* (1930), *The History of Susan Spray*, [*Susan Spray*] (1931), *The Children's Summer*, [*Summer Holiday*] (1932), *Ploughman's Progress*, [*Gipsy Waggon*] (1933), *Superstition Corner* (1934), *Gallybird* (1934), *Selina Is Older*, [*Selina*] (1935), *Rose Deeprose* (1936), *The Valiant Woman* (1938), *Faithful Stranger and Other Stories* (1938), *Ember Lane* (1940), *The Hidden Son*, [*The Secret Son*] (1941), *Tambourine, Trumpet and Drum* (1943), *Kitchen Fugue* (1945), *The Lardners and the Laurelwoods* (1947).

Andrew E. Malone, "The Novelist of Sussex: Sheila Kaye-Smith," *Fortnightly Rev.*, CXX (1926), 199-209; Karl Arns, "Sheila Kaye-Smith," *Zeitschrift für Englischen Unterricht*, XXVI (1927), 268-279.

Born in Plymouth, Devon, of Irish parentage, **Leonard Alfred George Strong (1896-   )** has been from boyhood equally at home in England and Ireland. He was educated at Brighton College and Wadham College, Oxford. At the latter his natural bent for writing was given a serious turn by his acquaintance with a number of literary undergraduates including Aldous Huxley, Richard Hughes, and Roy Campbell. Kept from military service in the First World War by physical disability, he took a temporary teaching post, and after graduation in 1919 became a master at Summer Fields School, writing in his spare time.

He first became known in 1921 for *Dublin Days,* racy poems of Irish life, and during the next few years published several more volumes of verse and one of short stories. In 1929 his reputation reached its highest point with *Dewer Rides,* his first novel, and *The English Captain,* his most popular volume of short stories. This success enabled Strong, married since 1926, to give up teaching and live by writing. Since then, although he has published a dozen novels, further stories, and a number of juvenile books, his reputation though on the whole well sustained has not increased. Of late years he has lived in London, where he has done a good deal of successful broadcasting.

Strong is definitely a poet, if a minor one, and his prose is rich in finely imaginative passages and rich descriptions of landscape. He has a deep feeling for nature and a power of evoking regional atmosphere that often makes the setting more memorable than the action of his longer works. He is a good story-teller in the shorter form but fails repeatedly in the construction of his novels, a defect that may be traced to the ill-health from which he has always suffered. That also may account for the brutality that intrudes—as it seems gratuitously—into his stories.

A versatile, industrious, and competent writer, Strong

seems, except in his verse, unable to realize his potentialities. There his quick sympathy, his Irish sense of humor, and his deftness of phrase do full justice to his admirable, if not great, abilities.

FICTION: *Doyle's Rock* (1925), *The English Captain* (1929), *Dewer Rides* (1929), *The Jealous Ghost* (1930), *The Big Man* (1931), *The Garden* (1931), *The Brothers* (1932), *Don Juan and the Wheelbarrow* (1932), *Sea Wall* (1933), *Corporal Tune* (1934), *The Seven Arms* (1935), *Tuesday Afternoon* (1935), *Mr. Sheridan's Umbrella* (1935), *The Last Enemy* (1936), *Laughter in the West* (1937), *The Swift Shadow* (1937), *The Open Sky* (1939), *The Absentee* (1939), *Sun on the Water* (1940), *The Bay* (1941), *The Unpractised Heart* (1942), *Slocombe Dies* (1942), *All Fall Down* (1944), *Othello's Occupation* (1945), *Travellers* (1945), *The Doll* (1946). VERSE: *Dallington Rhymes* (1919), *Dublin Days* (1921), *Twice Four* (1921), *Says the Muse to Me, Says She* (1922), *Eight Poems* (1923), *The Lowery Road* (1923), *Seven* (1924), *Difficult Love* (1927), *At Glennan Cross* (1928), *Northern Light* (1930), *Selected Poems* (1931), *March Evening* (1932), *Call to the Swan* (1936).

Bristol Public Libraries, *L. A. G. Strong: A Bibliography;* R. L. Megroz, "L. A. G. Strong" in *Five Novelist Poets of Today* (1933); Dayton Kohler, "L. A. G. Strong," *Bookman,* LXXIII (1931), 570-575.

Charles Morgan (1894-   ) was until 1913 an officer of the Royal Navy. Within a year after his resignation he was recalled to duty by the First World War and serving at the defense of Antwerp was taken prisoner and interned for the duration. Repatriated at the end of the war, he went to Oxford and in two years obtained his degree. In 1921 he joined the staff of the *Times* and in 1926 succeeded A. B. Walkley as its dramatic critic. In 1923 he married the novelist Hilda Vaughan; his home is in London.

Morgan's first novel, *The Gunroom* (1919), was withdrawn after publication because of its unfavorable picture of the

navy, and his second, *My Name is Legion* (1925), drew little
attention. *Portrait in a Mirror* (1929) was his first success
and his reputation was fully established by *The Fountain*
(1932), based on his experience when interned in Holland.
Since then he has written three more novels and a play, as
well as other miscellaneous works.

Though his books are comparatively few, Morgan is the
only novelist to whom the Femina Prize, the Hawthornden
Prize, and the James Tait Black Memorial Award have all
been given. His services to French cultural relations have
been rewarded with the Legion of Honor. Why his position
in critical and popular estimation has never been as secure
as these honors appear to warrant is hard to say. He is a
uniformly serious writer, interested in the subtler aspects
of personal ethics. To his ethical preoccupation there is
added a strong vein of mysticism, probably from his Welsh
blood. For many readers he is a "difficult" author, certainly
he is a demanding one. And for the close attention and
understanding he exacts from his reader his writing does
not offer much compensatory charm. An admirer of George
Moore, he is, like Moore, an ambitious but irregular stylist, capable of beautiful writing but also of serious lapses.
He is by no means an unimportant author, but he can
hardly be placed among the highly significant novelists
either for matter or manner.

FICTION: *The Gunroom* (1919), *My Name Is Legion* (1925), *Por-
trait in a Mirror* [*First Love*] (1929), *The Fountain* (1932), *Spark-
enbroke* (1936), *The Voyage* (1940), *The Empty Room* (1941),
The Judge's Story (1947). MISCELLANEOUS: *Epitaph on George
Moore* (1935), *Reflections in a Mirror* (1944), *Reflections in a
Mirror, Second Series* (1946).

W. G. Moore, "Mr. Morgan's *Sparkenbroke*," *Hibbert Jour.,*
XXXV (1936-37), 242-249.

J. B. Priestley (1894-   ) though known to most American readers only as a popular novelist, is a remarkably versatile prose writer who has done distinguished work in several fields without reaching the highest excellence in any.

John Boynton Priestley grew up in an uncongenial atmosphere of the textile trades in Bradford, Yorkshire. Against the pervading commercialism he was armored by the teaching of his father, a schoolmaster and a disciple of William Morris, who grounded him in old-fashioned socialism and formed his literary taste. As soon as he was through school he began to write weekly for the *Yorkshire Observer* over the signature Peter Pomfret. In 1914 at the age of twenty he enlisted in the Devonshire Regiment and served the entire war. His first book, *A Chapman of Rhymes,* was produced while he was in the service, but he ordered it destroyed before publication.

Discharged in 1919 he matriculated at Trinity Hall, Cambridge, where he contributed articles and essays to *The Cambridge Review, The London Mercury, The Outlook,* and other periodicals. In 1922, having taken honors in English literature, modern history, and political science, he began his literary career in London, publishing a selection of his essays as *Papers From Lilliput* (1922). For seven years he was known chiefly as a critic and essayist. To this period belong his volumes of familiar essays, *I for One* (1923), *Open House* (1927), *The Balconinny* (1929), and others. The essays show him "a humorist of the old order, tolerant but not without irony," fond of the color of life and amused by humanity. His critical talent appears in *Figures in Modern Literature* (1924), *The English Novel* (1927), and *The English Comic Characters* (1925), the last especially good. For the English Men of Letters Series he wrote biographies of Thomas Love Peacock and George Meredith.

Priestley's first novel, *Adam in Moonshine,* appeared in

1927, and two years later his third, *The Good Companions*
made his first popular success. This, a pioneer among modern long novels (not trilogies) is the hilarious story of a
group of strolling music hall entertainers, utterly improbable but producing by its infectious high spirits a "willing
suspension of disbelief" that carries the reader uncritically
through pages of sheer enjoyment. *Angel Pavement,* his next
novel, was a more serious study of London life; then followed, not counting two failures, *Far Away, They Walk in
the City,* and *The Doomsday Men.* In 1940 he tried to recapture some of the strolling gaiety of *The Good Companions,* in *Let the People Sing,* with a benevolent socialist
coloring, but the times were against it. There is good work
in all these later books, but Priestley has not yet been able
to repeat his triumph: his wartime novels, *Blackout in Gretley* and *Bright Day,* have been only moderately received.

The success of the dramatization of *The Good Companions* turned Priestley to the theater, and since 1932 he
has produced sixteen plays, nearly all of which have been
successful, especially *Dangerous Corner, Time and the Conways,* and *Music at Night.* He is proud of the fact that his
plays have been performed in twelve different languages.

In 1933 Priestley made a survey of working England, visiting the mining districts and industrial centers, in the
worst period of depression and unemployment. *English
Journey,* embodying his observations, is a grim book, unsparing in its presentation of fact and in its criticism. A
deep sympathy for the English people and the English scene,
even in their ugly aspects, gives it more than documentary
value. In 1937 a winter spent in Arizona for Mr. Priestley's
health resulted in *Midnight on the Desert,* a really remarkable book. Priestley once defined good talk as "autobiography enriched with ideas," a description that fits very well
this sustained and effective combination of reminiscence,
essay, and local color. The book is especially fine in its evo-

cation of the atmosphere and color of the Southwest. *Rain Upon Godshill,* a similar book written two years later, is not quite so good, but still a fine performance. These three books, with *The Good Companions,* contain Priestley's best work.

Early in the war Priestley delivered a series of BBC talks, addressed, as so much British utterance then, to the sympathies of America. In their published form, *Britain Speaks,* these show an interesting adaptation of the essay to the greater popularity and colloquialism suitable to the radio. They represent a new literary form in the making.

FICTION: *Adam in Moonshine* (1927), *Benighted* [*The Old Dark House*] (1927), *The Good Companions* (1929), *Angel Pavement* (1930), *The Town Major of Miraucourt* (1930), *Faraway* (1932), *Albert Goes Through* (1933), *Wonder Hero* (1933), *I'll Tell You Everything,* with Gerald Bullitt (1933), *Four-in-Hand* (1934), *They Walk in the City* (1936), *The Doomsday Men* (1938), *Let the People Sing* (1939), *Blackout in Gretley* (1942), *Daylight on Saturday* (1943), *Three Men in New Suits* (1945), *Bright Day* (1946), *Jenny Villiers* (1947). PLAYS: *Dangerous Corner* (1932), *The Roundabout* (1933) *Laburnum Grove* (1934), *Eden End* (1934), *Cornelius* (1935), *Duet in Floodlight* (1935), *Bees on the Boat Deck* (1936), *Time and the Conways* (1937), *Mystery at Greenfingers* (1937), *People at Sea* (1937), *I Have Been Here Before* (1938), *When We are Married* (1938), *Johnson Over Jordan* (1939), *Four Plays* [*Music at Night, The Long Mirror, They Came to a City, Desert Highway*] (1944), *How Are They At Home?* (1945), *An Inspector Calls* (1947). MISCELLANEOUS: *George Meredith* (1926), *Thomas Love Peacock* (1927), *English Journey* (1934), *Midnight on the Desert* (1937), *Rain Upon Godshill* (1939), *Russian Journey* (1946), *The Arts Under Socialism* (1947).

L. Alun Jones, "First Editions of J. B. Priestley," *Bookman,* LXXX (1931), 46; D. L. Mann, "J. B. Priestley: Servant of the Comic Spirit," *Amer. Bookman,* LXXIII (1931), 241-246; Edward Shanks, "Mr. Priestley's Novels," *London Mercury,* XXVI (1932), 240-247; T. Frederick, "J. B. Priestley," *English Jour.,* XXVII (1938), 371-380; R. W. Whidden, "Priestley and His Novels," *Queen's Quar.,* XLVIII (1941), 57-62.

Not a great writer, **John Buchan (Lord Tweedsmuir 1875-1940)**, is big enough to be named in company with Scott and Stevenson as one who has written the adventure story on a level worthy of the romances and the ballads.

Like many Scots who have made their mark in the world, Buchan was a child of the manse, his father being a free kirk minister in Perth and later in Glasgow. As a boy and youth he learned to love the Tweed country and throughout life was an enthusiastic fisherman, deer stalker, and tramper. Through these he developed a keen relish for Scottish character, local color, and tradition.

After completing his studies at the University of Glasgow, Buchan went on a scholarship to Brasenose College, Oxford, where he distinguished himself, becoming president of the Union, the usual prelude to a career in politics or the civil service. From Oxford he went to London in 1900 to study law and was admitted to the Bar in 1901. Then his career was interrupted for two years by service in the South African War.

Back in London again, Buchan was drawn to writing and publishing, of which he had already had some experience, rather than to politics. By 1907 he was a partner in the house of Thomas Nelson and Sons, Ltd., and had nine volumes of fiction, essays, and biography to his credit. By 1915 he was a successful man but very little known as a writer.

World War I called Buchan back into service, this time as a colonel in charge of news services at GHQ in France and later as Director of Information in London. It was during the war that he first became widely popular as an adventure writer with *Salute to Adventurers, The Thirty-nine Steps,* and *Greenmantle.* From 1915 to his death he produced a book or two a year with hardly an exception. His conspicuous public career did not begin until 1927, the year after the General Strike, when he entered Parliament as Conservative member for the Scottish universities. In 1933 he was appointed Commissioner to the Church of Scotland, and in 1935 was raised to the peerage as first Baron Tweedsmuir and appointed Governor General of Canada, a post which he held until his death.

Buchan's popularity as an author began with his creation of two adventurers, David Hannay and Edward Leithen. These with their associates, a gallery of portraits, really from his own acquaintance, he carries through a series of fast-paced adventures in war and international intrigue. Intensely masculine, conventional in their "sahib's" ideals, these stories seem superficially like others of their sort, only more cleverly contrived. But they soon reveal a marked superiority in the handling of character and the vivid presentation of scene. At rare times particular scenes approach the stark power of old ballads. Taken altogether, though, they would be no more than a fine achievement in story-telling were it not for the last and best, *Mountain Meadow*, called *Sick Heart River* in the English edition.

In this, written just before his death, Buchan shows Leithen, a dying man, going into the far north of Canada, to find a lost man whom he has never seen. As Leithen gains strength in his struggle with the killing north, the finding of Gaillard becomes less and less important, and the restoration of his own spirit more and more. He becomes the symbol of the Old War generation desperately seeking the cure of its sick heart. The art by which the story is lifted chapter by chapter to its austere climax is simple and sure. In its evocation of the fascination and terror of the north "beyond the barrens and rivers of no name" the book is a master-piece. In this book alone Buchan enters the company of the great romancers.

As a biographer Buchan is best known for his studies of Montrose and Cromwell, and his life of Sir Walter Scott, the best since Lockhart. His autobiography, *Pilgrim's Way* (1940), is among the notable modern books of its kind, espe-

cially fine in his enthusiasm for the scenes and traditions of
Scotland. Buchan has also written a variety of historical
works dealing with Scotland and with the First World War.
His essays, all of high quality, have been collected in three
volumes.

Calling forth equally the abilities of the scholar and the
artist, *The Path of the King* is an unusual, if not unique
book, an historical fantasy tracing the imaginary ancestry of
Abraham Lincoln, from a rude hamlet of Vikings in the
dark ages through all the intervening centuries in Europe
and America. It is sombre and intensely moving. Read together with *Mountain Meadow,* it leaves the conviction that
Buchan missed his calling—though that seems an absurd
thing to say of so successful a man. Yet certainly, if a writer
to whom fiction was little more than an avocation of his
lighter moments could produce two such books as these, he
would, had he given himself wholly to it, have been one of
the greater Georgian novelists.

AUTOBIOGRAPHY: *Memory Hold-the-Door* [*Pilgrim's Way*] (1940).
FICTION: *Sir Quixote of the Moors* (1895), *John Burnet of Barnes*
(1898), *Grey Weather* (1899), *A Lost Lady of Old Years* (1899),
The Half Hearted (1900), *The Watcher by the Threshold* (1902),
A Lodge in the Wilderness (1906), *Prester John* [*The Great Dia-
mond Pipe*] (1910), *The Moon Endureth* (1912), *Salute to Adven-
turers* (1915), *The Thirty-nine Steps* (1915), *Greenmantle* (1916),
The Power House (1916), *Mr. Standfast* (1919), *The Path of the
King* (1921), *Huntingtower* (1922), *Midwinter* (1923), *The Three
Hostages* (1924), *John Macnab* (1925), *The Dancing Floor* (1926),
Witch Wood (1927), *The Runagates Club* (1928), *The Courts of
the Morning* (1929), *Castle Gay* (1930), *The Blanket of the Dark*
(1931), *The Gap in the Curtain* (1932), *The Magic Walking Stick*
(1932), *A Prince of the Captivity* (1933), *The Free Fishers* (1934),
The House of the Four Winds (1935), *The Island of Sheep* [*The
Man From the Norlands*] (1936), *Sick Heart River* [*Mountain
Meadow*] (1941), *Lake of Gold* (1941). BIOGRAPHY: *Sir Walter
Raleigh* (1897), *The Marquis of Montrose* (1913), *Montrose: A
History* (1928), *Sir Walter Scott* (1932), *Julius Caesar* (1932),
Oliver Cromwell (1934), *Augustus* (1937).

(Arthur) Joyce (Lemel) Cary (1888-   ) was educated at Clifton School and Trinity College, Oxford. Later he studied art in Edinburgh. In the Balkan war of 1912 he served in the Montenegrin Battalion and afterward in the British Red Cross. The following year he joined the Nigerian Political Service, in which he remained, with an interval of military service (1915-16) in the Nigerian Regiment, until failing health obliged him to resign in 1920. He married, in 1916, Gertrude Margaret Ogilvie and has lived for some years in Oxford.

Though Cary's work has been known for some years in England, it is only recently that any of it has been published in the United States. His first novel, *Aissa Saved* (1932), was drawn from his memories of Africa; he later turned to English themes. His best known and most ambitious work is a trilogy of studies in self-deception, of which the first, *Herself Surprised* (1941), and the third, *The Horse's Mouth* (1944), are now available to American readers. The one is a study of a minor woman criminal, strongly suggestive of Defoe in matter and style, the other a robust burlesque centering in the tragicomic bohemian painter Gully Jimson. Together with the intermediate volume, *To Be a Pilgrim* (1942), they contain a memorable group of firmly created characters that place Cary securely among the serious writers of fiction.

NOVELS: *Aissa Saved* (1932), *The American Visitor* (1933), *The African Witch* (1936), *Castle Corner* (1938), *Mister Johnson* (1939), *Charley Is My Darling* (1940), *The House of Children* (1941), *Herself Surprised* (1941), *To Be a Pilgrim* (1942), *The Horse's Mouth* (1944), *The Moonlight* (1946), *A Fearful Joy* (1950).

Elizabeth (Dorothea Cole) Bowen (1899-   ) comes of an Anglo-Irish family of some antiquity and still owns Bowen's Court in County Cork, an estate given to the family by Cromwell. She was born in Dublin in 1899 and educated at

Downe House in Kent. At the age of nineteen, upon her father's second marriage, she left home and went to London where she lived until her marriage. She began writing short stories at twenty and published her first volume of them in 1923. In the same year she married Alan Charles Cameron, who afterward obtained a teaching position at Oxford. She is often at Bowen's Court, which she has made the subject of a book and used as a background for *The Last September*.

Miss Bowen is a much more important writer than the number of her titles or the length of this notice indicate. She has never written for popularity and all her work shows the restraint of a fastidious taste. Its material is restricted in range, for aside from a short period of war-nursing in 1918 and going to London a year later Miss Bowen has lived an unadventurous life. Her first novel, *The Hotel* (1927), was the result of a winter in Italy, where she has spent a good deal of time, but otherwise her experience has been largely limited by the upper-middle-class life of Ireland and England. Within these limits, however, she is a very acute and sensitive observer. She has especially a deep psychological sympathy with the disappointed and frustrated, and a power of presenting their unhappiness. Though her novels are well known, she is probably at her best in her short stories, such as *The Cat Jumps* (1934) and *Look at All Those Roses* (1941). These best show her gift for tragic atmosphere, her unexpected humor, and the delicate distinction of her style. It is natural to associate her with such writers as Virginia Woolf and Rosamund Lehmann.

NOVELS: *The Hotel* (1927), *The Last September* (1929), *Friends and Relations* (1931), *To the North* (1932), *The House in Paris* (1936), *The Death of the Heart* (1938), *The Heat of the Day* (1949). SHORT STORIES: *Encounters* (1923), *Ann Lee's* (1928), *Joining Charles* (1929), *Look At All Those Roses* (1941), *The Demon Lover* (1945), *Ivy Gripped the Steps* (1946), *Selected Stories* (1946).

MISCELLANEOUS: *Bowen's Court* (1942), *Seven Winters* (Dublin, 1942), *The English Novelists* (1942), *Anthony Trollope* (1946).

Edward Sackville-West, "Ivy Compton-Burnett and Elizabeth Bowen," *Horizon*, XIII (1946), 367-385.

In 1927 a young novelist, **Rosamund Lehmann (1903-   )**, attracted unusual attention by the power of her first book, *Dusty Answer*. During the twenty years since then she has published four more novels, a play, and a volume of short stories, the restrained product of a fastidious writer who values critical appreciation above popularity. She drew her attitude, as well as much of her technical skill, from a household in which the arts were domesticated and to do anything meant to do it remarkably well. Her father, Rudolph C. Lehmann, a lawyer by profession, was well known as a miscellaneous writer; a great uncle was a painter and a cousin a composer. Her brother John is a poet, critic, and publisher, and her sister Beatrix an actress. Her mother, Marie (Davis) Lehmann, was from Massachusetts, where Rudolph Lehmann once coached Harvard crews.

Dusty Answer exhibits the unfolding of a character from childhood to maturity through a variety of difficult and passionate relationships. Only after disappointment by all whom she has loved does the protagonist realize herself fully in her independence of others. A large part of the book treats of life at Newnham College, Oxford, where the author was educated. After *Dusty Answer* her second novel, *A Note in Music* (1930), was disappointing. Far less original, it is a chronicle of middleclass frustrations in an industrial town, too ordinary in conception to be saved by its distinction of style. Miss Lehmann next chose a severely restricted theme, the experiences of a young girl at her first big party. *Invitation to the Waltz* (1932) astonishes by the skill with which the usual meetings and emotions of such an affair, endowed with their full importance to the adolescent, are made to carry the story forward without any flagging of interest and with very little sense of strain. It is a less serious book than *Dusty Answer* but a strongly appealing one. In 1945 *The Ballad and the Source* secured beyond all question Miss Lehmann's position as a writer of major importance. A sombre story dominated by the enigmatic and tragic figure of Mrs. Jardine, it is conceived and treated with a classic severity that gives it great power. It was followed in a year by *The Gipsy's Baby* (1946), a volume of five shorter tales that had originally appeared in *New Writing*, edited by John Lehmann. These are all at the level of her best work in the novels.

Rosamund Lehmann has been an aloof writer, withdrawing behind her characters so that while an autobiographical element has been palpable in all her books, her true relation to her work has been hard to determine. Only in "The Red-Haired Miss Daintreys," the second story in her latest volume, has she admitted her readers at all to her confidence. She does not plan her work carefully beforehand, she says, but awaits receptively a memory of some person or scene that will quicken the imagination with its suggestion of the central mood or image of a story. From this central point the work develops according to its own principle of growth. The slow gestation this implies accounts for the slenderness, in bulk, of her production as well as for its unusual perceptiveness and the brooding quality, something like reverie, that is constantly felt in her pages.

Miss Lehmann's art is now fully mature, and though she has moved as yet in a rather narrow middle-class world, her principal themes, the tragic loneliness of the individual and the equally tragic persistence of life, have wide possibilities of interpretation.

NOVELS: *Dusty Answer* (1927), *A Note in Music* (1930), *Invitation to the Waltz* (1932), *The Weather in the Streets* (1936), *The Bal-*

lad and the Source (1945). SHORT STORIES: *The Gipsy's Baby* (1946). PLAY: *No More Music* (1939).

George Dangerfield, "Rosamund Lehmann," *Bookman,* LXXVI (1933), 172-176; Olive Warner, "Rosamond Lehmann," *Bookman,* LXXXVII (1934), 174.

"George Orwell" (Eric Blair, 1903-1950) was born at Motihari, Bengal, and like most Anglo-Indian children was sent back to school in England. After leaving Eton in 1921 he entered the Imperial Police in Burma in which he served from 1922 to 1927. He retired because of impaired health and disgust with the British imperial system. For the next few years he had a very hard time trying to find his feet as a writer and supporting himself in poverty by various odd jobs. The experiences of those years, which swung him far to the political left, may be followed in his first book *Down and Out in Paris and London* (1933). In 1934 he published his first novel, *Burmese Days,* a scathing and, it is said, accurate picture of "sahib" society in Burma. For the next two years he lived in the country writing and keeping a general store. He married in 1936. In 1937, having now published two more novels, he served in the Loyalist militia in Spain, becoming after a time as disgusted with leftist politics as with imperialism. In the end, because of the betrayal by the Communists of the POUM with which he served, he escaped from Spain just in time to avoid imprisonment. After that he lived in England repudiating politics but generally radical in his social sympathies.

Belonging himself to what he called "the middle middle class" George Orwell has an intimate and bitter knowledge of life at levels considerably lower, much of which will be found in the grim documentary record of *The Road to Wigan Pier* (1937). The world of his later novels is the world of Dickens with all the fun left out. He treats with considerable power the despair of lives caught in the poverty of cities or in the destroying monotony of lower-middle-class suburbanism. The material is often suggestive of Gissing and Swinnerton, but the handling is vigorous and individual. His political satire *Animal Farm* (1946) was overpraised at its appearance, but when it is no longer compared with Swift, will stand up as a piece of brilliantly conceived humor. Much stronger is his vision of the totalitarian state in *Nineteen Eighty Four* (1949). Among his few essays the studies of Henry Miller and Dickens are perceptive and interesting. *Homage to Catalonia* (1938) is an excellent account of service in the Spanish Civil War.

FICTION: *Burmese Days* (1934), *A Clergyman's Daughter* (1935), *Keep the Aspidistra Flying* (1936), *Coming Up For Air* (1939), *Nineteen Eighty Four* (1949). MISCELLANEOUS: *Down and Out in Paris and London* (1933), *The Road to Wigan Pier* (1937), *Homage to Catalonia* (1938), *Inside the Whale* (1940), *The Lion and the Unicorn* (1941), *Animal Farm* (1945), *Dickens, Dali and Others* (1946), *The Death of an Elephant* (1950).

V. S. Prichett, "George Orwell," in *Writers of Today,* ed. D. Val Baker (1947).

Since 1940 **Graham Greene (1904-   )** has been considered by many English critics among the foremost novelists of his generation. Educated at Berkhamstead School in Hertfordshire, of which his father was headmaster, and at Balliol College, Oxford, Greene entered literature by way of journalism, serving as subeditor of the *Times* from 1926 to 1930. His first novel, *The Man Within,* appeared in 1929.

A sensitive boy hurt by the minor brutalities of school life, Greene early developed a moral seriousness which was given final direction by his conversion to the Catholic Church. As a writer he is pre-eminently a moralist. The distinction between his "novels" and his "entertainments," the groups into which he divides his works, is largely one of ethical significance. In the former the problem is more subtle and the probing of will and conscience deeper; in the latter the conflict of good and evil is illustrated more simply in adventurous action. In both Greene exhibits the singular combination of gifts that is his greatest distinction. He has preeminently the journalist's sense of "story," of significant fact, and skill in rapid, tense narrative. With this he has the psychological insight usually reserved to the introspective novelist. Many of his books, such as *Stamboul Train* (1932) and *A Gun For Sale* (1936), may be satisfactorily read as fast-paced adventure stories, with little consideration of other values. At the same time they contain analysis of motive and conduct less impressive only because less elaborately developed than that in his more serious and mature works.

Greene's preoccupation with human weakness and his sense of the active power of evil are intense, and in these respects he has been compared to Joseph Conrad, though beyond them any likeness between the two writers breaks down. His favorite situation, the old and symbolic one of the man hunt, is an admirable vehicle for his purposes and at the same time makes vividly clear the tensions and fears that pervaded all European society after the middle thirties. Much of the contemporary estimation of Greene is no doubt due to his powerful expression of the feeling of the time and may not outlast the conditions that produced it. Only his most serious novels, *The Power and the Glory* (1940) and *The Heart of the Matter* (1948), seem strong enough to transcend this topicality, and in these there is a strong religious bias.

Well-traveled and of wide interests, Greene has escaped the provincialism of many English novelists. His stories are not restricted to any nation or class of society but give a sense of a world beyond the immediate scene and of the complexity of the forces whose interplay contributes to the moral and political tragedy of modern man.

Fiction: *The Man Within* (1929), *The Name of Action* (1930), *Rumor At Nightfall* (1931), *Stamboul Train* [*Orient Express*] (1932), *It's a Battlefield* (1934), *The Bear Fell Free* (1935), *The Basement Room* (1936), *A Gun For Sale* [*This Gun For Hire*] (1936), *Brighton Rock* (1938), *The Confidential Agent* (1939), *The Power and the Glory* (1939), *The Ministry of Fear* (1943), *The Heart of the Matter* (1948), *Nineteen Stories* (1949). Miscellaneous: *England Made Me* (1935), *Journey Without Maps* (1936), *The Lawless Roads* (1939), *British Dramatists* (1942).

Walter Allen, "Graham Greene," in *Writers of Today,* ed. D. Val Baker (1946); Arthur Calder-Marshall, "Graham Greene," in *Living Writers,* ed. G. H. Phelps (1947).

Among the younger English novelists none has as yet shown more substantial achievement or greater promise than **Henry Green (1905   )**, in private life Henry York. The son of a wealthy midland manufacturer and the nephew of a peer, he was educated at Eton and Oxford. While still at school he wrote his first novel, *Blindness,* a study not (autobiographical) of an adolescent facing the loss of sight. After Oxford he worked for a year in his father's Birmingham foundry and from the experience gathered there produced *Living,* a story of working-class life. Since then he has written five more novels, showing a steady growth in ideas and style, and a volume of reminiscences.

Green is a novelist of ideas, but one without the marked moral or political partisanship of some of his contemporaries. A strong influence of Kafka in the symbolism that is the heart of his work places him among the moderns, but his robust sense of comedy comes straight from the eighteenth-century tradition of the English novel. *Party Going* (1938) is a clever social satire on the middle class, a conversation piece reminiscent of T. L. Peacock and Aldous Huxley, but with a new note of austere symbolism that removes it from the derivative. *Caught* (1943) is a much grimmer tale reflecting Green's wartime experience in the Auxiliary Fire Service. *Loving* (1945), his finest work to date, again satirizes, under the thin disguise of a servants' hall comedy, the modern dilemma of the middle class. In satiric power and characterization it shows a great advance over *Party Going*. The confusion of the idealist after the war is the theme of *Back* (1946), and the bureaucratic state of the near future that of *Concluding* (1948).

The most impressive satiric novelist since the appearance of Huxley in the early twenties, Green, if less brilliantly witty than Huxley, has a richer humor and a greater power to create effective characters. His best have a life of their own beyond the qualities and ideas they serve to express, just as his novels while blended of satire and allegory are, with the exception of *Party Going,* good stories in their own right. His strongly individual style, though it has many roots in the past, is not conventionally traditional but thoroughly modern, an excellent medium to express the grim and foolish years in which he has written.

Novels: *Blindness* (1926), *Living* (1931), *Party Going* (1938), *Caught* (1943), *Loving* (1945), *Back* (1946), *Concluding* (1948), *Nothing* (1950). Reminiscences: *Pack My Bag* (1939).

Walter Allen, "Henry Green," in *Modern British Writing*, ed. D. Val Baker (1947); Philip Toynbee, "The Novels of Henry Green," *Partisan Review,* V (1949), 487-498.

Alfred Edgar Coppard (1878-   ) was born of working class parents at Folkestone in Kent. He attended school at Brighton until he was nine, when he was withdrawn because of poor health. He had no further formal education. Soon after, he was apprenticed to a tailor in Whitechapel, for whom he worked thirteen hours a day. From then on he worked steadily at anything he found to do: at various times he was an office boy, a messenger, a professional sprinter, and a clerk. He outgrew the sickliness of his childhood and made up for his lack of schooling by voracious reading. At length he qualified himself as an accountant, and in 1905, at the age of twenty-seven, he married. Two years later a position with an engineering firm took him to Oxford, where for the first time he found himself in an intellectual society.

Oxford stimulated a literary impulse latent in Coppard and about 1911 he began, half seriously, writing "poems and tales." After a while he made friends in a circle of literary undergraduates which included Aldous Huxley, L. A. G. Strong, and Richard Hughes. Occasionally W. B. Yeats attended the informal meetings at which they read and discussed books. The example of these younger men who were beginning to publish set Coppard to writing in earnest, and from 1916 onward his stories and verses appeared from time to time in magazines. By the end of the First World War, during which he worked in a munitions factory, he decided to give up clerical work for authorship. The first two years were discouraging; by the beginning of 1921 he was destitute and only an unexpected check from an American magazine saved his career. A few months later the Golden Cockerel Press began its publications with the issue of his first volume, *Adam and Eve and Pinch Me*. From that time on his success, though never spectacular, has been steady, his seventeen volumes of short stories being the most distinguished work in that genre during the fifteen years after the death of Katherine Mansfield.

Though a self-educated working man, Coppard is in no

ALFRED EDGAR COPPARD

sense a proletarian writer. His tales are often about working people and are grim with immediate knowledge of the harder aspects of life, but they are without bitterness or class consciousness. He is too objective an artist to be a propagandist, and his fantastic humor mitigates his deep and constant sense of the tragedy of most lives. The pervading emotion of his work is a sort of wry pity for those who are defeated through some tragic misapprehension of a situation or of the actions of their fellows.

Coppard is a thorough traditionalist. His model in narrative is the folk tale—and, reviewing his work, one would add the ballad. To analysis and the creation of atmosphere he prefers the revelation of character in action, and his tales generally march with military directness to their main events. He wants his reader to feel that he is being "talked to, not written at." His prose style, like that of his verse, strongly influenced by the seventeenth century, has the ease and grace of complete competence. Method and style together give to most of his tales an effect of austere poetry. In fact it is in the tales rather than in his verse, though that is often good, that one recognizes the essential poet in Coppard.

He turned like Katherine Mansfield away from the contrived short story of the French school, but by a different path, bringing back something of the old simplicity of narrative. His work is like fresh air in a time when the short story is increasingly influenced by the probings and intricate symbolisms of Kafka.

SHORT STORIES: *Adam and Eve and Pinch Me* (1921), *Clorinda Walks in Heaven* (1922), *The Black Dog* (1923), *Fishmonger's Fiddle* (1925), *The Field of Mustard* (1926), *Count Stefan* (1928), *Silver Circus* (1928), *The Man From Kilsheelan* (1930), *The Hundredth Story of A. E. Coppard* (1931), *Nixey's Harlequin* (1931), *Cheefoo* (1932), *Crotty Shinkwin* (1932), *Dunky Fitlow* (1933), *Ring the Bells of Heaven* (1933), *Emergency Exit* (1934), *Nine-*

penny Flute (1937), *Tapster's Tapestry* (1938), *You Never Know, Do You?* (1939). VERSE: *Hips and Haws* (1922), *Pelagea* (1926), *Yokohama Garland* (Philadelphia, 1926), *Collected Poems* (1928), *Cherry Ripe* (1935).

Jacob Schwartz, *The Writings of Alfred Edgar Coppard: A Bibliography* (1931); George Brandon Saul, *A. E. Coppard* (Phila., 1932).

"Katherine Mansfield" (1888-1923) was the pen name of Kathleen Mansfield Beauchamp, daughter of Sir Harold Beauchamp, a banker and business man of Wellington, New

KATHERINE MANSFIELD

Zealand. In the nineties her father was not so wealthy and prominent as he afterward became, and her childhood was somewhat like that of Kezia Burnell, the little girl who appears in several of her stories. She attended a local school in the suburban village to which her family had moved and later Wellington Girls College, where her stories, which she had been writing since the age of eight or nine, were published in the school magazine. At fifteen she was sent to complete her education at Queen's College, an old-fashioned finishing school in London. In 1906, school over, she went back to the family in New Zealand and spent the next two years in a fight to get away from it again. It was then that she adopted her pen name to sign her contributions to *The Native Companion*. At length her father reluctantly allowed her £100 a year on which to live in London.

Her early years in London were hard and discouraging.

Her health was delicate and her allowance inadequate. She found no encouragement in her work. In 1909, at twenty-one, she married, but left her husband almost immediately. In a desperate interval that followed she took a lover and was delivered of his still-born child at an obscure resort in Bavaria. Here she gathered the materials for her first literary success, a series of sketches of German bourgeois types which she contributed to *The New Age*. The next year these were published as her first volume, *In a German Pension* (1911). Later Katherine Mansfield was ashamed of these stories, and during the war would not allow them to be republished. They are caricatures, it is true, without the subtlety and sureness of her later work; they ridicule unkindly but not unjustly the weaknesses of the German character. But they are thoroughly good work.

In 1911 began the long and close relation with John Middleton Murry that, after her writing, was the most important thing in Katherine Mansfield's life. When they met he was a young journalist, poorer than she, trying to edit a literary magazine called *Rhythm,* to which she had offered a story, *The Woman in the Store*. Work for the magazine drew them together and she rented Murry a room in her flat. Before long they were living together, but it was not until 1918 that her husband would obtain a divorce so that they might marry. Though they were completely devoted to each other, their life together was always harassed by want of money, by her increasing ill-health, by separations, and by constant moving about. Katherine Mansfield had a restless spirit and even in love could not always accept the life of laborious poverty their circumstances enforced. They were completely happy only for a few months in 1915-16 when they took a small villa at Bandol in the south of France. Here she did some of her best work.

The spiritual pressure of the war and the death of a brother at the front turned Katherine Mansfield's mind back to her childhood as an escape from sorrow. Out of this came *Prelude,* written at Bandol, and later *The Garden Party,* drawn directly from memories of her home at Karori. But she could not escape for long: her restlessness and tubercular weakness increased and in 1918 she returned, alone, to France. *Je ne parle pas français* expresses her despairing mood at this time.

Recognition as an artist did not come to Katherine Mansfield until after the war, tragically too late. *Prelude* was published by Leonard and Virginia Woolf at the Hogarth Press in 1918, *Je ne parle pas français* appeared in 1919, and *Bliss* in 1920. She was married to Murry and was helping him by reviewing for the *Athenaeum,* of which he was now editor. But her tuberculosis had reached an advanced stage and it was too late to find the abiding peace for which they both had struggled desperately. She tried to achieve a calm of the spirit to compensate for her broken life. In October of 1922 she went to take the psychophysical therapy of the Gudjieff Institute near Fontainebleau. She died there January 9, 1923.

Katherine Mansfield was small and dark in person, aloof and reserved in manner. She had great warmth of sympathy and affection: as she wrote to Murry, "All I write or ever, ever will write will be the fruit of our love—." But there was something in her that she could not give to others, that insisted on separateness with a fierce independence, and she had the gift of sarcasm that sometimes belongs to quiet, clear-seeing women. She was wholly an artist, a good musician as well as a writer, a brilliant but not wholly integrated personality. Sustained happiness would probably have been impossible for her.

The work of Katherine Mansfield marks a critical change in the technique of the English short story. Conventionally a story was built upon a well-contrived incident, or a facet of a character. For this she substituted a technique in which

the implications of a story are more important than its statement, in which the "atmosphere" evokes a revealing central
mood, as in the familiar essay. This may be attributed partly
to the influence of Chekhov, whom she greatly admired, but
more to her own nature, writers being generally better explained by what they are than by what they read. She wrote
less from observation than from understanding, and this was
drawn from that withheld, secluded part of her character to
which things and people appeared inseparable from the
mood in which they were known. To her ability to create a
scene or a moment in its totality of experience, she adds
remarkable clarity of perception, a keen irony, and an unfailing instinct for simplicity of means that give her unpretentious stories their curious charm and power.

After her death Katherine Mansfield's journals, letters,
poems, and book reviews were collected and published by
Murry, as well as a selection of her stories. Her last volume,
Something Childish (called *The Little Girl* in the American
edition), appeared in 1924.

SHORT STORIES: *In a German Pension* (1911), *Prelude* (1918), *Je
ne parle pas français* (1919), *Bliss and Other Stories* (1920), *The
Garden Party* (1922), *The Doves' Nest* (1923), *The Little Girl and
Other Stories* (1924), *Something Childish* (1924), *The Aloe* (1930),
The Short Stories of Katherine Mansfield (1937). MISCELLANEOUS
WORKS EDITED BY J. MIDDLETON MURRY: *Poems* (1923), *The Jour-
nal of Katherine Mansfield* (1927), *The Letters of Katherine Mans-
field* (1928), *Novels and Novelists* (1930), *The Scrap Book of
Katherine Mansfield* (1940).

R. E. Mantz, *The Critical Bibliography of Katherine Mansfield*
(1931); R. E. Mantz and J. M. Murry, *The Life of Katherine
Mansfield* (1933); Edward Wagenknecht, "Katherine Mansfield,"
English Jour., XVII (1928), 272-284; Edward Shanks, "Katherine
Mansfield," *London Mercury*, XVII (1928), 286-293; Sidney Cox,
"The Fastidiousness of Katherine Mansfield," *Sewanee Rev.*,
XXXIX (1931), 158-169; S. J. Hubbell, "Katherine Mansfield and
Kezia," *Sewanee Rev.*, XXXV (1927), 325-335; George Jean-Aubry,
"Katherine Mansfield," *Revue de Paris*, XXXVIIIe An, 5 (1931),

57-72; Louis Gilet, "Katherine Mansfield," *Rev. des Deux Mondes,* VIIᵉ Per., 24 (1924), 929-942, " 'Kass,' ou la jeunesse de Katherine Mansfield," *Rev. des Deux Mondes,* VIIIᵉ Per., 19 (1934), 456-468; Marguerite d'Escola, "Katherine Mansfield," *Rev. Bleue,* LXXII (1934), 643-649; B. von Heissler, "Katherine Mansfield," *Die Literatur,* XL (1937), 16-21; Arnold Whitridge, "Katherine Mansfield," *Sewanee Rev.,* XLVIII (1940), 256-272; John Middleton Murry, *Katherine Mansfield and Other Literary Portraits* (1949); Sylvia Berkman, *Katherine Mansfield: A Critical Study* (New Haven, 1951).

Born in a Northamptonshire village of country-bred parents, **Herbert Ernest Bates (1905-**) has become one of the most sensitive portrayers of English rural life in his generation. After local schooling a few years' experience of business routine proved unbearably irksome and hastened his escape into the freer life his writing allowed him. He had been writing for six years when his first novel, *The Two Sisters,* was published in 1926. He was just twenty-one. Five years later he married and since then has lived in Kent close to the life he writes about. He served the Second World War in the RAF.

Like Katherine Mansfield, Bates was strongly influenced by Chekhov, and his stories, like hers, depend for their effect upon atmosphere and emotion rather than contrived incident. Less of a literary Brahmin than she, he misses something of her delicate sensitivity, but his greater robustness is suitable to his material. He writes of those aspects and moments of country life that have a poetic significance at best half comprehended by the actors in them, generally simple people of average character and capacity. He has an ability to express the poignancy of the "lyrical moment" that has made him conspicuously successful in the short story. In his novels, of which he has written ten, he is not always successful in sustaining his created mood.

One of the most thoroughly English writers of the present

both in his choice and his treatment of material, Bates was little read in the United States until the serialization of his novel *Spella Ho* in the *Atlantic Monthly* in 1938. Since then the amusing stories of *My Uncle Silas* (1939) and his romance of the war, *Fair Stood the Wind for France* (1944), have increased his popularity, but some of his books are still hard to obtain.

SHORT STORIES: *The Seekers* (1926), *The Spring Song* (1927), *Seven Tales and Alexander* (1929), *The Tree* (1930), *Mrs. Esmond's Life* (1931), *A German Idyll* (1932), *The Black Boxer* (1932), *The Woman Who Had Imagination* (1934), *Cut and Come Again* (1935), *Something Short and Sweet* (1937), *The Flying Goat* (1939), *My Uncle Silas* (1939), *Country Tales* (1940), *The Beauty of the Dead* (1940), *The Cruise of the Breadwinner* (1946). Under pseudonym "Flying Officer X": *The Greatest People in the World* (1942), *How Sleep the Brave* (1943), *Something in the Air* (1944). NOVELS: *The Two Sisters* (1926), *Catherine Foster* (1929), *Charlotte's Row* (1931), *The Fallow Land* (1932), *The Poacher* (1935), *A House of Women* (1936), *Spella Ho* (1938), *The Bride Comes to Evensford* (1943), *Fair Stood the Wind for France* (1944), *The Purple Plain* (1947).

Michael Williams, "H. E. Bates," in *Writers of Today*, 2 (1948).

THE DRAMA
1890—1950

FOR THE London theatergoer of the later nineties who asked more than entertainment the table was not bountifully spread. There was Shakespeare in the expert hands of Henry Irving and Ellen Terry, but little modern fare. The conviction of Oscar Wilde in 1895 had driven his plays temporarily from the stage and no heir to his brilliant, epigrammatic wit had appeared. George Bernard Shaw, now known for half a dozen plays, was also Irish and brilliant but with an uncomfortable difference. His wit was the lambent surface of a fierce puritanism that probed and questioned everywhere and raised disquieting thoughts. Beneath it he was too much like the serious foreigner Ibsen, with whose praises he belabored the public in the *Saturday Review.* London had put up a stout resistance to Ibsen. Ever since his discovery by Edmund Gosse in 1879, intelligent critics and managers had been trying to persuade the English public to accept him, but though the season of 1890-91 had seen five of his plays, audiences remained shy and the theatrical world had learned that he did not pay.

As an alternative to Shaw and Ibsen there were smoothly constructed and less disturbing social problem plays of Henry Arthur Jones and Arthur Wing Pinero. Jones, already a veteran who had been writing for twenty years, caused a sensation and something of a scandal in 1896 with *Michael and His Lost Angel,* a play dealing with clerical adultery. It closed after eleven nights but established for his plays a reputation greater than they deserved. For some years afterward he enjoyed great popularity. Pinero scored his greatest success with *The Second Mrs. Tanqueray* in 1893 and *The Notorious Mrs. Ebbsmith* in 1895, but *Trelawney of the "Wells"* (1898) and *The Gay Lord Quex* (1899) sustained his reputation, and in 1909 *Mid-Channel* was the most controversial play of the year. Both of these men were exceedingly deft technicians, whose plays owed more to skill of construction than to intellectual content. Their handling of social problems was far more timid than Shaw's and the old-fashioned conventionality of their work caused it to be quickly outmoded. Yet by putting the problem play in terms that were acceptable to English audiences they did more perhaps than Shaw's ruthless attack to prepare the public taste for a more serious drama, and they deserve credit for an important part in the effort to raise the English theater out of the low estate into which it had fallen in the nineteenth century.

In this effort the dramatist had the support of the Stage Society, which produced plays that could not get a hearing in the commercial theater, and of a group of brilliant journalists. Aware of how the continental drama was advancing in the hands of Ibsen, Strindberg, Maeterlinck, and Sudermann, the leading dramatic critics, Shaw, A. B. Walkley, William Archer, and soon Max Beerbohm, deplored the flaccidity of the London theater and labored hard to raise the standard of appreciation. There was no lack of theatrical talent: Johnston Forbes-Robertson, John Hare, Herbert Beerbohm Tree, Cyril Maude, Lilly Langtry, Janet Achurch, and Mrs. Pat Campbell were as fine a group of actors as the English stage has had at any time. All things were propitious for the revival of the drama which had already begun.

The first vigor of the new movement appeared in Dublin where W. B. Yeats, Douglas Hyde, Lady Gregory, and George Moore founded the Irish National Theater Society. Though denounced by young James Joyce in an early pamphlet, *The Day of the Rabblement* (1901), as a prostitution of art to political ends, the movement was artistically sincere and became practically effective with the opening of the Abbey Theater in 1904 under the management of Miss Annie Elizabeth Horniman to produce the plays of native authors. The dramatic strength of the Abbey Theater was supplied by the genius of John M. Synge, a discovery of Yeats's, who from its opening until his early death in 1909, wrote for it the finest plays that Ireland has yet produced. They sometimes offended the touchy patriotism of Dublin audiences, and *The Playboy of the Western World* (1907) caused rioting in theaters on both sides of the Atlantic by its alleged misrepresentation of the Irish character. Lady Gregory contributed short comedies of peasant life in the amusing "Kiltartan" dialect, some of them translations from the Gaelic writings of Douglas Hyde. Yeats's plays were too poetic in their conception to be effective on the stage and George Moore took no active part in the venture. In 1908 the Abbey produced *The Clancy Name,* a tragedy by a young playwright, Lennox Robinson. Two years later he became stage manager, taking the players to the United States in 1912. Later still from Belfast came St. John Ervine, whose *John Ferguson* was produced at the Abbey in 1914 and who succeeded Robinson as manager in the following year.

In 1908 Miss Horniman left Dublin to manage the Manchester Repertory Theater. Inspired by the success of the Abbey, this movement developed some able dramatists in the Midlands of whom the best were Stanley Houghton, Harold Brighouse, and Alan Monkhouse, all vigorous realists. Masefield's *Tragedy of Nan* (1909) was the theater's first sensation, and Houghton's *Hindle Wakes* its greatest success. Repertory theaters were also founded in Glasgow, Birmingham and Liverpool, but these were less important.

Meanwhile in London Harley Granville-Barker and J. E. Vedrenne, encouraged by J. T. Grein's experiment with the

Independent Theater, took over the management of the Royal Court Theater to produce plays of real merit, and were so successful that in 1907 they moved to the larger Savoy. The genius of Gordon Craig, Ellen Terry's son, was employed to furnish a new simple decor that broke away completely from the detailed realism that was then the established fashion in stage settings. Granville-Barker was himself a dramatist, having made his debut in the Stage Society's production of *The Marrying of Ann Leet* in 1901. By the time he retired from management in 1914 he had made a substantial reputation as a playwright with *The Voysey Inheritance* (1905), *Waste* (1907), and *The Madras House* (1910).

James Barrie, after the lavender and old lace of *Quality Street* (1901), had showed in *The Admirable Crichton* (1903) that he was capable of pointed social satire, and the next year had as great success with the best beloved children's play in the language, *Peter Pan*. At the Court Theatre in 1906 John Galsworthy began a successful dramatic career with *The Silver Box*. The problem plays of his first period were felt to be "challenging," like those of Pinero, and were for some time overestimated. So were the showy but ephemeral social plays of Alfred Sutro. Somerset Maugham was doing steady journeyman work, his successes *The Circle* and *The Letter* still far in the future after the war. These four writers, with Shaw, gave London its most serious plays, with a preponderance of social criticism, until the First War.

For the first few years of the century Stephen Phillips had a great name as a poetic dramatist. Paolo and Francesca was generally acclaimed by the critics in 1900, as were his three following plays, *Herod* (1901), *Ulysses* (1902), and *The Sin of David* (1904), after which, as their rhetoric and theatricality become more apparent, even praise for the genuine if slight talent in his work ceased. In 1910 he was eclipsed by Masefield, whose *Tragedy of Pompey the Great* promised more than his really narrative genius could sustain in the drama. Gilbert Murray's translations of the Greek dramatists, while attacked by scholars as betrayals of their originals, were, under Granville-Barker's management, dramatically effective. The exotic fantasies of Lord Dunsany, though their charm of "strange beauties and strange dooms" has not lasted, appealed strongly to the taste of the prewar public.

The war put an end to the demand for serious plays, life having quite enough problems for everyone. Galsworthy, engaged in war work, wrote only one trifle; Barrie furnished the sentimental with *The Well Remembered Voice, Barbara's Wedding,* and *The Old Lady Shows Her Medals.* Shaw, equal to any war, produced *O'Flaherty V. C., The Inca of Perusalem,* and *Augustus Does His Bit.* But for the most part the theater offered reviews and light diversion. *Chu Chin Chow,* a lavish oriental spectacle, ran to packed houses for over three years.

Shaw, Galsworthy, and Barrie were still the leading dramatists in the twenties, Galsworthy doing his best work with *Loyalties, The Skin Game,* and *Old English.* Frederick Lonsdale, who had been writing without great distinction since 1908, scored a success with *Aren't We All?* in 1923. His suavely sophisticated social dramas, in the tradition of Pinero with a postwar difference, held the stage until in the late thirties they began to seem outmoded. A similar belated success came to John Drinkwater, whose chronicle plays enjoyed a decade of popularity after the success of *Abraham Lincoln* in 1918.

The first of the new playwrights to appear was A. A. Milne, an established humorist of the staff of *Punch* who had begun his dramatic writing while in the army. His whimsical comedies with an exquisite sense of the ridiculous in situation and dialogue were just what audiences of the twenties wanted to help them forget the war. In 1924 the younger generation knocked unmistakably at the door with the appearance of *The Rat Trap,* the first play by Noel Coward. As his amazing versatility unfolded he showed perfect competence, and often more, in sophisticated comedy (*Private Lives, Design for Living*), drama (*The Vortex*), historical spectacle (*Cavalcade*), and fast-paced revue (*This Year of Grace, Words and Music*). His hard cleverness and nostalgic sentiment are intensely characteristic of his generation and he has become its most efficient spokesman in the theater. J. B. Priestley has appealed to a less sophisticated middle-class audience. He did not turn to the theater until 1932, when he was a well-established novelist, but the popular success of his plays has been as great as that of his books. A sturdy socialism and interesting experiments with time hardly relieve the mediocrity of his work, through most of which there runs a distinct reminiscence of Barrie. *An Inspector Calls* (1947) is an effective parable of social responsibility and probably his strongest play since *Dangerous Corner* (1932). John Van Druten was lost to the English theater through his emigration to the United States in 1926.

Meanwhile in 1923, at the end of Lennox Robinson's second period of management, the Abbey Theater had produced *The Shadow of a Gunman,* by Sean O'Casey. It was soon clear that he was the best Irish dramatist since Synge, but like Synge he offended national susceptibilities and *The Plough and The Stars* (1926) provoked the same sort of rioting that had greeted *The Playboy.* He has been better appreciated in England and the United States than in his own country.

As the thirties drew on there was a marked decline of new dramatic authorship. Here and there an isolated success was scored such as R. C. Sherriff's war play *Journey's End* in 1929 or Walter Greenwood's socialist document *Love on the Dole* in 1933, but they led to nothing. Lawrence Housman, who for thirty years had been writing unpopular, and often censored, religious plays, scored a remarkable success in 1934 with *Victoria Regina*. The Welsh actor Emlyn Williams appeared as author in 1930 and has written a number of steadily better plays of which *The Corn Is Green* (1938) is the best so far. Keith Winter showed considerable promise in *The Shining Hour* (1934) but has not sustained it in his later work. W. H. Auden and Christopher Isherwood have collaborated in three plays of very modern technique: *The Dog Beneath the Skin* (1935), *Ascent of F 6* (1937), and *On the Frontier* (1938). These, however, are more suitable for reading than for production. An interesting revival of the religious drama was instituted at the Canterbury Festival with plays presented in the Cathedral Chapter house. For this T. S. Eliot wrote *Murder in the Cathedral,* the martyrdom of St. Thomas à Becket, in 1935, and Dorothy Sayres *The Zeal of Thy House* in 1937 and *The Devil to Pay,* a version of the Faust story, in 1939.

The rehabilitation of the English drama since 1890 has been accomplished against serious obstacles. The low estate into which the nineteenth-century drama fell was due in part to the great vogue of the novel and in part to the wholesale pirating of foreign plays by London managers, both of which drove the best literary talent into the field of fiction. The English playwright has also had to support the incubus of the censor who, with his power to refuse a license for a play upon his unsupported judgment, has been a virtual dictator of the theater. The poor fare offered as a consequence to the Victorian theatergoer depressed and vitiated the public taste to such a degree that the education of the modern public to the appreciation of serious plays has been slow and often discouraging.

The period from 1890 to 1920 with the work of Wilde, Shaw, Barrie, Galsworthy and Synge, not to mention the lesser writers, was the most brilliant that the English theater had seen since the Restoration. In those thirty years the intellectual level was astonishingly raised. A public whose average taste was fairly represented by *Charlie's Aunt* had been brought to accept and support a drama of serious social criticism, to recognize wit above the level of farce, and to associate again the once wholly divorced worlds of the stage and of reality.

Since 1920 there has been a noticeable decline from the abundant excellence of the prewar period. In spite of many interesting technical experiments and many individually good plays there is a comparative thinness of dramatic achievement. So far only three men have produced substantial bodies of dramatic work and if one makes such a comparison as Milne with Barrie, Priestley with Galsworthy, and Coward with Wilde, it is only in the last instance that the younger man's work will bear it. Only time will allow this period to be correctly evaluated but from the uncertain standpoint of the present a peak appears to have been passed.

Among the British playwrights who were influenced by Ibsen whose dramas of social import were produced in London during the nineties, none was more popular than **Sir Arthur Wing Pinero (1855-1934)**. Between 1887 and 1928 he wrote more than thirty plays, some of which such as *The Second Mrs. Tanqueray* (1894), *The Notorious Mrs. Ebbsmith* (1895), *Trelawny of the "Wells"* (1898), and *Mid-Channel* (1909) had very long runs and have been frequently revived. As late as 1924 Ethel Barrymore gave one of her finest performances in *The Second Mrs. Tanqueray* as Paula, a role which had given Mrs. Patrick Campbell much of her fame. Although all of Pinero's social themes are no longer considered profound, and his management of them is now regarded as sketchy and superficial, his plays, especially the tragedies, are generally moving and theatrically effective.

Arthur Wing Pinero was born in London in 1855, the son of a well-to-do solicitor of Portuguese-Jewish ancestry. His education did not extend to the university, for soon after completing his classical studies at Birkbeck Institute he became interested in the theater, and at the age of twenty-four made his first appearance as an actor in Edinburgh. A few years later he was with Sir Henry Irving's company, with

ARTHUR WING PINERO

which he remained from 1876 to 1879 and in which he no doubt received much valuable training for his chosen profession of playwright. It was while he was associated with Irving's group that he wrote his first plays, but it was not until 1880 that he forsook his work as an actor to devote his time to writing for the stage. During the eighties and early nineties his plays were produced at frequent intervals, but it was with *The Second Mrs. Tanqueray* (1894) that he became famous. In 1909 he was knighted in recognition of his services to the English stage. His plays written after the First World War show ingeniousness but a perceptible falling off in dramatic effectiveness. He died in 1934.

Pinero's plays divide themselves into the dramas of social import such as *The Second Mrs. Tanqueray* and *Mid-Channel,* and the Comedy of Manners plays such as *The Weaker Sex* and *The Gay Lord Quex.* In the dramas of social import, problems are raised and in some measure answered. For example, Aubrey, in *The Second Mrs. Tanqueray,* risks marrying Paula, a woman with a past. The catastrophe becomes apparent when it is disclosed that Ellean, Aubrey's daughter by a previous marriage, has fallen in love with one of her stepmother's former lovers. Paula, who has tried in her way to be a good wife to Aubrey, sees no way out of the difficulty and commits suicide. Pinero's method of solving the problem seems real enough, but there is nothing of striking inevitability about the tragedy. In *Mid-Channel,* a more universal problem is presented, that of a childless couple who find upon reaching middle age little by way of common bond and no ideal or illusion toward which to strive. Pinero manipulates the characters and situation with great skill, with the result that the climax seems not only entirely plausible, but inevitable. Although even now it is not generally recognized, it was with light social comedy that Pinero did some of his finest work. Possessed of a talent for ingenious situation and witty lines, he wrote more than a score of comedies which in spite of their dated mannerisms are genuinely entertaining. In all of his work his resourcefulness as a technician is outstanding.

Mayfair (1885), *Lady Bountiful* (1890), *The Hobby-Horse* (1892), *Sweet Lavender* (1893), *The Second Mrs. Tanqueray* (1894), *The Weaker Sex* (1894), *The Notorious Mrs. Ebbsmith* (1895), *Trelawny of the "Wells"* (1898), *The Gay Lord Quex* (1899), *Iris* (1901), *The House in Order* (1905), *The Thunderbolt* (1909), *Mid-Channel* (1909), *The Big Drum* (1915), *The Enchanted Cottage* (1921), *A Private Room* (1926), *Child Man* (1928).

W. D. Dunkel, *Sir Arthur Wing Pinero: A Critical Biography* (Chicago, 1941); H. H. Fyfe, *Sir Arthur Wing Pinero's Plays and Players* (1930); Clayton Hamilton, *The Social Plays of Arthur Wing Pinero, with a General Introduction and a Critical Preface to Each Play* (1917-19); Wilibald Stöcker, *Pinero's Dramen: Studien über Motive, Charaktere und Technik* (Berlin, 1911).

Sir James Matthew Barrie (1860-1937) was born at Kirriemuir, Forfarshire, Scotland, the ninth of ten children of David Barrie, a poor handloom weaver. The death of an elder brother made him very early the favorite child of his mother Margaret Ogilvie (so called in the family by her maiden name, according to Scots custom) and his whole childhood and youth were shaped by his close and tender association with her.

Barrie had his schooling at Glasgow Academy, where his
brother was classical master, and later at Dumfries Academy,
still under the eye of his brother, now Inspector of Schools
for that district. He showed
some aptitude for writing and
more for amateur theatricals
of all kinds, and took a normal schoolboy interest in
sports. In his last years at
school he decided upon a literary career, disappointing his
mother's hopes of seeing him
a minister, and in 1878 entered the University of Edinburgh in order to study
English literature under Pro-

JAMES MATTHEW BARRIE   fessor David Masson. He was
now a very short, thin youth
of eighteen, shy among strangers because of his physical in-
significance, a good but not remarkable student. Like most
literary undergraduates he conceived numbers of literary
projects, but beyond his academic essays he wrote nothing
at the University except some dramatic criticisms for the
Evening Courant. He took his degree in 1882 without having made any mark in college life.

Barrie, now with his family's whole-hearted support, began his literary career as "leader" (editorial) writer for the
Nottingham Journal, which he joined in January, 1883. For
a weekly salary of £3 he produced twelve columns of matter, including, in addition to daily editorials, a weekly article and a column of notes. At the end of a year of this
servitude he left the paper—whether he resigned or was discharged is not clear—and thereafter remained a free lance.
He returned home for a while, and then, in 1885, encour-

aged by the sale of his articles, went to London. For the next four years he lived in the Bloomsbury district, working desperately hard, increasing his acquaintance among editors, and gradually establishing a reputation.

The work that first brought Barrie popular recognition began with an article entitled *An Auld Licht Community,* published in 1884. The "Auld Lichts" formed a very strict sect of Presbyterians to which Margaret Ogilvie had belonged before her marriage. It was from her reminiscences, for he never himself entered an "Auld Licht" church, that Barrie drew his material, filling it out with character and local color from his own knowledge of Kirriemuir. The success of the first sketch brought editorial requests for more, and in 1888 these were collected in a volume as *Auld Licht Idylls.* With the critical and popular appreciation of these, Barrie ceased to be an obscure journalist. He had found a rich vein in the atmosphere of his native place and he went on to exploit it fully in *When a Man's Single* (1888), *A Window in Thrums* (1889), and *The Little Minister* (1891). *Sentimental Tommy* (1895) and *Tommy and Grizel* (1900) brought him to the height of his power and of his reputation as a novelist. His success inspired a number of imitators, the so-called "kailyard school," exploiting the humor and pathos of humble Scottish life and the picturesqueness of the "lallans" speech, on the whole the most important group of new regional writers before 1900.

Meanwhile Barrie had been working away from fiction toward the theater. His first successful play, *Walker, London* (1892), dramatizing material drawn from *When a Man's Single,* ran for 511 performances. The heroine was played by Mary Ansell, who two years later became Barrie's wife. This play was followed by *The Professor's Love Story* (1895) and a dramatization of *The Little Minister* for Charles Frohman in 1897. All of these plays Barrie had regarded as experiments or potboilers, but from 1900 with Frohman as his producer and Maude Adams as his leading lady he seriously undertook the works that at once brought him enormous popularity. *Quality Street,* a delicate romantic comedy, appeared in New York in 1901 and a year later in London, where it was very soon followed by *The Admirable Crichton,* on the whole the best he ever did. The Christmas holidays of 1904 saw the historic first performance of *Peter Pan,* that all but immortal fantasy for children, that for more than a generation has been revived annually. To many now middle aged, Maude Adams as Peter Pan is an ineffaceable part of their childhood. His next important play, *What Every Woman Knows,* a comedy of Scottish character recalling his early stories, appeared in 1908 and brings to a close the first period of his dramatic work.

In 1909 Barrie's wife left him for Gilbert Cannan, the novelist, and was soon afterward divorced. The failure of his marriage was a severe blow to Barrie and for a while paralyzed his creative effort. For the next few years he produced chiefly one-act plays, of which the best known is *The Twelve-Pound Look.* In 1913, when the title meant little to him, he was made a baronet.

The war years 1914-18 saw him writing again with his former energy. In addition to three one-act plays, *The New Word, A Well Remembered Voice,* and *Barbara's Wedding,* he produced two of full length, *A Kiss For Cinderella* and *The Old Lady Shows Her Medals.* Apart from these "war plays," in 1917 was *Dear Brutus,* a serious comedy on the theme that "If there were second chances in this world, few of us would take them." For one scene drawn straight from Barrie's own childless unhappiness, this is his most powerful work. In 1920 appeared the only partially successful *Mary Rose* and two years later *Shall We Join the Ladies?,* a one-act thriller.

In the same year, 1922, Barrie was granted the Order of Merit, an honor then held only by Meredith and Hardy, and was elected Rector of St. Andrews University. He was now a wealthy man, living opposite Shaw in the Adelphi Terrace, and his career was all but over. He wrote one more prose story, *Farewell, Miss Julie Logan,* for the Christmas Eve supplement to the *Times* in 1931, and an unsuccessful biblical drama, *The Boy David,* in 1936. He died the following year.

Besides all these, and some minor pieces not mentioned, Barrie wrote *Margaret Ogilvie* (1896), an affectionate study of his mother, and his pleasant but unreliable autobiography, *The Greenwood Hat.* His exact relation to "Daisy Ashford's" hilarious *The Young Visitors,* of which he appeared as sponsor, remains a mystery.

With genuine pathos and humor, with a gift for telling a story dramatically and with an unfailing mastery of "good theater," Barrie was handicapped as a dramatist by weaknesses which have been attributed to his spiritual dependence on his mother. Certainly Margaret Ogilvie is responsible for the frequency in his plays of efficient, motherly women who dominate their men, and possibly for the escapism that he shares with D. H. Lawrence and Shaw, who were also much under maternal influence. But Barrie's sentimentalism, his greatest defect, is all his own. Before 1918 it was accepted and even applauded because it was exactly on the emotional level of the theater-going middle class, but in retrospect it seems so glaringly false as to vitiate a large part of his work. *The Admirable Crichton* contains good social satire, *What Every Woman Knows* humor of character, and *Dear Brutus* the genuinely pathetic figures of Dearth and his dream-daughter—enough to sustain them for some time to come. But it is doubtful whether even the wistful magic of Peter Pan still has its old appeal to children, and for the rest Barrie's inventions seem already to belong to a faded past.

COLLECTED WORKS: *Peter Pan Edition* (1929-31). FICTION: *Better Dead* (1887), *Auld Licht Idylls* (1888), *When a Man's Single* (1888), *A Window in Thrums* (1889), *The Little Minister* (1891), *A Holiday in Bed* (1892), *An Auld Licht Manse and Other Sketches* (1893), *A Powerful Drug* (1893), *A Tillyloss Scandal* (1893), *Two of Them* (1893), *A Professor's Love Story* (1895), *Sentimental Tommy* (1896), *Tommy and Grizel* (1900), *The Little White Bird* (1902), *Peter Pan in Kensington Gardens* (1906), *Peter and Wendy* (1911), *Farewell, Miss Julie Logan* (1932). PLAYS: *The Little Minister* (1898), *The Wedding Guest* (1900), *Walker London* (1907), *Quality Street* (1913), *The Admirable Crichton* (1914), *Half Hours* [*Pantaloon, The Twelve-pound Look, Rosalind, The Will*] (1914), *"Der Tag"* (1914), *What Every Woman Knows* (1918), *Echoes of the War* [*The Old Lady Shows Her Medals, The New Word, Barbara's Wedding, A Well-Remembered Voice*] (1918), *Alice Sit-by-the-fire* (1919), *A Kiss for Cinderella* (1920), *Dear Brutus* (1922), *Mary Rose* (1924), *Shall We Join the Ladies* (1928), *Peter Pan* (1928), *The Boy David* (1938). MEMOIRS: *The Greenwood Hat* (1937).

B. D. Cutler, *Sir James M. Barrie: A Bibliography* (1931); Herbert Garland, *A Bibliography of the Writings of Sir James Matthew Barrie, O. M.* (1928); Andrew Block, *Sir J. M. Barrie: His First Editions* (1933); F. J. Darton, *J. M. Barrie* (1929); W. A. Darlington, *J. M. Barrie* (1938); J. A. Hamerton, *Barrie: The Story of a Genius* (1929); James A. Roy, *James Matthew Barrie: An Appreciation* (1937); Denis Mackail, *Barrie* (1941); Thomas Moult, *Barrie* (1928); Patrick Braybrook, *J. M. Barrie* (1924); Hugh Kingsmill, "J. M. Barrie," *Horizon*, IV (1941), 43-49; James Agate, "The Genius of Barrie," *Saturday Rev.*, CXXXIII (1922), 517-518; J. Bailhache, "Le Sentimentalisme de Barrie," *Études Anglaises*, II (1938), 113-119; H. M. Walbrook, *J. M. Barrie and the Theatre* (1922); Walter Eschenhauer, *Sir James M. Barrie als Dramatiker* (Halle, 1929); Lionel Stevenson, "A Source for Barrie's 'Peter Pan,'" *Philological Quarterly*, VIII (1929), 210-214; E. Delavenay, "'Mary Rose' et le problème de la personalité chez Barrie," *Rev. Anglo-Americaine*, VI (1929), 327-343; Luise Lotze, *Stil und Sprache in den Erzählungen Barries* (Halle, 1931); Israel B. Kaplan, "A Scot in America," *Colophon* (Winter, 1936), 358-366.

George Bernard Shaw (1856-1950) at his death was much more than the Grand Old Man of English letters; like Queen Victoria he had become an institution. Two generations always had G. B. S. there to delight, frighten, stimulate, or exasperate them. He was a brilliant young arriviste of *Yellow Book* days; he debated with Belloc and Chesterton in their Edwardian prime; he commented on the First World War with authority, on the second as a sage. It was hard to believe that he had temporal origins.

GEORGE BERNARD SHAW

He was born in Dublin, the third child and only son of George Carr Shaw, a retired civil servant turned corn factor, an unsuccessful and sometimes intemperate man, who bequeathed his son little but his saving wit. The family was kept solvent largely through the efforts of Mrs. Shaw, the daughter of a Wicklow squire, a woman of great strength and independence and an accomplished musician. Up to the age of fourteen Shaw was given a haphazard education at the Wesleyan Connexional School and other institutions, but was idle and learned little. Music he got from his mother; literature from his wide and largely undirected reading.

At fifteen Shaw was put to work in a Dublin land agent's office, where he did so well that when, a year later, the cashier's position fell vacant, he was chosen to fill it. For four years he competently performed duties that were supposed to require maturity and experience. This was the first evidence of the business ability he showed throughout his life.

In 1876, at the age of twenty, Shaw left Dublin to join his mother in London, where she was teaching music. For nine years he tried to make a place for himself in literature and journalism without the least success. His statement: "I did not throw myself into the struggle for life: I threw my mother into it" is an exaggeration of course, but certainly she was his principal support in these years. Between 1879 and 1883 he wrote five novels, *Immaturity, The Irrational Knot, Love Among the Artists, Cashel Byron's Profession,* and *An Unsocial Socialist,* all of which except the first were published before 1890. *Immaturity* did not appear until 1930.

Journalism became his means of livelihood in 1885 when through William Archer he obtained a place on the reviewing staff of the *Pall Mall Gazette* and later as dramatic critic of *The World.* From 1888 to 1890 he contributed articles on music to *The Star* and from 1890 to 1894 to *The World.* His public reputation as a critic was made by his dramatic criticisms in the *Saturday Review* (1895-1898). It was confirmed by his two books *The Quintessence of Ibsenism* (1891) and *The Perfect Wagnerite* (1898). Out of his unsuccessful attempt to collaborate with William Archer in 1885 came also his first play, *Widowers' Houses,* performed and published in 1892. This was followed during the next four years by some of his best work, *The Philanderer, Mrs. Warren's Profession, Arms and the Man, Candida, The Man of Destiny,* and *You Never Can Tell.* All of these were published in 1898 in two volumes as *Plays: Pleasant and Unpleasant.*

Thus by 1898 Shaw had established a reputation as novelist, critic, and dramatist but he had severely overworked himself to do so. His health broke down completely. During a long convalescence, he married Miss Charlotte Francis

Payne-Townsend, a woman capable at once of caring for him, of appreciating his art, and of sharing his work in the Fabian Society. In these happier circumstances Shaw began the second, and most creative, period of his work.

This began with *The Devil's Disciple, Caesar and Cleopatra,* and *Captain Brassbound's Conversion,* published in 1901 as *Three Plays for Puritans. Man and Superman* followed in 1901, *John Bull's Other Island* and *Major Barbara* in 1905, and *The Doctor's Dilemma* in 1906. In these years he was gradually securing a theatrical as well as a reading public. At first his plays antagonized critics and audiences unused to intellectual satire and social propaganda, and performances of *Mrs. Warren's Profession* were forbidden on both sides of the Atlantic, but between 1905 and 1910 he won acceptance in the theatres of London and New York. Down to *Heartbreak House* in 1917 Shaw produced at least one remarkable play a year. It was then that the mythical figure of G. B. S., half genius, half bogey-man was formed in the public mind.

Shaw was now past fifty and recognized even by his severer critics as the foremost English playwright. He had managed his affairs well and was materially as well as artistically a successful man. His plays appeared less frequently and declined in quality. *Back to Methuselah* (1921) is really a sequence of five plays beginning in Genesis and ending in the forty-second century A.D. in a static, passionless world in which man, through knowledge, has almost escaped from the web of life. *Saint Joan* (1923) is an attempt to capture some of the sublimity of tragedy entirely beyond the scope of Shaw's purely comic genius, and insofar is a failure. The play becomes a treatise on toleration that obscures the human significance of the heroine. *The Apple Cart* (1929) is amusing but a trifle, and padded. His later plays have added nothing to his reputation.

If Shaw was for a long time resented and often misunderstood, it was largely his own doing. A witty Irish provincial without the cachet of an English public school—an outsider, in short—trying to break into the London literary world, he realized that to succeed he must advertise himself by eccentricity. His virgin red beard, his Jaeger clothing, his alpinstock, and such paraphernalia were all part of a calculated campaign to impress the public. So was much of his intellectual arrogance.

"For ten years past," he wrote in the *Saturday Review* in 1898, "with an unprecedented pertinacity and obstination, I have been dinning into the public head that I am an extraordinary witty, brilliant and clever man. That is now part of the public opinion of England . . ."

In all his long life he was never able to resist the Irishman's impulse to muddle and befool the Saxon, and the public was not greatly to blame if often it was not able to separate the superlative buffoon from the artist. But the artist beneath the baffling, irritating antics of the buffoon was of such consistent principle and purpose from the start that what was written of him forty-odd years ago may stand today without the alteration of a word.

Saved by his mother's energy and intelligence from the consequences of his father's fecklessness and kept under her influence until he was past forty, Shaw developed an abhorrence of wasteful, stupid, and sensual ways. He was ascetic, sexually prudish, a teetotaler, a nonsmoker, a vegetarian. Though he was never confirmed in any religion and came to recognize God only as a Life Force, his outlook has always been uncompromisingly puritan. In his eyes the contemporary world had fallen into a quagmire of false idealisms that made it incapable of managing its own affairs or even of seeing them realistically. Socialism seemed to him the only rational way for modern man and he became one of the earliest members of the Fabian Society. Throughout his career he was a revolutionist, a consistent propagandist for his own highly individual interpretation of Fabian principles.

Shaw's first two plays were direct attacks upon specific social evils; thereafter he gradually developed the idea of a realistically ordered society emancipated from the stupidity of idealism. But here he encountered the problem of all social planners, that of adequate direction. Who is to bring about the regeneration? The Webbs looked practically to a carefully selected and trained civil service; Wells revived the Platonic ideal of a dedicated aristocracy. Shaw was not a democrat; he never believed in the power of the mass of men to raise or guide themselves. He exalted the born leader, subtly intelligent, clear-sighted, self-confident, strong of will and completely free of prejudice. He has dressed this character in every sort of costume and shown him in every variety of situation; he is that "master of reality" through whose eyes Shaw looks at humanity, "the slaves of reality." Here as Chesterton pointed out (*Heretics,* 1905) is the fatal defect in Shaw's thought. The leader who is to free us from ideals is himself an ideal and an inhuman one that can furnish no solution to purely human problems. The most effective part of Shaw's work is iconoclastic; he swept up a lot of rubbish and knocked down a lot of idols, and it is good fun, but his Superman can build no new world. In *Back to Methuselah* the empty life of the Ancients, drained of all humanity and passion, is a virtual admission of defeat.

Like the morality plays, of which they continue the tradition, like the poetry of Browning, like the novels of Wells and Huxley—like all literature having the discussion of ideas for its purpose—the plays of Shaw tend toward dialogue and ultimately monologue. Action becomes merely accessory, to be imposed upon the dialogue by clever device or its absence covered by local color and the wit of the lines. To this the conventional playgoer finds it hard to adapt himself; he wants to "cut the cackle and come to the 'osses," but with Shaw the cackle is the 'osses and he has not the humorist's resources for involving it in significant action. For a humorist, however he may ridicule humanity, fundamentally accepts it and finds significance in whatever men do: to Shaw the humanity of human nature is too often an offense, and his moral situation becomes a monotonous opposition between Intelligence, represented by his brilliant spokesman, and stupidity variously manifested in most of the other characters. It is the greatest evidence of Shaw's power that with this serious limitation he has achieved so many characters that transcend their puppet origins and are memorable as created persons.

Like Dryden, Shaw has found the play form too narrow for the full expression of his thought and has overflowed into copious prefaces and appendices. They are the principal continuation of his critical work through his dramatic period and survey, not always accurately, a wide field of politics, sociology, and criticism. Other by-products of the time include such various books as *Socialism and Superior Brains* (1910), *Common Sense About the War* (1914), *The Intelligent Woman's Guide to Socialism and Capitalism* (1928), *Adventures of a Black Girl in Search of God* (1932), and *William Morris as I Knew Him* (1936). His musical criticisms and other fugitive writings have been collected, and a collected edition of his works appeared 1931-1934.

Shaw's later life was, except for public outcry at his provocative utterances, uneventful. He always maintained his eccentric pose, largely as a barrier to keep the public at a distance. He avoided the honors usually given to literary men, accepting only the Nobel Prize for literature in 1925. He generally resisted the popularization of his works. *Arms and the Man* was adapted as a musical comedy in 1911 as *The Chocolate Soldier*, but it was not until 1938 that he permitted any of his plays to be filmed. Since then *Pyg-*

malion, Major Barbara, and *Caesar and Cleopatra* have all
had marked success on the screen.

Shaw deliberately made himself hard to sum up partly
by allowing his mind at times to follow tracks only tangent
to his main line of thought, partly, like an Irishman, by
saying a lot of things that he only half meant. It may take
some time to distill the quintessence of Shavianism but it
is pretty clear that he was the best English dramatist since
the Restoration.

COLLECTED WORKS: Ayot St. Lawrence Edition (1930). NOVELS:
Cashel Byron's Profession (1886), *An Unsocial Socialist* (1887),
Love Among the Artists (Chicago, 1900), *The Irrational Knot*
(1905), *Immaturity* (1930). PLAYS: *Widowers' Houses* (1893), *Plays
Pleasant and Unpleasant* [*Widowers' Houses, The Philanderer,
Mrs. Warren's Profession, Arms and the Man, Candida, The Man
of Destiny, You Never Can Tell*] (1898), *Three Plays For Puritans*
[*The Devil's Disciple, Caesar and Cleopatra, Captain Brass-
bound's Conversion*] (1901), *Man and Superman* (1903), *John
Bull's Other Island, and Major Barbara; also How He Lied to
Her Husband* (1907), *Press Cuttings* (1909), *The Doctor's Di-
lemma, Getting Married, and The Showing Up of Blanco Posnet*
(1909), *Misalliance, The Dark Lady of the Sonnets, and Fanny's
First Play* (1914), *Androcles and the Lion, Overruled, Pygmalion*
(1916), *Heartbreak House, Great Catherine, and Playlets of the
War* (1919), *Back to Methusalah* (1921), *St. Joan* (1924), *Trans-
lations and Tomfooleries* (1926), *The Apple Cart* (1930), *The
Complete Plays of Bernard Shaw* (1931), *Too True to Be Good,
Village Wooing, and On The Rocks* (1934), *The Simpleton, The
Six, and The Millionairess* (1936), *Cymbeline Refinished* (1937),
Geneva (1938), *In Good King Charles's Golden Days* (1939).
MISCELLANEOUS: *The Quintessence of Ibsenism* (1891), *The Per-
fect Wagnerite* (1898), *The Author's Apology From Mrs. Warren's
Profession* (1905), *Dramatic Opinions and Essays* (1906), *The
Sanity of Art* (1908), *The Dying Tongue of Great Elizabeth*
(1920), *The Intelligent Woman's Guide to Socialism and Capital-
ism* (1928), *The Adventures of a Black Girl in Her Search For
God* (1932), *Major Critical Essays* (1932), *Pen Portraits and Reviews* (1932), *Our Theatres in the Nineties* (1932), *Music in London, 1890-94* (1932), *Prefaces* (1934), *London Music, 1888-89*

(1937), *Sixteen Self Sketches* (1949). Letters: *Letters from George Bernard Shaw to Miss Alma Murray* (1927), *Ellen Terry and Bernard Shaw: A Correspondence* (1931), *Some Unpublished Letters of George Bernard Shaw* (1939).

C. L. and V. M. Broad, *A Dictionary to the Plays and Novels of Bernard Shaw* (1929); Geoffrey H. Wells, "A Bibliography of the Books and Pamphlets of George Bernard Shaw," *Suppl. Bookman's Jour.*, XII (1925), 1-16, March, 17-24, April; Archibald Henderson, *George Bernard Shaw: His Life and Works* (1911), *Table Talk of G. B. S.* (1925), "The Real Bernard Shaw," *Virginia Quar. Rev.*, 111 (1927), 177-189, *Is Bernard Shaw a Dramatist?* (1929), *Bernard Shaw, Playboy and Prophet* (1932); Holbrook Jackson, *Bernard Shaw* (1907); G. K. Chesterton, *George Bernard Shaw* (1909), "George Bernard Shaw," *Fortnightly Rev.*, CXXXVI (1931), 150-159; Hesketh Pearson, *G. B. S.: A Full Length Portrait* (1942); Frank Harris, *Bernard Shaw* (1931); Edward Shanks, *Bernard Shaw* (1924); Richard Burton, *Bernard Shaw: The Man and the Mask* (1916); J. S. Collis, *Shaw* (1925); W. D. Dunkel, "George Bernard Shaw," *Sat. Rev. Lit.* (1942), 255-262; André Maurois, "Shaw," *Poets and Prophets* (1935); Edmund Wilson, "Bernard Shaw at Eighty," *Atlantic Monthly*, CXLI (1938), 198-215; Jaques Barzun, "Bernard Shaw in Twilight," *Kenyon Rev.*, V (1943), 321-345; S. Winston (Ed.), *G. B. S. 90;* Charles McM. Shaw, *Bernard's Brethren* (1939); R. H. Sherard, *Bernard Shaw, Frank Harris, and Oscar Wilde* (1937); Ellen Terry, *Ellen Terry and Bernard Shaw: A Correspondence* (1931); Joseph McCabe, *George Bernard Shaw: A Critical Study* (1914); R. P. Howe, *Bernard Shaw: A Critical Study* (1915); E. C. Wagenknecht, *A Guide to Bernard Shaw* (1929); Henry A. Jones, "Bernard Shaw as a Thinker," *English Rev.*, XXXVI (1923), 532-536, XXXVII (1923), 65-74, 227-231, 644-648, XXXVIII (1924), 345-350; T. D. O'Bolger, *George Bernard Shaw's Philosophy* (Phila., 1913); Helen Richter, "Die Quintessenz des Shawismus," *Englische Studien*, 46 (1913), 367-469; Eric Bentley, "Bernard Shaw's Politics," *Kenyon Rev.*, VII (1946), 347-371; Sen Gupta, *The Art of Bernard Shaw* (1936); Winfield Smith, "Bernard Shaw and His Critics (1892-1938)," *Poet Lore*, XLVII (1941), 76-83; Martin Ellehauge, *The Position of Bernard Shaw in European Drama* (Copenhagen, 1931); Wilhelm Rebach, *George Bernard Shaw als Dramatiker* (Leipzig, 1915); E. R. Bentley, "The Theory and Practice of Shavian Drama," *Accent*, V (1944), 5-18; A. J. Ropes,

"History as Shaw is Wrote," *Critical Rev.*, CXXVII (1925), 341-350; J. Van Kan, "Shaw's Saint Joan From an Historical Point of View," *Fortnightly Rev.*, CXXIV (1925), 36-46; Stephen Winsten, *Days With Bernard Shaw* (1949); A. C. Ward, *Bernard Shaw* (1950).

A master of the stage in all its aspects, **Harley Granville-Barker (1877-1946)** was best known as a producer, but at least four substantial plays assure him a good position among the serious dramatists of the Edwardian years. He was born in London and from the time he entered a dramatic school at thirteen was dedicated to the theater. From 1891 to 1910 he acted, appearing in the leading roles of several of Shaw's plays as well as in Shakespearean repertory. At the same time he was associated with the Stage Society, from 1900, and, from 1905, with J. E. Vedrenne in the management of the Court Theatre, which produced many of the plays of Shaw, Galsworthy, and Masefield. He made noteworthy experiments in producing Gilbert Murray's translations from the Greek dramatists, and Hardy's *The Dynasts.*

Granville-Barker's own first play *The Weather Hen* (1899), written in collaboration with Herbert Thomas, was not remarkable but within the next ten years he had written the four plays, *The Marrying of Ann Leete* (1901), *The Voysey Inheritance* (1905), *Waste* (1907), and *The Madras House* (1910), on which his reputation rests. Though his close association with Shaw is evident in some of his ideas, the plays are closer to the manner of Galsworthy. They deal seriously with social problems which the author presents but does not solve. They are notable for skill of construction, sympathetic treatment of character, and sensitive rather than brilliant dialogue. Not immediately impressive they are sound pieces of dramatic work that wear well.

After his retirement from active production in 1914 Granville-Barker wrote occasional plays until 1928, but these were lighter works that added nothing to his reputation. His serious later work is to be found in his books on the drama and in translations, done in collaboration with his wife, from foreign dramatists. He has received several academic distinctions and for some years before the Second World War was Director of the British Institute of the University of Paris. He was twice married, his first wife being Lillah McCarthy, the leading actress in many of his productions, his second Helen Manchester Gates.

PLAYS: *Prunella,* with Laurence Housman (1911), *Three Plays* [*The Marrying of Ann Leete, The Voysey Inheritance, Waste*] (1909), *The Madras House* (1910), *Three Short Plays* [*Rococo, Vote By Ballot, Farewell to the Theatre*] (1917), *The Harliquinade,* with D. C. Calthrop (1918), *The Secret Life* (1923), *His Majesty* (1928). CRITICISM: *The Exemplary Theatre* (1922), *From Henry V to Hamlet* (1925), *Prefaces to Shakespeare* (1927-29), *A National Theatre* (1930), *On Dramatic Method* (1931), *Associating With Shakespeare* (1932), *The Study of Drama* (1934), *On Poetry in Drama* (1937), *Quality* (1938), *The Use of the Drama* (Princeton, 1945).

Dixon Scott, "Mr. Granville-Barker and An Alibi," in *Men of Letters* (1916).

Laurence Housman (1865-   ), younger brother of the poet A. E. Housman, differs from the author of *A Shropshire Lad* in both personality and achievement. A. E. Housman was in no way disparaging his brother's talents but rather expressing the essential contrasts in their natures when he said, "Knowing my brother Laurence is no introduction to me." Whereas the elder Housman's poetry is contained in three small volumes, Laurence Housman has been prolific and versatile; and whereas the elder was a perfectionist in form, the younger, although by no means a slipshod craftsman, has not shown stylistic excellence consistently. He has written poetry, novels, short stories, essays, children's books, and almost forty plays, some of which, however, do not run to more than one act. He was born at Bromsgrove, Warwickshire, in 1865, educated at the local schools, and instead of going to Oxford as did his older brother, he went to London to study art, for which he showed considerable talent. He studied at the Lambeth School and at the National Art College. Much of his illustrating done in this period shows a marked Pre-Raphaelite quality. Before the turn of the century, however, he had discovered his talent in a different *métier,* and with *An Englishwoman's Love Letters,* published anonymously in 1900, he was assured by the wide circulation of the novel that his talent was recognized. Although he has written much since this work appeared, he is often still identified with the *Love Letters.* His early poetry shows something of the Pre-Raphaelite influence and something of the Decadents; and in curious contrast to his ornamented verse and plays, there were novels in which political satire plays an important part, and essays on social problems. His concern with woman's place and rights is reflected in his essays "Articles of Faith in the Freedom of Women" (1910), "The Immoral Effects of Ignorance in Sex Relations," (1911), and "The Moving Spirit in Womanhood" (1914). His work in the drama has varied in theme and quality. The dramatic cycle of plays about St. Francis of Assisi, *The Comments of Juniper* (1926) and *Little Plays of St. Francis* (1931), are tasteful pieces which are possibly more effective when read than when produced. The one-time popular *Victoria Regina: A Dramatic Biography* (1934) shows Housman's skill and limitation as a playwright. It is better integrated than the stage adaptation which Walter Pritchard Eaton made from Lytton Strachey's *Queen Victoria,* although there is nothing memorable about the lines. Housman's talents suffer somewhat from diffuseness, but he is generally competent in craftsmanship and winning in his approach to his varied subjects.

VERSE: *Green Arras* (1896), *Rue* (1899), *Mendicant Rhymes* (1906), *Selected Poems* (1908), *The Heart of Peace and Other Poems* (1918), *The Love Concealed* (1928). NOVELS: *Gods and Their Makers* (1897), *An Englishwoman's Love Letters* (1900), *Sabrina Warham* (1904), *The Sheepfold* (1918), *Trimblerigg: A Book of Revelation* (1924). PLAYS: *The Comments of Juniper: Six plays from the Life and Legend of St. Francis of Assisi* (1926), *Little Plays of St. Francis*, 2nd Series (1931), *Victoria and Albert*, Palace Plays, 3rd Series (1933), *Victoria Regina: A Dramatic Biography* (1934).

Anna Rudolf, *Die Dichtung von Laurence Housman* (Berlin, 1930), with bibliography; Edmund Blunden, *Votive Tablets: Studies Chiefly Appreciative of English Authors and Books* (1932), 91-98; and for comments concerning the once widely circulated *An Englishwoman's Love Letters*, see Arthur Eliot, *Blighted Billet-doux* (1902).

SOME MINOR DRAMATISTS

Of the "Midland dramatists" developed by the Manchester Repertory Theatre, **Stanley Houghton (1881-1913)** was the most promising. The son of a Manchester textile merchant, he entered his father's business at the age of sixteen. For recreation he joined an amateur dramatic society, for which he acted and wrote light plays for several years. Later he turned to dramatic criticism. His first play to be professionally produced was *The Dear Departed* (1908). Three other good plays followed and then *Hindle Wakes* (1912), the sensation of its season in London. Tragically Houghton died within a year of his success of an infection caught while travelling abroad.

Allan Monkhouse (1858-1936) born in Durham, wrote his plays during the thirty years (1902-32) when he was dramatic critic for *The Manchester Guardian*. His situations are either tragic or ironic and his treatment the starkness and downrightness traditionally attributed to the north countryman. They are, with one or two exceptions, the sort of plays more likely to be respected by critics than acclaimed by audiences.

Harold Brighouse (1882-   ) was also a member of the *Guardian* staff but made his theatrical debut in Glasgow with *Dealing in Futures* (1909). For more than thirty years he was a prolific writer and having a more popular style than Monkhouse enjoyed a wider audience. Like Houghton he had been in the cotton trade before turning to journalism and knew industrial Lancashire thoroughly, though he often went outside it for the backgrounds and characters of his plays.

The Manchester dramatists did for the industrial Midlands on the stage much what Arnold Bennett did for them in the novel. The robust, colorful Lancashire character, the racy dialect, and the conflicts of industrial life offered a rich field of regional material of which they made the most. Though the Manchester theater never had the brilliance of the Abbey, its men produced a very substantial body of excellent work.

S. HOUGHTON. COLLECTED WORKS: *The Works of Stanley Houghton* (1914). PLAYS: *The Dear Departed* (1910), *The Younger Generation* (1910), *Independent Means* (1911), *Hindle Wakes* (1912), *Five One Act Plays* [*The Dear Departed, Fancy Free, The Master of the House, Phipps, The Fifth Commandment*], *A Tartar Caught* (c. 1937).

A. J. Ellis, "Stanley Houghton: The Man and His Work," *English Rev.*, XVI (1914), 274-277; Edward Storer, "Dramatists of Today: Stanley Houghton," *Living Age*, CCLXXX (1914), 413-417.

A. MONKHOUSE. PLAYS: *Mary Broome* (1912), *The Education of Mr. Surrage* (1913), *Four Tragedies* [*Resentment, Reaping the Whirlwind, The Hayling Family, The Stricklands*] (1913), *War Plays* [*Shamed Life, Night Watches, The Choice*] (1916), *The Conquering Hero* (1916), *First Blood* (1924), *The Grand Cham's Diamond* (1924), *Sons and Fathers* (1925), *O Death Where Is Thy*

Sting? (1926), *The King of Barvender* (1928), *The Rag* (1928), *Nothing Like Leather* (1930), *Paul Felice* (1930), *Cecelia* (1932). NOVELS: *A Deliverance* (1898), *Love in a Life* (1903), *Dying Fires* (1912), *Men and Ghosts* (1918), *True Love* (1919), *My Daughter Helen* (1922), *Marmaduke* (1924), *Suburb* (1925), *Alfred the Great* (1927), *Farewell Manchester* (1931). MISCELLANEOUS: *Books and Plays* (1894), "The Words and the Play," *Essays and Studies,* XI (1925), 32-48.

H. BRIGHOUSE. PLAYS: *The Oak Settle* (1911), *The Price of Coal* (1911), *The Odd Man Out* (1912), *Spring in Bloomsbury* (1912), *Dealing in Futures* (1913), *Graft* (1913), *Garside's Career* (1914), *Lonesome-like* (1914), *Hobson's Choice* (1916), *Maid of France* (1917), *Converts* (1920), *Followers* (1922), *The Happy Hangman* (1922), *Once a Hero* (1922), *The Apple Tree* (1923), *"The Bantam V. C."* (1925), *Mary's John* (1925), *Little Red Shoes* (1925), *Open Air Plays* (1926), *The Little Liberty* (1927), *What's Bred in the Bone* (1927), *When Did They Meet Again?* (1927), *Behind the Throne* (1929), *Coincidence* (1929), *The Stoker* (1929), *The Sort-of-a-Prince* (1929), *Safe Among the Pigs* (1930), *Six Fantasies* (1931), *A Bit of War* (1933), *Smoke Screens* (1932), *Back to Adam* (1935), *Passport to Romance* (1937), *The Funk Hole* (1938), *British Passport* (1939), *Air-raid Refugees* (1939), *The Man Who Ignored the War* (1940), *London Front* (1941), *The Golden Ray* (1941).

Alan Alexander Milne (1882-   ) was born at Henley House, Kilburn, London, a private school of which his father was headmaster and where for a while H. G. Wells —"too clever and too impatient"—taught science. After learning his rudiments at home, he went to Westminster School and thence to King's College, Cambridge, where he achieved his one ambition, to edit the undergraduate magazine *The Granta.* His work attracted the attention of Rudolph Lehmann of the staff of *Punch,* who encouraged him to try his hand at humorous journalism. When Milne graduated in 1903 his father wanted him to become a civil servant or a schoolmaster, but he had chosen his career and decided to live on his capital of £320 until he could establish himself as a journalist. He succeeded, and in 1906 became assistant editor of *Punch*.

For the next nine years Milne was known chiefly as a humorous essayist; his first volume of collected pieces, *The Day's Play* appearing in 1910. He made a great many literary friends, of whom Barrie and E. V. Lucas were the closest. In 1913 he married Dorothy de Selincourt and settled in Chelsea. Some time later he sent a one-act play to Barrie for criticism. Barrie in turn sent it to Granville-Barker who accepted it and urged Milne to write a full-length play at once.

Then, in spite of pacifist convictions, Milne joined up and was commissioned in the 4th Battalion, Royal Warwickshire Regiment. His first play, *Wurzel-Flummery*, was written in training camp, revised after he was invalided home from France, and produced in April, 1917. Before his discharge he wrote three more plays, of which the last, *Belinda*, appeared in April, 1918.

On leaving the service Milne did not return to *Punch*. He had not only become a dramatist; he was for the moment the only new dramatist of any promise. He gave his whole time to his plays and to dramatic criticism for *The Outlook*. The opening of *Mr. Pim Passes By* on January 4, 1920 with Irene Vanbrugh in the leading role marked his arrival at unquestioned success. His *First Plays* had already been published, as well as a detective story, *The Red House Mystery* (1922). For the next ten years his plays appeared rapidly, the best being *The Dover Road* (1923), *The Truth About Blayds* (1923), and *The Fourth Wall* (in America *The Perfect Alibi*) (1928). As the twenties drew to a close, however, Milne's plays began to seem rather old-fashioned beside those of Noel Coward, and with *Michael and Mary* (1930) he virtually ended his work as a dramatist.

Milne's most characteristic work is based on some absurd or whimsical situation, such as a man's inheriting a fortune if he will change his name to Wurzel-Flummery, or the discovery that a great and revered poet has been a wretched fraud. His treatment is delicately humorous and sometimes sentimental—rather in the school of Barrie. The result is a comedy that can be seen or read with complete enjoyment, but that leaves no very strong impression. *The Perfect Alibi* is a tour-de-force of detective drama in which a murder is committed under the eyes of the audience in the first act, yet the suspense of detection is maintained throughout the play.

Milne may be remembered less for his plays than for his books for children, first written for his son Christopher Robin. The verses of *When We Were Very Young* and *Now We Are Six* and the nursery animal adventures of the "Pooh" stories belong to the small group of juvenile books that show a real understanding of the child's imagination. They have won the affection of the adults who read them as much as of the children to whom they are read.

In his essays Milne shows the sort of quiet humor and light touch made popular by E. V. Lucas but with a keener sense of fun and an occasional ironic turn that gives him distinction. A few are serious, notably his pacifist "pamphlet"—to use his own term—*Peace With Honor* (1934). Like many English pacifists he modified his views on the outbreak of the Second World War.

AUTOBIOGRAPHY: *It's Too Late Now* [*Autobiography*] (1939). PLAYS: *First Plays* [*Wurzel-Flummery, The Lucky One, The Boy Comes Home, Belinda, The Red Feathers*] (1919), *The Romantic Age* (1920), *Second Plays* [*Make Believe, Mr. Pim Passes By, The Camberley Triangle, The Stepmother*] (1921), *Three Plays* [*The Dover Road, The Truth About Blayds, The Great Broxopp*] (1922), *The Artist,* a duologue (1923), *The Man in the Bowler Hat* (1923), *Four Plays* [*To Have the Honor, Ariadne, Portrait of a Gentleman in Slippers, Success*] (1926), *The Ivory Door* (1928), *The Fourth Wall* (1929), *Toad of Toad Hall* (1930), *Michael and Mary* (1930), *Plays* (2 v. 1930-31), *Other People's*

Lives (1935), *Miss Elizabeth Bennett* (1936), *Sarah Simple* (1939). CHILDREN'S BOOKS: *When We Were Very Young* (1924), *A Gallery of Children* (1925), *Winnie-the-Pooh* (1926), *Now We Are Six* (1927), *The House at Pooh Corner* (1928).

As author, composer, producer, and actor, **Noel Coward** (1899-) has acquired a more intimate knowledge of the theater than any other modern English playwright. He was born at Teddington, but spent most of an unsettled childhood in London where he attended the Chapel Royal School. His father, an unsuccessful piano salesman who gave up his struggle with the world rather easily, left the support of the family largely to his wife, who took boarders and encouraged her little son's talent for music and dancing. At the age of nine he obtained a small part in a children's play and so determined his career. The rest of his life he spent in the theater, scrambling his education into the intervals between engagements. When the horizons of most youngsters are bounded by home and school his precocious intelligence was being matured by the hard discipline and easy comradeship of the stage. Rehearsal rooms, trains, and boarding houses were efficient teachers. He outgrew children's roles, appeared in musicals, legitimate dramas, and, as a super, in films. By 1916 he was a promising young actor with an adequate social experience.

Coward's war service in 1918 was brief but trying, much of it being spent in hospitals as the result of an injury while in training. As soon as he was discharged he returned to the stage, but a widening acquaintance among literary people confirmed a growing desire to write, and he sold enough of the magazine stories he now turned out to keep him going while he learned the craftsmanship of playwriting. In 1920 *I'll Leave It to You,* written to order for Gilbert Miller, after opening in Manchester, played for five weeks in London. It was not a success but it was encourage-

ment. In 1923 after a rather disappointing five months in
New York, he took the leading part in his own play *The
Young Idea,* inspired by Shaw's *You Never Can Tell,* which
had a slightly longer run. His first real success, at the age
of twenty-five, was *The Vortex,* which opened in November, 1924. Within the year he had three plays running simul-
taneously: *The Vortex, Fallen Angels,* and the Charlot revue
London Calling, of which he had done the greater part.
An equal triumph in New York followed and the first collection of his work, *Three Plays,* was published. *The Queen
Was in the Parlour* and *The Rat Trap,* his first serious play,
written when he was eighteen, confirmed his reputation as
an astonishingly brilliant young playwright. His next play,
Sirocco (1928), was a ghastly failure, being violently hissed
and booed from the stage on the first night. He recovered
public favor and his self-confidence with the musical comedy *Bitter Sweet* and *This Year of Grace,* the first of his
big revues for the producer Charles Cochran. While they
were running he took a long trip to the Orient, during which
he wrote *Private Lives* and his war play *Post Mortem.*

The production of *Private Lives* after his return was followed by *Cavalcade,* a chronicle of thirty years of England
and an English family conceived with all the elaborate
staging of the old Hippodrome spectacles. Its recapture of
well-remembered scenes, such as the embarkation of troops
for South Africa and Queen Victoria's funeral, was received
with the greatest enthusiasm. Coming as it did at the blackest time of the depression, it carried precisely the emotional
stimulus the public wanted and it succeeded beyond anything of its kind. Since *Cavalcade* Coward's career has been
evenly successful: he has had no more spectacular triumphs
and nothing nearer to disaster than the partial failure of
Point Valaine (1935). *Design For Living* (1933) enhanced
his reputation for comedy and *Blithe Spirit* (1941) sustained
it: the musical comedies *Operette* and *Conversation Piece*

have been not so appealing as *Bitter Sweet*. The one-act plays collected in *To-night at 8:30* (1936) show his wit in its most engaging light.

Coward's versatility has not been approached in the modern theater. His forte is Restoration comedy in a modern manner, but he has also showed dramatic power in *The Vortex* and parts of *Cavalcade,* and a mastery of nostalgic sentiment in *Bitter Sweet.* He did not abandon the stage when he became an author, but showed by his performance in his own plays that he would have made a first rate reputation as a comic actor if he had never written a line. As a light theatrical composer he has done more than creditably: *I'll See You Again, A Room With A View,* and *Mad Dogs and Englishmen* are among the classics of their kind.

The largest element in his success has been his emotional understanding of his own generation, that which passed its adolescence before the First World War. He has caught its detestation of convention, its uninhibited love of the ridiculous, its wise-cracking sophistication, and its concealed but devastating sentimentality. He can manage these as he pleases to create the very form and pressure of the time, but for that very reason his characters are fatally limited. They are the people of their age seen with pitiless clarity, but few of them could be imagined as existing outside it. Coward's genius is as unmistakable as Oscar Wilde's, but like Wilde's, it is a genius exhausting the spirit of its time and exhausted by it. One feels that his plays may have the same ephemeral history as *Lady Windermere's Fan* and amuse another generation only as period revivals. In any case he is the only genius the English theater has produced since the First War.

AUTOBIOGRAPHY: *Present Indicative* (1937). PLAYS: *"I'll Leave It to You"* (1920), *The Rat Trap* (1924), *The Young Idea* (1924), *Fallen Angels* (1925), *Hay Fever* (1925), *The Vortex* (1925), *Easy Virtue* (1926), *The Queen Was in the Parlour* (1926), *"This Was a Man"* (1926), *The Marquise* (1927), *Home Chat* (1927), *Sirocco* (1927), *Bitter Sweet* (1929), *Private Lives* (1930), *Post Mortem* (1931), *Collected Sketches and Lyrics* (1931), *Cavalcade* (1932), *Design for Living* (1933), *Conversation Piece* (1934), *Point Valaine* (1935), *To-Night at 8:30* [*We Were Dancing, The Astonished Heart, "Red Peppers," Hands Across the Sea, Fumed Oak, Shadow Play, Ways and Means, Still Life, Family Album*] (1936), *Operette* (1938), *Blithe Spirit* (1942), *Present Laughter* (1943), *This Happy Breed* (1943), *Peace in Our Time* (1947).

Patrick Braybrooke, *The Amazing Mr. Noel Coward* (1933); Edgar M. Lustgarten, "Noel Coward," *Adelphi,* IV (1927), 488-492; Homer E. Woodbridge, "Noel Coward," *So. Atlantic Quar.,* XXXVIII (1938), 239-251; J. C. Furnas, "The Art of Noel Coward," *Fortnightly Rev.,* CXXXIX (1933), 709-716; A. G. Macdonell, "The Plays of Noel Coward," *Living Age,* CCCXLI (1932), 439-446.

One of the cleverest playwrights of the school of Wilde, **Frederic Lonsdale (1881-   )** was throughout the twenties Noel Coward's only serious rival for the favor of sophisticated audiences. Born in the Channel Islands, he went to sea in his youth as a merchant seaman and also served an enlistment in the South Lancashire Regiment.

His career as a dramatist began with *The Early Worm* in 1908 and by the end of the First World War he had enjoyed two popular successes, *The Balkan Princess* (1912) and *The Maid of the Mountains* (1916). The first of his comedies in a new vein was *Aren't We All?* (1923), after which for a decade others followed annually, bringing him by 1930 a somewhat too high reputation. These later plays are ingeniously plotted comedies of aristocratic life dealing lightly and wittily with social situations but carefully avoiding problems. They are never very serious, but sometimes, as in *The Last of Mrs. Cheney* (1925), achieve tenseness of action without melodrama. Their charm lies in the wit of the dialogue and their suave, sophisticated atmosphere.

In the thirties Lonsdale's popularity declined and an attempt to meet the changed taste of 1938, *Once Is Enough,* was not successful. He belonged to the "postwar I" theater for which he had exactly the appropriate gifts.

PLAYS: *The Early Worm* (1908), *The King of Cadonia* (1908), *The Best People* (1908), *The Balkan Princess* (1910), *Betty* (1915), *Maid of the Mountains* (1916), *Aren't We All?* (1924), *The Fake* (1924), *The Street Singer* (1924), *Spring Cleaning* (1925), *The Last of Mrs. Cheney* (1925), *On Approval* (1927), *The High Road* (1927), *Canaries Sometimes Sing* (1930), *Never Come Back* (1932), *Once Is Enough* (1938), Undated: *Lovers Courageous, The Lady of the Rose, Another Love Story, But for the Grace of God, Films, The Devil to Pay.*

OTHER PROSE
1890–1950

In Victorian hands the essay had become almost exclusively formal and didactic. Between Leigh Hunt and Stevenson only Thackeray and Alexander Smith kept alive the tradition of the familiar essay. But when in the eighties and nineties a lighter type of literary periodical began to supplant the ponderous reviews there was a brisk revival of the informal essay in all its varieties: familiar, satiric, apprecitive, and picturesque. The field of the essay then became once more, as it had been in the seventeenth century, a literary Everyman's Land which all might, and did invade at will. Thus the twentieth century, rich in general prose writers, has comparatively few essayists in the strict sense of that classification, and has seen a general relaxation of the formal distinctions of the various types of the essay.

Essay writing in the eighteen-nineties was marked by the estheticism and preciousness of style that permeated the entire "Decadence" and that were derived chiefly from Pater's *Renaissance*. The arts of pagan Greece or neopagan Italy interpreted with exquisite discernment inspired a great deal of work that was polished and charming but too fragile for survival. Above the general level of beautiful triviality rose Oscar Wilde's *Intentions* (1891), Maurice Hewlett's *Earthwork Out of Tuscany* (1895), the early essays of W. B. Yeats, and those of Lionel Johnson, collected in *Post Liminium* (1912). Above all rose Max Beerbohm, a young Oxonian brilliantly impudent in *The Yellow Book*, affecting to be *passé* in 1895, and delicately reminding the public at intervals for the next thirty years that he was the most accomplished familiar essayist of the twentieth century. His latest volume *Mainly on the Air* (1946) shows that in his radio talks before and during the Second World War there was no failure of the gifts that have delighted two generations.

Among works of less popular appeal than Beerbohm's but enjoyed by the bookish of two generations were the fastidious essays of Alice Meynell, often too precious in style, the delicate eighteenth-century studies of Austin Dobson, and the scholarly ironic judgments of Augustine Birrell.

Between 1900 and 1930 the regular appearance of certain essayists in weekly periodicals brought something like a renewal of the popularity the light journalistic essay had enjoyed in the eighteenth century. G. K. Chesterton in *The Illustrated London News,* E. V. Lucas and A. A. Milne in *Punch,* Robert Lynd in *The New Statesman,* and Edmund Gosse in *The Times Literary Supplement* were the most talented of a group, each of which had a regular following of readers. Their contributions, of varying degrees of popularity, the challenging paradoxes of Chesterton, the pleasant connoisseurship of Lucas, the literary causeries of Gosse— appealed to all sorts of tastes.

Chesterton and Hilaire Belloc were foremost among the Edwardian writers of general prose. A curious pair, the one sturdily English, the other as sturdily Gallic, they were united by their religious and political views. Between them they covered a wide range of biography, criticism, controversy, and familiar commentary with a trenchancy that won the public by its very defiance of public sentiment and prejudice. At the opposite pole was the moody, donnish sentimentalism of A. C. Benson's self-revelation which were much admired until the war shattered the gentle academic world in which he mused. By that time the more vigorous academic mind of Dean Inge had begun to impress the public with the outspoken criticism of modern life and society that was later to make him famous as "The Gloomy Dean."

Robert Cunninghame-Graham and W. H. Hudson were less popular but stood higher in critical estimation. The characters of both had been formed in the spacious pampas of the Argentine that stamped them forever aliens in modern commercial England. Cunninghame-Graham contemned with aristocratic scorn a world emptied of all graciousness; Hudson ignored it and went freely among unspoiled natural things.

H. M. Tomlinson published *The Sea and the Jungle* in 1912, but recognition of it as one of the great works of English travel was delayed for some years. Though nothing that he wrote afterward quite equalled it in quality, his vigorous thought and rich individual style have secured him the foremost place among the essayists of his generation. The reputation as stylists of the brothers John Cowper Powys and Llewellyn Powys, once high, has declined somewhat, and while Llewellyn's work especially is often excellent in both matter and art it does not approach the force and originality of Tomlinson's.

A great many notable essays, of course, were written throughout the period by authors better known in other fields. Among the novelists Galsworthy, Aldous Huxley, D. H. Lawrence, Virginia Woolf, E. M. Forster, and William McFee stand out; among the poets, Masefield and Edmund Blunden.

In the early twenties the writing of biography was revolutionized by the work of Lytton Strachey. In *Eminent Victorians* (1918) and *Queen Victoria* (1921) Strachey, abandoning the biographer's traditional reserve and reverence, gleefully played skittles with hallowed reputations. Often blemished by prejudice and caricature, his work was salutary and spectacularly effective in humanizing and popularizing biography. His influence can be seen in the work of Phillip Guedalla, Gamaliel Bradford, André Maurois, Emil Ludwig and others who have created a public appetite for biography second only to that for fiction. Charles Whibley, a master of the short biography, known for his contributions to the *Dictionary of National Biography* as well as for his general essays, is chiefly interesting as the last of the essayists to express uncompromising Toryism. Winston Churchill's *Marlborough* is a major biography in the traditional style.

In 1907 appeared an anonymous autobiography *Father and Son* that treated with admirable candor and restraint the spiritual struggle of its author's youth. When later it was honored by the French Academy it proved to be the work of Edmund Gosse. In its kind it has been equalled only by Joyce's *Portrait of the Artist as a Young Man*. These are, as literature, the best self-studies that the period has produced. In memoirs, war books aside, the best work has been done by Osbert Sitwell and Siegfried Sassoon.

Among the critics at the beginning of the century the romantic Arthur Symons stands out for his breadth of interest and reasoned esthetic consistency. He is best known for his treatments of the Romantic Movement in England and the Symbolist Movement in France. In scholarly criticism, Professor W. P. Ker of London University occupied a high place as an authority on mediaeval literature. Sir Edmund Gosse and Professor George Saintsbury were bookmen rather than critics, widely read scholarly gossips of literature valuable for their service in bringing authors to readers. Also a bookman and essayist, Holbrook Jackson showed himself a capable critic in his studies of Shaw and William Morris, as well as a bibliophile capable of communicating his enthusiasms in books and reading. On the whole, however, Edwardian criticism, aside from book reviewing, which was excellently done, was not remarkable.

The pure esthetic doctrine had proved inadequate, but no new principle had been defined or old one restored.

In the twenties there appeared a number of vigorous young critics stimulated rather than inspired by the American, T. S. Eliot. Of these John Middleton Murry and Herbert Read have attained the most widely recognized authority. Both are humanists with romantic leanings, Murry excelling in biographical interpretation, Read having, like Symons, a wide scope of artistic knowledge and sympathy. The distinguishing features of the newer criticism are a more sensitive social consciousness and an increasing use of the aid of psychology in critical analysis. It has brought little change in fundamental esthetic principles but rather a larger understanding of them that promotes the appreciation of new works of unorthodox form.

The rapid growth of interest in psychology during the years between the wars gave momentum to an increasing stream of full-length lives and biographical essays in which the authors were primarily concerned with the inner forces in man's nature which shape personality and achievement. The American Gamaliel Bradford went so far as to call his studies of personality "psychographs" in order to differentiate his essays from the factual records of events which had been the biographers' traditional approach. In such portrait studies as Bonamy Dobree's *Essays in Biography* (1925), F. L. Lucas's "Dorothy Osborne" in *Studies French and English* (1934), Virginia Woolf's "Miss Ormerod" in *The Common Reader* (1925), and Harold Nicholson's "Hindenburg" in *The Yale Review* (Summer, 1931), there are evidences of the psychological approach. Full-length biography was influenced as well, as for example in the several sustained studies of Byron by Peter Quennell. Although many biographers held to the traditional manner, including Winston Churchill in his substantial *Marlborough* (1933-38), the trend of the times was toward the manner of the fiction writers, a manner supported if not originated by Strachey in such passages as the death-bed scene in *Queen Victoria* (1921) and by the influence of the French André Maurois in *Ariel* (1923). The tendency to adopt the methods of the novelist became so prevalent that in 1934 Hugh Walpole expressed the hope that "there will not be too many biographies so gayly imaginative that there is nothing to differentiate them from fiction." Walpole's hope has in some measure been realized: the biographies which appeared in the late thirties and forties show something of a reaction. Although the two schools of biographical writing continue to flourish—the well documented traditional life and the fictionized narrative which often adopts a psycho-analytical approach, the best of the more recent biographies show a fusion of the two, with relatively few of the extremes which were prevalent in the mid-twenties.

Since 1930 there has been a general decline of essay-writing thoughout the English speaking world, as the temper of the time has discouraged the habit of leisurely cultivated reading that the essay requires. Though many of the older essayists have kept on writing, few new ones have appeared. The most spectacular of these is C. S. Lewis, an Oxford don known through his critical writings for some years before he became immensely popular during the Second World War as a Christian apologist. Cyril Connolly, editor of *Horizon*, who writes under the pseudonym of "Palinurus," and George Orwell attracted attention as essayists during the forties, but in general the scarcity of good new work in this field is discouraging. In the past the essay has often been most vigorously written immediately after great wars: the work of Addison and Steele followed the victories of Marlborough, that of Lamb, Hazlitt and Hunt followed Waterloo. There was an abundance of good essays after the First World War, but as yet there is no such prospect after the Second.

(Joseph) Hilaire (Pierre) Belloc (1870-   ) was born on the family estate near Fontainebleau. His father, Louis Swanton Belloc was an advocate. His mother, Bessie Parkes Belloc, was a young English woman of strong and independent character, a descendant of Joseph Priestly and a pioneer of women's rights. Belloc, though educated in England, was brought up a French citizen. He was schooled at the Oratory School, Edgbaston (near Birmingham), where he came under the influence of Newman. From the Oratory he went to Balliol, reading history and taking a First in his subject as well as winning the Brachenbrey Scholarship. In 1892 he interrupted his education to perform his obligatory service in the French army as a driver in the 3rd Battery, 6th Field Artillery. Belloc had a peculiar pride in the military history of France; four of his ancestors were generals in the armies of Napoleon, and though he had only the ordinary experiences of a recruit, his year of service made a lasting impression on him.

After leaving Oxford in 1895, Belloc made a trip to the United States, where he married Elodie Hogan of Napa Valley, California. They returned to England and have made their permanent home at King's Land, Sussex.

In 1903 Belloc became a British subject by naturalization, and from 1906 to 1910 represented South Salford in Parliament. Except for the part he played with Cecil Chesterton (G. K. C.'s brother) in exposing the "Marconi Scandal" in 1912 after he had left the House of Commons, his political career was undistinguished. Repudiating the major parties of his day as merely different groups of the same aristocratic political machine, Belloc developed a political theory based on the personal responsibility of monarchy coupled with democratic institutions. He bitterly hates the control of politics throughout the world by international financiers, and it is from this that his strong but not violent anti-Semitism arises.

Belloc's most ambitious writings are historical. After completing Lingard's unfinished History of England in 1915, he wrote his own in four volumes between 1925 and 1931. More generally read are his historical biographies. All of these develop the thesis that European culture is a single whole, essentially Latin and essentially Christian, derived from the Roman Empire and preserved by the Catholic Church. European destiny he finds in the lives of men such as Richelieu, Milton, James II, and Napoleon, who have affected the growth or decline of this culture. Though not esteemed for accuracy by some historians, these books are capably and vigorously written, and are good correctives to uncritical acceptance of conventional views.

With an historian's sense of time and a soldier's eye for terrain, Belloc is an admirable writer of books of travel and survey. Such books are often picturesque and trivial, but in Belloc's the description and personal adventure are mixed with a deep feeling for the earth and the tragedy and glory of the men who have lived on it. *The Path to Rome* is his best; *Towns of Destiny* and *Esto Perpetua* are good.

As an essayist he is in many of his moods too dogmatic to be pleasing, but when he can lose himself for a moment in his subject the result is absolutely first rate. The *Mowing of a Field* has become, deservedly, a minor classic and there are half a dozen others of comparable quality. The essays of *Hills and the Sea* are among the best in this century, and through a couple of dozen later volumes to *The Silence of the Sea,* his latest before the war, there is enough to keep a fastidious reader satisfied. The selection made from them by Father Dineen, while not perfect, will serve as a good introduction. There are, regrettably, few critical essays among them, for, though Belloc has generally refrained from literary criticism, in his *Milton* and elsewhere through his work there is evidence of great competence in this field.

In satire and verse he is far less successful. He is too

heavy-handed for the first, belaboring the obvious to weariness, and insufficiently subtle in his responses for the second. With a few exceptions—his *Tarentella* has made a delightful concert piece—his poems are high-keyed and rhetorical and are not in the ballad style that makes these faults forgivable. When unrestrained robustness is in order, as in his classic vituperation against the don, they cease to be faults at all, but Belloc seems never to have recognized his limitations in verse.

Belloc's sociopolitical works are not especially pertinent to this survey except *The Contrast,* which in its analysis of British and American institutions points to some significant differences generally neglected on both sides of the Atlantic.

In spite of his versatility and appeal to readers of many different interests Belloc has not been a widely popular author. He is opinionated and iterative, forcing his views upon the reader in and out of season. But if these irritating qualities are put in their proper place of unimportance, the reader will be impressed by a mind as tough and vigorous as any of our day and a style that is genuinely classical in its clarity. Belloc has variety and substance, and the strength that comes of controlled emotion. The excellence of his style is the firm Latin beauty of monumental carving.

HISTORY AND BIOGRAPHY: *Danton* (1899), *Robespierre* (1901), *The Eyewitness* (1908), *Marie Antoinette* (1909), *The French Revolution* (1911), *High Lights of the French Revolution* (1915), *The Last Days of the French Monarchy* (1916), *The House of Commons and Monarchy* (1920), *A Shorter History of England* (1924), *The Campaign of 1812 and the Retreat from Moscow* (1924), *Miniatures of French History* (1925), *A History of England,* 4 v. (1925-41), *Oliver Cromwell* (1927), *James the Second* (1928), *How the Reformation Happened* (1928), *Joan of Arc* (1929), *Richelieu* (1930), *Wolsey* (1930), *Cranmer* (1931), *Six British Battles* (1931), *Napoleon* (1932), *Charles the First, King of England* (1933), *William the Conqueror* (1933), *The Tactics and Strategy of the Great Duke of Marlborough* (1933), *Cromwell* (1934), *Milton* (1935),

The Battleground [*The Battleground; Syria and Palestine*] (1936), *Characters of the Reformation* (1936), *The Crusade* [*The Crusades*] (1937), *Monarchy: A Study of Louis XIV* [*Louis XIV*] (1938), *The Great Heresies* (1938), *The Last Rally: A Story of Charles II* [*Charles II: The Last Rally*] (1940), *Elizabethan Commentary* [*Elizabeth: Creature of Circumstance*] (1942). ESSAYS: *Hills and the Sea* (1906), *On Nothing* (1908), *On Something* (1910), *On Everything, On Anything* (1910), *First and Last* (1911), *This that and the Other* (1912), *At the Sign of the Lion* (1916), *On* (1923), *Short Talks With the Dead* (1926), *A Conversation With an Angel* (1928), *Survivals and New Arrivals* (1929), *Essays of a Catholic Layman in England* [*Essays of a Catholic*] (1931), *A Conversation With a Cat* (1931), *The Silence of the Sea* (1941). MISCELLANEOUS: *The Path to Rome* (1902), *Avril* (1904), *Esto Perpetua* (1906), *The Historic Thames* (1907), *The Pyrenees* (1909), *The River of London* (1912), *The Servile State* (1912), *Europe and the Faith* (1920), *The Contrast* (1923), *The Cruise of the Nona* (1925), *The Catholic Church and History* (1926), *An Essay on the Nature of Contemporary England* (1937), *On the Place of Gilbert Chesterton in English Letters* (1940), *The Catholic and the War* (1940). VERSES: *Verses and Sonnets* (1896), *Verses* (1910), *Sonnets and Verse* (1923).

Norah Nicholls, "The First Editions of Hilaire Belloc," *Bookman*, LXXXI (1931), 62, 126-127; C. C. Mandell and Edward Shanks, *Hilaire Belloc: The Man and His Work* (1916); Patrick Braybrooke, *Some Thoughts on Hilaire Belloc* (1924); Robert Hamilton, *Hilaire Belloc* (1948); Raymond Las Vergnas, "Une personalité anglo-française: Hilaire Belloc," *Revue des Deux Mondes*, VIIIe Per. 28 (1935), 401-422; Osbert Burdett, "Hilaire Belloc," *London Mercury*, XXX (1935), 133-142; Stanley B. James, "Hilaire Belloc—the Good European," *Catholic World*, CLI (1940), 288-293; Sister M. Madeleva, "Belloc as a Biographer," *Amer. Bookman*, LXII (1931), 607-612.

Gilbert Keith Chesterton (1874-1936) grew up in the unexciting comfort of a middle-class London home. Except for his perpetual arguments with his brother Cecil there was little that was stimulating in his environment. But much of his time was spent in a private world of the marvelous, full of the color and surprise that actuality failed to give him, and in this world he continued to move throughout his life.

After attending St. Paul's School he studied at the Slade School of Art and heard lectures at University College. At this time he began reviewing for the *Bookman* and soon found himself drawn from art, for which he had a lively but amateur talent, to letters.

During the nineties Chesterton established himself as a journalist, writing for the *Daily News,* the *Speaker,* the *Academy,* and the *Outlook.* His first verses and his first play were published in 1900, and his first volume of essays, *The Defendant,* appeared in 1901. In 1905 he began the weekly contributions to the *Illustrated London News* which continued until his death. By 1906 G. K. C. was well known as poet, essayist, and satirist. After 1909 he averaged three volumes a year.

In his art school days Chesterton became dissatisfied with the Victorian world and Universalist faith in which he had been raised. For a while, under the influence of William Morris, he thought socialism the way to a brighter and more hopeful order, but he was soon disappointed. He remained spiritually adrift until 1896 when he met Frances Blogg, an Anglo-Catholic, whose certainty of faith gave him the stability he sought. They were married in 1901, and after eight years in London, during which Chesterton with his operatic hat, cloak, and sword-stick became the most picturesque figure in Fleet Street, moved to Beaconsfield, where they made their home. Here Chesterton was able to take more carefully his spiritual soundings, but it was not until 1922 that he was received into the Roman Catholic Church. His wife followed him four years later.

Chesterton was deeply religious and aggressively controversial. He wrote to convince his reader that the right kind of belief about the spiritual foundations of life is necessary to sanity. But he was an artist rather than a reasoner, and his romantic revolt against the drabness of modern society and modern religion led him to confuse the significant with the marvelous and colorful. His thought is so involved with impulse that his best arguments, generally brilliant and stimulating, are only occasionally persuasive, seldom convincing. He has been called "too big for his books" and certainly on the platform—in his debates with Shaw, for instance—the force of his personality, his tremendous vitality and exuberant wit, often carried a point that would not bear scrutiny in print and even made the mannerisms of his style acceptable. Though his verse, with the exception of one or two fine things like *Lepanto,* is mediocre, it is for poetic quality, for single sentences of exquisite comprehension and splendid phrasing that one remembers his prose. He is therefore at his best in works of fantasy and appreciation. Stories such as *The Napoleon of Notting Hill* and *The Man Who Was Thursday* are inimitable in their kind; Father Brown has a secure place among the beloved detectives. It is through his appreciative studies of Cobbett, Blake, and Dickens that one should approach him. There the largeness of the man, who was magnanimous in the truest sense, gets thoroughly written into the book.

Politically, Chesterton was a "little Englander" and a staunch champion of the rights of the ordinary man. He advocated "distributism"—"breaking all the big businesses up into little businesses"—and a repudiation of the exclusive secularism that he felt was driving the modern world mad. But though he meant his politics quite seriously, there was in them, as in everything else in his life, an element of fun. He said, "I like the sound of breaking glass."

Like Dr. Johnson, Chesterton owes much of his influence to his being superlatively English. He belongs to the pre-Victorian England of *Pickwick Papers* and *Rural Rides.* In him one finds the robust humor, the eccentricity, the one-sidedness, the provincialism, the uncompromising regard for the rights of man that give its enduring power to the national character.

Autobiography (1936). FICTION: *The Napoleon of Notting Hill* (1904), *The Club of Queer Trades* (1905), *The Man Who Was Thursday* (1907), *The Ball and the Cross* (1909), *The Innocence of Father Brown* (1911), *Manalive* (1912), *The Flying Inn* (1914), *The Perishing of the Pendragons* (1914), *The Wisdom of Father Brown* (1914), *The Man Who Knew Too Much* (1922), *Tales of the Long Bow* (1925), *The Incredulity of Father Brown* (1926), *The Secret of Father Brown* (1927), *The Return of Don Quixote* (1927), *The Sword of Wood* (1928), *The Poet and the Lunatics* (1929), *The Moderate Murder and the Honest Quack* (1929), *Four Faultless Felons* (1930), *The Ecstatic Thief* (1930), *The Scandal of Father Brown* (1935), *The Paradoxes of Mr. Pond* (1937). ESSAYS: *The Defendant* (1901), *Heretics* (1905), *All Things Considered* (1908), *Orthodoxy* (1908), *Tremendous Trifles* (1909), *Alarms and Discussions* (1910), *What's Wrong With the World* (1910), *A Defence of Nonsense* (1911), *A Shilling For My Thoughts* (1916), *Utopia of Usurers* (1917), *The Uses of Diversity* (1920), *The Superstition of Divorce* (1920), *Eugenics and Other Evils* (1922), *Fancies vs. Fads* (1923), *The Superstitions of the Skeptic* (1925), *The Outline of Sanity* (1926), *Generally Speaking* (1928), *Come To Think of It* (1930), *All Is Grist* (1931), *All I Survey* (1933), *Avowals and Denials* (1934), *The Well and the Shallows* (1935), *As I Was Saying* (1936), *The Common Man* (1950). BIOGRAPHY AND CRITICISM: *Twelve Types* (1903), also published as *Varied Types; Robert Browning* (1903), *Charles Dickens: A Critical Study* (1906), republished as *Charles Dickens, the Last of the Great Men* (1932), *George Bernard Shaw* (1909), *William Blake* (1910), *Appreciations and Criticisms of the Works of Charles Dickens* (1911), *A Miscellany of Men* (1912), *The Victorian Age in Literature* (1912), *St. Francis of Assisi* (1923), *William Cobbett* (1925), *Robert Louis Stevenson* (1927), *Chaucer* (1932), *St. Thomas Aquinas* (1933). MISCELLANEOUS: *Irish Impressions* (1920), *The New Jerusalem* (1920), *What I Saw In America* (1922), *The Everlasting Man* (1925), *The Catholic Church and Conversion* (1926), *The Thing* (1929). VERSE: *Greybeards At Play* (1900), *The Wild Knight* (1900), *The Ballad of the White Horse* (1911), *The Ballad of St. Barbara* (1923), *The Queen of Seven Swords* (1926), *The Collected Poems of G. K. Chesterton* (1927).

PLAYS: *Magic* (1913), *The Judgment of Dr. Johnson* (1927), *The Turkey and the Turk: A Christmas Play* (1930).

"Bibliographies of Modern Authors, G. K. Chesterton," *London Mercury*, I (1920), 496-497; Maisie Ward, *Gilbert Keith Chesterton* (1943); Anon. (Cecil Chesterton) *Gilbert K. Chesterton: A Criticism* (1908); Ada E. Chesterton (Mrs. Cecil Chesterton), *The Chestertons* (1941); Hilaire Belloc, *On the Place of Gilbert K. Chesterton in English Letters* (1940); Maurice Evans, *G. K. Chesterton* (Cambridge, 1939); Patrick Braybrooke, *Gilbert Keith Chesterton* (1922), *The Wisdom of G. K. Chesterton* (1929); W. R. Titterton, *G. K. Chesterton: A Portrait* (1936); Julius West, *G. K. Chesterton: A Critical Study* (1916); André Maurois, "Chesterton," in *Poets and Prophets* (1935); Raymond Las Vergnas "G. K. Chesterton," *Revue des Deux Mondes*, VIIIe per., 23 (1934), 404-433; Monsignor J. O'Connor, *Father Brown on Chesterton* (1937); G. Fauvin, "L'oeuvre de G. K. Chesterton," *Revue de l'Enseignement des Langues Vivants*, LIV (1937), 289-301; W. F. R. Hardie, "The Philosophy of G. K. Chesterton," *Hibbert Jour.*, XXIX (1931), 449-464; Marshall McLuhan, "G. K. Chesterton: A Practical Mystic," *Dalhousie Review*, XV (1936), 455-464; H. J. Waring, "G.K.C.: Prince of Essayists," *Fortnightly Rev.*, CXLVIII (1937), 588-595; Hugh Kenner, *Paradox in Chesterton* (1947).

(Sir Henry) Maxwell Beerbohm (1872-   ) was the son of Sir Julius Beerbohm by his second wife Eliza (Draper) Beerbohm. He was educated at Charterhouse, which had counted Addison and Thackeray among its pupils, and at Merton College, Oxford. While still young he made a brilliant reputation as an essayist, which he sustained, adding to his achievements those of critic, satirist, and caricaturist. In 1910 he married Florence Kahn of Memphis, Tennessee, and for the next twenty-five years lived chiefly in Italy. He was knighted in 1939 and at the outbreak of the Second War returned to live in England. Beyond these facts biographers and critics seem to know very little about what Sir Henry very rightly considers his own business and none of the public's.

On the other hand the life of Max Beerbohm is patent to

everyone in a few delightful volumes of essays and caricatures and in the gossip of literary acquaintants. Max, still
an undergraduate, was discovered by Aubrey Beardsley and
enrolled among the contributors to the first volume of the
Yellow Book (April, 1894). The essays that he wrote during
the next two years placed him among the most brilliant
young men of the nineties. In 1896 seven of these were published in a volume entitled *The Works of Max Beerbohm.*
The concluding essay, *Dimmuendo,* pictures the author, an
outmoded relic of "the Beardsley period," about to retire to
a suburban villa. "And I, who crave no knighthood, shall
write no more." *More,* a collection of twenty essays, appeared
in 1899.

These two books show a precocious youth seeking in vain
the aesthetic world of Pater in an Oxford that was "a bit of
Manchester through which Apollo had once passed." He is
witty, sophisticated, pleasantly affected, but unlike nine-
tenths of the young men of the period capable of seeing
himself from without.

Through his half-brother, Sir Herbert Beerbohm-Tree,
Max had an excellent entrée to the theatrical world, and in
1898 he succeeded Bernard Shaw as dramatic critic of the
Saturday Review. For twelve years he wrote criticism very
different in manner from Shaw's but of equal quality. In
1930 these criticisms were published in two volumes entitled
Around Theatres.

Yet Again (1909) was Beerbohm's next volume of essays,
and with *And Even Now* (1920) and *A Variety of Things*
(1928), shows the maturity of his work in this form. These
essays are unmistakably the work of the same hand that
wrote *More* but the hand has begun upon its "second manner." There is the same fastidiousness, the same delicately
impish humor, but the range of interest and material is
much wider, the words are ballasted with experience, the
affectations judiciously curbed. They are no longer period

pieces but, with very few exceptions, those delicately humorous comments on the timeless minor comedy of life that is the familiar essayist's province. In all, the five volumes named contain about a hundred essays (how few compared to the output of men who have published a couple of volumes a year) and of the hundred there are very few that one would sacrifice. Of the rest more than half are masterpieces, never final—the familiar essay cannot be—but perfect within their limits. The limits are those of civilized men who live in cities with leisure enough to enjoy intellectual pleasures and the sense to draw much of their sustenance from the arts.

In addition to the essays Beerbohm is the author of four miscellaneous volumes of fantasy and satire. *The Happy Hypocrite: A Fairy Tale for Tired Men* (1896) and *Zuleika Dobson* (1911) are delightful fooling, the one dealing with high life of the Regency, the other with undergraduate life at Oxford. Both have been widely reprinted. *A Christmas Garland* (1912) is one of the cleverest works of parody in English. Its form imitates the "keepsake," the genteel Christmas annual with its contributions by "eminent hands." The hands here parodied include Hardy, Meredith, Kipling, Bennett, Gosse, and others, most of whom are so accurately hit off in matter and manner that passages from the specimens can hardly be told from originals. *Seven Men* (1919) consists of six character sketches, the seventh being the author himself, present in all of them. They range from *Enoch Soames,* a modern Faust—and incidentally interesting as Beerbohm's retrospective view of the nineties—to *Savonarola Brown,* satirising not only pseudo-Elizabethanism but all that is weak in the genuine article.

In his essay on *Lytton Strachey* (1943) Beerbohm says of himself, "In the year 1900 I had been considered a rather clever and amusing young man. . . . In 1918 I was young no longer, and I think I amused people less than I had. I had

subsided into sober irony." He has always written in this
vein of self-depreciation, but it is not to the credit of his
readers and critics that they have echoed his ironic estimate
of himself as a "petit maître" who has "made a charming
little reputation." Consider the implications of *Ichabod,* for
example, or *A Club in Ruins*—beneath the wit the one is
humiliating, the other tragic. The experiences they reveal
are universal. They are not profound but they are far more
perceptive and thoughtful than the persiflage usually associated with "the incomparable Max."

And yet the adjective is right; he is incomparable. Thoroughly traditional, he is not at all derivative. One may note
in his work qualities of Addison, of Lamb, and so on, but
one can call none of them his model; by force of personality
Beerbohm is wholly original. He has not been successfully
imitated nor is he likely to be. His style has survived the
wars, but it belongs to the time before them; no one could
have begun to write as he does after 1915. Moreover the
familiar essay today is becoming as dated an art form as the
pastoral. It belongs to a more leisurely world than ours and
one of different culture. What can be salvaged for present
use has been pre-empted by the radio commentator and the
columnist. It can hardly be considered a means to literary
reputation today. Max Beerbohm may be remembered as
the last of the pure familiar essayists.

COLLECTED WORKS: *The Works of Max Beerbohm* (1922). ESSAYS:
The Works of Max Beerbohm (1896), *More* (1899), *Yet Again*
(1909), *And Even Now* (1921), *A Variety of Things* (1928), *Mainly
On The Air* (1946). MISCELLANEOUS: *The Happy Hypocrite* (1897),
Zuleika Dobson (1911), *A Christmas Garland* (1912), *Seven Men*
(1919), *Herbert Beerbohm-Tree* (1920), *Around Theatres,* 2 v.
(1924), *The Dreadful Dragon of Hay Hill* (1928), *Lytton Strachey*
(1943), *Seven Men and Two Others* (1950). CARICATURES: *Caricatures of Twenty-five Gentlemen* (1896), *The Poets' Corner* (1904),
A Book of Caricatures (1907), *The Second Childhood of John
Bull* (1911), *Fifty Caricatures* (1913), *A Survey* (1921), *Rossetti*

and His Circle (1922), *Things Old and New* (1923), *A Survey* (1925).

"Bibliographies of Modern Authors, Max Beerbohm," *London Mercury,* I (1920), 626; Bohun Lynch, *Max Beerbohm in Perspective* (1921); Dixon Scott, "Beau Beerbohm" in *Men of Letters* (1916); G. S. Layard, "An Open Letter to Max Beerbohm," *Bookman,* LXV (1923), 168-170; Annie K. Tuell, "The Prose of Mr. Beerbohm," *So. Atlantic Quar.,* XXX (1931), 190-199; John Shand, "Max Beerbohm as Prophet," *Adelphi,* III (1925), 439-443.

Edward Verall Lucas (1868-1938) was born at Eltham in Kent, but grew up in Brighton. His family were solid, middle-class Quakers. He attended various schools until he was sixteen, when his father stopped his education and apprenticed him to a bookseller. In 1889, his apprenticeship completed, Lucas joined the staff of the *Sussex Daily News,* and two years later left home for London, where the kindness of his uncle enabled him to attend University College. In 1893 he joined the *London Globe* and published his first prose work, *Bernard Barton and His Friends,* a pleasant but unimportant book.

For the next twenty years he worked hard at whatever came to hand, anthologies, essays, light novels, publishers' reading and editorial work. He joined the editorial staff of *Punch* in 1904. During the First World War he wrote propaganda satires and served the Red Cross on the Italian Front. In all this period he was remarkably productive and by 1919 he was prosperous and sufficiently popular to make a lecture tour around the world.

Lucas lived in London and in Sussex. He was a sociable but reserved man with many acquaintances and few intimate friends. He was an enthusiastic cricketer and an intelligent amateur of art. Early in life he had withdrawn from the Society of Friends and thereafter maintained a saddened agnosticism. In 1925 he became chairman of the publishing house of Methuen and Co.; in 1932 he was made Companion of Honour and later LL.D. of St. Andrews. He died June 26, 1938.

From his boyhood reading of the *Essays of Elia* Lucas was interested in Charles Lamb. In 1887 he wrote some verses on *Old China*. The Bernard Barton book increased his interest in Lamb and his circle. Later a publisher commissioned him to do a book on Lamb and the Lloyds. For Methuen he wrote an introduction to the *Essays of Elia* and in 1900 prepared a new pocket edition with a new biography. His *Life of Lamb* (1905) has blemishes but is the best and fullest work on the subject. It was reissued in 1935 and was followed by the *Letters of Charles and Mary Lamb* in 1936. *At the Shrine of St. Charles* (1934), stray papers on Charles Lamb, is a charming book. These constitute his most important work.

Lucas is most widely popular through his familiar essays, issued in some thirty volumes from 1901 to 1934. These have sometimes been compared with the *Essays of Elia,* but the reader will not find in them the delicate grace of Lamb nor his depth of feeling. Urbanity and wit are their chief merits and they have a limpid charm that justifies their reputation. As a cicerone of pictures and cities Lucas is admirable. In the first group his books on Vermeer are the best, in the second those on London. For the rest his novels, satires, and miscellaneous works are of no great merit.

His autobiography, *Reading, Writing and Remembering,* is merely, as he said of it, "a selection intended to entertain." Real understanding of his background may be gained from *The Old Contemporaries* (1935). More may be gathered from *E. V. Lucas: A Portrait,* by Audrey Lucas (1939).

Essays: *The Friendly Town* (1905), *Fireside and Sunshine* (1906), *Character and Comedy* (1907), *One Day and Another* (1909), *Old Lamps for New* (1911), *A Little of Everything* (1912), *Loiterer's Harvest* (1913), *Harvest Home* (1913), *Landmarks* (1914), *Cloud and Silver* (1916), *A Boswell of Baghdad* (1917), *'Twixt Eagle and Dove* (1918), *The Phantom Journal* (1919), *Mixed Vintages* (1919), *Adventures and Enthusiasms* (1920), *Specially Selected* (1920), *Urbanities* (1921), *Giving and Receiving* (1922), *You Know What People Are* (1922), *Luck of the Year* (1923), *Encounters and Diversions* (1924), *Events and Embroideries* (1926), *A Fronded Isle* (1927), *A Rover I Would Be* (1928), *Out of a Clear Sky* (1928), *Turning Things Over* (1929), *Traveller's Luck* (1930), *Down the Sky* (1930), *If Dogs Could Write* (1930), *French Leaves* (1931), *Visibility Good* (1931), *". . . and such small deer"* (1931), *Lemon Verbena* (1932), *At the Sign of the Dove* (1932), *Saunterer's Rewards* (1933), *English Leaves* (1933), *At the Shrine of St. Charles* (1934), *Pleasure Trove* (1935), *Only the Other Day* (1936), *All of a Piece* (1937), *Adventures and Misgivings* (1938). MISCELLANEOUS: *Bernard Barton and His Friends* (1893), *The Life of Charles Lamb* (1905), *A Wanderer in Holland* (1905), *A Wanderer in London* (1906), *A Wanderer in Paris* (1909), *A Wanderer in Florence* (1912), *London Lavender* (1912), *The British School* [*British Pictures and Their Painters*] (1913), *Roving East and Roving West* (1921), *Vermeer of Delft* (1922), *A Wanderer Among Pictures* (1924), *A Wanderer in Venice* (1924), *John Constable* (1924), *Introducing London* (1925), *London* (1926), *A Wanderer in Rome* (1926).

Audrey Lucas, *E. V. Lucas: A Portrait* (1939); J. C. Farrar, with others, *E. V. Lucas Appreciations* (1926); Grant Overton, "That Literary Wanderer E. V. Lucas," *Bookman,* LIX (1924), 270-276; A. E. Newton, "E. V. Lucas," *Atlantic Monthly,* CLXII (1938), 616-624; Agnes I. Smith, "E. V. Lucas," *Sewanee Rev.,* XLVIII (1940), 221-235.

Arthur Christopher Benson (1862-1925) was the son of the Rev. E. W. Benson, bishop of Lincoln, then of Truro, and finally Archbishop of Canterbury. He was educated at Eton and King's College, Cambridge, where he took a classical first in 1884. The following year he returned to Eton as a master. For eighteen years he remained a conscientious but uninspired teacher, contemptuous of public school life with its narrow classical training and worship of athletics. The next two years he spent editing, with Viscount Esher, Queen Victoria's letters. In 1905 he accepted a Fellowship at Magdalene College, Cambridge. Here he remained until his death in 1925, becoming Master of the college in 1915, and devoting himself wholeheartedly to its interests. His academic life was twice interrupted, in 1907 and in 1917 by severe nervous breakdowns, but was otherwise a happy and effective one. He was a big shy man, most at home in academic walls, content to live a physically uneventful life, but ceaselessly active in his curious, restless mind. He had a wide acquaintance, including Queen Victoria and Ruskin, but few close friends.

Benson's literary activity began in boyhood, at school and in the family circle, and continued throughout life. Though he wrote three or four novels and some passable verse, Benson's chief work was in biography and the essay. He had a gift of sympathy that enabled him to convey character effectively. His studies of Ruskin and Pater are especially good. His essays, widely read on both sides of the Atlantic before 1920, are pleasant reflections of the ordered, sheltered life that vanished with Benson's generation. They were written after school hours for relaxation, much as he poured out his thoughts to his voluminous diary; consequently they are often verbose in style and commonplace in content. But the patient reader will be rewarded with passages of great delicacy and charm, and a humor so quiet that it may pass unappreciated. Unfortunately the mood for reading such essays has largely passed with the life they depict and today they receive little attention.

ESSAYS AND BIOGRAPHIES: *William Laud* (1887), *Essays* (1896), *The Schoolmaster* (1902), *The House of Quiet* (1903), *Alfred Tennyson* (1903), *Rossetti* (1904), *Edward Fitzgerald* (1905), *The Upton Letters* (1905), *The Thread of Gold* (1905), *From a College Window* (1906), *The Gate of Death* (1906), *Walter Pater* 1906), *The Altar Fire* (1907), *Beside Still Waters* (1907), *At Large* (1908), *The Silent Isle* (1910), *Ruskin* (1911), *The Leaves of the Tree* (1911), *Thy Rod and Thy Staff* (1912), *Joyous Gard* (1913), *Along the Road* (1913), *Where No Fear Was* (1914), *The Orchard Pavilion* (1914), *Escape* (1915), *The Happy Warrior* (1917), *The Trefoil* (1923),

Memories and Friends (1924), *Rambles and Reflections* (1926).
VERSE: *Collected Poems* (1909), *Selected Poems* (1924).

E. H. Ryle, *Arthur Christopher Benson As Seen By His Friends*
(1926).

Of **William Ralph Inge** (1860-   ), Dean of St. Paul's,
a wag once wrote:

> Hark the herald angels sing
> Timidly because Dean Inge
> Has arrived and seems to be
> Bored with immortality.

It is ironical that Dean Inge, an intellectual aristocrat of
the highest breeding, a fine scholar, and one of the best
modern interpreters of mysticism, should be known to the
public only as "The Gloomy Dean," a parson-publicist, a
captious and unfriendly critic of the age. His father, the
Rev. William Inge, D.D., was Provost of Worcester College,
Oxford; his mother's family, the Churtons, produced four
notable generations of scholars and divines. His career was
virtually inevitable. From Eton he entered King's College,
Cambridge, and from 1880 to 1885 gathered prizes, honors,
and scholarships with amazing rapidity. From 1884 to 1888
he was an assistant master at Eton, liking it no better than
his contemporary and friend there, A. C. Benson. From 1886
to 1904 he was a Fellow, first of his own college and then of
Hertford College, Oxford. From 1907 to 1911 he was Lady
Margaret Professor of Divinity at Oxford. In short, of the
twenty-five years following his ordination in 1886, only four
(1903-1907) were spent in parish duty; during all the rest he
was a teacher and scholar. When in 1911 he was appointed
Dean of St. Paul's he brought to his task the equipment of
a thinker rather than of a preacher or an administrator.

The books that he wrote down to the end of World War
I contain his most valuable and permanent work. Unfor-

tunately they belong to the literature of religious philosophy and have no place in the present survey. In the tradition of Christian Platonism which Dean Inge follows, they show him as "belonging to the right wing of theological liberalism," an orthodox but wholly candid and independent thinker.

It was after the war, in 1919, that Dean Inge began the essays which earned him his soubriquet. Appearing originally in the *Quarterly Review,* the *Edinburgh Review,* and the *Hibbert Journal,* they were published in two volumes, *Outspoken Essays* (1919) and *Outspoken Essays: Second Series* (1922). They follow the style of formal essay writing developed in the serious journals of the nineteenth century and deal about equally with social and religious questions. Looking at Western civilization, the Dean, not alone among his contemporaries, found it in a bad way. Mechanization, he felt, was being paid for by social parasitism and racial deterioration which endangered the white man's advantage over his competitors of other races. As a remedy he proposed the scientific application of eugenics and birth control to the improvement of the stock of Western nations. To the buoyant mood of the twenties his view of society seemed unduly sombre; after nearly a generation it no longer does. The essays on religious topics, of which his "Confessio Fidei" is the most important, are more popular treatments of materials considered in his earlier works. The five essays grouped under the title "The State, Visible and Invisible" were delivered in the series of Hibbert Lectures at Oxford in 1920 and survey the various historical conceptions of the relations of church and state.

Dean Inge's later essays, down to the eve of World War II, became mellower and less formal, often pleasantly and amusingly reminiscent. Further essays on religious topics contributed to the *Edinburgh,* the *Quarterly,* and the *Contemporary Review* are collected in *The Church in the World*

(1925). *Everyman's Bible* (1931) is an anthology from the scriptures, with an admirable introduction and commentary.

GENERAL: *Society in Rome Under the Caesars* (1888), *Outspoken Essays* (1919), *The Idea of Progress* (1920), *Outspoken Essays: Second Series* (1922), *The Victorian Age* (1922), *Lay Thoughts of a Dean* (1926), *England* (1926), *Science and Ultimate Truth* (1926), *Scientific Ethics* (1927), *Assessments and Anticipations,* Am. ed. *Labels and Libels* (1929), *More Lay Thoughts of a Dean* (1931), *The New Twilight of the Gods* (1932), *Liberty and Natural Rights* (1934), *Vale* [autobiographical] (1934), *Greeks and Barbarians* (1934), *A Rustic Moralist* (1937), *Modernism in Literature* (1937), *Our Present Discontents* (1938), *A Pacifist in Trouble* (1939), *The Fall of the Idols* (1940), *Possible Recovery?* (1941), *Talks in a Free Country* (1942).

Sidney Dark, *Five Deans* (1928); J. P. D. Llwyd, "The Gloomy Dean," *Dalhousie Review,* VII (1928), 466-472; Arthur McDowall, "Three Philosopher Prophets," *London Mercury,* IV (1921), 164-172; J. Scott Lidgett, "The Philosophy of Dr. Inge," *Critical Rev.,* CXXIII (1923), 301-311; Robert Shafer, "Dean Inge and Modern Christianity," *Amer. Rev.,* V (1935), 1-30, 209-233.

Robert Lynd (1879-1949) was born and raised in his father's manse in Belfast. As the son of a Presbyterian minister in Ulster he was taught by his childhood associates to be a good, that is an intolerant, Orangeman. But there was a breadth of sympathy in his character and an affection for his country that made him by the time he was mature a serious Nationalist. It may have been this that led him when he had taken his M. A. at Queen's College, Belfast, in 1899 to leave Ulster for England. He has told almost nothing of his early days there—he appears to have worked for a while in the Midlands—but he soon became a journalist in London and has followed this career successfully ever since. One gathers from his books that he was married, was rejected for service in World War I, had a wide spectator interest in sports, and was a discriminating reader.

Mr. Lynd's books fall into three groups. First there are

four volumes intended to promote a better understanding
of Ireland. *Ireland: A Nation* (1919) is a sympathetic and
realistic presentation of Ireland's case for political and social
autonomy. The others are local-color and travel sketches.
His essay "If the Germans Had Conquered England," drawing, in the midst of the war and the Irish troubles, a parallel
between Ireland under the English and England under the
Germans, was a courageous and illuminating piece of work.
He avoided the common excesses of the convert and was
that rare person, an Irishman who could write about Ireland
with restraint. His patriotism did not absorb his critical
sense.

"The good critic," writes Mr. Lynd, "communicates his
delight in genius." His business, in other words, is synthesis
rather than analysis, the recreation for his reader of the best
he has found in a work of art. Mr. Lynd's criticism was sometimes brilliant, always sound, and pleasantly free from the
preciosity of some of the moderns. He took the reading of
books for granted and was interpretative rather than informative. His own reading was wide and his sympathy
failed only toward illiberal authors.

Above all Mr. Lynd was a familiar essayist. For a generation readers enjoyed his work in the *New Statesman* over the
signature "Y.Y."—a childhood nickname. They have been
issued in a series of volumes whose titles—*The Blue Lion,
The Peal of Bells, The Orange Tree, The Green Man, The
Cockleshell*—carry a genial echo of tavern signs. Their range
of subject and mood is wide, but all are marked by an un-
obtrusive, whimsical humor pointing an eminently sane
philosophy and an unfailing enjoyment of all sorts of human
activity and character. He had the rare gift of self-revelation
without egotism, and of making fun without dispraise. Of all
contemporary familiar essayists Mr. Lynd is nearest to Lamb.
This does not imply equality with Elia, but it puts him in

very good company. Like all journalistic essayists who have
had to furnish their weekly essays year after year, Mr. Lynd
did some inferior work, but his general level is high, and
among his best "The Herring Fleet" is unexcelled in its
kind. An admirable selection of these essays, "Y.Y." (1933),
has been made by Eileen Squire.

Mr. Lynd is not so widely read and appreciated in the
United States as he should be. He was well known in England as the literary editor of the London *News Chronicle,*
as an editorial writer for the *New Statesman and Nation,*
and as a contributor to *John O'London's Weekly.* His wife,
Sylvia Lynd, is known as a poet and novelist.

ESSAYS: *Irish and English Portraits and Impressions* (1908), *The
Book of This and That* (1915), *If the Germans Conquered Eng-
land* (1917), *The Pleasures of Ignorance* (1921), *Solomon In All
His Glory* (1922), *The Sporting Life* (1922), *The Blue Lion* (1923),
Selected Essays (1923), *The Peal of Bells* (1924), *The Money Box*
(1925), *The Little Angel* (1926), *The Orange Tree* (1926), *The
Goldfish* (1927), *The Green Man* (1928), *It's a Fine World* (1930),
Rain, Rain, Go to Spain (1931), *The Cockleshell* (1933), *"Y Y"*
[Selected Essays] (1933), *Both Sides of the Road* (1934), *I Tremble
To Think* (1936), *In Defence of Pink* (1937), *Searchlights and
Nightingales* (1939), *Life's Little Oddities* (1941), *Essays on Life
and Literature* [Everyman's Library] (1951). CRITICISM AND
SKETCHES: *Home Life in Ireland* (1909), *Rambles in Ireland*
(1912), *Ireland, a Nation* (1919), *Old and New Masters* (1919),
The Art of Letters (1920), *The Passion of Labour* (1920), *Books
and Authors* (1922), *Dr. Johnson and Company* (1927).

F. E. Schelling, "A Sound British Critic," in *Appraisements and
Asperities* (1922).

The sons of Charles Francis Powys, a clergyman of the
Church of England, and descended on their mother's side
from the poets Cowper and Donne, the brothers **John
Cowper** (1872-   ), **Theodore Francis** (1875-   ), and
Llewelyn (1884-1939) **Powys** are a remarkable trio of indi-

vidualists to have come from one household. All have distinction as men and writers, all have eccentricities and limitations that have kept them definitely minor figures in letters.

The best known, John Cowper Powys, was for about thirty years a popular and effective lecturer on the University Extension and other platforms in England and the United States. An appreciative rather than a judicious critic, he had a gift of communicating his enthusiasms, a sensuous prose style strongly influenced by Walter Pater, and above all a compelling presence with his romantic appearance and intense nervous energy. At the age of twenty-eight he published his first course of lectures—on Carlyle, Ruskin, and Tennyson—and followed them with others until 1905. Then for nine years he lived wholly by lecturing, until 1914, since when he has published regularly. Without the benefit of his delivery his literary essays often suffer: the matter often seems adapted to a popular audience and the style superficially impressive. Yet at times they contain excellent passages, sincere and vigorous in thought and expression. Between 1915 and 1940 he produced ten novels, romantic, redundant, and most of them rather dull. His gift is not creative; he is at his best in the interpretation of esthetic experience. A curious mixture of mystic and rationalist, he is profoundly affected by the poetry of religion while his mind remains sceptical.

Theodore Francis Powys after completing Dorchester Grammar School remained for some time at home. While yet in his twenties he chose to settle down to a quiet country life in a Dorsetshire village. Religious, simple in his tastes, a brooding observer of life, he was content with obscurity and an honorable poverty. He married, raised a family, and for many years wrote without finding a publisher. It was not until he was forty-eight that his first volume, containing three novelettes, appeared; it has been followed by twenty-five others, novels, novelettes, and short stories in a steady stream.

T. F. Powys has never been a popular writer. His books deal largely with village life in Dorset, with much the same scene and social conditions depicted in Hardy's Wessex novels, and with abundant irony but of a different sort. They have suffered by the comparison. They are capably written but lacking adequately created characters they remain realistic statements, sometimes humorous, sometimes grim, of English rural life.

Llewelyn Powys, the youngest brother, is the ablest writer of the three. He followed John Cowper at Sherborne School and Corpus Christi, and in 1909, three years after graduation, to the lecture platform. After a season in America he returned to England in failing health. His disease proved to be tuberculosis and he spent two years in Swiss sanatoria fighting for his life, an experience he has vividly described in *Skin for Skin*. By 1914, his disease arrested, he went to British East Africa, where for the next five years he managed a cattle ranch. In 1920 he again joined his brother in the United States, living in Greenwich Village and later in California, and making the beginning of his literary reputation with the publication of *Ebony and Ivory*. Disappointed at his lack of success in this country, Powys, after marrying Alyse Gregory, returned in 1925 to England. Here he remained until 1936, when his health required him to return to Switzerland. At Clavadel, Davos Platz, he spent his last three years of life.

Purely an essayist—his two excursions into fiction are negligible—Llewelyn Powys is notable for the love of life and the earth that pervades everything he wrote, the passionate love of a man who held life on precarious tenure. When he writes of nature, beautiful and cruel, on the African Veldt, or of an autumn evening in New York, or of the English country, one feels beneath the surface of the scene, brilliantly depicted, the bones of earth and the old generations of men with whom he expected to go down to annihilation. Most of all he loved Dorset; wherever he might find his subjects, in the end he was drawn back to Montacute and the vicarage of his childhood, to obscure places known with the quiet intimacy of a countryman. And if his love of life sometimes betrayed him into weakness, his love of earth was the source of strength in nearly all his best work. If any books of the Powys brothers have lasting value they are those such as *Dorset Essays* and *Earth Memories* that contain Llewelyn's most characteristic essays.

J. C. POWYS. *Autobiography* (1934). ESSAYS: *Visions and Revisions* (1915), *Confessions of Two Brothers,* with Llewelyn Powys (1916), *Suspended Judgments* (1916), *One Hundred Best Books* (1916), *The Complex Vision* (1920), *Psychoanalysis and Morality* (1923), *The Art of Happiness* (1935), *The Religion of a Skeptic* (1925), *The Meaning of Culture* (1929), *In Defense of Sensuality* (1930), *Dorothy M. Richardson* (1931), *A Philosophy of Solitude* (1933), *The Pleasures of Literature* [*The Enjoyment of Literature*] (1938). FICTION: *Wood and Stone* (1915), *Rodmoor* (1916), *Ducdame* (1925), *Wolf Solent* (1929), *The Owl, the Duck, and— Miss Rowe! Miss Rowe!* (1930), *A Glastonbury Romance* (1932), *Weymouth Sands* (1934), *Jobber Skald* (1935), *Maiden Castle* (1936), *Morwyn* (1937), *Owen Glendower* (1940). VERSE: *Odes and Other Poems* (1896), *Poems* (1899), *Wolf's-bane* (1916), *Mandragora* (1917), *Samphire* (1922).

T. F. POWYS. NOVELS: *Black Briony* (1923), *Mark Only* (1924), *Mr. Tasker's Gods* (1925), *Mockery Gap* (1925), *Innocent Birds* (1926), *Mr. Weston's Good Wine* (1927), *Kindness in a Corner* (1930), *Unclay* (1931), *Captain Patch* (1935), *Make Thyself Many* (1935), *Goat Green* (1937). SHORT STORIES: *The Left Leg* (1923), *Feed My Swine* (1926), *A Strong Girl* (1926), *A Stubborn Tree* (1926), *What Lack I Yet?* (1927), *The Rival Pastors* (1927), *The Dewpond* (1928), *The House With the Echo* (1928), *Fables* (1929), re-issued as *No Painted Plumage* (1934), *Christ in the Cupboard* (1930), *The Key of the Field* (1930), *Uriah on the Hill* (1930), *The White Paternoster* (1930), *The Only Penitent* (1931), *Uncle Dottery* (1931), *When Thou Was Naked* (1931), *The Tithe Barn*

(1932), *The Two Thieves* (1932), *Bottle's Path* (1946). MISCEL-LANEOUS: *The Soliloquy of a Hermit* (1916), also published as *Soliloquies of a Hermit* (1918), *An Interpretation of Genesis* (1929).

LLEWELYN POWYS. MISCELLANEOUS: *Confessions of Two Brothers*, with J. C. Powys (1916), *Ebony and Ivory* (1923), *Thirteen Worthies* (1923), *Black Laughter* (1924), *Honey and Gall* [Haldeman-Julius Book No. 534] (1924), *Cupbearers of Wine and Hellebore* [Haldeman-Julius Book No. 782] (1924), *Skin For Skin* (1925), *The Verdict of Bridlegoose* (1926), *Henry Hudson* (1927),) *The Cradle of God* (1929), *The Pathetic Fallacy* [*An Hour on Christianity*] (1930), *A Pagan's Pilgrimage* (1931), *Impassioned Clay* (1931), *The Life and Times of Anthony à Wood* (1932), *Now That the Gods are Dead* (1932), *Glory of Life* (1934), *Earth Memories* (1934), *Damnable Opinions* (1935), *Dorset Essays* (1935), *The Twelve Months* (1936), *Somerset Essays* (1937), *Rats in the Sacristy* (1937), *A Baker's Dozen* (1939), *Swiss Essays* (1947). NOVELS: *Apples Be Ripe* (1930), *Love and Death* (1939).

Louis N. Wilkinson, *Welsh Ambassadors* (1936), *The Brothers Powys* (1947); Richard H. Ward, *The Powys Brothers* (1935), John C. Powys, "Four Brothers," *Century,* CX (1925), 553-560; Gilbert E. Govan, "The Powys Family," *Sewanee Rev.,* XLVI (1938), 74-90; Malcolm Elwin, *Life of Llewelyn Powys* (1946), Donald MacCampbell, "The Art of T. F. Powys," *Sewanee Rev.,* XLII (1934), 460-473.

The most prominent English essayist since 1940 has been **Clive Staples Lewis (1898-   )**. He was born in Belfast and attended local schools. Only sixteen when the First World War broke out, he served in the latter part of it as lieutenant in the Somerset Light Infantry. In 1918 he matriculated at University College, Oxford, where he became a lecturer in 1924. The next year he was elected Fellow and Tutor of Magdalen College, a post that he still holds. He is one of the most popular teachers in the university.

Lewis's first literary interests were in poetry and criticism and it was only with the publication of the tremendously popular *Screwtape Letters* in 1943, that his present reputation as a Christian apologist began. Lewis was raised in the Church of Ireland (Anglican) but at the age of twelve called himself an atheist. Then at eighteen he fell under the spell

of George Macdonald's *Phantastes* (1858), which, as he says, converted his imagination. An intellectual reconcilement to the entirety of Christian dogma followed.

Lewis's religious experience was a primarily emotional one confirmed by rationalization. The same sequence may be found in his books; they are admirably logical, premises being granted, but their power and appeal are due far less to Lewis' persuasiveness than to his capture of the imagination by concrete drama.

CLIVE STAPLES LEWIS

The analysis of Christian morals in *The Screwtape Letters* is given humorous point by being embodied in the correspondence of a devil in hell with a junior colleague on earth. The bus ride to heaven in *The Great Divorce* is as vivid as an episode in *Pilgrim's Progress*. In the *Perelandra* trilogy the conflict between good and evil is cast into a Wellsian setting of war among the planets. Possibly a Welsh grandfather who built ships in Belfast may be responsible for both the imaginative power and the religious seriousness that are Lewis's driving forces.

Like several other modern essayists Lewis has gone on the air and proved an effective speaker, reaching—and holding—a large audience. Some of his radio talks have since been published in *The Case for Christianity* and *Beyond Personality*.

Lewis's popular reputation has been rapidly made and has obscured his older one as a critic of distinction. While his *Preface to Paradise Lost* remains obscure, *The Screwtape Letters* ran through twenty printings in England and fourteen in the United States in three years. In a little longer time he has produced a dozen books. That sort of reputation is often transient and it is probable that the more journalistic part of Lewis's work will not last, but in the rest he has written fine prose without qualification and has assured himself a place in the history of English letters.

CRITICISM: "What Chaucer Really Did to Il Filostrato," *Essays and Studies,* XVII (Oxford, 1932), 56-75; "The Personal Heresy in Criticism," *Essays and Studies,* XIX (Oxford, 1934), 7-28; *The Allegory of Love* (1936), "An Open Letter to Dr. Tillyard," *Essays and Studies,* XXI (Oxford, 1936), 153-168; *Rehabilitations* (1939), "The Fifteenth Century Heroic Line," *Essays and Studies,* XXIV (Oxford, 1939), 28-41; *A Preface to Paradise Lost* (1942), *Hamlet, the Prince or the Poem* (1942), "Psycho-analysis and Literary Criticism," *Essays and Studies,* XXVII (Oxford, 1942), 7-21; *The Abolition of Man* (1943). RELIGION: *The Pilgrim's Regress* (1933), *Out of the Silent Planet* (1938), *The Problem of Pain* (1940), *The Screwtape Letters* (1942), *Broadcast Talks* (1942), [*The Case for Christianity*] (1943), *Perelandra* (1943), *Christian Behaviour* (1943), *Beyond Personality* (1944), *That Hideous Strength* (1945), *The Great Divorce* (1945), *Miracles: A Preliminary Study* (1947). VERSE: *Dymer,* under pseud. Clive Hamilton (1926).

Chad Walsh, *C. S. Lewis Apostle to the Skeptics* (1949); *Time,* L, 10 (Sept. 8, 1947), 65-74; Victor M. Hamm, "Mr. Lewis in Perelandra," *Thought,* XX (1945), 271-290.

"A traveller in little things," a phrase he liked and used as a title for a book, very aptly characterises **William Henry Hudson (1841-1922)**. He was all his life a traveler, a migrant without fixed habitat. Though he liked to call himself "an Exeter man," his grandfather had been an emigrant from England to Massachusetts. His father was from Marblehead, his mother a Kimball from Maine. His parents migrated

from New England to the Argentine pampas west of Buenos
Aires and there Hudson was born. He was a solitary
child, as later in spite of wife and friends he was a solitary
man, and drew his early education more from the open
country around his father's store near Quilnes than from the
itinerant tutors who from time to time stayed for a while to
give the Hudson children a little schooling. In *Far Away and
Long Ago* he has left a delightful record of this childhood.

Of Hudson's youth and early manhood little is known
definitely. He visited Patagonia and perhaps other parts of
South America. His father died in 1868 and two years later
Hudson came to England, but for a long time remained
obscure. His almost superstitious reluctance to recall unpleasant things made him always reticent about these years.
He married in poverty and after a succession of dismal lodg-
ings, managed a down-at-heels apartment house, moving
from flat to flat as they fell vacant. He did not become a
British subject until 1900.

Hudson's writing began in 1885 with *The Purple Land
That England Lost,* a romance of Uruguay, but for some
time it went unrecognized. By the time he received a Civil
List pension in 1901 he had nine books to his credit, including *A Naturalist in La Plata, Idle Days in Patagonia,* and
Nature in Downland. And it was not until the success of
the American edition of *Green Mansions* in 1915 that his
earnings became adequate. Long recognized as a master of
prose by his fellow writers, he received little public appreciation in England and almost none in America until
toward the close of his life.

"My flesh and the soil are one, and the heat in my blood
and in the sunshine are one, and the winds and the tempests
and my passions are one," wrote Hudson. "I feel the 'strangeness' only with regard to my fellow men, especially in towns,
where they exist in conditions unnatural to me but congenial to them." He was pre-eminently a field naturalist with

a lifelong knowledge of plants and animals and birds, especially of birds keenly observed and interpreted by temperamental sympathy. He could comprehend anything in nature and had a quick instinctive friendship for peasants and children and such, who, like himself, lived simply and quietly in touch with natural things. The pageantry of life had little appeal for him: he had seen the beaten army of Rosas streaming across the pampas, and had cared for it less than for the ombu trees or the rising of a heron from a lake.

It is about little things that he writes best, things to be found in the homes of villages, in the talk of children and shepherds, in watching a deer at the edge of a wood. He found them over years, cycling or afoot through the byways of England, storing his exact, vivid memory with what others passed by. And at the last the little things gave him a wonderful understanding of the great things. When he died he had all but finished *A Hind in Richmond Park*. The book is an exploration backward through the senses and instincts of animals to the mind of primitive man and the origins of the artistic impulse. It is impressive not only for its encyclopedic nature lore but for the vistas it opens into remote, dim regions of the human mind.

Though he is known chiefly as an ornithologist, and birds fill the greater part of his work, there is hardly an aspect of nature and rural life in the south of England or on the South American plains that he has not treated in faithful detail in his volumes of essays, sketches, and stories written over thirty years. The general reading public, however, has cared most for what are really less characteristic works, his two South American romances, *The Purple Land* and *Green Mansions*. By the time he died the latter had achieved the rank of "classic," and Epstein's much abused sculpture of Rima adorns the bird sanctuary in Hyde Park dedicated to his memory in 1925. Few more haunting stories have been written than this of the bird woman, Rima, found and loved

by a European in the Venezuelan jungle and lost to him by
the malice of hostile savages. Not a woman but something
unutterably beautiful seems to have perished when the
flames sweep Rima's forest, where she should have lived
forever, passionately loved but never possessed, a symbol of
eternal desire.

Something, it is true, must be withdrawn from Hudson's
credit as an inventive artist since Carlos Baker has shown
that the story in general and in detail is closely copied from
Lady Morgan's all but forgotten novel *The Missionary*. (See
"The Source Book for Hudson's Green Mansions," *PMLA,*
LXI, 1946.) But if this study leaves Hudson convicted of
something very like plagiarism, it does not touch the power
of the treatment, wholly lacking in Lady Morgan. *Green
Mansions* is a story, said Galsworthy, "which immortalizes,
I think, as passionate a love of all beautiful things as ever
was in the heart of man."

Much of the charm of all Hudson's work is due to the
intensity of his feeling and the quietness of his style that
Conrad compared to the growth of grass. He is not an easy
author to quote, for his goodness is diffused throughout the
whole and does its surprising work unperceived. He was like
that himself, a tall, intense, quiet man, deliberate, certain
of what he was to do and doing it simply. Though he had
a large circle of friends—Conrad, Cunninghame Graham,
Galsworthy, Edward Garnett, and Belloc among others—he
always moved apart in an element of his own. Even after he
had escaped from poverty and was famous he lived un-
fashionably in a shabby part of London.

The spirit of independence that Huson brought from the
pampas had nothing of the fierceness of Cunninghame
Graham's; he neither denounced nor satirized the alien culture of cities in which he was obliged to live. Instinctively as
an animal would, he kept himself apart from it and avoided
it when he could. There was not a grain of the political

man in him; if human polity disgusted him it was a fact of nature like the polity of a rabbit warren. He turned from it to find the eternal interest of simple things.

Essays and Nature Studies: *Argentine Ornithology,* with P. L. Sclater (1888-89), *The Naturalist in La Plata* (1892), *Idle Days in Patagonia* (1893), *Birds in a Village* (1893), *British Birds* (1895), *Birds in London* (1898), *Nature in Downland* (1900), *Birds and Man* (1901), *Hampshire Days* (1903), *The Land's End* (1908), *Afoot in England* (1909), *A Shepherd's Life* (1910), *Adventures Among Birds* (1913), *Far Away and Long Ago* (1918), *Birds in Town and Village* (1919), *The Book of a Naturalist* (1919), *Birds of La Plata* (1920), *A Traveller in Little Things* (1921), *A Hind in Richmond Park* (1922), *Men, Books and Birds* (1923). Fiction: *The Purple Land That England Lost* (1885), *A Crystal Age* (1887), *Fan,* as Henry Harford (1892), *El Ombu* (1902), reissued as *South American Sketches* (1909), and again with two additions as *Tales of the Pampas* (1916), *Green Mansions* (1904), *A Little Boy Lost* (1905), *Dead Man's Plack* (1920), *Ralph Herne* (1923).

George F. Wilson, *A Bibliography of the Writings of W. H. Hudson* (1922); Morley Roberts, *W. H. Hudson: A Portrait* (1925); H. C. Goddard, *W. H. Hudson, Bird Man* (1928); Richard Curle, "W. H. Hudson," *Fortnightly Rev.,* N. S. CXII (1922), 612-619; Violet Hunt, "The Death of Hudson," *English Rev.,* XXXVI (1923), 23-35; Cornelius Weygandt, "Out-of-door Essays of Mr. W. H. Hudson," *University Lectures, 1919-20* (Univ. of Pennsylvania, 1921), 327-348; Robert H. Charles, "The Writings of W. H. Hudson," *Essays and Studies,* XX (1935), 135-151; H. J. Massingham, "The Art of W. H. Hudson," *Nation-Athenaeum,* XXXI (1922), 708-709; James V. Fletcher, "The Creator of Rima, W. H. Hudson," *Sewanee Rev.,* XLVIII (1933), 908-918; E. M. Nicholson, "W. H. Hudson's 'Birds in a Village,' " *Cornhill,* LIX (1925), 24-35.

Robert Bontine Cunninghame Graham (1852-1936) was born in London. His immediate ancestry, aristocratic but not illustrious, was three-quarters Scotch, one-quarter Spanish. His early training he had from his maternal grandmother, who formed him in the school of Spanish gentlemen. Later he was sent to Harrow, but unhappy and ill-suited to the life of an English school, he left when he was sixteen. For the next sixteen years he lived a life of adventure in South America, Mexico, and Texas, ranching, living with gauchos on the pampas, teaching fencing. He became a splendid horseman. In 1879 he married a Chilean, Gabriela de la Balmondiere.

Five years later, at the age of thirty-two, he inherited the debt-encumbered family property at Gartmore and returned to Scotland to farm the estate and clear the debt. In 1886 a chivalrous championship of the working man and a hatred of modern commercialism led him into politics and he was elected to Parliament as Liberal member for Lanark. In the House he consistently supported "labour" measures. In the Bloody Sunday riots in Trafalgar Square, that climaxed the dockers' strike of 1887, he led a charge of strikers against the police. He was arrested and sentenced to two months in jail. Thereafter he found himself without influence in Parliament and withdrew from politics in 1892.

Though he had written articles for newspapers (his first published work appeared in the *San Antonio Times*), Cunninghame Graham's career as a writer did not begin until he was forty-three, when he published *Notes on the District of Menteith*. The next year, in collaboration with his wife, he produced a volume of short stories, *Father Archangel of Scotland*. This was followed at intervals until 1932 by fifteen volumes of "tales and sketches." In form they are like the similar work of Galsworthy, sometimes approaching the short story, sometimes the essay; in material they draw upon a cosmopolitan experience as varied and rich as Kipling's. A knifing on the pampas, a starving beggar in London, provide him occasion to pour contempt on the vulgarity, brutality, and impotence of the modern sophisticated world.

A second group of Cunninghame Graham's works deals with the history of South America and the lives and exploits of the Conquistadores. These his Spanish blood and his adventurous youth enabled him to understand and to interpret sympathetically. *The Conquest of New Granada* is a really splendid book.

Two books of travel complete his works. *Mogreb-el-Acksa* (Morocco of the West) is the account of a trip undertaken in 1898 to reach Tarudant, a city then forbidden to Europeans. *Cartagena and the Banks of the Sinu* describes aspects of Colombia observed during the First World War when the author was buying remounts there for the British service.

Cunninghame Graham was a Spanish hidalgo of the fifteenth century strayed into the twentieth. He saw the world through the eyes of a free man who carries his honor through a world open to his fortune. The degradation of the individual in regimented societies dominated by money provoked his scorn. In such a world success is vulgar, only defeat is honorable. In his style he is afraid neither of the sentiment that is the complement of Scottish dourness nor of the high rhetoric of Spanish prose. But his prevailing tone when writing of the modern world is one of fierce aristocratic contempt. These qualities have won the appreciation of the few he esteemed but have denied him any wide popularity.

SKETCHES AND STORIES: *Father Archangel of Scotland,* with Mrs. Cunninghame Graham (1896), *Aurora La Cujini* (1898), *Thirteen Stories* (1900), *Success* (1902), *Progress* (1905), *His People* (1906), *Faith* (1909), *Hope* (1910), *Charity* (1912), *A Hatchment* (1913), *Scottish Stories* (1914), *Brought Forward* (1916), *The Dream of the Magi* (1923), *Inveni Portum, Joseph Conrad* (1924), *Redeemed* (1927), *Writ in Sand* (1932), *Mirages* (1936). SELECTIONS FROM THESE: *Thirty Tales and Sketches* (1929), *Rodeo* (1936). BIOGRAPHY: *Hernando do Soto* (1903), *Bernal Diaz del Castillo* (1915), *A Brazilian Mystic* (1920), *Doughty Deeds* (1925), *Pedro de Valdivia* (1926), *José Antonio Paez* (1929), *Portrait of a Dictator* (1933). HISTORY AND TRAVEL: *Notes on the District of Mentieth* (1895), *Mogreb El Acksa* (1898), *The Ipané* (1899), *A Vanished Arcadia*

(1901), *Cartagena and the Banks of the Sinu* (1921), *The Conquest of New Granada* (1922), *The Conquest of the River Plate* (1924), *The Horses of the Conquest* (1930).

H. F. West, *Cunninghame Graham: His Life and Works* (1932); A. F. Tschiffely, *Don Roberto: The Life of R. B. Cunninghame Graham* (1937).

Though **Charles Montague Doughty (1843-1926)** lived the greater part of his life and wrote his most important book in the nineteenth century, he is by accident of delayed recognition as well as by a late developing poetic gift virtually a writer of our own times.

He came of "county" families on both sides, his father being the Rev. C. M. Doughty of Theberton Hall, Suffolk, squire and parson in one, his mother a Beaumont of the East Riding of Yorkshire. Both of them died while Doughty was still a little boy and he was brought up by an uncle and an aunt.

Intensely patriotic from boyhood, Doughty determined to enter the navy and was heartbroken when he was rejected for a speech defect. At eighteen he entered Cambridge, devoting himself principally to geology. His first published work (1866) was a monograph on the glaciers of Norway. Upon taking his degree in the same year he transferred his interest from geology to literature and spent the next four years in intensive reading.

In 1871 Doughty began his travels, going first to Holland and progressing easily by way of France, Italy, Spain, and Greece to Palestine and Egypt, studying as he went. This occupied him until 1875. He then wanted to visit and report upon the monuments of Medain Salih in the Arabian desert and, his family being no longer wealthy, tried to secure the backing of the Royal Geographical Society for an expedition. Failing in this he set out in 1876 privately in the character of a Syrian physician. He went with the Haj (the

Mohammedan pilgrim caravan) to Medain Salih and then, leaving it, spent eighteen months wandering with Bedouins in the desert. He was in poor health, he underwent great hardships, and his life was in constant danger from Arab fanaticism, but he reached Jidda and thence India safely and returned to England in 1879.

This remarkable adventure produced one of the most remarkable of modern books, *Travels in Arabia Deserta*. Published, after many delays and disappointments, by the Cambridge University Press in 1888, it remained almost unknown to the general public until the glamor of T. E. Lawrence's desert campaign created a wide interest in Arabian adventures. New editions in England and the United States were immediately popular and the work was belatedly recognized as a great English classic.

Arabia Deserta is not a light book to read either for the matter or the manner. It tells of wanderings in remote places and among obscure tribes and often the reader is fairly bewildered in a maze of uncouth names. The mind avid of action will grow impatient at the deliberate chronicling of campfires, wild Arab characters, and mean cruelties, though the cumulative effect is impressive. Moreover Doughty believed that good English began with Chaucer and ended with the Elizabethans, and in this belief created a style unique in modern letters. It is direct, dignified, and quaintly archaic, but not easy. But the whole book is like its subject; it holds one by its very austerities and leaves him with a sense of great experience.

Doughty's later years were almost placid. He married, settled in the country, travelled genteelly on the continent, and, living entirely apart from the contemporary world, devoted himself to writing ambitious poems. These, hitherto, neglected except by a few admirers, will probably never be as widely read as *Arabia Deserta,* for they are far more difficult without great compensating beauty. *The Dawn in*

Britain (1906) recounts the Celtic resistance to Rome from the campaign of Brennus to the conquest of Britain. It fills four volumes of the most crabbed verse in English. *Adam Cast Forth* followed in 1908; then two patriotic poems, *The Cliffs* (1909) and *The Clouds* (1912), and an allegory, *The Titans* (1916). His last poem was another allegory, *Mansoul: or the Riddle of the World* (1920, revised 1923).

World War I brought Doughty to the brink of poverty but his distress was relieved by a small Civil List pension until a bequest and the returns from his great work gave him a competence again. He died in 1926.

TRAVEL: *On the Jostedal Brae Glaciers* (1866), *Documents epigraphiques recuellis dans le nord de l'Arabie* (1884), *Travels in Arabia Deserta* (1888), *Wanderings in Arabia,* excerpts from *Arabia Deserta* (1908). POETRY: *Under Arms* (1900), *The Dawn in Britain* (1906), *Adam Cast Forth* (1908), *The Cliffs* (1909), *The Clouds* (1912), *The Titans* (1916), *Mansoul* (1920), *Mansoul,* revised (1923).

D. G. Hogarth, *The Life of Charles M. Doughty* (1928); Barker Fairley, *Charles M. Doughty: A Critical Study* (1927); "Charles Doughty: 1843-1926," *Univ. Toronto Quar.,* XIII (1943-1944), 14-25.

Thomas Edward Lawrence (1888-1935) was one of the most fascinating and baffling characters of this century. He was born at Tremadoc, Wales, second son of Thomas Lawrence. During his early childhood the family moved about the British Isles and France, but in 1896 settled in Oxford for the education of the boys. For eleven years Lawrence attended the Oxford High School, at the end passing high (thirteenth) among the Firsts in the Oxford Local Examination.

In a household that encouraged plain living and high thinking, Lawrence was conspicuously Spartan, caring little for comfort and showing fortitude under pain. His daring led him into risky adventures. With a boy's activity he combined an interest in local archeology that before he left school grew into a mature interest in Norman military architecture. He spent his holidays of 1906 and 1907 cycling in France and studying castles, and later while in college extended his study to Syria.

From 1907 to 1910 he was an undergraduate in Jesus College, Oxford, pursuing history, but getting less from the university curriculum than from those independent studies that he embodied in his first work, *Crusader Castles,* written in the winter of 1909-10.

THOMAS EDWARD LAWRENCE

Between graduation and the war Lawrence worked as an archeological assistant to D. G. Hogarth at the Carchemish dig, which yielded such valuable knowledge of the Hittites, and for a while with Flinders Petrie in Egypt. Early in 1914 he went with C. L. Woolley on an expedition to Sinai which was a thinly-veiled British reconnaissance. Before he had completed his report of this survey (*The Wilderness of Zin*) the war had broken out and he was called to the War Office. By the end of 1914 he was attached to Intelligence at Cairo, where he quickly demonstrated his amazing abilities and his incapability of military discipline.

After nearly two years his superiors were glad to release him to work with Storrs in raising the Arab tribes to rebellion. It was this operation, probably the last picturesque campaign in modern war, that made Lawrence one of the most famous men of his generation. He returned from the

East to find that Lowell Thomas had made "Lawrence of Arabia" almost a legend. After his work at the Peace Conference, in the interests of the Arabs, he could not take up his life where he had left it.

A poor man after all his achievements, he accepted a fellowship that All Souls College, Oxford, offered him so that he might work on his projected book about the Arabian campaign. But he was not to be let alone. In the spring of 1921 he was called to the Colonial Office by Winston Churchill, and gave valuable aid in settling some of the lamentable trouble the war had left in the Near East. A career was open to him but he declined it as he had declined honors for his war service, and once more he tried to live privately.

Lawrence was bitter. Britain and France had broken their pledges to the Arabs, and he felt that he was placed in an intolerably false position. To escape the world and his own identity he turned to the army as in another age he would have turned to a monastery. As Aircraftman Ross he enlisted in the RAF late in 1922, but was discharged after a few months when his identity was discovered. In March, 1923, he enlisted again, this time in the Royal Tank Corps, under the name of Shaw, which he later legally assumed by deed poll. In 1925 he obtained a transfer back to the RAF and remained in it for ten years, including a year's service in India.

Upon leaving the service in 1935 he went to a cottage at Clouds Hill, Dorset, which he had bought during his days in the Tanks. Here he had solitude and a choice library of books and records. But he had a passion for speed that he indulged by furious motor-cycling. In May 1935 he died shortly after the crack-up of his latest machine.

Seven Pillars of Wisdom was begun at the Peace Conference and continued until the end of the year, when the

completed manuscript—the whole except two books—was lost
in the Reading railway station. Lawrence's amazing memory
enabled him to reproduce it correctly with all its multiple
detail in some 400,000 words. This text was then reworked
into literary form, and of it eight copies were printed by the
Oxford Times. In 1926 the first edition, a reduction to
280,000 words, was published by subscription and an abridg-
ment of about half that length, was made public in the following year under the title *Revolt in the Desert.* The public
edition of *Seven Pillars* appeared after Lawrence's death in
1935.

In 1932 Lawrence, in need of funds, translated Homer's
Odyssey into approximately contemporary prose, an interesting but not altogether successful piece of work. At about
the same time he was writing *The Mint,* a realistic narrative
of his RAF experiences, which was not to be published until
1950. It has not been published, but the MS may be con-
sulted in the Library of Congress. His miscellaneous writings
with a selection of his war photographs were published in
Oriental Assembly (1940). Since then *Crusader Castles* and
Secret Despatchers from Arabia have been published in
England in a limited edition.

There have been other modern Englishmen, such as
Colonel Leachman and Glubb Pasha, whose military exploits among the Arabs have been nearly as amazing as
Lawrence's, but they have been limited by their profession.
England has had greater soldiers than Lawrence, but none
who could fight a campaign and write about it with equal
competence. *Seven Pillars,* like *Arabia Deserta,* is an inimitable work of modern prose, but unlike it, is easily readable.
One cannot forget the beautifully fought battle of Tafileh,
or the army of Feisal on the march with the tribesmen chant-
ing antiphonally from wing to wing any more than one can
forget Doughy's picture of the column of the Haj winding

into the desert from Damascus. To begin to appreciate the fascinating and elusive character of Lawrence, however, it is necessary to read further. Two books are especially recommended, *The Letters of T. E. Lawrence* and *T. E. Lawrence By His Friends.*

Seven Pillars of Wisdom, Limited ed. (1926), Trade ed. (1935), *Revolt in the Desert* (1927), *The Odyssey of Homer,* translation (1932), *Crusader Castles* (1936), *The Diary of T. E. Lawrence,* MCMXI (1937), *The Letters of T. E. Lawrence,* edited by David Garnett (1938).

E. W. Duval, *T. E. Lawrence: A Bibliography* (1938); T. German-Reed, *Bibliographical Notes on T. E. Lawrence's Seven Pillars of Wisdom and Revolt in the Desert* (1928); Basil H. Liddell-Hart, *T. E. Lawrence in Arabia and After* (1934); Robert Graves, *Lawrence and the Arabs* (1927), [*Lawrence and the Arabian Adventure*] (1928); A. W. Lawrence, ed., *T. E. Lawrence By His Friends* (1937); Lowell Thomas, *With Lawrence in Arabia* (1924); Herbert Read, "Lawrence of Arabia" and "The Seven Pillars of Wisdom," in *A Coat of Many Colours* (1945); R. P. Blackman, "T. E. Lawrence," in *The Expense of Greatness* (1940).

Henry Major Tomlinson (1873-   ) was born in Poplar when that parish in the East End of London was inhabited by unpretentious people like his own—families of shipmasters, engineers, and others connected with the sea. His youth saw the passing of the sailing ship, on which the prosperity of Poplar was founded, and with it the color of an era and the simple standards of life to which he had been bred. That life had no superfluity; it was natural that he should go to work at twelve in a shipping office. His nineteen years of clerkship were a drudgery, connected tenuously with the ships he had come to love, but none the less drudgery from which he worked hard to escape. A steady reader from boyhood of Emerson, Melville, and Thoreau, he had apprenticed himself to letters and at length, after years of writing for exercise, had his contributions accepted by a London paper.

In 1904, at the age of thirty-one, he left shipping for journalism, joining the staff of the *Morning Leader,* with which he remained, except for one short interruption, until the middle of the First World War.

In 1912 Tomlinson made a voyage in a freighter across the Atlantic and two thousand miles inland up the Amazon and its tributary the Madeira to the head of navigation at the San Antonio Falls in the heart of Brazil. An unusual voyage, it produced an unusual book, *The Sea and the Jungle,* now a classic, some think the greatest, of modern travel literature. Published in the autumn of 1912, however, the book failed to attract attention in the troubled days that preceded the war and was remaindered at half a crown a copy.

HENRY MAJOR TOMLINSON

When the war broke out, Tomlinson was sent to France as correspondent by the *Morning Leader.* Later he became official correspondent at British Headquarters, but there he proved too outspoken and truthful for the command and in 1917 he was back in London. He became literary editor of the *Athenaeum,* continuing under Middleton Murry's editorship until the periodical was sold in 1923.

Tomlinson's work as correspondent had attracted wide attention and had made his literary reputation. The *Sea and the Jungle* was "discovered" by critics and its quality recognized. In 1918 Tomlinson issued some war sketches with earlier journalistic work in *Old Junk,* and three years later his colorful essays on the "dockland" of his early love, *London River.* His position among modern prose writers was now assured and after leaving the *Athenaeum* he remained a free lance, devoting himself entirely to his books. These appeared steadily but without sign of haste: another book of travel *Tide Marks* (1924) and three volumes of essays, *Waiting for Daylight* (1922), *Gifts of Fortune* (1926), *Out of Soundings* (1931). Besides these there was *Under the Red Ensign* (*The Foreshore of England* in the American edition), a survey of the shipping depression in 1926, and shorter works, his lecture *Between the Lines* (1928) and *Norman Douglas* (1931). After *South to Cadiz* (1934) Tomlinson's work shows signs of fatigue: the shadow of approaching war, which he saw more clearly than many of his contemporaries, lies over *Mars His Idiot* (1935); and *The Wind is Rising* (1941) and even *The Turn of the Tide* (1946), though their vivid reporting of another war often recalls his grim pictures of Flanders, have not emerged from it.

Meanwhile Tomlinson had appeared as a novelist with *Gallions Reach* in 1927. This and its half dozen successors have all been well received but have added little to his reputation, his genius being reflective and reminiscent rather than creative. His novels are thoughtful, but the narrative is often sluggish and few of the characters come to life or remain in the reader's memory.

There is a sense in which Tomlinson can be said to have a very narrow range; certain fundamental ideas and even the images and phrases that express them reappear frequently in his writing. Nearly all that he was to say, early or late, can be found in his origins. Poplar gave him his standards of plain living and high thinking, his independent attitude, his love of ships, his hatred of war, and his suspicion of the too rapid growth of the modern world. What his native place began was confirmed by the formative authors of his youth —Melville, Thoreau, and Whitman. He remains among these few first things, whether commenting on war or favorite books or surveying the world from China to Peru—but in no case do they restrict his mental horizon. When one considers the symbolism of the essays in his most mature volume, *Out of Soundings,* one feels that what he has to say is neither small nor narrow. Mankind has lost its way ("The Changeling") because mechanism has replaced human values in the modern world ("Beauty and The Beast") from which wisdom has departed ("A Brown Owl"). Our culture is derelict on a lee shore but something may be salvaged ("The Wreck") by an arduous strengthening of the spirit that will raise us to a higher plane of perception ("Gilolo"). He prefers to speak by symbols and parables and to the literal and imperceptive his meaning is not always clear.

To express his sense of the impermanence of the material world Tomlinson has developed a highly individual style and imagery. An essay will begin as simply as the best journalism and before we know it the prose will have passed imperceptibly into a stately largo in which phrase after phrase, image after image demolishes the solid world about us. Light fills space in solid cubes and wedges or blends land and clouds, sea and sky into a single continuum, the present dissolves before the past; everywhere matter attenuates until we find ourselves in a world of pure perception. It approaches poetry as nearly as writing can without ceasing to be authentic prose, and yet at all times it remains natural, with those colloquial rhythms that have always linked the best essay writing with the best talk. Tomlinson's excellence as a prose stylist is generally admitted; his right to be considered among the great English essayists rests on a broader basis.

Essays and Travel: *The Sea and the Jungle* (1912), *Old Junk* (1918), *London River* (1921), *Waiting For Daylight* (1922), *Tide Marks* (1924), *Gifts of Fortune* (1926), *Under the Red Ensign,* [*The Foreshore of England*] (1927), *A Brown Owl* (1928), *Illusion: 1915* (1928), *Thomas Hardy* (1929), *Côte d'Or* (1929), *Between the Lines* (1930), *Out of Soundings* (1931), *Norman*

Douglas (1931), *South to Cadiz* (1934), *Below London Bridge* (1934), *The Wind Is Rising* (1941), *The Turn of the Tide* (1946), *The Face of the Earth* (1950). Novels: *Gallions Reach* (1927), *All Our Yesterdays* (1930), *The Snows of Helicon* (1933), *Mars His Idiot* (1935), *All Hands!*, Am. ed. *Pipe All Hands!* (1937), *The Day Before* (1939), *Morning Light* (1946).

There has been no major study of Tomlinson, though it was reported in 1949 that one was under way in England.

John Freeman, "Mr. H. M. Tomlinson," *London Mercury,* XVI (1927), 400-408; F. P. Mayer, "H. M. Tomlinson: The Eternal Youth," *Virginia Quar. Rev.,* IV (1928), 72-82; Helen and Richard Altick, "Square Rigger on a Modern Mission," *College English,* V (1943-44), 75-80; Robert Lynd, "Mr. H. M. Tomlinson," in *Books and Authors* (1923).

Of the recent biographers none is of more historical significance and of more literary worth than **(Giles) Lytton Strachey (1880-1932).** Although his Lives—both the full-length pieces *Queen Victoria* (1921) and *Elizabeth and Essex* (1928) and the biographical essays in *Eminent Victorians* (1918), *Books and Characters* (1922), and *Portraits in Miniature* (1931)—show a pronounced inclination toward revealing the weak rather than the strong elements in human nature, they did much to bring biography away from the cold, factual records with their prevailing tone of eulogy to a readable, well-integrated interpretation of personality; and they showed an unmistakable brilliance of style. In his Preface to *Eminent Victorians,* he stated:

The art of biography seems to have fallen upon evil times in England. We have had, it is true, a few masterpieces, but we have never had, like the French, a great biographical tradition. . . . With us, the most delicate and humane of all the branches of the art of writing has been relegated to the journeyman of letters; we do not reflect that it is perhaps as difficult to write a good life as to live one. Those two fat volumes, with which it is our custom to commemorate the dead—who does not know them, with their ill-digested masses of material, their slipshod style, their tone of tedious panegyric, their lamentable lack of selection, of detachment of design? They are as familiar as the *cortege* of the undertaker, and wear the same air of slow, funereal barbarism. ... The studies in this book are indebted, in more ways than one, to such works—works which certainly deserve the name of Standard Biographies. For they have provided me not only with much indispensable information, but with something even more precious—an example. How many lessons are to be learned from them! But it is hardly necessary to particularize. To preserve, for instance, a becoming brevity—a brevity which excludes everything that is redundant, and nothing that is significant—that, surely, is the first duty of the biographer. The second, no less surely, is to maintain his own freedom of spirit. It is not his business to be complimentary, it is his business to lay bare the facts of the case as he understands them. That is what I aimed at in this book— to lay bare the facts of some cases as I understand them, dispassionately, impartially and without ulterior intentions. ...*

Giles Lytton Strachey was born in London in 1880, the son of Sir Richard and Lady Jane Strachey. He was educated by tutors before entering Trinity College, Cambridge, where he distinguished himself by his studies in History and Literature, including the French, and by winning the Chancellor's Medal with his poem "Ely" in 1902. Although an avid reader and of marked literary interests and talent, he did not produce anything to attract attention

LYTTON STRACHEY

until 1918, when *Eminent Victorians* appeared. It is possible that the disillusionment fostered by the war was responsible for the prompt and wide circulation of the volume, for in

* Lytton Strachey, *Eminent Victorians*. Reprinted with permission of Harcourt, Brace and Co.

the four portraits—Cardinal Manning, Florence Nightingale, Dr. Arnold, and General Gordon—the author demonstrated very persuasively that these English idols had feet
of clay. The attempts at refutation of Strachey's characterization of Cardinal Manning in the Catholic journals
have only recently subsided. With the appearance of *Queen
Victoria* (1921) Strachey's fame was secured. It is generally surmised that the author originally intended to use
the Queen as a target for his satirical talent; but although
Victoria's weaknesses are exposed, she emerges a personable and likeable figure. Someone has called Victoria's conquest of Lytton Strachey the most remarkable phenomenon
of modern biography. The brilliant essays in *Books and
Characters: French and English* (1922) were interesting,
chiefly to Strachey enthusiasts—of whom a considerable
number had grown up—, for the subjects considered, such
as Madame du Deffand, Thomas Beddoes, and Lady Hester
Stanhope, were of limited appeal. Most of the biographical essays in this collection had been written long before
the volume appeared. *Elizabeth and Essex* (1928) added
considerably to the author's stature, for it indicated that
his insight was not confined to the Victorian scene, and
that he was a consistent master of a compelling style. The
brief pieces in *Portraits in Miniature,* which appeared the
year before his death in 1932, although concerned largely
with minor figures, are all admirable examples of Strachey's
ability to select the highly significant and integrate the
details into a consummate whole.

Strachey has often been judged severely and justly on
account of his satirical attitude toward many of the characters he portrayed. It is true that in his attempt to break
away from the panegyrical tone of most of the Victorian and
early twentieth-century biographies, he went often to the
other extreme. The motto he introduced into *Eminent Victorians* is generally applied: *"je n'impose rien; je ne propose*

rien: j'expose." Although his interest in exposing the motives of characters is plain, Strachey was more concerned with selection and unification than he was with the uses to which irony and the devices of fiction could be put. His selection of detail was invariably highly discriminating; and in the presentation of detail he employed the talent he admired so much in Racine: of making each word say everything that that one word can say. With epigram and nimbly turned phrases he did not deal; it was rather the beauties of restraint, clarity, refinement, and precision that he sought and attained.

BIOGRAPHY: *Eminent Victorians* (1918), *Queen Victoria* (1921), *Elizabeth and Essex* (1928), *Portraits in Miniature and Other Essays* (1931). ESSAYS, CHIEFLY CRITICAL: *Landmarks in French Literature* (1912), *Books and Characters, French and English* (1922), *Characters and Commentaries* (1933).

Max Beerbohm, *Lytton Strachey* (1943); Mark Longaker, "The Art of Lytton Strachey," in *Contemporary Biography* (Phila., 1934); Cyril Clemens, "Lytton Strachey," *Dalhousie Rev.,* XX (1940), 29-36.

Differing from Lytton Strachey and from the other writers who adopted the methods of fiction and the psychoanalytical approach, **Philip Guedalla (1889-1944)** produced many biographical essays which are to be found in *Supers and Supermen* (1920), *A Gallery* (1924), and *Bonnet and Shawl* (1928); and several full-length lives, notable among which are *Palmerston* (1926) and *Wellington* (1931). In many respects, Guedalla was a traditionalist, for he rejected entirely the devices of the so-called "new biography" in order to view his subjects in the strong light of their historical background. "The first essential of sound portraiture," he observed in his sketch of Washington in *Fathers of the Revolution* **(1926),** "is background. The park, the looped curtain, the invariably decisive sea-fight behind him may tell so much about a sitter that is concealed by his impenetrable stare. Yet history, disdainful of significant detail, is lamentably apt to divorce her favorite characters from their surroundings; to present them in statuesque isolation that is all pedestal and no perspective; to leave them, insulated and gasping for air, in a sort of historical vacuum. Perhaps that is why, in her stately pages, they so rarely contrive to live. . . . Background, the full and accurate rendering of *milieu,* is the first element of historical portraiture."

Philip Guedalla was born in 1889, educated at Rugby and Balliol College, Oxford, where in 1911 he was president of the Union. He practiced law from 1913 until 1923, and during the First War he was a legal adviser in the War Office. He contested for Parliament unsuccessfully during the mid-twenties, and was actively engaged in the English political and economic scene. In addition to his active participation in politics, he was a tireless student of history, especially that of nineteenth-century England and France. This interest in history is reflected in his numerous contributions to the London periodicals and his works which appeared in book form. Recognition came to him chiefly from his full-length biographies of which *Wellington* (1931), published in England under the title *The Duke,* was widely circulated on both sides of the Atlantic. He lectured in America in the early thirties, and held audiences spellbound by his compelling and often brilliant delivery. He died in London in 1944.

Guedalla did his least effective work in his short pieces in which he was frequently too given to stylistic mannerisms. Possessed of a sparkling wit of which he was well aware, he often sacrificed substance for trimly turned phrases. He justified his manner in the sketches by insisting that his essays were "after all, only studies casually detached from a prose-writer's notebook." In the essays in *Masters and Men, Supers and Supermen,* and *A Gallery* the author at times exasperates the reader by the deliberately casual way in which he toys with his subject. Too often the subject provides him with a framework on which he performs his stylistic calisthenics. There is at times discernment in these essays, however, and in the full-length lives there is substance as well as brilliance of style. *Palmerston* is not only a penetrating interpretation of the personality of the Prime Minister, but an illuminating record of the times, with biography and history working happily together to produce a well-integrated result. *Wellington* is equally valuable as a skillful fusion of biography and history, and there are sustained passages which show the author's talent for brilliant phrase and resonant prose.

ESSAYS: *Supers and Supermen* (1920), *Masters and Men* (1923), *A Gallery* (1924), *Fathers of the Revolution,* Published in England as *Independence Day* (1926), *Bonnet and Shawl* (1928), *The Missing Muse and Other Essays* (1929). BIOGRAPHY: *The Second Empire* (1922), *Palmerston* (1926), *Mary Arnold* (1929), *The Duke* [*Wellington*] (1931).

Mark Longaker, "Erudition and Epigram: Mr. Philip Guedalla," in *Contemporary Biography* (Phila., 1934); Leonard Woolf, "Philip Guedalla," *Nation and Athenaeum,* XL (1926), 339-344.

The reputation of **Sir Edmund Gosse (1849-1928)** has sunk greatly since his death, but during the first twenty years of the century he was an important figure in the literary world. He was the son of Philip Henry Gosse, a poor but able marine biologist, who raised his son in the severe and narrow discipline of the Plymouth Brethren. At the age of seventeen Edmund Gosse obtained, through the kindness of Charles Kingsley, a minor post in the British Museum. With independence and new friendships among men of letters Gosse broke with his father and renounced the beliefs of his youth. Making himself officially acceptable, he passed from the Museum to the Board of Trade as translator, and in 1910 became librarian of the House of Lords.

He first attracted literary notice in 1879 by his apprecia-

tive study of Ibsen, whom he was the first to introduce to
English readers. Gosse's causeries on literature, polished and
informative, were widely read. In 1886 he was appointed
Clark Lecturer in literature at Cambridge. The lectures,
published as *From Shakespeare to Pope,* drew severe stric-
tures for inaccuracy of scholarship that damaged Gosse's
reputation and for a while shook his self-confidence. Reputation and confidence were not fully recovered until the recognition by the French Academy of his masterpiece *Father and
Son.* This book, published anonymously in 1907, tells in
great detail of his youth, his spiritual struggle with his
father's narrow, puritan views. It is candid without bitterness and ranks with the best autobiographical works in
English. During his later years Gosse had great authority
with the reading public and his judgments upon new books
were widely accepted. His critical essays were a weekly feature of the *Sunday Times* from 1919 until his death.

"Gosse is a showman," his biographer says, and in a good
sense that is true. He was omnivorous of literary excellence
and could communicate his enthusiasms to his readers. Nor
were his enthusiasms static; acquainted in his youth with
Tennyson and Swinburne, he welcomed sympathetically new
writers of ability whenever they appeared. Along with
Arnold Bennett, whose judgments had equal weight with
the reading public, he did much to establish the reputations
of those young writers of the twenties who are still regarded
as the best. Gosse had his faults as a scholar but as an interpreter and popularizer he served his times well.

In the European world of letters Gosse knew everyone of
note, and though his unsparing sarcastic wit was widely
feared he was generally known and welcome all over the
continent. No British man of letters has ever carried as many
foreign decorations and distinctions as he. His value as a
critic apart, Gosse is an entertaining personality to include in
one's reading.

ESSAYS AND CRITICISM: *Studies in the Literature of Northern Europe* (1879), *Seventeenth Century Studies* (1883), *From Shakespeare to Pope* (1886), *A History of Eighteenth Century Literature* (1889), *Northern Studies* (1890), *Gossip in a Library* (1891), *Questions at Issue* (1893), *The Jacobean Poets* (1894), *Critical Kit-Kats* (1896), *A Short History of Modern English Literature* (1897), *English Literature*, 4 v., with Richard Garnett (1903), *French Profiles* (1905), *Portraits and Sketches* (1912), *Collected Essays*, 5 v. (1913), *The Future of English Poetry* (1913), *Two Pioneers of Romanticism: Joseph and Thomas Warton* (1915), *Inter Arma* (1916), *Three French Novelists* (1918), *Some Diversions of a Man of Letters* (1919), *Malherbe and the Classical Reaction* (1920), *Books on the Table* (1921), *Aspects and Impressions* (1922), *The Continuity of Literature* (1922), *More Books on the Table* (1923), *Silhouettes* (1925), *Leaves and Fruit* (1927), *Selected Essays* (1928). BIOGRAPHY: *Gray* (1882), *Raleigh* (1886), *The Life of William Congreve* (1888), *Robert Browning: Personalia* (1890), *The Life and Letters of John Donne* (1899), *Jeremy Taylor* (1904), *Coventry Patmore* (1905), *Sir Thomas Browne* (1905), *Ibsen* (1907), *Father and Son* (1907), *The Life of Algernon Charles Swinburne* (1917), *Tallemant des Réaux* (1925).

"Bibliographies of Modern Authors, Edmund Gosse," *London Mercury,* III (1920), 212-213; Evan Charteris, *The Life and Letters of Sir Edmund Gosse* (1931); George Saintsbury, "Some Memories of Edmund Gosse," *London Mercury,* XVIII (1928), 264-268; Virginia Woolf, "Edmund Gosse," *Fortnightly Rev.,* CXXXV (1931), 766-773, reprinted in *The Moment* (1947); John Drinkwater, "Edmund Gosse," *Quarterly Rev.,* v. 257 (1931), 116-132; J. C. Squire, "Sir Edmund Gosse," *London Mercury,* XVIII (1928), 114-119; Osbert Sitwell, "A Short Character of Sir Edmund Gosse," *Horizon,* V (1942), 243-266; V. S. Prichett, "A Plymouth Brother," in *The Living Novel* (1946).

The dean of the elder critics in 1900 before whom even Edmund Gosse walked delicately was **George (Edward Bateman) Saintsbury (1845-1933)**. Born in Southampton, he attended school in London and took his degree from Oxford in 1868. There followed eight years of school teaching and five more of journalism before his name became well known. From the appearance of his *Primer of French Literature* in

1881 until his death critical works and essays poured from him steadily. His best known and most ambitious are *A History of Criticism and Literary Taste in Europe* (1900-4) and *A History of English Prosody* (1906-21). In 1895 he was appointed to a chair of English at the University of Edinburgh which he held until he reached the age of retirement in 1915. At the close of the First World War Saintsbury lost a great deal of money, so that he was obliged to sell his splendid library and live cheaply in Bath. The books that he wrote from 1920 on are the pot boilers of an old and discouraged man.

Like Gosse, Saintsbury is of the school of Saint Beuve. He was a prodigious reader, as he believed every critic should be, since on no other basis can adequate generalizations and comparisons be made. Well read in most European literatures, he was, like most of the older critics, especially so in the French, which he knew nearly as well as English. He contemned narrowness of critical theory and especially any attempt to treat criticism as a pseudo-science, preferring to rest it on broad comparative judgments. He generally justifies the method in his practice, which shows him, within his limits, a sound and appreciative critic. Less of a gossip than Gosse, he had not the elasticity of mind that enabled Gosse to receive new writers sympathetically to the end of his days. Saintsbury's is always the voice of the nineteenth century with a strongly conservative tone. Politically he was a Tory and though he deprecated political criticism, the irritating attitude expressed in his "Thoughts on Republics" (*Miscellaneous Essays,* 1893) often pervades his work.

A Primer of French Literature (1880), *Dryden* (1881), *A Short History of French Literature* (1882), *A History of Elizabethan Literature* (1887), *Essays in English Literature, 1780-1860* (1890), *Essays on French Novelists* (1891), *Miscellaneous Essays* (1892), *Essays in English Literature, 1780-1860, Second Series* (1895),

Corrected Impressions (1895), *A History of Nineteenth Century Literature, 1780-1895* (1896), *The Flourishing of Romance and the Rise of Allegory* (1897), *Sir Walter Scott* (1897), *A Short History of English Literature* (1898), *A History of French Literature* (1899), *Matthew Arnold* (1899), *A History of Criticism* (1900-1904), *The Earlier Renaissance* (1901), *Minor Poets of the Caroline Period* (1905-1921), *The First Half of the Seventeenth Century* (1906), *A History of English Prosody* (1906-1910), *A History of Elizabethan Literature* (1906), *The Later Nineteenth Century* (1907), *Historical Manual of English Prosody* (1910), *A History of English Prose Rhythm* (1912), *The Historical Character of the English Lyric* (1913), *The English Novel* (1913), *The Peace of the Augustans* (1916), *A History of the French Novel* (1917-1918), *Some Recent Studies in English Prosody* (1919), *Collected Essays and Papers of George Saintsbury, 1875-1920* (1923-1924), *George Henry Borrow, 1803-1881* (1924), *A Consideration of Thackeray* (1931), *Prefaces and Essays* (1933), *Shakespeare* (1934), *French Literature and Its Masters* (1946).

"Bibliographies of Modern Authors, George Saintsbury," *London Mercury*, I (1919-20), 238-239; Introduction to *The Memorial Volume* (1945); J. B. Priestley, "Mr. George Saintsbury: An Appreciation," *London Mercury*, VI (1922), 502-512; Robert Lynd, "Two English Critics, Mr. Saintsbury," in *The Art of Letters* (1921); Herbert Read, "George Saintsbury," in *A Coat of Many Colors* (1945).

An uncompromising conservative, **Charles Whibley (1859-1930)** was, curiously, a graduate of Cambridge, the more liberal of the two great English universities. A young literary journalist in London of the eighties, he became an early contributor to the *Scots Observer* and soon the friend of its editor, W. E. Henley, the two being drawn together by their common hatred of sham as well as by their politics. For some years Whibley continued to work closely with Henley as contributor to the *National Observer* and as co-editor of the *Tudor Translations* from 1892.

In 1900 he began his best known and best sustained work

of literary journalism, the "Musings Without Method," which appeared in 347 issues of *Blackwood's Magazine* from their inception until shortly before his death in 1930. Over some of these years he also contributed to the London *Daily Mail* his *Letters of an Englishman,* which were issued anonymously in 1911 and 1912. It is to be regretted that T. S. Eliot never made the selection from the "Musings" which he long ago projected. Their considerable literary merit aside, these two groups of occasional writings are among the best sustained works of English journalism in the twentieth century, and, as Professor Altick has pointed out, valuable sources of reference for the social and political history of England as seen by a representative of a dying class and political party.

Whibley's more substantial work is to be found in his biographical writing. This includes sound, if old-fashioned, studies of Thackeray (1903), Pitt (1906), Swift (1917) and Lord John Manners (1925) as well as numerous biographical essays collected in such volumes as *A Book of Scoundrels* (1897), *The Pageantry of Life* (1900), and *Essays in Biography* (1913). These latter are especially good, for he was a master of the form. No one has known better how to convey the essence of a character within the limits of an essay, not bleakly but with the color of the age his subject lived in. A marked individualist, Whibley preferred to write of unusual and colorful characters, especially of the seventeenth and eighteenth centuries.

A Tory of the old pattern, Whibley outlived his age and often offends the modern reader by the narrowness and vindictiveness of his political and social views. Yet to those who can overcome their resentment, he discloses himself as an able and utterly sincere writer of great ability. He is never cheap. He is urbane and scholarly, master of a richly traditional prose style, and, within the limits of his convictions, a sound judge.

A Book of Scoundrels (1897), *The Pageantry of Life* (1900), *William Makepeace Thackeray* (1903), *Literary Portraits* (1904), *William Pitt* (1906), *American Sketches* (1908), *Studies in Frankness* (1910), *The Letters of an Englishman, First Series* (1911), *Second Series* (1912), *Essays in Biography* (1913), *Jonathan Swift* (1917), *Political Portraits, First Series* (1917), *Literary Studies* (1919), *Political Portraits, Second Series* (1923), *Lord John Manners and His Friends* (1925).

T. S. Eliot, "Charles Whibley," in *Selected Essays* (1932); Richard D. Altick, "Toryism's Last Stand! Charles Whibley and His 'Musings Without Method,' " *So. Atlantic Quar.,* XLI (1942), 297-312.

John Middleton Murry (1889-   ) made his name as a brilliant young critic at the time of the First World War. He was born in Peckham, London, the son of a poor government clerk. His father, obsessed by insecurity, wished his son to rise in the world and to that end educated him ferociously. Murry learned to read at two, and when he entered the Board (public) School at two-and-a-half could write his multiplication table. In 1901 he was admitted on a scholarship to Christ's Hospital, the famous Blue Coat School, where Coleridge, Lamb, and Leigh Hunt had got the rudiments of their learning. Here he remained until, again on a competitive scholarship, he went on to Brasenose College, Oxford.

As the university brought him closer to the career in the Civil Service for which his father intended him, he became increasingly discontented and he left his college in 1911, returning only to take his examinations for his degree. With a college friend he had undertaken to produce a literary magazine, *Rhythm,* which was to be "the *Yellow Book* of the modern movement." This and reviewing for the *Westminster Gazette* were his introduction to journalism. They brought him little money and for some time no recognition, but important friendships with Frank Harris, W. L. George, D. H. Lawrence, and Katherine Mansfield (q.v.) whom he later married. *Rhythm* lasted through 1912 and was succeeded by the even shorter lived *Blue Review*. Book-reviewing served him better, and soon he was reviewing for the *Daily News* and for the *Times Literary Supplement*. In 1916 he was appointed translator in the Political Intelligence Department of the War Office and at the end of three years had become Chief Censor. The war was an agony of spiritual depression and overwork but by the end of it he had made a name as journalist and critic.

In 1917 Murry had met H. W. Massingham and had been asked by him to write for the *Nation*. In 1919 he was appointed editor of the *Athenaeum,* also controlled by Massingham, which until it was merged with the *Nation* two years later was the most brilliant English literary weekly. In 1923 he founded the successful *Adelphi*. In the same year he suffered a heavy loss in the death of Katherine Mansfield, to whom he had been married since 1918.

Murry's creative work begins virtually in 1920: before that he had published only a novel, a study of Dostoievsky, and one volume of criticism. His thirty-seven volumes since then include biography, ethics, literary criticism, and, latterly, public affairs. He has written studies of his favorite English classics, Shakespeare, Keats, and Blake, and of his friend D. H. Lawrence. His five volumes on religious subjects include the brilliant, but unorthodox, *Life of Jesus* (in the American edition *Jesus, Man of Genius*). He was the literary executor of Katherine Mansfield and collaborated in her biography. Of his critical essays the best known are *Aspects of Literature* and *Countries of the Mind* (First and Second Series).

If labels must be attached, Murry is a humanistic critic. The one valuable experience of his Oxford days was his surrender to Plato. But whereas to Wells Plato pointed the way to the realization of the world state, to Murry he disclosed the ultimate values and their relations, an eternally valid basis of judgment. He believes that "the values of literature, the standards by which it must be criticised, and the scheme according to which it must be arranged, are in the last resort moral." This does not imply any authoritarian categories like those of T. S. Eliot; it simply means that in the light of Plato aesthetic and ethic are inseparable and the critic whose duty it is to establish the one cannot ignore the other, since art "has reference to a more perfectly human morality than any other activity of man." Upon this qualitative basis the critic founds the judgments which "establish a definite hierarchy among the great artists of the past, as well as test the production of the present" and so bring order into the intellectual confusion of the modern world.

Since the death of Katherine Mansfield, Murry has been twice married and has four children. He lives quietly in the country. His autobiography, written in 1935, carries his story only to his thirtieth year.

AUTOBIOGRAPHY: *Between Two Worlds* [*The Autobiography of John Middleton Murry*] (1938). CRITICISM: *The Critic in Judgment* (1913), *Fyodor Dostoevsky: A Critical Study* (1916), *The Evolution of an Intellectual* (1920), *Aspects of Literature* (1920), *Countries of the Mind* (1922), *The Problem of Style* (1922), *A Neglected Heroine of Shakespeare* (1922), *Pencillings* (1923), *Discoveries* (1924), *Keats and Shakespeare* (1925), *Studies in Keats* (1930), *D. H. Lawrence, Two Essays* (1930), *Countries of the Mind, Second Series* (1931), *Son of Woman: The Story of D. H. Lawrence* (1931), *Reminiscences of D. H. Lawrence* (1933), *The Life of Katherine Mansfield,* with Ruth E. Mantz (1933), *William Blake* (1933), *Shakespeare* (1936), *Heroes of Thought* (1938), *Katherine Mansfield and Other Literary Portraits* (1949).

Rayner Heppenstall, *Middleton Murry* (1934); Orlo Williams, *Contemporary Criticism of Literature* (1924); R. J. Dingle, "Murry Contra Ecclesiam," *Nineteenth Century,* CXXIX (1941), 85-91.

Herbert Edward Read (1893-   ) was born and passed his first ten years on his father's farm in Yorkshire, a place little touched by the outside world, where life was remarkably simple for modern times. Upon his father's death he was sent to boarding school, a rather bleak establishment, where until he was fifteen he had few pleasures but acquired his first taste for reading and writing. During these years his home had been broken up and his mother had moved to Leeds. On leaving the school at the end of his fifteenth year he took a post as junior clerk in a bank. Here he worked for £20 a year, educating himself in night schools and the public library until 1912, when he matriculated at the University of Leeds. He had no definite intentions beyond acquiring a sound education, majoring in Law and Economics. He did not finish his course, for in 1914 the outbreak of war found him in summer camp with the University OTC unit. A few months later he was commissioned in the Yorkshire Regiment and went to France in 1915.

After the war, in which he served with credit as adjutant of his battalion, receiving the DSO and Military Cross, Read obtained a clerkship in the Treasury, an excellent post by civil service standards, but one which left him no leisure for the literary work on which his heart was set. After a few years and at a considerable sacrifice of salary, Read exchanged it for another in the ceramics department of the Victoria and Albert Museum which allowed him greater freedom. The knowledge of the arts gained in his museum work led to a professorship of fine art at the University of Edinburgh from 1931 to 1933 and later to lectureships at Liverpool and Cambridge.

Read began as a poet, his earliest verse having been published in 1915 in an edition that was pulped after twenty-two copies had been sold. Influenced at first by Blake and Yeats, later by Donne and Browning, he worked his way toward poetic maturity through *Naked Warriors,* his war poems. His ultimate allegiance was to the Imagists, with whom he has been regularly identified.

It is as a critic, however, that Read is best known. Fundamentally a humanist with romantic leanings, he has acquired from his dual connection with literature and the plastic arts a fastidious sense of form. Among his strongest preferences, he says, "are poets like Arnold and Hopkins, novelists like Flaubert and Henry James, and painters like Poussin and Seurat, in all of whom formality is almost an obsession." His practice, however, is less strict than this statement indicates, and though his sympathies are imperfect in some directions —as are those of all critics—his range of perception and receptivity is wide. In common with most modern critics he has availed himself fully of the resources of psychology, and interprets the concrete result in terms of the conceiving mind. His judgments are expressed in a wide variety of forms from the full-length study *Wordsworth* (1930) to the brief essays of *A Coat of Many Colours*. His criticism, however, is not confined to literature. His interest in the plastic arts is as wide and the authority of his judgment as high.

For Read art and morals have a common law in the highest expression of the individual. Consequently he calls himself a philosophic anarchist. He envisions a society ordered in conformity with natural law in which every man shall have the fullest opportunity of spiritual development. It is not very different, really, from the more liberal sorts of liberalism. In his criticism his philosophy appears without doctrinal implications but simply as an integrating spirit. He is ready to welcome any work of art for what it is and to examine it as understandingly as possible, seeing all artists and arts as the variant expressions of a common impulse. A purely intellectual critic, he is never difficult or repellently highbrow. His autobiography, *The Innocent Eye*, which contains some of his best writing, offers the best approach to an understanding of his work.

For the six years before the Second World War Read edited the *Burlington Magazine*. He lives in London and has been twice married.

CRITICISM: *Reason and Romanticism* (1926), *English Prose Style* (1928), *The Sense of Glory* (1929), *Wordsworth* (1930), *Julien Benda and the New Humanism* (1930), *The Meaning of Art* (1931), *Form In Modern Poetry* (1932), *Art Now* (1933), *In Defense of Shelley* (1935), *Art and Society* (1936), *Poetry and Anarchism* (1938), *Collected Essays in Literary Criticism* (1938), *A Coat of Many Colours* (1941), *Coleridge As Critic* (1949). VERSE: *Collected Poems* (1926), *Poems, 1914-1934* (1935), *Thirty-five Poems* (1940), *World Within a War* (1945). MEMOIRS: *The Innocent Eye* (1933), *Annals of Innocence and Experience* (1940).

C. I. Glicksburg, "Herbert Read: Reason and Romanticism," *Univ. Toronto Quar.*, XVI (1946-47), 60-70.

ADDITIONAL MINOR FIGURES

Barker, George (1913-   ), named the most promising of the younger poets by C. Day Lewis in 1939, has only in fair measure progressed beyond the plane reached in such a fine poem as "Munich Elegy Number 1." His representative work is to be found in *Janus* (1935), *Poems* (1935), *Calamiterror* (1937), *Lament and Triumph* (1940), *Sacred and Secular Elegies* (1943), and *Eros in Dogma* (1944). There is no doubt that Barker has an energetic talent, as his procession of volumes indicates, but this talent has taken no particular direction or theme, nor has it progressed in manner. Severe discipline continues to be lacking: there is much which can be deleted as inept and even tasteless. Illustrative of his distinctive manner, including his lapses into mere word play, is the poem "The Amazons." The collection *Sacred and Secular Elegies* is probably Barker at his best.

Cecil, Lord David (1902-   ), literary biographer, author of *William Cowper* (1932), *Sir Walter Scott* (1933), *Early Victorian Novelists* (1934), *Jane Austen* (1935), and *The Young*

Melbourne (1939). He is a younger son of the Fifth Marquess of Salisbury and has been a Fellow of Wadham College, Oxford.

Comfort, Alex (1920-   ), a practicing physician, educated at Highgate School and Trinity College, Cambridge, is one of the younger poets from whom more is sure to come. He has written both prose and verse: his critical perceptions are demonstrated in his brief consideration of contemporary fiction, *The Novel and Our Time* (1947); and the themes and manner of his verse appear in large part in *The Song of Lazarus* (1945). His forceful "Notes for My Son," a warning to the new generation about the deceptions of warmongers, is hardly so characteristic of his usual themes as the poems in which he is concerned with metaphysical inquiry.

Empson, William (1906-   ), known in America chiefly as a critic, was considered for a time the pole-star around which the younger poets of Cambridge circled. In this respect for a time he was compared with W. H. Auden. His measures are frequently those of the traditionalists, with only slight modifications and adaptations; but his themes are presented with little regard for traditionalist imagery and logical sequence. *Poems* (1935), *The Gathering Storm* (1940), and the recent *Selected Poems* (1948) indicate his latitude of theme and manner.

Gascoyne, David (1916-   ), identified for a time with the surrealists, although still given to the extreme use of free association rather than logical sequence, has added considerably to his stature as a poet in his later work in which his manner is aloof and stately in treating themes which seem to be essentially religious. His *Short History of Surrealism* is a notable contribution to the critical literature which concerns this curious and ephemeral movement. His early volume *Man's Life is His Meat* (1936) is plainly experimental. It is in *Poems: 1937-1942* (1943) that one finds a clearer indication of his direction and talent.

George, W. L. (1882-1926). Novelist, born in France of English parents and educated there. Remembered for his savage caricature of Lord Northcliffe in *Caliban* (1920). Author of fifteen novels besides short stories and a great deal of miscellaneous prose.

Godden, Rumer (1909-   ). English born but has lived the greater part of her life in India, the background of three of her novels. Became generally known in 1939 with appearance of *Black Narcissus*. *Take Three Tenses* (1945) is an interesting technical experiment in the handling of time. Has also written *Chinese Puzzle* (1936), *The Lady and the Unicorn* (1938), *Gipsy, Gipsy* (1940), and *Breakfast With the Nikolides* (1942).

Gogarty, Oliver St. John (1878-   ), the original of "Buck Mulligan" in James Joyce's *Ulysses,* in addition to his work as a physician has written a sizeable amount of prose and verse in which there is a distinctive flavor. It has been reported that he never liked Joyce especially, but that he was on intimate and friendly terms with Yeats and the chief figures of the Celtic Renaissance. His memoirs *As I Was Going Down Sackeville Street* (1937) are not only illuminating of the author's life and personality, but the work makes very good reading. *Poems and Plays* (1920), *An Offering to Swans and Other Poems* (1924), *Wild Apples* (1930), *Selected Poems* (1933), *Elbow Room* (1939), and *Mad Grandeur* (1941) illustrate his themes and manner in which there is an unmistakable tone which varies between the light and the bold. In recent years he has lived in the United States, where on occasion he lectures on literature.

Grigson, Geoffrey (1905-   ), editor, anthologist, essayist, and poet, has been a considerable force among the younger generation of writers. As editor of *New Verse,* he provided poets of the advance guard with a receptacle for their offerings and exercised a moderating influence. The anthology *New Verse* (1939), and the recent collection *Poetry of the Present* (1949) indicate his preferences. His own poetry is to be found in *Several Observations: Thirty-one Poems* (1939), and the more conventional *The Isles of Scilly* (1946). His prose, often terse to the point of abruptness, is largely devoted to an attempt to illuminate and justify recent developments and movements in the arts. *The Arts Today* (1938), the introductory piece in *The Romantics* (1942), and *The Harp of Aeolus and Other Essays on Art, Literature, and Nature* (1948) show his variety of interests and critical perceptions.

Hulme, T. E. (1886-1917), although killed in action in the First World War before his theories and talent were completely developed, has been the subject of much critical attention. After leaving Cambridge, he established himself as one of the experimental poets in London. Five of his poems appeared along with Ezra Pound's *Ripostes* in 1915. Herbert Read collected and edited some of Hulme's precepts concerning his art under the title *Speculations* (1924), and supplemented them in a pamphlet *Notes on Language and Style* (1929). Hulme's poetry, slight in volume, but interesting historically, scarcely warrants the critical emphasis which has been placed on it.

Lewis, Wyndham (1886-   ). Born in Maine of English parents but educated in England. Known chiefly as an artist and critic. Editor before the First World War of *Blast,* which he founded with Ezra Pound. Author of *Tarr,* a novel which made some stir in 1918. He had a large influence on

the younger men, especially the poets, of the wartime generation. He is often confused with the journalist D. B.
Wyndham Lewis (1894-   ).

Murray, Gilbert (1866-   ), classical scholar and translator,
born in Australia and educated in England at Merchant
Taylor's School and Oxford. Professor of Greek at Glasgow
University, 1889-1908; Regnis Professor of Greek at Oxford,
1908-36; Charles Eliot Norton Professor of Poetry at Harvard, 1926. He is known for his translations of the Greek
dramatists, especially for his renderings of Euripides in Swin-
burnian measures. Highly readable, these are not always
looked on with favor by his fellow classicists. See, besides his
translations, *Euripides and His Age* (1913), *The Classical
Tradition in Poetry* (1927), *Aristophanes, A Survey* (1933),
and *Aeschylus: The Creator of Tragedy* (1940).

Quiller-Couch, Sir Arthur (1863-1948), King Edward VII
Professor of English Literature at Cambridge since 1912. For
many years he wrote stories and novels of his native Cornwall under the pen name "Q." He is better known for his
later lectures and critical essays, among which are *Studies
in Literature* (1918, 1922, 1929), *The Art of Reading* (1920),
and *Charles Dickens and Other Victorians* (1925).

Scarfe, Francis (1911-   ), educated at Durham University
and the Sorbonne, and a member of the tutorial staff at Cambridge University for a time, has written discerningly about
his contemporaries in *Auden and After: The Liberation of
Poetry* (1942). His verse in *Inscapes* (1940), a title which
suggests at once Gerard Manley Hopkins, is more interesting
to the experimentalist than to one who is seeking a significant theme presented in a readily comprehensible way.

Thirkell, (Mrs.) Angela (1890-   ), was born Angela Mackail, daughter of J. W. Mackail, classicist and professor of
poetry at Oxford. Like her brother Denis Mackail, she is a

popular novelist. Though she first published in 1930 she was not well known to American readers until 1939. Her novels of genteel country life closely imitate those of Anthony Trollope but though amusing have none of his solid quality.

Waddell, Helen J. (1889-   ), medieval scholar born in Japan of Irish parents and educated in Belfast. She taught and lectured for many years at Oxford and at Bedford College, London, and has received a great many academic distinctions. Her principal book is *The Wandering Scholars* (1927) but her translations from medieval Latin and her novel *Peter Abelard* (1933) are nearly as well known.

Williams, Emlyn (1905-   ), Welsh actor-dramatist, author of *Night Must Fall* (1935), *The Corn is Green* (1938) and other less-well-known plays, some of them as yet unpublished.

Williamson, Henry (1897-   ), miscellaneous writer of considerable ability, known for his studies of nature, especially *Tarka the Otter* (1927) and *Salar the Salmon* (1935). These are not juvenile books, as their titles might suggest.

BIBLIOGRAPHY

If not otherwise indicated, place of publication is London or New York

HISTORICAL AND SOCIAL BACKGROUND

Graves, Robert, and Hodge, Alan, *The Long Week End* (1941)
Gretton, R. H., *A Modern History of the English People, 1880-1922* (1930)
Marriott, A. R., *Modern England, 1885-1945* (1948)
Maurois, André, *The Edwardian Era* (1933)
Somervell, D. C., *Modern Britain, 1870-1939* (1941)
Spender, J. A., *Great Britain, 1886-1935* (1936)
Wingfield-Stratford, Esmé, *The Victorian Sunset* (1932), *The Victorian Aftermath* (1934)

BIOGRAPHICAL AND BIBLIOGRAPHICAL REFERENCES

Kunitz, Stanley J. and Haycroft, Howard, *British Authors of the Nineteenth Century* (1936), *Twentieth Century Authors* (1942)
Millett, Fred B., *Contemporary British Literature.* (Third revised and enlarged edition, based on the second revised and enlarged edition by John M. Manly and Edith Rickert, 1944)
Pine, L. G., *The Authors' and Writers' Who's Who and Reference Guide* (1948-1949)

GENERAL SURVEYS

Buck, Philo M., *Directions in Contemporary Literature* (1942)
Charques, R. D., *Contemporary Literature and Social Revolution* (1933)
Cunliffe, J. W., *English Literature in the Twentieth Century* (1923)

493

Mackenzie, Compton, *Literature in My Time* (1933)

Reade, A. R., *Main Currents in Modern Literature* (1935)

Routh, H. V., *English Literature and Ideas in the Twentieth Century* (1948)

Swinnerton, Frank, *The Georgian Scene* (1934)

Tindall, W. Y., *Forces in Modern British Literature* (1947)

Ward, A. C., *The Nineteen Twenties* (1930)

POETRY

Critical Commentaries and Works Which Deal With Theory and Technique

Abercrombie, Lascelles, *The Idea of Great Poetry* (1925), *Principles of English Prosody* (1926), *Poetry: Its Music and Meaning* (1932)

Archer, William, *Poets of the Younger Generation* (1903)

Bowra, C. M., *The Background of Modern Poetry* (Oxford, 1946)

Boyd, Ernest A., *Ireland's Literary Renaissance* (1918)

Brenner, Rica, *Ten Modern Poets* (1930)

Brooks, Cleanth, *Modern Poetry and the Tradition* (Chapel Hill, 1940)

Bullough, Geoffrey, *The Trend of Modern Poetry* (1934; 3rd ed., revised, 1949)

Burdett, Osbert, *The Beardsley Period* (1925)

Collins, H. P., *Modern Poetry* (1925)

Daiches, David, *Poetry and the Modern World* (Chicago, 1940)

Davison, Edward, *Some Modern Poets* (1928)

De la Mare, Walter, *Poetry in Prose* (1936)

Dobree, Bonamy, *The Lamp and the Lute* (Oxford, 1929)

Drew, Elizabeth, *The Appreciation of Poetry* (1940)

Drinkwater, John, *The Muse in Council* (Boston, 1925)

Elliott, G. R., *The Cycle of Modern Poetry* (Princeton, 1929)

Ellis, A. W., *An Anatomy of Poetry* (1922)

Evans, B. Ifor, *English Poetry in the Later Nineteenth Century* (1933)

Garrod, H. W., *Poetry and the Criticism of Life* (Cambridge, Mass., 1931)

Gawsworth, John, ed., *Ten Contemporaries* (1932)

Graves, Robert, *On English Poetry* (1922), *Poetic Unreason and Other Studies* (1925), *Contemporary Techniques of Poetry* (1925); with Laura Riding, *A Survey of Modernist Poetry* (1927)

Harris, Frank, *Contemporary Portraits,* first series (1915), second series (1919), third series (1920)

Hind, Lewis, *Authors and I* (1921), *More Authors and I* (1922)

Housman, A. E., *The Name and Nature of Poetry* (1933)

Hughes, Glenn, *Imagism and the Imagists* (Stanford University, Cal., 1931)

Jackson, Holbrook, *The Eighteen Nineties* (1914)

Jones, Llewellyn, *First Impressions* (1925)

Kernahan, Coulson, *Six Famous Living Poets* (1933)

Leavis, F. R., *New Bearings in English Poetry* (1932)

Lewis, Cecil Day, *A Hope for Poetry* (1934; enlarged ed., 1939); *The Poetic Image* (1948)

Lowes, John Livingston, *Convention and Revolt in Poetry* (Boston, 1919)

MacNeice, Louis, *Modern Poetry* (1939)

Megroz, R. L., *Modern English Poetry, 1882-1932* (1933), *Five Novelist Poets of Today* (1933)

Monro, Harold, *Some Contemporary Poets* (1920)

Morton, David, *The Renaissance of Irish Poetry, 1880-1929* (1929)

Murdoch, W. B., *The Renaissance of the Nineties* (1911)

Newbolt, Sir Henry, *A New Study of English Poetry* (1919)

Noyes, Alfred, *Some Aspects of Modern Poetry* (1924)

Palmer, Herbert, *Post-Victorian Poetry* (1938)

Pearson, Hesketh, *Modern Men and Mummers* (1921)

Phelps, William Lyon, *The Advance of English Poetry in the Twentieth Century* (1918)

Pottle, Frederick, *The Idiom of Poetry* (Ithaca, N. Y., 1946)

Powell, Dilys, *Descent From Parnassus* (1934)

Priestley, J. B., *Figures in Modern Literature* (1924)

Read, Herbert, *Form in Modern Poetry* (1933)

Riding, Laura, and Graves, Robert, *A Survey of Modernist Poetry* (1927)

Savage, D. S., *The Personal Principle* (1944)

Scarfe, Francis, *Auden and After: the Liberation of Poetry* (1942)

Sitwell, Edith, *Aspects of Modern Poetry* (1934)

Southworth, J. B., *Sowing the Spring* (Oxford, 1940)

Sparrow, John, *Sense and Poetry* (1934)

Spender, Stephen, *The Destructive Element* (Boston, 1936)

Squire, Sir John, *Younger Poets of Today* (1932)

Strong, L. A. G., *Common Sense About Poetry* (1932)

Sturgeon, Mary C., *Studies of Contemporary Poets* (1919)

Symons, Arthur, *The Symbolist Movement in Literature* (1899), *Studies in Prose and Verse* (1904)

Weygandt, Cornelius, *Tuesdays at Ten* (Philadelphia, 1928), *The Time of Yeats* (1937)

Wilder, Amos N., *The Spiritual Aspects of the New Poetry* (1940)

Williams, Charles, *Poetry at Present* (Oxford, 1930)

Williams, Harold, *Modern English Writers* (1918)

Wilson, Edmund, *Axel's Castle* (1931)

ANTHOLOGIES

Abercrombie, Lascelles, *New English Poems* (1931)

Andrews, C. E., and Percival, M. O., *Poetry of the Nineties* (1926)

Auden, W. H., and Garrett, John, *The Poet's Tongue* (1937)

Church, Richard, *Poems of Our Time* (1946)

Clarke, George H., *The New Treasury of War Poetry* (Boston, 1943)

Coblentz, Stanton A., *Modern British Lyrics* (1925)

Drinkwater, John, Canby, H. S., and Benét, William Rose, *Twentieth Century Poetry* (Boston, 1929)

Eberhard, Richard, and Rodman, Selden, *War and the Poet* (1945)

Ford, Ford Madox, and Hughes, Glenn, *An Imagist Anthology* (1930)

Friar, Kimon, and Brinnin, John, *Modern Poetry* (1951).

Garrity, Devin A., *New Irish Poets* (1948)

Grigson, Geoffrey, *Poetry of the Present* (1949)

Lewis, C. Day, and Strong, L. A. G., *A New Anthology of Modern Verse* (1948)

Marsh, Sir Edward, *Georgian Poetry*. (Five year-books, 1912, 1915, 1917, 1919, and 1922)

Megroz, R. L., *A Treasury of Modern Poetry* (1936)

Monro, Alida K., *Recent Poetry: 1922-1933* (1933)

Monroe, Harriet, and Henderson, Alice Corbin, *The New Poetry* (1917, revised and enlarged ed., 1936)

Osborne, E. B., *The Muse in Arms* (1919)

Rexroth, Kenneth, *The New British Poets* (1949)

Rittenhouse, Jessie B., *The Little Book of Modern British Verse* (1924)

Roberts, Michael, *The Faber Book of Modern Verse* (1936)

Rodman, Selden, *A New Anthology of Modern Poetry* (1938)

Sanders, Gerald, and Nelson, John Herbert, *The Chief Modern*

Poets of England and America (1929, revised and enlarged ed., 1943)

Squire, Sir John, *Selections from Modern Poets* (1924)

Untermeyer, Louis, *Modern British Poetry* (1920; revised and enlarged ed., 1942; mid-century ed., revised and enlarged, 1950)

Williams, Oscar, *The War Poets* (1945), *A Little Treasury of Modern Poetry* (1946)

THE NOVEL

Beach, Joseph W., *The Twentieth Century Novel* (1932)

Bullett, Gerald W., *Modern English Fiction* (1926)

Chevalley, Abel, *Le Roman Anglais de Notre Temps* (Paris, 1921)

Daiches, David, *The Novel and the Modern World* (Chicago, 1939)

Ford, Ford Madox, *The English Novel* (1929)

Forster, E. M., *Aspects of the Novel* (1927)

Frierson, William C., *The English Novel in Transition, 1855-1940* (Norman, Okla., 1942)

Henderson, Philip, *The Novel Today* (1934)

Hoare, Dorothy M., *Some Aspects of the Modern Novel* (1940)

Muir, Edwin, *The Structure of the Novel* (1929)

Myers, Walter L., *The Later Realism* (Chicago, 1927)

Pritchett, V. S., *The Living Novel* (1946)

Weygandt, Cornelius, *A Century of the English Novel* (1925)

THE SHORT STORY

Bates, H. E., *The Modern Short Story* (1941)

Ward, A. C., *Aspects of the Modern Short Story* (1924)

THE DRAMA

Agate, James E., *A Short View of the English Stage, 1900-1926* (1926)

Archer, William, *The Old Drama and the New* (1923)

Chandler, F. W., *Aspects of Modern Drama* (1914)

Clark, Barrett H., *A Study of the Modern Drama* (1925)

Dickinson, Thomas H., *The Contemporary Drama of England* (1931)

Ellehauge, Martin, *Striking Figures Among Modern English Dramatists* (1931)

Ervine, St. John, *Some Impressions of My Elders* (1922)
Jameson, Storm, *Modern Drama in Europe* (1920)
McCarthy, Desmond, *The Court Theatre, 1904-1907* (1907)
Phelps, William Lyon, *Essays on Modern Dramatists* (1921)
Robinson, Lennox, *The Irish Theatre* (1939)
Vernon, Frank, *The Twentieth Century Theatre* (1924)
Weygandt, Cornelius, *Irish Plays and Playwrights* (1913)

BIOGRAPHY

Longaker, Mark, *Contemporary Biography* (Phila., 1934)

INDEX

Pages in italics indicate principal reference

499